LONDON RECORD SOCIETY
PUBLICATIONS

VOLUME LVI

RECORDS OF THE JESUS GUILD IN ST PAUL'S CATHEDRAL,

c. 1450–1550

AN EDITION OF OXFORD, BODLEIAN MS TANNER 221, AND ASSOCIATED MATERIAL

EDITED BY

ELIZABETH A. NEW

LONDON RECORD SOCIETY
THE BOYDELL PRESS
2022 for 2021

Editorial material © Elizabeth A. New

First published 2022

A London Record Society publication
Published by The Boydell Press
an imprint of Boydell & Brewer Ltd
PO Box 9, Woodbridge, Suffolk IP12 3DF, UK
and of Boydell & Brewer Inc.
668 Mt Hope Avenue, Rochester, NY 14620–2731, USA
website: www.boydellandbrewer.com

ISBN 978-0-900952-62-3

A CIP catalogue record for this book is available
from the British Library

The publisher has no responsibility for the continued existence or
accuracy of URLs for external or third-party internet websites referred to
in this book, and does not guarantee that any content
on such websites is, or will remain, accurate or appropriate

This publication is printed on acid-free paper

Printed and bound in Great Britain by
TJ Books Limited, Padstow, Cornwall

MIX
Paper from
responsible sources
FSC® C013056
www.fsc.org

CONTENTS

ILLUSTRATIONS

The editor, contributors and publisher are grateful to all the institutions
and persons listed for permission to reproduce the materials in which
they hold copyright. Every effort has been made to trace the copyright
holders; apologies are offered for any omission, and the publisher will be
pleased to add any necessary acknowledgement in subsequent editions.

This book is produced with the generous assistance of a grant from the Richard III and Yorkist History Trust.

ACKNOWLEDGEMENTS

This volume originated as a postdoctoral project and, in the twenty years since, I have accrued a significant number of debts of thanks. First and foremost, I am grateful to Professor Caroline Barron for introducing me to the Jesus Guild manuscript as a central source for my PhD, for suggesting it as an edition for the London Record Society, and for providing unfailing support and encouragement during the long gestation of this edition. Dr Clive Burgess has proved to be an invaluable 'critical friend', first as my PhD advisor and more recently as series editor, generously commenting on the full text and correcting my idiosyncratic modern spelling. Numerous archivists and librarians have facilitated my research and preparation of this edition, and I would especially thank Dr Martin Kauffmann and Dr Steven Freeth for advice and assistance. Elizabeth McDonald, Caroline Palmer and Christy Beale at Boydell and Brewer smoothed the final stages of the project and calmed an apprehensive editor. I am grateful to the Isobel Thornley Bequest Fund for a grant towards the cost of illustrations, including the cover image. The Introduction draws in part on a paper I gave at the Institute of Historical Research Medieval and Tudor London seminar, and I thank participants for helpful questions and comments. Colleagues and friends (confirmed medievalists and otherwise) have been unfailingly helpful and supportive during this extended project. Some are mentioned in the text for specific assistance, but I would especially acknowledge Dr Hannes Kleineke for his advice as series editor in an early attempt to complete this edition, Dr Christian Steer for advice, comparing notes as a fellow LRS editor and wickedly entertaining conversation, and Dr Marie-Hélène Rousseau for all things St Paul's; the late Professor Peter Borsay, Dr Claire Daunton, Dr Rachael Harkes, Dr Phillipa Hoskin, Dr Eryn White, and members of Caroline Barron's 'medieval group'; Sue Howlett, Robin LaTrobe, Rebecca Prashad and Heather Thorpe (much missed). My family are remarkably tolerant of my medieval interests and supportive of my work, so with love I thank Margaret, Michael and Jo, and Millicent and Winnifred. This volume is dedicated in loving memory of my mother, Jennifer (Jenny) New, always unconditionally supportive of and encouraging in all aspects of my life, and never doubting that this volume would be published even when I almost gave up.

Shrewsbury, Feast of St Boniface 2021

ABBREVIATIONS

BL	British Library, London
BRUC	*A Biographical Register of the University of Cambridge to 1500,* A. B. Emden (Cambridge, 1963)
BRUO	*Biographical Register of the University of Oxford*, A. B. Emden, 4 vols (Oxford, 1957–74)
CPR	*Calendar of Patent Rolls*, 54 vols (London, 1891–1939)
EETS	Early English Text Society
LMA	London Metropolitan Archives
LRS	London Record Society
MED	Medieval English Dictionary, online at https://quod.lib.umich.edu/m/middle-english-dictionary
ODNB	*Oxford Dictionary of National Biography*, eds. H. C. G. Matthew, B. Harrison and others (Oxford, 2004–) online at http://www.oxforddnb.com/
OED	Oxford English Dictionary
TNA	The National Archives, London
VCH	*Victoria History of the Counties of England*

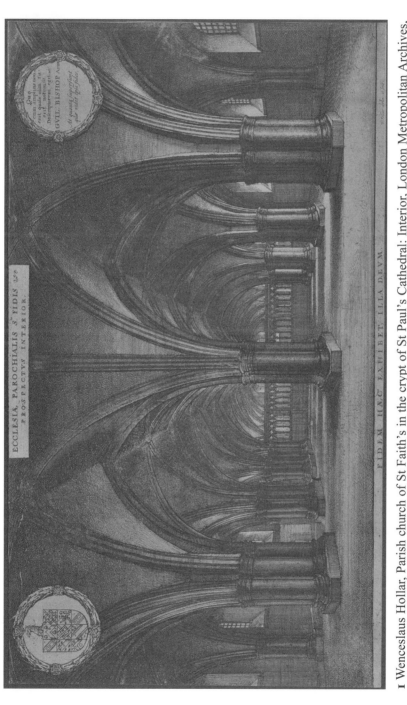

1 Wenceslaus Hollar, Parish church of St Faith's in the crypt of St Paul's Cathedral: Interior, London Metropolitan Archives, Metropolitan Prints Collection, © London Metropolitan Archives. The Jesus Chapel previously had occupied this space.

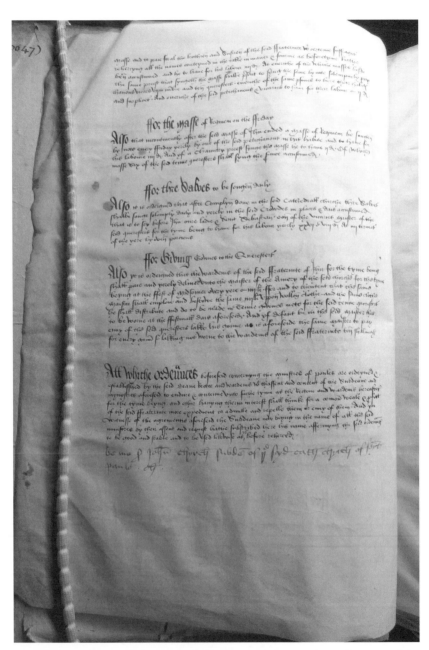

2 Oxford, Bodleian MS Tanner 221 f.7v. Part of the 1506/7 Ordinances of the Jesus Guild, folio signed by John Church, subdean of St Paul's Cathedral. Photograph: the author. Reproduced by permission of The Bodleian Library.

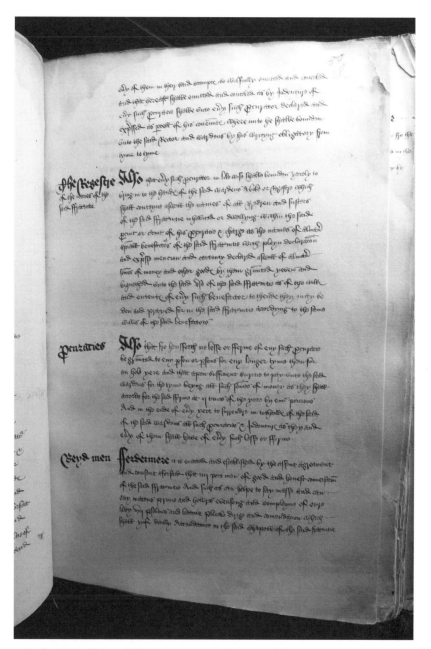

3 Oxford, Bodleian MS Tanner 221 f.28. Part of the c.1514 Ordinances of the Jesus Guild. Photograph: the author. Reproduced by permission of The Bodleian Library.

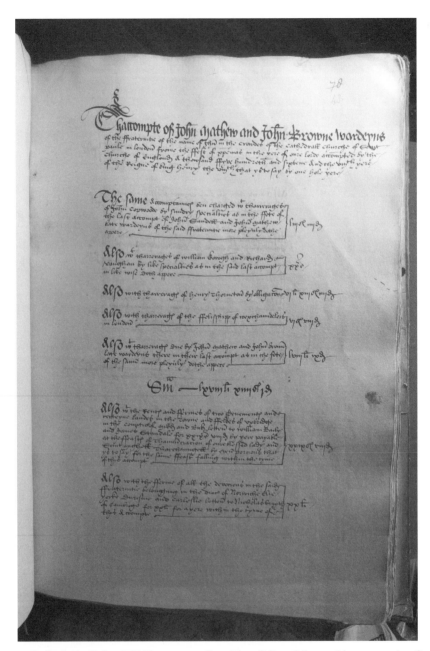

4 Oxford, Bodleian MS Tanner 221 f.43. First folio of the 1516/17 accounts of the Jesus Guild. Photograph: the author. Reproduced by permission of The Bodleian Library.

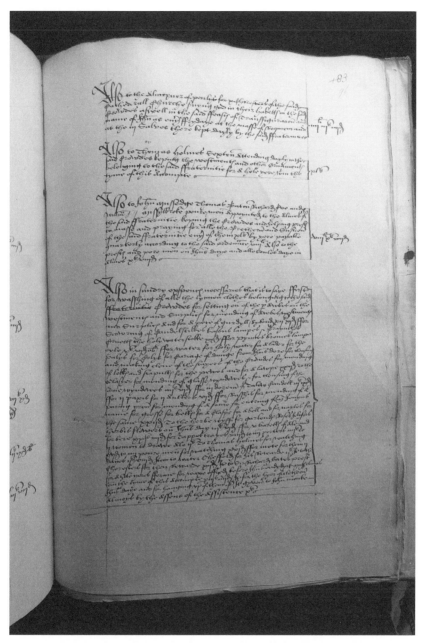

5 Oxford, Bodleian MS Tanner 221 f.96. Part of the expenditure from the 1526/27 account of the Jesus Guild. Photograph: the author. Reproduced by permission of The Bodleian Library.

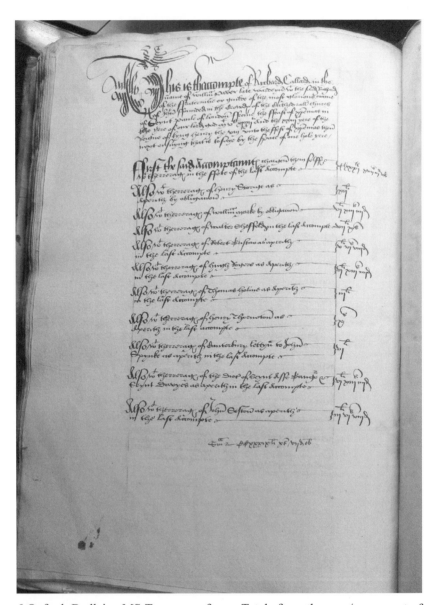

6 Oxford, Bodleian MS Tanner 221 f.121v. Totals from the 1530/31 account of the Jesus Guild. Photograph: the author. Reproduced by permission of The Bodleian Library.

INTRODUCTION

The text edited in this volume publishes the surviving records of the Fraternity of the Holy Name, otherwise known as the Jesus Guild, in the crypt of St Paul's Cathedral; these records derive principally from the second, third and fourth decades of the sixteenth century, but also include copies of some fifteenth- and early sixteenth-century documents.[1] While there may be no surviving membership lists or bede rolls (although both existed [4.i, 22.d]), the ordinances, memoranda, copies of Letters Patent and land deeds and, above all, the twenty consecutive years of accounts contain a wealth of detail about this singular organisation. Indeed, short extracts from Bodleian MS Tanner 221 were published in the late nineteenth century by William Sparrow Simpson, the sub-dean of St Paul's Cathedral who was also an antiquarian, and the Jesus Guild has drawn comment from a number of scholars in the light of its rich records.[2] Nonetheless, the records have remained out of reach to many, and this edition is intended to open up this valuable source to as wide a readership as possible. Included as Appendix I [200–214] is the certificate produced by the parish of St Faith, also located in the crypt of St Paul's, in response to the Royal Commission into church goods of 1552. This document contains detailed descriptions of the Jesus Chapel where the Guild met which, when read in conjunction with the accounts, provide a poignant coda to the activities of the religious fraternity. Finally, Appendix II provides short biographies for all the Guild wardens who can be identified in the edited text.[3]

---

[1]   Both Fraternity and Guild names were used by the association itself but, for the sake of brevity, 'Jesus Guild' is used as the principal name in this introduction and the appendices.

[2]   *Registrum Statutorum et Consuetudinum Ecclesiae Cathedralis Sancti Pauli Londinensis*, ed. W. S. Simpson (London, 1873), 435–62. Simpson employed a rather minimalist editorial style for the English sections of the manuscript that he included, for example ignoring all terminal abbreviation marks. It also appears that on occasion he may have been working from a transcript rather than directly from the manuscript. As emerges in this introduction, both Brigden and Swanson have drawn upon the Jesus Guild records in their respective studies – S. Brigden, *London and the Reformation* (Oxford, 1991), and R. N. Swanson, *Indulgences in Late Medieval England: Passports to Paradise?* (Cambridge, 2007).

[3]   For wardens identified from other sources see E. A. New, 'The Cult of the Holy Name of Jesus in Late Medieval England, with Special Reference to the Fraternity in St Paul's Cathedral, London, c.1450–1558' (unpub. Ph.D. thesis, University of London, 1999), Appendix 4, 403–23.

THE JESUS GUILD IN CONTEXT I: FRATERNITIES IN LATER MEDIEVAL ENGLAND

The Jesus Guild was a prestigious religious fraternity dedicated to one of the more popular devotions of the century and a half leading up to the Reformation, and it was unusual in some important respects. Religious fraternities were a common phenomenon in later medieval England, almost always founded and dominated by the laity and generally open to both men and women.[4] They ranged from a small group of neighbours augmenting worship at an altar to associations that attracted hundreds of members and which were dominated by the great and good in their locale and beyond; they generally exhibited social as well as religious aspects, esteeming good reputation, mutual support and respect as highly as overt piety. The great majority of medieval English religious fraternities were established in a parochial context, however, and the Jesus Guild stands out as one of a limited number located within a cathedral.[5] Following its reorganisation in 1506/7, the Jesus Guild did not employ its own priest, also setting it apart from the majority of religious fraternities, most of whom paid a dedicated priest to spend some or all of his time working for that association. Furthermore, while many religious fraternities provided assistance for brothers and sisters in need and, above all, with guaranteed attendance at or assistance with burial, this was not offered by the Jesus

---

4   The terms 'fraternity', 'brotherhood' (even for those that accepted women as full members) and 'guild' were all used by such associations, often interchangeably, as they are by modern historians. In the historiography of medieval England, the term 'confraternity' is usually reserved for associations connected with, and often instituted by, religious houses or orders. The pioneering studies are *English Gilds*, ed. L. Toulmin Smith, EETS o.s. 40 (1870), and H. F. Westlake, *The Parish Gilds of Mediæval England* (London, 1919); Toulmin Smith covers trade, craft and mercantile guilds, and those connected with civic governance, as well as 'religious (or social) gilds'. G. Rosser, *The Art of Solidarity in the Middle Ages: Guilds in England, 1250–1550* (Oxford, 2015), is one of the few recent publications to take a national perspective, driven by questions about the individual and community in medieval society. Most studies published in the late twentieth and early twenty-first centuries have focused on a region or specific fraternity: see, for example, R. C. Harkes, 'Joining a Fraternity in Late Medieval England: The Case of the Palmers' Guild of Ludlow, c. 1250–1551', (unpub. Ph.D. thesis, University of Durham, 2020); J. Freeman, 'The Religious Fraternities of Medieval Middlesex', *Transactions of the London and Middlesex Archaeological Society* 62 (2012 for 2011), 205–49; K. Farnhill, *Guilds and the Parish Community in Late Medieval East Anglia, c.1470–1550* (York, 2001); D. F. Crouch, *Piety, Fraternity and Power: Religious Gilds in Late Medieval Yorkshire, 1389–1547* (York, 2000); V. Bainbridge, *Gilds in the Medieval Countryside: Social and Religious Change in Cambridgeshire c.1350–1558*. Studies in the History of Medieval Religion 10 (Woodbridge, 1997); J. Mattingly, 'The Medieval Parish Guilds of Cornwall', *Journal of the Royal Institution of Cornwall* n.s. 10.3 (1989), 290–329.

5   Various other lay fraternities were based in cathedrals, but as the exception rather than the norm; see E. A. New, 'Fraternities in English Cathedrals in the Later Medieval Period' in *Social Attitudes and Political Structures in the Fifteenth Century*, ed. T. Thornton, Fifteenth Century 5 (Stroud, 2000), 33–51.

Guild in the period for which its records survive.[6] Instead, it offered elaborate and high-profile liturgical celebration, the public commendation of souls, and prayers for benefactors and members, all located at the heart of the nation's capital city.

What the Jesus Guild in St Paul's did have in common with other religious fraternities was record-keeping. It is impossible to know just how common this practice was, but it is clear that even modest associations had written regulations and it would presumably have been necessary to keep a record of membership in all but the very smallest fraternities.[7] Through deliberate action and good fortune, records survive for a not insignificant number of religious fraternities, although, as in the case of the Jesus Guild, these are often fragmentary.[8] The current edition adds to those extant fraternity records made accessible through publication, but contributes another dimension because of the differences between the Jesus Guild in St Paul's and the great majority of religious fraternities in medieval England.

THE JESUS GUILD IN CONTEXT II: DEVOTION TO THE HOLY NAME IN LATE MEDIEVAL ENGLAND

The Jesus Guild in St Paul's Cathedral was perhaps the most prominent organisational expression in fifteenth- and sixteenth-century England of the cult of the Holy Name, a complex and multi-faceted devotion that flourished as part of the upsurge in Christocentric piety during the later Middle Ages. Devotion to the 'Holy Name' focuses upon the Second Person of the Trinity, with the Name seen to represent the power and glory of God and divinity incarnate, Jesus the living and suffering man. The devotion has New Testament origins and was developed in the early Church as Christianity spread across Europe.[9] Evidence of the use of three letters, the 'sacred trigram' (more commonly, if inaccurately, referred to

---

6   Very occasional exceptions can be seen, when for example John Monk, waxchandler and past warden of the Jesus Guild, was granted alms in 1526/7 **[138]**.

7   Reference may be made to the various ordinances and other written records itemised in the calendar of the 1389 Guild Returns in Westlake, *Parish Gilds*, Appendix.

8   Two previous London Record Society publications focus on a religious fraternity, *Parish Fraternity Register: Fraternity of the Holy Trinity and Ss. Fabian and Sebastian in the Parish of St Botolph without Aldersgate*, ed. P. Basing, LRS 18 (1982), and *The Bede Roll of the Fraternity of St Nicholas*, ed. N. W. and V. A. James, LRS 39, 2 vols (2004). Other recent edited records of religious fraternities include *The Accounts of the Guild of the Holy Trinity, Luton 1526/7–1546/7*, ed. B. Tearle, Bedfordshire Historical Record Society 91 (Woodbridge, 2012), and *The Register of the Guild of the Holy Cross, St Mary and St John the Baptist, Stratford-upon-Avon*, ed. M. MacDonald, Dugdale Society 42 (2007).

9   For example, Philippians 2:10–11. For an overview of the devotion's development from the days of the early Church until the fourteenth century, see A. Cabassut, 'La Devotion au Nom de Jesus dans L'Eglise d'Occident', *La Vie Spirituelle* 86 (1952), 46–69, and New, 'Cult of the Holy Name', 17–19.

as the 'sacred monogram'), to represent the Holy Name is found from the second century and, by the sixth century, was used throughout the Christian world.[10] In the Western Church, Saints Augustine, Ambrose and Anselm all played a role in promoting honour to the Holy Name, which further developed during the twelfth and thirteenth centuries under the auspices of Saints Bernard, Francis and Louis IX.[11] Evidence of what might be described as a 'cult' really emerges in Western Europe during the fourteenth century, with the devotion promoted in particular by the German Dominican Heinrich Suso, by the Blessed Giovanni Colombini of Siena, and by the English mystics Richard Rolle and Walter Hilton.[12] Rolle and Suso also wrote extensively about the Holy Name, both through devotional literature and liturgical texts, with this material circulating widely and sometimes being adapted by others. Early in the fifteenth century, the Franciscan St Bernardino of Siena (1380–1444) further promoted the devotion, especially reverence for the sacred monogram.[13] There was no uniform Europe-wide progression of the cult of the Holy Name but, instead, a striking regionalisation of the devotion. The cult in England expressed elements of the emotive and mystical strands of devotion but was, as Richard Pfaff suggested, more overtly orthodox than elsewhere in Western Europe.[14]

The earliest surviving text of the Mass so far identified in an English context is in a missal made for Sir William Beauchamp in the mid-1380s, and liturgical celebration of the votive Mass and Office seems to have spread rapidly during the late fourteenth and early fifteenth centuries.[15] Altars and chapels established in honour of, or rededicated to, the Holy Name (usually referred to as 'Jesus' altars or chapels) proliferated in the fifteenth century, in cathedral, monastic and parochial contexts.[16]

---

[10] H. Blake et al., 'From Popular Devotion to Resistance and Revival in England: The Cult of the Holy Name of Jesus and the Reformation' in *The Archaeology of Reformation, 1480–1580*, ed. D. Gaimster and R. Gilchrist (Leeds, 2003), 175–203 (at 175).

[11] Blake et al., 'From Popular Devotion', 176.

[12] Blake et al., 'From Popular Devotion', 176; D. Renevey, '"Name Above Names": The Devotion to the Name of Jesus from Richard Rolle to Walter Hilton's Scale of Perfection', in *The Medieval Mystical Tradition in England, Ireland and Wales. Exeter Symposium VI*, ed. M. Glasscoe (Cambridge, 1999), 103–21.

[13] Cabassut, 'Devotion au Nom de Jesus', 60–2.

[14] R. W. Pfaff, *New Liturgical Feasts in Later Medieval England* (Oxford, 1970), 62.

[15] For the mass, see Oxford, Bodleian, Trinity College MS 8, f. 286r. It is worth noting that Beauchamp had originally been destined for a career in the Church and was, for a while, a canon of Salisbury Cathedral. See New, 'The Cult of the Holy Name', 27–30; Pfaff, *New Liturgical Feasts*, 79; and J. Catto, 'Sir William Beauchamp between Lollardy and Chivalry', in *The Ideals and Practice of Medieval Knighthood* III, ed. C. Harper-Bill and R. Harvey (Woodbridge 1990), 39–48.

[16] New, 'The Cult of the Holy Name', 32, 36, 39–42; and, for a detailed investigation of the development and expression of devotion to the Holy Name, see also E. A. New, *The Holy Name and Christocentric Piety in Later Medieval England and Wales* (forthcoming).

The earliest identified religious guild in honour of the Holy Name was established at Sheringham (Norfolk) in 1387; from the middle of the fifteenth, and especially at the end of the fifteenth and early sixteenth centuries, a plethora of Jesus fraternities was founded across the country.[17] Devotional writing, private prayer and contemplation were also key features of the evolving cult and have received considerable scholarly attention, including an interest from those seeking to find unorthodox religious sentiment among devotees.[18] The Holy Name also pervaded the visual and material culture of late medieval England, although by the early sixteenth century it can be challenging to discern true devotion from pious fashion.[19] The English ecclesiastical authorities finally acknowledged the strength of popular feeling by adding the feast of the Name of Jesus to the official calendar of Canterbury in 1488 and of York in the following year. Convocation in both Provinces ordered that the Feast should be celebrated on 7 August, the day after the Transfiguration, setting England apart from the rest of Europe, where the feast was celebrated in early January in conjunction with the Circumcision.[20]

THE JESUS GUILD IN ST PAUL'S CATHEDRAL: FOUNDATION AND EARLY HISTORY

The Fraternity of the 'most glorious Name of Jesus' was founded in St Paul's Cathedral in the mid fifteenth century, probably under the auspices of Dean Thomas Lisieux who, in 1450, requested burial in what was by then known as the Jesus Chapel in the crypt – or, as contemporaries often called it, the Crowdes.[21] It is possible that the earlier Guild of St Anne, also located in the crypt, was absorbed

---

[17] New, 'Cult of the Holy Name', 30–2, 36–44; Blake et al., 'From popular devotion', 177. The Jesus Guild in St Paul's was one of the earliest of these 'second wave' fraternities.
[18] See, for example, D. Renevey, 'The Name Poured Out: Margins, Illuminations and Miniatures as Evidence for the Practice of Devotions to the Name of Jesus in Late Medieval England', *Analecta Cartusiana* 130.9 (1996), 127–47; C. A. Carsley, 'Devotion to the Holy Name: Late Medieval Piety in England', *Princeton University Library Chronicle* 53 (1992), 156–72; R. Lutton, '"Love this Name that is IHC": Vernacular Prayers, Hymns and Lyrics to the Holy Name of Jesus in Pre-Reformation England', in *Vernacularity in England and Wales c. 1350–1550*, ed. E. Salter and H. Wicker, Utrecht Studies in Medieval Literacy (Turnhout, 2011), 115–41.
[19] Blake et al., 'From popular devotion', 177–88.
[20] Blake et al., 'From popular devotion', 176–7.
[21] E. A. New, 'Fraternities: A Case Study of the Jesus Guild' in *St Paul's. The Cathedral Church of London, 604–2004*, ed. D. Keene, A. Burns and A. Saint (New Haven & London, 2004), 162–3 (at 162). The Jesus Chapel, solely occupied by the Guild by 1506 at the latest, took up the whole of New Work undercroft, with the parish of St Faith occupying the western Romanesque Old Work crypt until 1551; see C. Cragoe Davidson, 'Fabric, tombs and precinct, 1087–1540' in *St. Paul's*, ed. Keene, Burns and Saint, 127–42 (at 136 and fig. 68); E. A. New, 'The Jesus Chapel in St Paul's Cathedral,

into the Jesus Guild, or that the agreement between that fraternity and the Dean and Chapter influenced arrangements between the later organisation and the cathedral.[22] The earliest direct reference to the Jesus Guild is found in the codicil of the will of Thomas Batail, a mercer, made in 1455, where he bequeathed 40s. to 'susteyn the Brotherhoode',[23] and in January 1459 the Guild received Letters Patent from Henry VI, who took upon himself the role of patron [**2.a and 2.c**]. There are scattered references to the Guild and its members throughout the second half of the fifteenth century, including one to Edmund Appleyard who was 'made a brother' of the fraternity in 1489, implying an induction ceremony of some kind.[24]

Apart from enrolled and later copies of the Henry VI Letters Patent and copies of deeds relating to land granted to the Guild in Uxbridge [**2.a, 2.c and 10.a–10.d**], no fifteenth-century records produced by the Jesus Guild itself have been identified, but it is possible to piece together an outline of how the Guild may have operated in this period. Whether or not he was directly concerned with the foundation, Thomas Lisieux, as dean of the Cathedral, presumably authorised the establishment of the Guild in its prestigious location, a combination suggestive of a high-status association from the outset. The earliest-known wardens of the Guild were both royal servants: Henry Benet, a clerk of the Privy Seal (who would have known Lisieux through the latter's appointment as Keeper of the Privy Seal), and Richard Ford, a Remembrancer of the Exchequer [**227**].[25] People associated with the Jesus Guild in this period included, among others: Robert Heworth, undersheriff of London; Johanna, widow of Edward Kervile, grocer; John Brankynbrugh, a wealthy and well-connected vicar of Hendon (Middx.); John Mirfyn, 'gentleman of London'; and John Wood, archdeacon of Middlesex, who bequeathed 40s. '*pro pictura*

London: a reconstruction of its appearance before the Reformation', *Antiquaries Journal* 85, (2005), 103–24 (at 105–6).

22 LMA, CLC/313/L/H/001/MS25121/0513, Agreement between the Dean and Chapter of St Paul's and the Brothers of the Guild of St Anne, 18 July 1371. I am grateful to Dr David Rollenhagen for a transcript of this document and to Professor Caroline M. Barron for drawing my attention to it. The Guild of St Anne was not mentioned in the 1388/9 Returns and may already have failed by that date; see C. M. Barron and M.-H. Rousseau, 'Cathedral, City and State, 1300–1540', in *St Paul's,* ed. Keene, Burns and Saint, 33–44 (at 38).

23 New, 'Fraternities: A Case Study', 162; and TNA, PROB 11/4/107. I am grateful to Dr Anne Sutton for this reference.

24 E. S. Dewick, 'On a Manuscript of a Sarum Prymer which belonged to a Brother of the Jesus Gild at St Paul's, London', *Transactions of the St Paul's Ecclesiological Society* 5 (1905), 170–1; E. Duffy, *The Stripping of the Altars. Traditional Religion in England c.1400–1580* (New Haven and London, 1992), 224–5. The current whereabouts of this manuscript is unknown.

25 Lisieux, who also served as chaplain to Henry VI, was Keeper of the Privy Seal from 1452 until 1456, the year he died; see J. L. Kirby, 'Lisieux, Thomas (d. 1456), administrator and dean of St Paul's' in *ODNB*.

tabernaculi Jhu in criptu' (for painting the tabernacle of Jesus in the crypt).[26] Although the evidence is fragmentary, it provides an impression of a guild that attracted the wealthy and well-to-do.

In addition to well-heeled supporters, the Jesus Guild received income from tenements and lands from the later fifteenth century, albeit in part through the failure of another pious venture. In 1471, John Hart alias Chapman had bequeathed land to fund beds for four poor men in his house in Uxbridge (Middx.), to be placed under the direction of his wife, Elizabeth, with the proviso that if, after Elizabeth's death, her executors did not want to maintain the beds, the lands should go to support the Mass of Jesus in St Paul's.[27] John Wood, archdeacon of Middlesex, was the overseer of Hart's will and, it might be inferred, the person who made this valuable suggestion. The other Uxbridge lands and two tenements belonging to the Jesus Guild had also been held by John and Elizabeth Hart, although these reverted to the three men who officially granted them to the Fraternity shortly after John's death [10.a–10.d]. The Guild kept the tenements and land until at least 1535, and they provided a decent annual rent of between 29s. 8d. and 40s. The Jesus Guild also held the Bull's Head tavern in St Martin's Lane from the 1460s until it was sold in 1507 to a member of the Guild, the vintner John Hatfeld alias Pilborough, who held it until at least 1518 and possibly until his death in 1520.[28] The extant Guild records do not name the benefactor who gave the Bull's Head, just that he was to be prayed for [14], which raises some interesting questions about institutional memory and could reflect the degree of administrative disruption that precipitated the 1506 reorganisation. The Bull's Head had, in fact, been bequeathed by Richard Ewen, a canon of St Paul's, who wished to be buried before the Jesus altar in the crypt chapel, and on condition that the Guild should pray for him and celebrate six Masses of Jesus.[29] Although the stated aim in selling the Bull's Head was to raise money to buy a meeting hall for the Guild, this was never done; feasts were usually held in the crypt of the Cathedral or, in the 1530s, in the newly constructed Saddlers' Hall [190, 197].

As well as revenue from property and bequests, the Guild farmed out the right to collect 'offerings' on its behalf, a practice that provided the bulk of its income after its early sixteenth-century refoundation. This procedure, usually done in association with offering an indulgence (as

---

[26] Heyworth, Commissary Court MS 9171/5/316; Johanna Kervile, TNA PROB 11/8/112 (I am grateful to Professor Caroline M. Barron for this reference); Brankynbrugh, PROB 11/8/117 (I am grateful to Dr Jessica Freeman for this reference); Mirfyn, TNA, PROB 11/6/147; Wood, TNA, PROB 11/6/282.

[27] TNA, PROB 11/6/37. I am grateful to Dr Jessica Freeman for this reference.

[28] John Hatfeld alias Pilborough took an action for unpaid rent against another vintner in a case dated 1518x29; he died in 1520 – see, respectively, TNA C1/481/1 and TNA PROB 11/20/127.

[29] TNA, PROB 11/5/69. Ewen made his will in 1461 and it was proved in 1464.

was the case for the Jesus Guild), was quite often adopted by fraternities, as well as by hospitals and religious houses, and could be an
excellent source of income.[30] Problems could arise, however, and this is
how we know that the Jesus Guild operated in this way during its first
incarnation. In 1485/86, Thomas Sandell of London, named in a case in
Chancery as 'proctor of the Frathernite of Jhesu in London', claimed
that he had been falsely arrested by one John Balsere of Canterbury out
of 'old malice and rankour' while on pilgrimage to St Thomas Becket's
shrine, a pious journey that he combined with gathering offerings for the
Jesus Guild.[31] The case was brought before the bishop of Winchester, but
unfortunately the outcome is unknown. Another Chancery case reveals a
murkier side to the practice of farming the right to collect devotions and,
perhaps, provides a partial explanation of why the Jesus Guild needed to
be re-established in the early sixteenth century. At some point between
1475 and 1485, a Chancery case was brought by John Duffton, a bedesman
(presumably of the Jesus Guild), who accused the sheriffs of London and
Middlesex of detention without due cause.[32] Duffton had been arrested
because Martin Jolyff, named as 'preste and keper of the gilde of Jhesus',
had taken an action of trespass out against him.[33] Duffton claimed that
he was the injured party, and that the truth of the matter was that when
he (Duffton) paid for the right to collect alms for the Guild, Jolyff had
provided sealed licences which were for some reason invalid. The men
to whom Duffton had sub-contracted to collect the alms were imprisoned
but, despite repeated entreaties, Jolyff would not provide new licences
and instead had Duffton arrested and charged with trespass.

THE JESUS GUILD FROM REFORMATION TO REFORMATION

Again, we do not know the outcome of the Duffton case but, whoever
the guilty party really was, it is clear that the Jesus Guild was in
serious trouble by the first years of the sixteenth century, with wardens
apparently embezzling money and the common seal being misused

---

[30]   This practice is investigated in detail in Swanson, *Indulgences*, 113–78; the farmed-out
       collecting procedure employed by the Jesus Guild in St Paul's during the period
       for which its records survive is used extensively by Professor Swanson to illustrate
       various points.
[31]   TNA, C1/78/73. The vintner John Sandell was active in the Jesus Guild between 1514
       and 1532 and may have been a kinsman of Thomas.
[32]   TNA, C 1/66/25.
[33]   It is unclear whether this is the same Martin Jolyff who features in the Uxbridge deeds
       [**10.a–10.d**], where he is identified as a layman, although it has been suggested that
       the Martin Jolyff who served as chamberlain and keeper of the bakehouse at St Paul's
       was ordained to the priesthood late in life, see *The Estate and Household Accounts of
       William Worsley, dean of St Paul's Cathedral 1479–1497*, ed. H. Kleineke and S. R.
       Hovland, LRS 40 (2004), 154–5.

[4.k]. Reform-minded Dean John Colet was not about to tolerate a sub-standard association within his own cathedral and, in 1506 and under Colet's auspices, the Jesus Guild was reorganised.[34] New ordinances were drawn up and things generally put in order, with royal licences, land grants and memoranda concerning prayers to be said for benefactors carefully copied, and with annual accounts kept from that time onwards: a selection from these documents yields the text edited in this volume.

It is unclear whether the 1506 ordinances **[4.a–4.k, 6.a–6.m, 8.a–8.i]** expanded upon previous regulations or represented a root-and-branch overhaul, but they are detailed and contain provisions for dealing with problems that might arise. While the hand of Colet may be discerned in the reformation of the Guild, the precise language and careful formulae of the ordinances speak more of an association which, from this date onwards, was run by men used to the regulation of crafts and trades. The governance and financing of the Guild are clearly one priority of the ordinances, but more time is spent specifying liturgical provision, and the extant accounts confirm that this remained a priority. However, the 1506 refoundation did not immediately solve all the problems faced by the Guild, for in 1514 new ordinances were drawn up. The partial set of regulations that survives among the records **[22.a–22.h]** lack their crucial first folio or two, but on palaeographic grounds and from the internal evidence of the extant accounts **[36]**, it may be assumed that these are the 'new' set.[35] Among the changes implemented in the new ordinances was the stipulation that the right to gather devotions would be renewed annually, an eminently sensible provision because previously the Guild had farmed the devotions for longer periods and was clearly losing out as a result. Indeed, Swanson has noted that the profits accruing to the Jesus Guild as the result of this practice were now substantial, and that it was one of the few fraternities that extended such procedure during the reign of Henry VIII.[36] The 1514/15 account also records significant work undertaken in the Jesus Chapel **[34]**, and it is possible that 1514 marked the real turning-point for the revived Guild. A reference to 'reformacione of dyvers matters' concerning the Guild occurs, however, in the 1516/17 account **[54]**, indicating that further minor adjustments to

---

[34]   Re-organising the Jesus Guild was part of a programme of reform undertaken by Colet; see J. Arnold, *Dean John Colet of St Paul's. Humanism and Reform in Early Tudor England* (London, 2007), 14, 89–92.

[35]   It is interesting to note that the account for 1514/15 includes payment for 'translatyng' the ordinances for the brethren **[35]**, although it is unclear whether this indicates a translation from Latin or French to English, or if 'translating' actually meant 'moving' (i.e. copying them into the main records).

[36]   Swanson, *Indulgences*, 370, 476. Swanson also notes that, unlike many religious fraternities, in its revised ordinances the Jesus Guild closed a 'loophole' by insisting that gifts and bequests be itemised separately from standard 'devotions', Swanson, *Indulgences*, 222.

the running of the Fraternity were required following two years' trial of the new ordinances.

In both sets of ordinances and in the twenty years' worth of surviving accounts, liturgical provision looms large and emerges as one of the main attractions of the reformed fraternity. After 1506, the Guild kept no dedicated priest of its own, but instead paid cathedral clergy to attend and perform all services, with precise numbers and attire clearly stipulated [6.c–6.f, 6.j–6.l]. In addition to the various clergy who participated on a daily and weekly basis, at the annual celebration of the Feasts of the Transfiguration and Holy Name (6 and 7 August) no fewer than thirty-seven cathedral clerics attended service in the Jesus Chapel, with all those in major orders wearing copes for the procession. Furthermore, the cathedral's choristers were supplied with special gowns, presumably to wear when attending Guild services [6.m]. As well as singing and saying Mass and the Divine Office, a cardinal (one of the senior minor canons) was to read out the names of departed brothers and sisters in his weekly Mass, and the sub-dean was to preach a sermon on the feast of the Holy Name. If the sub-dean was unavailable, one of the cathedral cardinals was to preach the sermon, but the Guild insisted that, if he did so, he should wear his grey amice, the symbol of his office [6.e].

Even this standard of liturgical provision might be improved, for choristers from the Chapel Royal were paid to sing in the chapel on several occasions and, in 1524/25, a Franciscan friar was paid to preach a sermon to the members of the Guild, at the express invitation of the assistants [123]. That the music in the Jesus Chapel was of the highest standard is clear from the presence of the highly trained choristers and vicars choral, from the numerous repairs made to the organs, and from frequent payments for the compilation and repair of various liturgical manuscripts. One mass book was given to the Guild by the noted composer Robert Fayrfax [162], and it may be that Fayrfax's surviving Mass *O bone Jesu* is the setting that he composed for the Fraternity, perhaps to coincide with its reorganisation in 1506.[37]

The Jesus Guild took care to publicise its celebrations, paying the six London waits to process around the city and suburbs of London playing their instruments to give 'warnyng and knowlage' of the upcoming feasts of the Transfiguration and Name of Jesus [8.b]. The Guild supplied the waits with banners and gowns adorned with the Holy Name, better to advertise the celebrations and, presumably, to stir devotion among those who did not attend the Guild celebrations on a more frequent basis. The chance survival of a flyer in a 1522 Almanac demonstrates that the Jesus Guild went to considerable lengths to advertise its liturgical celebrations,

---

[37] D. Mateer and E. A. New, '"In Nomine Jesu": Robert Fayrfax and the Guild of the Holy Name in St Paul's Cathedral', *Music and Letters* 81 (2000), 507–20 (at 514–15).

and the prayers and indulgence offered to members [71].[38] It is significant that this 'advertisement' gives precise details, commending the role of the bedesmen, the daily antiphons, and the prayers at the Paul's Cross sermons, but with the indulgence, usually the focus of such advertisements, relegated to the very end. As well as its own indulgence, the Jesus Guild also went to some trouble and expense to acquire the *Scala Coeli* indulgence for its members [54].[39]

Clearly all the members of the Jesus Guild had at least some religious motives for joining, even if the social prestige and networking opportunities were also attractive – indeed, Susan Brigden went so far as to describe members of the Fraternity 'as conservative in religion as they were wealthy'.[40] This was perhaps exemplified by Richard Callard, a Painter-Stainer who acted as assistant and warden of the Jesus Guild [223], and who, in his will of 1544, specifically requested that a 'Catholycke Doctor or Bacheler of Dyvyntie' should preach at his Requiem Mass and month's mind (a Requiem Mass celebrated one month after death).[41] Another warden, William Paver, was also a committed Catholic and clearly deeply troubled by the increasing attacks, as he saw them, on traditional religion. Paver, the common clerk of London,[42] had been involved with the Jesus Guild since its reorganisation in 1506/7 and was elected warden in 1530 [233]. On May Day 1533 he oversaw the execution of Richard Bainham, a relapsed heretic and, according to the chronicler Edmund Hall, Paver vehemently refuted Bainham's speech justifying his beliefs.[43] Paver further declared that if the Gospel was allowed in English he would kill himself and, a few weeks later, did indeed commit suicide.[44]

Very few members of the Guild can be identified as being as fervent as Callard and Paver, but many come across as more than usually pious. Although, as a number of scholars have demonstrated, problems can accompany the incautious use of wills, these documents nevertheless can offer basic guidance as to religious sentiment.[45] So, for example, John Hatfeld alias Pilborough, who served the Jesus Guild as an assistant,

---

[38] London, BL, Huth 54. I am grateful to Professor Mary Erler for drawing my attention to this.

[39] For a discussion of the *Scala Coeli* indulgence, see Duffy, *Stripping of the Altars*, 375–6, and Swanson, *Indulgences*, 54–6, 410–12; and Swanson, *Indulgences*, 139 explicitly discusses the Jesus Guild's acquisition of *Scala Coeli*.

[40] S. Brigden, 'Religion and Social Obligation in early sixteenth-century London', *Past & Present* 103 (1984), 67–112 (at 100).

[41] TNA, PROB 11/30/209.

[42] C. M. Barron, *London in the Later Middle Ages* (Oxford, 2004), 364.

[43] E. Hall, *Hall's Chronicle: Containing the History of England &c.* (London, 1809), 806.

[44] Hall, *Chronicle*, 806 revealed that Paver 'brake promes' to cut his throat, (he hanged himself) but commented, in a rather more sympathetic tone, 'of what mynde and intent he did so, God judge.' The incident is discussed in Brigden, *London and the Reformation*, 217–18.

[45] See, for example, C. Burgess, 'Late Medieval Wills and Pious Convention: Testamentary

began his notably pious will by commending his soul to God and to 'his blessid mother Saynt Mary Virgin, Quene of Hevyne, Lady of the worlde and Empress of hell'.[46] Another example of the testamentary piety expressed by members of the Jesus Guild is provided by Elizabeth Reed, widow of Sir Bartholomew, who commended her soul to God 'beleving that he created me and also by the aspercion of his precious blod and by his moost paynfull passion hath redemed me and all mankynde'.[47] The rest of her long and detailed will included a wide array of pious bequests, ranging from fraternities and parish churches, to named nuns who were to pray for her, and which amply fulfilled the obligations of the seven corporal works of mercy.

Testamentary evidence provides only a snapshot of personal piety, however, and here the surviving records of the Jesus Guild come into their own by revealing lifetime giving. The devout Elizabeth Reed added considerably to the 10 marks that her husband, Sir Bartholomew Reed, bequeathed to the Jesus Guild in 1505, for example [20]. Sometimes money was given for specific purposes, such as the gifts received in 1518 from John Sandell and Thomas Nichols for making a new pair of silver shoes for the image of Jesus in the chapel [60]. Such gifts afford a salutary reminder that even the most comprehensive testamentary evidence never provides more than a glimpse of an individual's pious activity, for neither Sandell nor Nichols made any reference to the Jesus Guild in their wills.[48]

In common with most religious fraternities, the Jesus Guild also had a social side, with food and drink provided at the main feasts and frequent 'drinkings' for Guild officers. The opportunity to rub shoulders (quite literally, in what must at times have been an overcrowded chapel) with potential business contacts and those with wealth and civic power must have been a draw for some members. Association through kinship and friendship may also be discerned and would have been of importance to the Jesus Guild, which could not rely upon neighbourly support in the way that a parochial fraternity often could. Two wardens of the Guild were kinsmen: William Campion, warden 1525–27, and William Brothers, warden 1527–29, were cousins, and it is interesting to note that William Osbourne, the priest who gave money to the Guild in 1517/18 [60], was parson of Campion's parish, St Mary Magdalen Milk Street.[49] Thomas Hynd, a sheriff of London who served as warden, assistant, and

---

Evidence Reconsidered', in *Profit, Piety and the Professions in Later Medieval England*, ed. M. A. Hicks (Gloucester, 1990), 14–33.

46   TNA, PROB 11/20/127.
47   TNA, PROB 11/24/303.
48   TNA, PROB 11/24/235, 11/22/409.
49   TNA, PROB 11/24/152; G. Hennessy, *Novum Repertorium Ecclesiasticum Parochiale Londinense; or London Diocesan Clergy Succession from the Earliest Times to the Year 1898* (London, 1898), 319.

auditor of the Jesus Guild, left memorial rings to three members of the Fraternity, and named two others as executors.[50] None of these men were of the same parish as Hynd (St Antholin), and although three, Benjamin Dygby, Thomas Baldry and William Botry, were fellow mercers, the other two were a haberdasher (John Browne) and a scrivener. The scrivener, John Worsopp [235], a brother of the Fraternity who served as warden in 1526–28, provides a clear link between several members of the Guild. Worsopp witnessed the wills of four fellow members, including three fellow wardens (William Botry, John Browne and Thomas Hynd), and also received bequests from William Bromwell, another warden.[51] Indeed, while Worsopp on the one hand may just have been recommended as a reliable scrivener by one client to another, it is on the other hand very likely that he facilitated some important connections through the Jesus Guild, especially since he drew up many of the annual accounts (see below).

During its second incarnation the Jesus Guild attracted men from a wide range of occupations, from liveried members of the wealthiest companies to those engaged in more modest economic activities. It was a prestigious association, and the very poorest seem deliberately to have been kept away from the Guild in what might be deemed a rather un-Christian manner. In 1529/30, for example, the 'bedille of the beggers' was paid for keeping poor people out of the Jesus Chapel [162]. The Guild members comprised, as one might imagine, a considerable number of high-status brothers and sisters, including several mayors and sheriffs, and liveries were given to and donations received from the king and other members of the royal household [52].[52] A score of mercers can be identified as members, and between five and ten each of merchant tailors, haberdashers, goldsmiths and grocers; eleven brothers of the Jesus Guild were also members of the Merchant Adventurers' Company.[53] A total of twenty-four occupations have been identified among the London-based brothers of the Jesus Guild, excluding clergy of various kinds, demonstrating a notably diverse membership base.[54]

The connection with the Mercers' Company appears to have been particularly strong, albeit informal, not only in terms of the numbers of mercers who were members of the Jesus Guild, but also through the refoundation under Colet's auspices.[55] John Colet's father, Henry,

50 TNA, PROB 11/23/75.
51 Botry, TNA, PROB 11/25/428; Browne, PROB 11/24/296; Hynde, PROB 11/23/75; Bromwell, PROB 11/27/23; Thurston, PROB 11/20/149.
52 For example, *Privy Purse Expenses of Henry the Eighth from November 1529 to December 1532: with Introductory Remarks and Illustrative Notes,* ed. N. H. Nicolas (London, 1827), 46; *Privy Purse Expenses of the Princess Mary, Daughter of King Henry the Eighth, afterwards Queen Mary,* ed. F. Madden (London, 1831), 115.
53 New, 'Cult of the Holy Name', 122–9.
54 New, 'Cult of the Holy Name', 128, table 2.2.
55 The suggestion that the Jesus Guild may have formed an unofficial religious association

was a prominent mercer who served as one of their wardens on several occasions, and the dean himself was admitted to the company in 1508.[56] The wardens of the Mercers' made detailed arrangements for prayers to be said by the Jesus Guild for John Stile and Thomas Wyndout [13], and the latter, significantly, had been apprenticed to Henry Colet.[57]

There was, however, a much clearer association between the Guild and the Waxchandlers' Company. In the 1506 Guild ordinances, the 'Felishippe of Wexchaundelers' (presumably the senior members of the Company) were among those supplied with liveries each year [8.f], and payments for such liveries occur in all the surviving accounts. A separate agreement made between the Waxchandlers' and the Jesus Guild in 1508 specified that the former should find certain lights and pay an annual fee to the Guild [12]. Such annual payments are recorded in the accounts of both the Jesus Guild and the Waxchandlers' Company, although payments were often made by the Guild for wax other than that supplied by the Company (for example [42]). The Waxchandlers' accounts also record extra expenses relating to the Jesus Chapel not listed in the accounts of the Jesus Guild, and they also maintained the 'great light of Jesus' (possibly a candelabra stand).[58] The Feasts of the Transfiguration and the Holy Name were important to the Waxchandlers', for the company elected its officers on the former day and held obits for dead guild members on the latter.[59] The Waxchandlers' also joined the Jesus Guild for communal celebrations on these days, and fined its members who were late for these combined events.[60] The Jesus Guild also numbered among its brethren individual waxchandlers, including two masters of the Company, John Monk and Stephen Ward, both of whom also served as wardens of the Guild. It is not clear when the Waxchandlers' started using the Jesus Chapel, but it may have coincided with, or just preceded, the re-organisation of the Fraternity in 1506, since Monk was one of the re-foundation wardens [1]. After the 1547 dissolution of the Jesus Guild, the Waxchandlers' abandoned the cathedral and transferred its religious services to the parish church of St John Zachery, near to their company hall.[61] The Waxchandlers'

---

for the Mercers' is rejected by Anne Sutton but given more credence by Arnold: New, 'Cult of the Holy Name', 122–3; A. F. Sutton, *The Mercery of London: Trade, Goods and People, 1130–1578* (Aldershot, 2005), 381–3 (and esp. n. 16); Arnold, *Dean John Colet*, 89–92.

56   Sutton, *Mercery*, 557–8, 360–1.

57   Sutton, *Mercery*, 382.

58   LMA, CLC/L/WB/D/001/MS09481/001, for example f.16r.

59   J. Dummelow, *The Wax Chandlers of London: A short history of the Company* (Chichester, 1973), 33.

60   Several members of the Waxchandlers' Company were, for example, fined for being late for the procession to the Jesus Chapel on the feast of the Holy Name in 1534–36, GL MS 9481/1, f.23r.

61   Dummelow, *Wax Chandlers,* 169.

may have had 'corporate' membership of the Fraternity but, despite the close links between them, it is clear from the records of both that they were separate organisations.

THE JESUS GUILD DURING THE REFORMATION

The Jesus Guild entered the choppy waters of the mid-1530s relying on people being willing and able to pay for prayer, liturgy and indulgence but also, increasingly, on promissory income, as will be explained below. After the declaration of royal supremacy over the Church in England in 1534, the Guild made efforts to protect its principal source of income by obtaining letters of protection for its proctors across the country. As well as a copy of the 1535 letters themselves [19],[62] the trouble and expense of obtaining these can be seen through the payments made in the accounts for 1533/34 [190]. In the following year, the Jesus Guild arranged a letter of protection specifically for the proctor and his agents in the province of York [21]. In the same period the Guild paid for copies of its records to be made, perhaps to be submitted as part of the process of securing the licences [190]. The Guild continued to operate the 'farm of devotions' through the 1540s but faced increasing problems and, in 1547, a letter of protection to William Loxeley to gather devotions in Oxfordshire and Buckinghamshire forbade any mention of an indulgence.[63] In common with all religious fraternities, the activities of the Jesus Guild came to an end in 1548 when it was dissolved by Act of Parliament. The Chantry Certificate for the Jesus Guild claimed a total income of only £3 15s. *per annum*, and this may indeed have been truthful considering its reliance on farming the right to collect devotions.[64]

Most unusually, however, the Jesus Guild was re-founded with royal assent in 1556, albeit with a radically altered constitution.[65] A president, vice-president and rector were all to be clerics (although not from the cathedral clergy), while two masters and four wardens, two senior and two junior, were to be elected from the laity, with twelve assistants to advise them.[66] In marked contrast to its composition in the first half of the sixteenth century, only the two junior wardens were London merchants (John Cawood a stationer, and William Bull a haberdasher), while the senior wardens and masters were lawyers. Richard Lyell, one of the masters, was an advocate in the Court of Arches, and Thomas

---

[62] Swanson, *Indulgences*, 494 notes that the declaration that none of the Jesus Guild's privileges came from the pope was false.

[63] TNA, LR 14/774; Swanson, *Indulgences*, 496.

[64] *London and Middlesex Chantry Certificate, 1548*, ed. C. J. Kitching, LRS 16 (1980), 51.

[65] *CPR 1555–57*, 274–6.

[66] Brigden, *London and the Reformation*, 582 notes how the officers of the Marian-era Guild exhibited decidedly conservative leanings, and with vice-president Thomas Darbishire later becoming a Jesuit.

Argall, the other master, was registrar of the Prerogative Court of Canterbury; Roger Huntte and John Lewys, senior wardens, were both proctors of the Court of Arches.[67]

Another clear distinction between the Marian-era Guild and its previous incarnation was its close association with the parish of St Faith, which had moved into the more spacious Crowdes in 1552, rather than with the cathedral (see Appendix I).[68] Christopher Hawke, the rector of the re-founded Guild, was rector of this parish, while all four wardens were parishioners.[69] Furthermore, the license for refoundation specified that henceforth the two masters and two of the wardens were to be chosen 'from the senior and more discreet parishioners' of St Faith's, and also that the fraternity be called the 'gild of Jesus in the said parish church'.[70] Before the Reformation there appears to have been some antipathy between St Paul's and St Faith's, with papal intervention required to solve a dispute in the fifteenth century and very few parishioners known to have left bequests to the cathedral.[71] Moreover, only one ambiguous reference indicates any personal connection between those who lived in the parish of St Faith and the pre-Reformation Jesus Guild – indeed, a certain grim satisfaction can be read in the churchwardens' record of clearing the crypt chapel after the Guild was dissolved [201], so it may be that the re-establishment of the Jesus Guild was undertaken with these sensitivities in mind.[72] A final difference between the pre-Reformation and Marian iterations of the Jesus Guild was corporate attendance at funerals, with Henry Machyn recording several at which brethren and officials of the Guild wore hoods and liveries.[73] Upon Elizabeth's accession, it may be assumed that the Jesus Guild was quietly dissolved for a final time.

[67] Brigden, *London and the Reformation*, 582.
[68] The dean and chapter leased 'a certain vault under the Cathedral of St Paul's called the Crowdes or Jesus Chapel' to the churchwardens of St Faith's on 1 March 1552; see 'Edward VI – Volume 14: March 1552', in *Calendar of State Papers Domestic: Edward VI, Mary and Elizabeth, 1547–80*, ed. R. Lemon (London, 1856), 38.
[69] *CPR 1555–57*, 275. Huntte and Lewys were said to be 'the senior parishioners' of St Faith's.
[70] *CPR 1555–57*, 275.
[71] *Calendar of Entries in the Papal Registers Relating to Great Britain and Ireland: Papal Letters vol. XII, A.D. 1458–1471* (London, 1933), 650; New, 'Cult of the Holy Name', 359–60.
[72] Richard Langer, barber and parishioner of St Faith, bequeathed the sum of 4s. to a Fraternity of Jesus in 1469, but did not specify the location of this guild, LMA, DL/C/B/004/MS09171/6, f. 64v. The royal license to re-establish the Guild indicates that the Jesus Chapel had been used for storage at some point between 1552 and 1556, which is perplexing since the parish claimed that it had occupied the Chapel because the New Work undercroft was more spacious and much lighter, *CPR 1555–57*, 274–5.
[73] Brigden, *London and the Reformation*, 582–3 for discussion.

THE OFFICERS AND STAFF OF THE JESUS GUILD

The Jesus Guild maintained its organisational structure through its first two incarnations, with the dean of the cathedral as governor (renamed rector in 1506) and two laymen as wardens. Apart from Colet's involvement with the 1506 reorganisation, there is scant evidence that the dean's role was anything other than honorary in terms of how the Guild was run, and even the responsibility for keeping one of the treasure-chest keys passed to a senior assistant in 1514 [22.b].

During the fifteenth century, wardens could and did serve for some years, for Henry Ford and Henry Benet, wardens when the Henry VI Letters Patent were issued in 1459 [2.a, 2.c], were still in office when the Guild acquired the Uxbridge lands in 1471 [10.a–10.d]. There clearly had been problems with some wardens prior to the 1506 reorganisation, however, and the new ordinances stipulated that they be elected annually and render their accounts within their year in office [4.a, 4.c]. In fact, the accounts disclose that each warden served for two consecutive years, in his first year as junior and in the second year as senior official. This practice of overlapping periods of wardenship operated in the parochial context, too, and must have been helpful both in terms of stability and in enabling each man to 'learn the ropes' before taking over.[74] During the period covered by the surviving Guild records, wardens discharged a range of duties and responsibilities, including keeping two of the three keys to the treasure chest[75] and making certain payments [4.b], as well as rendering annual accounts in a timely manner. They were, however, handsomely rewarded with a stipend of £4 and a gown, as well as a feast in their honour [4.g].

Although dominated by royal servants in the fifteenth century, the wardens of the Jesus Guild were drawn from a wide range of occupations in the first half of the sixteenth century: four were haberdashers and three mercers, while the goldsmiths, grocers, merchant tailors and waxchandlers each provided two wardens. The remaining eight included such diverse occupations as the common clerk of London, an innholder, and a painter-stainer (see Appendix II). However, the two wardens who served in any one year were always from different crafts or trades. This could, of course, have been a coincidence, but plausibly suggests a decision to prevent any one company exercising undue influence, and making sure that the Jesus Guild did not become too closely associated in people's minds with any occupation.

In common with parish and occupational guild practice, the Jesus Guild had men (although membership was open to women, none served as officers) who acted as assistants, aldermen, auditors and

---

[74] For example, K. L. French, *The People of the Parish. Community Life in a Late Medieval English Diocese* (Philadelphia, 2001), 76–7.
[75] In 1514/15 the chest was for a time kept in warden John Monk's house [35].

proctors. We know least about the aldermen, in part because some of the references to them are ambiguous, with the individual involved sometimes having served in the civic office of the same name. The 1514 ordinances specify that the 'alderman assistants' should wear different-coloured gowns from the rest [22.g], possibly suggesting that these men were the senior members, and perhaps past wardens.[76] We know more about the assistants, mentioned in both sets of ordinances [4.a, 22.a], and who feature extensively in the accounts. Assistants were a feature of many London craft and mercantile associations and provided useful support for, and potential oversight of, the wardens.[77] The accounts reveal that they occasionally acted independently of the wardens – for example, inviting a Franciscan friar to preach in the Jesus Chapel in 1524/5 [123]. The 1514 ordinances increased the number of assistants from twelve to twenty-four [22.g], presumably to ensure that an adequate number would always be available if needed. According to the ordinances, the auditors were to be chosen by the rector and assistants to oversee rendering the annual accounts [4.e], and the signatures of those who served in this capacity are preserved in seventeen of the twenty of the extant records. There is no indication of what qualified someone to discharge this role, but presumably men of good reputation and with some financial experience would have been the best candidates.[78]

The oath of the proctors, or procurators, of the Jesus Guild is recorded at the end of the administrative section of the 1506 ordinances [5] and was presumably taken by the 'farmers of the devotions' when they first paid to collect in their particular area. The expectation was that those from outside London would usually travel to the capital in person to deliver an annual record of those who had paid 'devotions' and given gifts or bequests, and on several occasions the Guild pursued those who defaulted. But there are instances where a London-based individual shared the payment for farming the devotions with someone from the region in question and may well have acted as the conduit for the records as well as money. There could also be a combination of in-person and proxy representation for regional proctors. Four men from Liskeard, John, William and Walter Mark, and John Phillip, were licenced to collect donations on behalf of the Jesus Guild in the Diocese of Exeter between 1514 and 1535. The Liskeard proctors may have had direct links with London, but in many years farmed the devotions in conjunction

---

76 There is no indication that the Guild aldermen had previously served as proctors, as was supposed to happen in the Stratford-upon-Avon Holy Cross Guild, see *Register of the Guild of the Holy Cross*, ed. MacDonald, 31; indeed, in the St Paul's Jesus Guild the role of proctor emerges as quite junior.

77 Barron, *London*, 226–7.

78 It may, however, be noted that some auditors made a mark rather than signing their names [58, 66].

with London-based members of the Jesus Guild. In 1515/16 **[40]** and other years, for example, William Mark was joined as a farmer of the diocese of Exeter by John Lake, a London grocer, and Henry Thorneton, a sergeant of arms in the City, both of whom held lands in Devon and presumably provided a convenient liaison with the Jesus Guild.[79] Occasionally a Londoner seems to have acted only as a middle-man for a provincial proctor. In 1516/17 the proctor of the diocese of St David's was Rice ap Howell, but his payment was delivered to the Fraternity 'by the handes' of London waxchandler Richard Lynne **[50]**. Indeed, some regional proctors or their families revealed connections with the Jesus Guild that went beyond the financial, such as the gift of 10s. towards making new pews in the chapel **[110]** received from Katherine, the wife of Nicholas Smyth in 1524, the year in which he died.[80] However they were collected, farming out the devotions provided a crucial source of income for the Jesus Guild and, while prosecuting proctors for failings **[183]**, it went to some lengths to protect its collectors during the difficult years of the mid-1530s **[19]**.

The proctor of London occupied a different position within the Guild as an important junior officer. According to the 1506 ordinances, the proctor of London was obliged to render annual accounts to the Wardens **[8.i]**, and such a practice can be seen explicitly in some accounts and inferred from others (for example **[27]**). This proctor summoned brothers and sisters of the Guild when necessary, paid various clergy, secular staff and workmen, and lit the bonfire and cresset light outside the Jesus Chapel on the vigil of the Holy Name **[8.c, 8.d]**. The London proctor also gathered devotions in the local area. From 1514/15 to 1516/17 devotions were gathered at Court and at the Inns of Court and of Chancery as well as from the City of London but, from 1517/18 onwards, this was reduced to just the City. From 1514/15 to 1518/19 the London-based collections were made on a commission basis, but from 1519/20 until the end of the extant accounts the sum was farmed at a fixed rate.[81] Three men occupied the position of proctor of London during the period for which Guild records survive. Thomas Holmes, a cathedral sexton, acted as proctor of London from at least 1514, but, in 1517/18, he was arrested by the Guild and an action taken against him **[63]**. The details of Holmes' misdemeanour were not stated, and he remained sexton, undertaking duties for the Jesus Guild until he died or retired in 1534. Following this incident John Tyler, named as 'clerk of Jesus' (see below), briefly took over the duties as proctor of London **[69]**, but Holmes's long-term

---

[79] TNA, PROB 11/20/370 (Lake), PROB 11/25/7 (Thorneton).

[80] Katherine was named only as the wife of Nicholas Smyth in the Guild account. She was co-executor of her husband's will, and although Nicholas made no mention of the Jesus Guild in his will, this 'gift' may have been at his request, TNA, PROB 11/21/339.

[81] Swanson, *Indulgences*, 435–6 speculates that the Guild found this 'share-cropping' system unsatisfactory.

replacement was Walter Sheffelde [69], an apparently conscientious man who could also afford to pay for the licence to collect alms in parts of Middlesex and Essex [120].[82]

The 'clerk of Jesus' remains a rather shadowy figure in the administration of the post-1506 Guild. John Tyler was given this title in the 1517/18 accounts for collecting offerings in London for three-quarters of the year [60]. In the same year the assistants elected a 'new clerk' [65], but it is not clear whether this was Tyler, and other references to clerks are vague. It is possible that the Guild employed a dedicated clerk, but it may be that Tyler was a clerk associated more with the Jesus Chapel, and that the other clerks mentioned in the accounts were various men paid on an *ad hoc* basis.

The Jesus Guild also supported almsmen. According to the 1506 ordinances, the Guild was to pay an 'aged and honest man to help priests' and perform a number of other duties [8.a]. Although not explicitly called an almsman, receiving a salary rather than stipend, and with no mention of accommodation, this figure could have been a quasi-bedesman. Whatever transpired between 1506 and 1514, the revised ordinances explicitly established support for four bedesmen [22.f]. These four men were to be 'such as can helpe say Masse', say the Hours, and 'Lataine placebo, dirige and commendacion', suggesting that they may have been in minor Orders, or perhaps had previously worked as cathedral servants, so that they might be expected to possess some familiarity with the liturgy. Some bedesmen may even have been in major Orders. William Bromwell, a mercer who served as warden of the Jesus Guild on three occasions, bequeathed items of his 'wering gere' to 'father Penyfather'.[83] Thomas Penyfather was bedesman of the Fraternity from 1532–35 (when the accounts cease), and it is possible that Bromwell may have used 'father' as an abbreviation of the more usual 'ghostly father', a spiritual director who was normally a priest, although it is possible that he used the term 'father' simply because Penyfather was an old man. Regardless of whether he was a priest or a layman, Penyfather was evidently respected, for he was honoured with a courtesy title by someone as wealthy and influential as Bromwell. The almsmen were remembered by some other members of the Jesus Guild, including the skinner John Josson who left 4d. to each of them, suggesting that they were considered an important part of the fraternity.[84]

---

[82]   Sheffelde, who died in 1544, named his curate (in St Andrew Holborn) as his 'goostelie father', suggestive of a spiritual advisor. We also catch a glimpse of the man in his wish that the residue he left to his 'welbiloved wyf' Elizabeth 'were 100 times more', LMA, DL/C/B/004/MS09171/11, f. 125v.

[83]   TNA, PROB 11/27/23.

[84]   TNA, PROB 11/21/324. Josson also bequeathed 26s. 8d. to the Jesus Guild more generally.

Evidently the bedesmen were provided with lodging, since they would lose their room if caught begging or committing other offences on three occasions [22.f], but the accounts make no mention of this accommodation and its location remains unclear. The almsmen were named in all the accounts, and so it is possible to trace their association with the Guild. While occasional changes probably indicate the death of one of the almsmen, in the 1519/20 account all four were different to those in the previous year. If they lived in close quarters, it is possible that disease could have carried off most of them, but the payment of 10s. to William Bamen 'by the comaundement of the Assistence at the discharging hym of his servyce of the said Fraternitie' [80] means that at least he survived and suggests that something else had transpired.

In addition to its own officers and almsmen, the Jesus Guild engaged cathedral servants to carry out specific duties and supported poor laymen and impoverished priests through almsgiving ([64] for example). The 1506 ordinances stipulated that the sexton of St Paul's, called 'keeper of the vestry', the four cathedral vergers and two of the bellringers should be paid for various duties [6.h, 6.i], and the annual accounts reveal how this happened. The vergers attended and assisted with the daily services, while the bellringers were given responsibility for opening and closing the chapel doors, operating organ bellows and lighting candles, all in addition to ringing the bells.

THE ACCOUNTS OF THE JESUS GUILD

Twenty years' worth of the Guild's annual accounts survive in a continuous sequence, from 1514/15 to 1534/35, forming the bulk of the manuscript in this edition.[85] All the accounts are fair copies, compiled from bills, receipts and working accounts, in a similar manner to practices found in churchwardens accounts and the records of other religious fraternities.[86] The first extant account is labelled with a running header declaring it the ninth, indicating that the sequence would have begun in 1506/7, in line with the reorganisation overseen by Colet. The revision of the ordinances in 1514 raises the possibility that the first eight may deliberately have been 'lost' because of irregularity, but the attrition may equally have been an accidental result of the manner in which they were compiled and kept.[87] The first three extant accounts all begin on a new folio, even if the verso of the previous account's final

---

85   The final two accounts are bound out of sequence, as discussed below.

86   For example, Basing, *Parish Fraternity Register*, xxviii; *Reading St Laurence Churchwardens' Accounts 1498–1570*, ed. J. Dils, Berkshire Records Society 19 (2013), xii.

87   It may also be coincidental, but John Monk and Henry Hill, wardens of the Jesus Guild in 1513/14 (and assuming that the subsequent practice of each warden serving for two years was operative), were named in a Chancery case relating to the farm of charitable

folio is blank; but, from 1517/18, new accounts start on the next available blank side of a folio, often the verso. The first folios of the 1514/15 to 1516/17 accounts also have a round, reddish mark that can be identified as the traces of wax from an applied seal subsequently removed. This indicates that the Guild had the fair copy of its account written up in the form of a small booklet, then witnessed by the auditors and sealed (presumably with the Guild seal) for authentication.[88] At some stage it must have been recognised that keeping accounts separately increased the risk of loss or damage, and that binding them all into a book was both safer and more practical. This would explain why the first eight accounts have been lost and why the seal had to be removed from the 1514/15 to 1516/17 accounts.

All twenty accounts follow the same format, starting with a standard introduction naming the two wardens. The year was given in both calendar and regnal forms, sometimes rendered in words and sometimes numerals. In the accounts for 1514/15 through to 1521/22, the calendar year was described as being accounted by the Church of England, a curious and unusual (possibly unique) qualifier for which there is no obvious explanation.[89] The accounting year ran from Christmas to Christmas, thus covering part of two years, and the account was submitted for examination on the 26th March, in accordance with the ordinances. Only the first calendar year was given in the introduction even though the accounts were drawn up in the second calendar year, which introduced the potential for confusion with, for instance, the 1523/24 accounts being incorrectly labelled '1524' [109].

Single-entry bookkeeping is used for all the accounts, which always begin with the surplus from the previous year followed by repaid debts received within the time of the account, income, expenditure, and debts owing. The account for 1531/2 provides an exception, where a leaf, presumably with the debts recorded, was removed at some point before the manuscript was paginated. Roman numerals are used throughout, with standard abbreviations for denominations of money, weights, and measures. Sub-totals are provided for different sections, and these (rather than the sums next to individual items) tended to be used to calculate final totals.[90] All accounts use sub-headings of various kinds, and a number employ brackets on one or both sides of the text-block further to identify

---

collections in the diocese of Winchester. The document recording this is badly damaged, so that unfortunately the details of this case remain obscure, TNA, C 1/377/60.

[88]   The churchwarden's accounts for St Andrew Hubbard were also compiled as annual booklets, *The Church Records of St Andrew Hubbard, Eastcheap, c1450–c1570*, ed. C. Burgess, LRS 34 (1999), xiii.

[89]   I am grateful to Dr Clive Burgess, Dr Claire Daunton, Dr Philippa Hoskin and Dr Eryn White for helpful discussions on this matter.

[90]   There may also be other explanations for the discrepancies between the totals calculated by adding all the individual figures and the overall totals provided; see New, 'Cult of the Holy Name', chapter 3 (and at 193 and 220).

discrete sections. These were often added after the main text had been written because they break around words that extend slightly beyond the end of the line (for example, on folio 41). Conversely, it would appear from a number of erasures that the brackets and sub-headings were drawn before the text was added in the 1515/16 account.[91] The accounts are written in English, but some scribes occasionally used standard Latin words and phrases, and *le* instead of 'the' (for example [63]). As is to be expected for the period, the English spelling and word form often varies, although, if read aloud, one can almost hear the voice of the scribe or person rendering the account.

Indeed, reading aloud is of relevance to how the accounts were compiled. As mentioned, the auditors witnessed the final accounts, usually with a sign manual (a signature or mark made by the individual), at what was clearly a formal affair that even included the provision of food and drink. Before that point, however, drawing up the financial records of the Guild involved various stages. In some years, reference was made to payments being made either by one of the wardens or by the proctor of London (for example [32], where the scribe initially recorded payment being made by the proctor, corrected to the name of the warden), the inference being that each kept a separate record. In the 1533/34 account, reference is explicitly made to a clerk helping Walter Sheffelde, the proctor of London, to 'overloke the bokes' [197]. Moreover, although presented as the accounts of both wardens, the senior man evidently took charge, at least of the payments. In 1514/15, for example, it was Henry Hill, in his second term, who paid various expenses [35], and when in 1532/33 the Guild had to cope with a warden dying in office, reference was made to the compilation of William Paver's account as separate from the final fair copy [182]. There are also numerous – and, for the historian, frustrating – references to written bills from workmen, and to expenditure itemised in more detail in 'books of parcels', to which the auditors presumably had access if they wished to check. A clerk was often paid for sitting with the London proctor to 'know' the receipt of his account (for example, [183]), indicating careful recording of the disparate documents, perhaps with verbal queries. There was also a clear distinction between drawing up the accounts and writing them. In sixteen of the annual records, the scrivener John Worsopp was paid for making the accounts.[92] In ten of those years, along with another year (1515/16) where there was no separate reference to 'making', Worsopp was also paid for 'engrossing' the accounts; in a further three, he and his servant or clerk were paid jointly for this, while in the remaining three 'Worsopp accounts' only his servant was paid for engrossing. In

---

[91] This account contains a higher than usual number of corrections and erasures; it is understandable that a different scribe was employed for the following year's account.

[92] 1517/18–1530/31 and 1532/33 and 1533/34; in 1523/24 a servant was also mentioned, and in 1532/33 Worsopp was joined by his clerk.

this context, 'making' presumably implies preparation but, although 'engrossing' might at first glance seem to infer writing up, in four years of accounts a separate payment was made for the actual writing; moreover, on palaeographic grounds there appear to have been different scribes for many other years when this payment was not explicitly made. It would seem that for the Jesus Guild 'engrossing' meant recording in full in written form, and that the fair surviving copy was, on occasion, a third stage.[93] Furthermore, internal evidence from the manuscript hints that the scribe who wrote the fair copy may have heard the account (being read out loud), rather than reading it, at least on some occasions. In the 1516/17 account, for example, the scribe initially wrote a numeral two, but immediately corrected it as the word 'to' [51], a mistake that could only be made if listening to rather than reading the original.

INCOME AND EXPENDITURE

The accounts enable us to investigate the financial situation and day-to-day working of the Jesus Guild in the early sixteenth century, and provide a wealth of information about trade, crafts and victualing in London during this period, as well as glimpses of a range of people who came into contact with the prestigious fraternity.

The Jesus Guild received regular income through rent for their Uxbridge lands and property, and from an annual 'rent' from the Waxchandlers'.[94] Although the Guild sold the Bull's Head in 1507, there is an ambiguous reference in the 1519/20 account to the possible acquisition of another property from a Master Shelley [54]. While there is no further evidence about this in the extant accounts, it is possible that the Guild received the property after 1534/35 (when extra income would have been particularly important) because, in 1548, one Edward Acredde was in possession of a 'messuage with houses' in the parish of St Mary and St Gabriel Fenchurch 'whiche belonged to the late fraternity called Jesus Brotherheade...beneath St Paul's Cathedral'.[95] The Guild, as noted, received a number of lifetime gifts and bequests, although not all of these made it into the final version of the accounts. For example, the haberdasher Ellis Draper, who served as warden and assistant of the Jesus Guild, bequeathed it the not insignificant sum of 40s. in his will of 1527, while the priest John Graunte left the Guild a printed missal according to his 1516 will, although neither is

---

93 The Middle English Dictionary defines engrossing as '(a) The drafting, writing, or consummation (of an agreement or contract) in legal form [cp. **engrossen** v., sense **3.**]; (b) the action of recording receipts, expenditures, etc.'.
94 For a more detailed discussion of the income and expenditure of the Jesus Guild, see New, 'Cult of the Holy Name', chapter 3.
95 *CPR Edward VI* v.2, 1548–9, 47.

recorded in the extant accounts.[96] In addition to these standard sources of income, the Jesus Guild occasionally sold items surplus to their requirements and, in 1519/20, invested in a set of satin hoods [81] hired out in subsequent years.

It was, however, the farming out of the right to collect offerings and membership fees on behalf of the Jesus Guild that accounted for the bulk of its income. This process was both popular and lucrative; based on the average receipts and, assuming that the 'pardon' cost 4d., Robert Swanson has calculated that the Jesus Guild received somewhere in the region of 5,000 donations each year.[97] Even if the average cost exceeded this estimate, thereby somewhat reducing the number of individual payments, this would still suggest that a remarkable number of people wished to access the spiritual benefits of this fraternity.

The Jesus Guild farmed the right to collect on its behalf across England and Wales, although this had to be approved by the relevant ecclesiastical authorities, occasionally causing friction. In 1516/17, for example, the Guild obtained a letter from the bishop of London to the bishop of Exeter on behalf of the proctor in that diocese [54]. For a time the Jesus Guild also farmed the devotions in the Irish dioceses, although in 1528 had to admit defeat here, allowing John Mastok of Dublin to be released from his payment of £5 for his licence because the Irish bishops would no longer allow the collection [148]. Most farms were for a diocese or groups of dioceses, but Middlesex and Essex were farmed as counties, as was Hertfordshire (sometimes incorrectly recorded as Herefordshire) in many years. There are annual references to the farm of 'Kant', sometimes recorded as a county but on other occasions as a diocese, and it is probable that this was a reference to the dioceses of the county of Kent (Canterbury and Rochester); certainly Rochester is the one English diocese never mentioned by name.[98]

The income from specific areas varied slightly across the twenty extant accounts, presumably reflecting profitability for both the Guild and the farmers. That it was profitable is clear from the number of years for which the same individual(s) paid for the right to farm, the evidence of 'dynastic farming' (for example, John Tyler senior and junior, [149]), and a widow's willingness to take over the farm from her late husband (Blanche Leicester [172]; Blanche was joined by her son, Hugh Bardesley, in the following year [194]). On occasion, those responsible for gathering devotions were bound by obligation to produce

---

[96] Draper, TNA, PROB 11/24/306; Graunte, *London Consistory Court Wills, 1492–1547*, ed. I. Darlington, LRS 3 (1967), 38. It is of course possible that the executors failed to honour the testator's wishes, or that insufficient funds were available (unlikely in Draper's case).

[97] Swanson, *Indulgences*, 370.

[98] I am grateful to Dr Clive Burgess for suggesting this explanation for references to 'Kant'.

registers of Guild members in their allotted areas; presumably, despite their oath [5], they had failed to do so. John Seston was a notable repeat offender (for example [149]), whilst London haberdasher Roger Robyns provided three silver goblets as pledge for his debt [132] for several years. The profitability of farming the devotions is also seen through the losses incurred in 1524/25, when most of the farms were declared void because of the Jubilee [125], and through the Guild's acquisition of a licence to continue collecting [123].[99] This licence may only have been temporary, however, for in 1527/28 many farmers were released from debts for their payments 'consydering the yere of Jubely' [148].[100] Those named as farmers almost always sub-contracted, although this process is barely visible in the extant records of the Jesus Guild, the clearest evidence being from the Letters of Protection issued to Henry Hasilwood [21].[101] It is, however, clear from other sources that this could cause problems for the principal farmer, as it did for Henry Thorneton at some point between 1529 and 1531, when he took an action against Emanuel Symson and Harry Kynge for arrears related to gathering the devotions in Cornwall.[102] It is possible that this was one of the issues that caused serious financial problems for Richard Inskyppe who, after farming the devotions for the diocese of Chichester for several years with apparent success, died an imprisoned pauper [148].

In addition to 'real' income, the surplus from the previous year's transactions was included as part of the income for the year covered by each annual account, providing a proportion of the money available for expenditure. This 'float' formed a valuable reserve should other forms of income decrease, as indeed they did in 1529/30. Great care was taken over the safety of this sum, with part of it usually being entrusted to a reliable individual, such as a London alderman who was also a member of the Jesus Guild – as in 1526/7, when John Browne was given £40 of the surplus to keep until the following year [125]. The £40 in question was delivered to Browne in angel nobles, from which transfer the Guild benefited thanks to royal intervention in 1526 to stop bullion haemorrhaging abroad and attempting to peg English and foreign coinage by increasing the value of gold coins; by the following year, this sum had increased in value to £45 [132].[103]

---

99   During the years of a papal Jubilee, all other indulgences were suspended, see Swanson, *Indulgences*, 423.

100   Swanson, *Indulgences*, 423 n.8 suggests that the Jesus Guild 'possibly' had a licence, insofar as it is clear from the accounts that collecting continued for at least some of the Jubilee period.

101   Swanson, *Indulgences*, 204–6, 215–16 for discussion of the procedures by which the Jesus Guild farmed the devotions.

102   TNA, C 1/680/16.

103   G. C. Brooke, *English Coins*, 3rd edn (London, 1950), 175. It is possible that the money was deliberately changed into nobles precisely because an inflation in their value was predicted.

In addition to the surplus, income from farming the devotions was recorded as having been paid, regardless of whether it had been received, and so the Guild operated a system of making payments based partly upon promissory income. This might seem a risky strategy and, indeed, became so when the winds of religious change stared to blow; but such procedure was familiar to the merchants who dominated the Jesus Guild in its second incarnation.[104] A further complication of this system was that the same sum of money was on occasion counted twice, once as the payment to farm and once as a repaid debt. Despite these complexities, the Guild's income increased substantially across the twenty years' worth of extant accounts – a considerable achievement in a period that witnessed both economic instability and inflation.[105]

The expenditure of the Jesus Guild was recorded in detail and occupies approximately two-thirds of the extant annual accounts.[106] It is, however, complicated by the promissory income and debts accrued and, in some years towards the end of the run of accounts, the debts still owed to or remitted by the Guild outstripped the payments made in the same year for goods and services. In 1534/5, for example, less than one-third of the total expenditure was cash spent by the Guild, with unpaid and remitted debts accounting for the remainder. Despite this, in the years for which annual accounts survive, the Guild maintained sufficient funds to pay for a wide range of services and activities; these included the maintenance of the Jesus Chapel, which the Guild seems to have furnished and fitted out, as well as used, as its own, perhaps following the model of the later fourteenth century Guild of St Anne. In an agreement of 1371, the Dean and Chapter had granted free rein to the earlier fraternity to install, maintain or remove fixtures, fittings and equipment in the Jesus Chapel as deemed necessary, and such actions can still be perceived through the Jesus Guild accounts.[107] By contrast, the parish of St Faith agreed a ninety-nine-year lease with the Dean and Chapter when it occupied the chapel in the crowdes [202].

As discussed above, liturgical celebration (in its broadest sense) was a priority for the Jesus Guild, and the expenses section of the accounts always starts with extensive payments relating to religious services, sermons and the annual feast days of the Transfiguration and Holy Name. Various officers and staff of the Guild, along with a number of

---

[104] Both the Mercers' and Grocers' allowed a new shop-holder to obtain his initial stock on credit, see S. Thrupp, *The Merchant Class of Medieval London* (Ann Arbor, 1948), 104–5.

[105] See, for example, S. Rappaport, *Worlds Within Worlds: Structures of Life in Sixteenth-century London* (Cambridge, 1989), 155 and table 5.4.

[106] For a more detailed discussion of the expenditure, see New, 'Cult of the Holy Name', chapter 3.

[107] LMA, CLC/313/L/H/001/MS25121/0513. At the time of writing the author has been unable to identify any formal agreement between the Jesus Guild and the Dean and Chapter pertaining to the occupation of the crowdes chapel in the Cathedral's extensive records.

cathedral staff, received payments or 'rewards', generally following the ordinances very closely. Indeed, when these stipulations were not adhered to, for example if a cleric of a different status from that specified took part in a service, this was noted, and payment sometimes reduced as a result [51].

The payments in the accounts were often detailed and provide a wealth of information, especially about the trades and 'service industry' in London in the first half of the sixteenth century. In almost every year, a range of carpenters, plasterers, glaziers, metalsmiths and labourers were paid for the general maintenance of the large and, because of its semi-subterranean location, presumably damp Jesus Chapel.[108] The accounts for 1524/25 were typical, with 6s. 8d. paid for a new bell-clapper, 6s. 6d. for fitting two bells, 5s. 6d. to a glazier for mending and cleaning the windows, and 2s. 2d. to a plasterer and his servant for 'whyting of the Crowdes by the space of 2 days' [123]. Vestment-makers [162] and organ-makers [34] were among the more specialised trades employed, both for routine maintenance of the fittings, liturgical plate and fabrics, and for replacements and new acquisitions. The regular upkeep indicates diligence and care on the part of the Guild, and the quantities of material removed and sold by the parish of St Faith when it took possession of the Crowdes suggest that standards were maintained right up until the fraternity was dissolved (Appendix I, [201–203]).

As well as maintenance, security was also an issue for the Jesus Guild, and concerns can be traced through the accounts. The treasure chest specified in the ordinances was moved in and out of the chapel, its locks repaired and, in 1529/30, it was reinforced with an iron bar [162]. A paten was stolen from an altar on Christmas Day 1527 or 1528 [146], and a window barred with iron in 1534/35 [197]. No doubt as a response to the spate of break-ins, the final three extant accounts record that certain treasures belonging to the Guild were kept by one of the Wardens. The victualing trades also did well from the Jesus Guild, with frequent 'potacions' at various hostelries, such as the 9d. paid for the 'drinking' following the arrest of John Spynke in 1531/2 [183]. The feasting after the annual celebration of the Holy Name required not only the purchase of quantities of ale, beer, and food, but also people to serve it. In the earliest surviving accounts these were men but, for most of the 1520s and 1530s two women were engaged to draw the ale and beer and keep the taps. Most of these servants, craftsmen and traders were anonymous, but very occasionally a name appears, such as Robert Nelson, glazier, who was paid 30s. 2d. in 1514 [34].[109]

---

[108] See New, 'Jesus Chapel', 107.

[109] He may have been the same workman as, or a kinsman of, the Robert Nelson who, in 1537/8, was paid for glazing the hall of a property in Cheapside owned by the Bridge House, see *London Bridge: Selected Accounts and Rentals, 1381–1538*, ed. V. Harding and L. Wright, LRS., 31 (1995), **472**.

The sundry payments section of the accounts is the most varied, and provides insights into how the Guild operated, as well as its litigious side. For example, 11s. 6d. was spent in 1517/18 for taking an action against John Savage in 'my lord of Canterbures courte' for slandering the fraternity [63].[110] Sundry payments also included ephemeral and everyday items which were recorded in detail, even down to new brooms and thread, providing a glimpse of an active association led by men used to 'keeping tabs' on even the slightest expenditure. The more formal and set expenses relating to liturgy or requirements in the ordinances were made directly in cash, but sundry payments were occasionally made in kind, with fish being the preferred currency. In 1534/35, for example, the Guild paid 3s. 4d. for half a conger eel and a turbot given to 'Master Popley' (William Popler) because he had obtained the king's seal for various documents, and gave him conger eel, two plaice, two soles, a turbot, a gurnard, and a chain and a quarter of fresh salmon at other times during the year [197].

The final text edited in this volume as Appendix I is the 1552 inventory of church goods submitted by the parish of St Faith in response to an official request for this information ahead of a national confiscation of material in 1553.[111] The Certificate for St Faith's includes details about the Jesus Chapel, to which the parish gained access after the dissolution of the Jesus Guild and, in part because of its rarity as a survival, provides an invaluable coda to the information that can be gleaned from the Jesus Guild records.[112]

THE JESUS GUILD MANUSCRIPT

Provenance

The extant records of the Jesus Guild in St Paul's Cathedral now comprise Bodleian Library MS Tanner 221, part of the large collection of medieval manuscripts bequeathed to the library by the antiquarian

---

[110] He was not given an honorific in the Guild records, but it is tempting to speculate whether this might be the Sir John Savage (VII) who, in 1517, appeared before King's Bench indicted with murder, and would therefore have been in London at the time. Considering Sir John's general demeanour and behaviour, he may very well have slandered a prestigious religious guild, see T. Thornton, 'Savage family (per. *c.* 1369–1528), gentry', *ODNB*.

[111] For discussion of the 1552 Commission and the value of the inventories it produced, see E. Duffy, 'The End of It All: The Material Culture of the Late Medieval Parish and the 1552 Inventories of Church Goods', in *The Parish in Late Medieval England*, ed. C. Burgess and E. Duffy, Harlaxton Medieval Studies 14 (Donington, 2006), 381–99.

[112] Extracts from the certificate are reproduced in H. B. Walters, *London Churches at the Reformation* (London, 1939), 274–8; however, as well as excluding much of the detail about the stripping out and refurbishing of the Crowdes, Walters relied on a (not always accurate) transcript by F. C. Ecles.

Thomas Tanner, bishop of St Asaph (1674–1735).[113] There is unfortunately no clear evidence of how or when the records of the Jesus Guild came into the possession of Bishop Tanner, nor of how they survived both the Reformation and the Great Fire of London, although some suggestions may be made.[114]

John Stow mentions the Jesus Guild in his *Survey of London*, and cites not only Henry VI's grant of letters patent to the Guild in 1459 and Henry VII's confirmation of this document, but also the letters patent granted by Henry VIII in 1535, all of which were copied into MS Tanner 221.[115] Enrolled copies of these documents were at the time held by the Royal Chancery so Stow may have seen them there, but it is quite possible that he had direct access to the Jesus Guild records in the form of the manuscript now known as MS Tanner 221.[116] If so, this would strongly suggest that the Guild records were still in London in the late sixteenth century, perhaps preserved among the archives of St Paul's Cathedral. Thomas Tanner was a native of Wiltshire and a graduate of Oxford University who spent most of his career in the diocese of Norwich before being ordained bishop of St Asaph in 1732. In 1694 he was, however, examined for diaconal ordination by the bishop of London Dr Henry Compton (1631/2–1713) in the presence of the chapter of St Paul's, and he was a long-term friend of Edmund Gibson, bishop of London (1669–1748). If the records of the Jesus Guild were still within the library at St Paul's in the early eighteenth century, it is possible that Tanner acquired them through his connections with the cathedral and, especially, his friendship with Gibson. Bishop Gibson shared Tanner's interest in history and may have 'loaned' the manuscript to Thomas Tanner. It is also possible that Tanner, an enthusiastic collector of manuscripts and books, purchased the Jesus Guild records from another source, perhaps in relation to his *Life of John Colet*, published in 1724.[117]

Codicology, palaeography and diplomatic.

The present binding of MS Tanner 221 dates from the first half of the eighteenth century, and is similar to that of a number of the Tanner

---

[113]   See R. Sharp, 'Tanner, Thomas (1674–1735), bishop of St Asaph and antiquary', *ODNB*.

[114]   MS Tanner 221 is described simply as '*Codex partim membranaceus, partem characeus, in fol. majori ff.131*', in *Catalogi Codicum Manuscriptorum Bibliothecae Bodleianae. Pars Quarta Codices Viri Admodum Reverendi Thomae Tanneri, S.T.P., Episcopi Asaphensis, Complectens*, ed. A. Hackman (Oxford, 1860; reprinted with corrections, 1966), 643. MS Tanner 221 was not part of the collection acquired by Thomas Tanner from Archbishop Sancroft, and no provenance is given in the catalogue.

[115]   J. Stow, *A Survey of London*, ed. C. L. Kingsford, 2 vols (Oxford, 1908) i, 328–9.

[116]   Stow cites Henry VI's letters patent in English but, although the Guild also provided an English translation of them in MS Tanner 221, the text is not identical. Stow may well have made his own translation from the enrolled Chancery copies, but there remains the intriguing possibility that his 'translation' was based on his notes from the Guild's own records; see Stow, *Survey*, i, 328–9.

[117]   R. Sharp, 'Tanner, Thomas (1674–1735), bishop of St Asaph and antiquary', *ODNB*.

manuscripts; it may, therefore, be assumed either that Bishop Tanner had the manuscript bound while it was in his possession, or that it was bound soon after its acquisition by the Bodleian Library.[118] The manuscript is bound inside boards covered in brown leather with an open panel design and black-tooled foliate and geometric decoration typical of the period. The spine has subsequently been repaired, probably in the late nineteenth or early twentieth century. The whole volume, inclusive of bindings, measures 40 x 28.5cm, and is approximately 3.5cm thick. The manuscript is 132 folios in length, exclusive of a post-medieval title page bearing the inscription 'Guild at St Paul's', which has been inserted immediately inside the upper cover. It was paginated in ink in its current order after the leaf between folios 125 and 126 had been removed; to judge from the script, it looks likely that this was done either by Tanner or when it was acquired by the Bodleian Library. The modern foliation indicates that there are 131 folios, but neither this nor the ink pagination includes the blank leaf between folios 29 and 30 even though the paper appears to be from the same supply as the rest of the manuscript and has water-staining in the gutter consistent with surrounding folios.

Folios 1–16 are of parchment and measure 38cm x 24.2–28cm. The first few folios are stained and creased, possibly as the result of being exposed to water or another liquid.[119] Folios 17–131 (as foliated; see previous paragraph) are of paper. Folio 17 is smaller than the rest, measuring 22.7 x 34.2cm; folios 18–131 are all approximately 39.5 x 27.3cm. The paper is of a uniform quality, and a number of folios throughout the manuscript have the same watermark, a crowned eagle within a circle measuring 43mm in diameter.[120] This mark has not otherwise been identified, but suggests that the Jesus Guild either bought in bulk or acquired its paper from the same supplier throughout the time of the accounts, perhaps from one of the stationers based in St Paul's churchyard.[121]

The manuscript is ruled in hard-point and ink, written in dark brown or black ink throughout, with no rubrication; the text is reasonably plain, although some initial letters for the start of main sections, especially

---

[118] I am grateful to Dr Martin Kauffmann for his advice and comments upon the binding of MS Tanner 221. Tanner bequeathed his collection of manuscripts and books to the Bodleian Library, which received them in 1736 (the year following Tanner's death).

[119] Some of Tanner's manuscripts and books suffered water damage on route to Oxford in 1731, but the water damage to MS Tanner 221 is limited to the parchment booklet and therefore unlikely to be related to this incident.

[120] The watermark resembles C.-M. Briquet, *Les Filigranes: Dictionnaire historique des marques du papier des leur apparition vers 1282 jusqu'en 1600*, 2nd edn (Leipzig, 1923), nos 7193 and 8000, but is somewhat neater, and the eagle has a more distinct beak and a larger crown. See the Gravell Watermark Archive EAGLE.290.1 and EAGLE.293.1. https://www.gravell.org/index.php.

[121] A number of printers and stationers had shops or stalls in St Paul's churchyard, see E. G. Duff, *A Century in the English Book Trade: Short Notices of all Printers, Stationers, Book-binders and Others Connected with it from the Issue of the First Dated Book in 1457 to the Incorporation of the Company of Stationers in 1557* (London, 1905), xvii.

many of the accounts, are decorated with pen-flourishing, some of it quite elaborate. There may have been some decoration on folio 1 verso, for a wash of red and yellow covers the first few words, suggesting that the initial T of 'This booke' [1] was originally coloured, but that the colour washed out when the manuscript was wet.

The Jesus Guild records are written entirely in cursive script, ranging from neat 'free' hands to those with extensive secretary features.[122] As an unsurprising result of their compilation in current form, at least nine, and perhaps as many as fourteen, hands can be identified through the extant Jesus Guild records. Sections 1–8 (folios 1v–8v) are in the same hand, but a different scribe wrote sections 9–18 (folios 10r–14v); interestingly, three separate scribes appear to have copied in sections 19–21 (folios 15r, 16r, 16v). Sections 24–48 (folios 27r–42r) are written in a very similar small, neat hand quite distinct from the hands in the rest of the manuscript and almost certainly the work of the same scribe. Hugh Fourness was paid for drawing up and engrossing ordinances in 1514/15 [36] so might possibly be the scribe of this section but, on the basis that 'engrossing' does not necessarily equate with 'writing', this cannot be said with certainty. We then enter ambiguous territory, with certain years of accounts where the hands are similar, but with enough differences in the script, choice of letters and variants of spelling, and in some cases *mis-en-page*, to suggest a variety of scribes. Sections 49–75 (folios 43r–58r) may well be in the same hand, with sections 76–99 (folios 58v–73r) quite similar but with some features that suggest at least one other hand at work. A clearer distinction can then be seen between this block and sections 100–178 (folios 73v–125v), which may also have been the work of one scribe.[123] Sections 179–199 (folios 126r–131v and 17r–26v) are in a very similar hand and may be the same scribe. If so, then he can be identified as Thomas Pierson, servant of the scrivener John Worsopp, for he was paid for writing the 1534/5 account [197].

As mentioned above, on seven occasions a servant or clerk of John Worsopp is paid for writing the account, clearly differentiated from payments for making and engrossing the same. Worsopp was, however, paid for writing other documents, including in 1534/5 for 'entryng into the boke 2 patentes and for diverse other wrytinges' [197]. This might be associated with the letters of protection issued in 1535 [19], but this hypothesis can be challenged. Worsopp signed, and possibly wrote, the wills of two nuns of the Franciscan abbey outside Aldgate (the Minories) in London; but, although similar to the letters of protection and other parts of the Jesus Guild records, the hand in these wills is not an exact

---

[122] For a good summary of later fifteenth- to mid sixteenth-century cursive script in England, see L. C. Hector, *The Handwriting of English Documents*, 2nd edn (London, 1966), 57–61.

[123] Significantly, the dating clause changes at the same point that a shift in hands can be discerned.

match.[124] It is possible that Worsopp's hand changed in the twenty-four years between the documents but, equally, we know that the Jesus Guild records are fragmentary, and it may be that the 'wrytinges' he was paid for in 1534/5 have not survived. A further mystery is the payment made to Worsopp in the 1533/34 account for 'writing in parchment 2 tymes the corporacion of the said Fraternitie graunted by Kynge Henry the VIth and the confirmacone of kynge Henry the 7th' [190]. At first glance, this would appear to confirm the scribe and date of compilation for the first sections of the current manuscript (folios 2r–3v, [2.a–2.c]) but there is a problem here, because these folios appear to be in the same hand as folios 3v–8v [3–8.i] and folio 7v [7] is signed by John Church, the subdean of St Paul's who died in 1509,[125] providing an unequivocal *terminus ad quem* for the compilation of that section of the parchment booklet which survives in Tanner 221.

The most likely solution to all these puzzles is that most of the current manuscript was written under Worsopp's direction by scribes trained by, or working for, him, and who therefore would be likely to produce hands close to his own. Indeed, Worsopp is known to have had apprentices during the time with which he was involved in the Jesus Guild, bequeathing two of them his books of precedent and other professional manuals.[126]

In its current form, the manuscript is bound out of order.[127] The first folio of MS Tanner 221 is in the form of a cover and title page, dated 1507 in Arabic numerals (in different ink than the rest of the folio and probably in a later hand), and names Dean John Colet as the rector and William Bromwell and John Monke as the wardens of the Fraternity of the Holy Name in St Paul's Cathedral [1]. This introductory paragraph states that the 'booke' was acquired upon the recommendation of Dean Colet, and that within it are to be recorded copies of the letters patent and subsequent confirmations granted by royal authority, all the ordinances of the Fraternity, and any deeds and accounts relating to the Jesus Guild. Folios 1 to 16 form this parchment booklet, with folios 1r and 16v noticeably dirtier and in worse condition than the others, indicating that it was kept separate from the other records for some time. This booklet

---

[124] The earlier of these wills is discussed and illustrated in J. Luxford, 'The Testament of Joan FitzLewes: A Source for the History of the Abbey of Franciscan Nuns without Aldgate', in *Medieval Londoners. Essays to mark the 80th birthday of Caroline M. Barron*, ed. E. A. New and C. Steer (London, 2019), 275–91. I am grateful to Dr Philippa Hoskin for comments about the hands in TNA, LR 15/2 and MS Tanner 221 f. 15r.

[125] TNA, PROB 11/16/190.

[126] See Appendix II for Worsopp's biography, and E. A. New, 'The prosopography of piety: personal and professional connections between officers of the Jesus Guild', forthcoming.

[127] The current order had been established by the time that Alfred Hackman described the contents in the mid nineteenth century, although his listing can at first glance be confusing – see *Catalogi codicum manuscriptorum Bibliothecae Bodleianae*, ed. Hackman, 643–4.

contains copies of royal letters patent [**2.a–2.c**], a set of ordinances [**3–8.i**], and miscellaneous deeds and memoranda [**9–22.h**]. Subsequent accounts and other documents are recorded on paper, and the whole of what is now MS Tanner 221 would appear to have been combined later as a single volume. The quires are of varying lengths, folios 16 and 131 appear to be singletons, and (as noted) a leaf was removed from between folios 125 and 126, but the current binding is quite tight and, as a result, an accurate collation would be challenging and not presented here.[128]

Immediately following the parchment booklet are the accounts for 1533/34 and 1534/35 [**188–199**], as noted above written in a different hand to that of the letters patent, ordinances and memoranda. The first folio of the 1533/34 account is rather dirty and creased (and noticeably smaller than the remainder of the manuscript, suggesting trimming at some stage) and the final folio of the 1534/35 account is very worn and dirty, suggesting that these records were kept together but separately from the remainder of MS Tanner 221 for some time.

Folios 27 to 29 comprise a another, partial, set of ordinances, which relate to the organisation and staff of the Jesus Guild [**22.a–22.g**]. These ordinances begin mid-sentence and it is clear that at least one and possibly more folios have been lost, along with crucial direct evidence of when they were compiled. They are, however, in the same, or at least an extremely similar, hand to that of the 1514/15 and 1515/16 accounts; certainly, Hugh Fournesse was paid for 'engrossing' a set of ordinances in 1514/15 [**36**] and the 1514/15 and 1515/16 accounts [**28, 42**], so he presumably oversaw both documents. References in the accounts, and the names of those who served as officers of the Guild at the time of their compilation, also suggest that the partial set of ordinances date from 1514.[129] The accounts for 1514/15 to 1532/33 follow these ordinances and run consecutively through to the end of the manuscript, comprising folios 30r to 131v. The final two folios of the manuscript as currently bound are damaged and worn, seemingly in confirmation of the suggestion that the last two years' worth of extant accounts were kept separately for some time.

---

[128] It is anticipated that the manuscript will undergo conservation in the near future, at which point a full collation should be possible.

[129] A date of 1514 is suggested by the sum of 20s. 10d. paid in the 1514/15 account for expenses incurred at the Mitre Tavern 'when the Assistentes assembled there for makyng of the ordenances', [**36**]. One of the Assistants present was haberdasher Henry Hill [**228**], who died in 1521, providing a *terminus ad quem* for this occasion.

EDITORIAL CONVENTIONS

OXFORD, BODLEIAN MS TANNER 221.

In terms of format, a sense of the shape of the manuscript has been preserved, but in general the layout for receipts and payments in the accounts has been standardised for ease of reading. For example, within the accounts entries for farming the devotions are presented as a list when in this form in the manuscript, albeit without blank spaces between them, but are presented as a paragraph if written in that manner. Notes are made when the text-block is bracketed but no attempt is made to replicate that on the printed page, and sub-headings are presented within the main text even if they were written in the margins, although again a note is made of this; running-headers are treated in a similar manner. Bold text is used for headings and sub-headings for ease of reading, generally reflecting the original scribal practice. Section numbers have been introduced where seems most sensible, especially when the manuscript indicates a new section or has a sub-heading, but not all divisions within accounts are in the same place for each year. Capitalisation has been standardised and modernised in the sections in English, and limited modern punctuation has been added for readability. Apart from the heading on folio 1v Roman numerals were used throughout the manuscript but have been changed to Arabic to assist the modern reader, and signs for various denominations have been standardised in line with usual editorial conventions. In some year's accounts many of the individual payments have been underlined and this has been replicated in the edition, with attendant inconsistencies (although these are flagged up in footnotes). Curly brackets have been used to signal the end of an individual accounting entry (income and expenditure) for the sake of clarity and consistency, although in the manuscript the various scribes sometimes employed a dash or simply left a small gap between the entry and the amount. Scribal terminal brackets have been replaced by a full stop when it is clear that they provide 'punctuation' to avoid confusion with a missing sum of money (which is indicated by an editorial intervention). Round brackets indicate a contemporary scribal interlineation, often following an erasure which is indicated by strikethrough of the letter(s) or word(s). Square brackets indicate an editorial insertion or in-text comment, with more extensive editorial comments provided in footnotes.

Although predominately written in English the manuscript is macaronic, and this is reflected in the editorial process. The Latin text of the Henry VI Letters Patent and Henry VII confirmation is kept in full because the Jesus Guild itself provided a translation. In the instances where only Latin text for a whole document or series of documents is recorded, these sections have been calendared in English to facilitate use of the edition by a range of readers. Some Latin and occasional French words and phrases are included in the accounts, and these have been italicised but left in the original, with a note if the meaning is not obvious from the context. For the English text, a minimal amount of tidying-up has been undertaken in terms of standardising letters; 'u' / 'v' and 'i' / 'j' were used interchangeably by all scribes, and these have been standardised according to modern conventions for reliability. No further attempt has been made to translate the English, however, with the aim of preserving the sometimes strikingly different 'voices' of the scribes, and for the benefit of readers interested in the development of English in the crucial period covered by the manuscript.

The English text contains a considerable number of abbreviations, mainly employing the standard marks used for Latin but even in these cases leading to occasional ambiguity. Words with suspension and abbreviation marks have been expanded as seems most logical, usually by adding a final 'e' for a suspension unless the standard 'es' abbreviation mark has been employed or in instances where this could lead to confusion.[1] The only words for which this has not been done are 'London' and 'John'; both are almost always provided with a terminal suspension mark but neither are ever expanded in the main text when English is employed and the presumption is that the scribes were simply used to providing an abbreviation mark for these common names because this was required in Latin.[2] Contraction marks are most often employed for proper nouns and words ending in 'acion' / 'ation', and in these instances editorial judgement has been employed, wherever possible based on the scribe's rendition of unabbreviated words. Other standard abbreviation marks (for example, 'er') have been expanded as they would be in Latin, although the 'per' / 'par' symbol has been expanded as seems most sensible in English sections, taking into account the form of unabbreviated words written by the same scribe.[3] Where there is an ambiguous abbreviation mark at the end of a word, which could stand for different forms or lead to a potentially confusing expansion, or where a sign may just be a flourish, an inverted comma has been employed. As

[1] For example, 'on' (when the meaning clearly is 'on' and not 'one') is expanded as 'onn'.

[2] A few signatures clearly use *Johannis* rather than John, and this is preserved in the edition.

[3] Some scribes also employ a curious hybrid of the 'par' / 'per' and 'pro' symbols; these have been expanded as seems most sensible and a note made to alert the reader.

noted above, the Sacred Trigram was a key visual identifier of the later medieval cult of the Holy Name. Despite this, and its use as a header in a number of fifteenth and sixteenth century ordinances and accounts, it does not appear in the records of the Jesus Guild.[4] However, the name 'Jesus' was used throughout in the Guild manuscript in a surprisingly wide range of forms. Since on occasion this may be related to the item or activity in question, such as the livery badges distributed to various groups of people, the original scribal form has been retained in all instances rather than attempting to impose a standardised version.

THE 1552 ST FAITH'S INVENTORY MANUSCRIPT (APPENDIX I)

TNA E117/4/5 is a paper booklet of eight folios, written in cursive script with many elements of secretary hand and almost certainly by one scribe. The first leaf is blank, with the text beginning on folio 2, and the booklet is now bound out of order; the original sequence has been restored for this edition. There is some staining on the leaves, especially folio 2, and damage to the fore edges of the leaves. The manuscript is written in English apart from a handful of highly conventional Latin terms. The editorial conventions are the same as for Bodleian MS Tanner 221, with two exceptions. First, in the Jesus Guild records þ is rendered in a form distinct from the letter y, but in the St Faith's 1552 Inventory the scribe employs a letter indistinguishable from the letter y when þ clearly is intended, for example in the word 'the'. In order to make the text as accessible as possible, in such cases the letter y has been rendered as 'th', but within square brackets to indicate that this is an editorial intervention. Second, the St Faith's scribe was haphazard in the extreme when providing terminal dashes or brackets at the end of an item or section; for ease of reading, this has been standardised as a curly bracket since this is the most common form in the manuscript. The entire text has been presented in this volume because it is not always clear when items sold, or work undertaken, refer to the parish or the newly acquired space in the Crowdes which had been occupied by the Jesus Guild.

---

4   It is, for example, found as a heading in the fifteenth century accounts of the Grocers Company, sometimes combined with a longer devotional phrase, *Facsimile of the First Volume of Manuscript Archives of the Worshipful Company of Grocers of the City of London, A.D. 1345–1463,* ed. J. A. Kingdom, 2 vols (London, 1886), i, 30, 94 and ii, 165, 169.

RECORDS OF THE JESUS GUILD (OXFORD, BODLEIAN MS TANNER 221)

LICENCES, ORDINANCES AND MISCELLANEA OF THE JESUS GUILD

f.1r – blank
f.1v

Anno 1507[1]

[1] This booke boughte[2] and ordeigned by Maister John Colett, Doctour of Divinite, deane of the cathedralle chirche of Poules, and Rectour of the Fraternite and Guilde of Jhus in the crowdes of the seid chirche. William Bromewelle and John Monke, Wardeins of the same, recordethe & shewethe the copies of certeine lettres patentes of kyngis and ordenaunces for the fundacion and corparacion[3] of the foreseid Fraternite, and also the copies of divers chartres and dedys, with accomptes & othir necessaries whiche hereafter are to be hadde, entitled & remembred for the behof of the seid Fraternyte and Guylde.

f. 2r

[2.a] The graunte of king Harry the Sixt for the fundacion & corp[orati]on[4]

Henricus, Dei gracia Rex Anglie et Francie et Dominus Hibernie, omnibus ad quos presentes littere pervenerint, salutem. Mediator Dei et hominum Jesus Cristus, Filius Dei vivi, ut in prothoplausto lapsum vidit universum genus hominum eterne gehenne suppliciis Dei de-

---

1   Possibly later hand than main text ('modern' 7 used).
2   'This booke boughte' covered in a yellow-orange wash, perhaps indicating decoration of initial(s). First initial ornately pen-flourished.
3   Scribe of first section (certainly fols. 1–6) uses 'par' when writing full words in English that usually begin 'per' (e.g. 'parson' rather than 'person') so per par abbreviation mark expanded as latter in English in all cases for these folios.
4   Recorded in *CPR 1452–61*, 480.

creto cruciandum, immencissime misericordiarum thesauris nostre reparacionis salutare produxit remedium, atque ut, eterna redempcione inventa, totum salvaret hominem, glorie sue participem regni denique celestis faceret coheredem, nichil, cum Deus ipse Deo equalis esset, non subeundum statuit quod in predictum precium restitucionis nostre Deo Patri potuit immolare, disrupit, inquam, celos et descendit intra inviolate puelle viscera, formam indui non dedignatus humanam; et ex Apostolicis verbis si loquimur, semetipsum exinanivit formam accipiens servi, habituque inventus ut homo omnia tulit humana, eciam usque ad mortem factus est obediens. Mortem itaque pro maculosis passus Agnus Ipse sine macula, in sacrosanctis militantis Ecclesie thesauris interminabilem reposuit copiam meritorum, propter quod et Deus exaltavit Eum et donavit Illi Nomen quod est super omne nomen, ineffabile Nomen illud Jesus, potestatis maxime, auctoritatis immense, magestatis infinite, cui merito genuflectit omne celestium, terrestrium, et infernorum. Neque enim aliud est nomen sub celo datum hominibus in quo oporteat eos salvos fieri. In cujusque Nominis honore quamplures ligei nostri, Cristi fideles, spiritu devocionis ducti et excitati, in quodam Ecclesie Cathedralis Sancti Pauli Londoniarum loco vocato *le Crowdes* quandam fraternitatem sive Gildam inter se, et de se, ac aliis de Fraternitate sive Gilda illa esse affectantibus devote inchoarunt, que sic inchoata usque in presens continuata existit pacifice et quiete, ut accepimus. Jamque per dictos ligeos nostros metuentes, quod Fraternitas sive Gilda predicta rite et legittime juxta juris exigenciam fundata et stabilita non existit; et si sic, tunc totum et quicquid est inde subsecutum irritum est et vacuum, Nobis igitur humilime supplicaverunt quatenus pro debita et celeri fundacione et stabilimento ejusdem Fraternitatis sive Gilde, caritatis et pietatis intuitu providere, nomenque fundatoris et onus recte fundacionis Fraternitatis sive Gilde illius, super nos assumere, et solum fundatorem ejusdem esse dignaremur; Nos autem digna consideracione premissorum supplicacioni dictorum ligeorum nostrorum in hac parte inclinati, volentes ea que ad laudem et honorem prelibati Nominis Jesu sunt vel esse possunt multipliciter augmentari, et fraternitatem sive Gildam predictam, sic pie et devote, ut predictum est, inchoatum, juxta juris exigenciam fore perpetuam cupientes, nomenque fundatoris fraternitatis, sive Gilde illius, et onus fundacionis ejusdem super nos assumentes ad laudem, gloriam, et honorem Omnipotentis Dei Patris et Filii et Spiritus Sancti, et specialius in honore illius Nominis Jesu Filii, Salvatoris nostri, in cujus eciam Nominis honore fraternitas sive Gilda predicta, ut premittitur, inchoata existit, eandem fraternitatem, sive Gildam, de uno Rectore viro idoneo ecclesiastico, et duobus Gardianis, personis secularibus, ac aliis personis utriusque sexus quibuscumque in ejusdem Fraternitatis sive Gilde, fratres et sorores in presenti admissis, et decetero pro perpetuo admittendum, in supradicto loco vocato *le Crowdes* quousque nobis aut hujusmodi Rectori, Gardianis, fratribus et sororibus, vel successoribus suis de uberiore, utiliore, apciore et convenienciore loco in hac parte habendum, licencia, consensu, et assensu omnium et singulorum quorum intererit primitus intervenientibus et habitis, provisum fuerit, tenore presencium facimus, fundamus, ordinamus, et stabilimus perpetuis futuris temporibus duraturam: Et Willielmum Say, Sacre Theologie Professorem, Decanum Ecclesie predicte, Rectorem et pro Rectore ipsius Fraternitatis sive Gilde, ac Ricardum Forde unum Rememoratorium Scaccarii nostri, et Henricum Benett unum Clericorum de Officio Privati Sigilli nostri, Gardianos et pro Gardianis ejusdem Fraternitatis sive Gilde, cum dictis fratribus et sororibus, in fraternitatem, sive Gildam illam, ut predictum est, jam admissis, fratres et sorores ejusdem fraternitatis sive Gilde, et pro fratribus et sororibus ejusdem, per presentes preficimus, creamus, et ordinamus. Et ulterius volumus et concedimus per presentes quod fraternitas, sive Gilda antedicta fraternitas sive Gilda Nominis Jesu in Civitate London imperpetuum nuncupetur. Et similiter, quod predicti Rector, Gardiani, fratres et sorores fraternitatis, sive Gilde illius, perpetuam habeant successionem; et quod ipsi et successores sui imperpetuum Rector et Gardiani, fratres et sorores fraternitatis, sive Gilde, Nominis Jesu in Civitate London similiter nuncupentur; et quod sint unum corpus in se, et per nomen et sub nomine Rectoris, Gardianorum, fratrum et sororum fraternitatis, sive Gilde, Nominis Jesu in Civitate London sint persone perpetue habiles et capaces in lege ad impetrandum, recipiendum, et perquirendum terras, tenementa, redditus, servicia, et emolumenta quecumque, jura et possessiones spiritualia et temporalia, tenendum eis et eorum successoribus imperpetuum. Et insuper, quod ipsi et successores sui per nomen predictum implacitare possint et implacitari, ac prosequi omnimodas causas, querelas, et acciones reales et personales ac mixtas, cujuscumque generis vel nature fuerint, necnon respondere et responderi, ac defendere se sub nomine predicto in eisdem causis, querelis, et accionibus coram judicibus secularibus et ecclesiasticis quibuscumque,

f. 2v

in quibuscumque curiis, placeis, et locis nostris et heredum nostrorum, ac in curiis, placeis, et locis aliorum quorumcumque infra regnum nostrum Anglie, secundum leges et consuetudines ejusdem regni, et ad omnia alia facienda et recipienda prout, et eodem modo, quo ceteri ligei nostri persone habiles et capaces infra idem regnum nostrum implacitant et implacitantur, ac faciunt et facere poterunt, in curiis, placeis, et locis predictis, secundum leges et consuetudines predictas. Et quod idem Rector, Gardiani, fratres et sorores, et eorum successores imperpetuum habeant unum commune sigillum pro negociis et factis suis agendum et sigillandum serviturum. Et quod ipsi et successores sui hujusmodi Gardianos ad regendum et gubernandum fraternitatem, sive Gildam predictam, de seipsis, ac ceteros fratres et sorores de aliis personis, in fraternitatem, sive Gildam illam de anno in annum, ac quando et quociens pro commodo et honore ejusdem fraternitatis, sive Gilde, fuerit expediens, eligere et facere, ac dictos Gardianos ab eorum officiis removere et expellere, necnon alios Gardianos de seipsis in officia predicta eligere et facere valeant; proviso semper, quod predictus Decanus dicte Ecclesie Cathedralis Sancti Pauli, et quilibet successor suus Decanus ejusdem Ecclesie, sit semper et continue Rector Fraternitatis sive Gilde antedicte, absque aliqua eleccione inde per predictos Gardianos, fratres et sorores qualitercunque fiendam. Et quod predicti Rector, et Gardiani, fratres et sorores, et eorum successores congregaciones licitas et honestas de seipsis, ac statuta et ordinaciones licita pro salubri gubernacione Fraternitatis sive Gilde supradicte, secundum necessitatis exigenciam, quociens et quando opus fuerit, facere valeant, licite et impune, sine occasione, impedimento, perturbacione, vel molestacione nostri vel heredum nostrorum, Justiciariorum, Escaetorum, Vicecomitum, aut aliorum Ballivorum seu Ministrorum nostrorum vel heredum nostrorum quorumcumque; Et insuper, de uberiore gracia nostra concessimus et licenciam dedimus, pro nobis et heredibus nostris, per presentes prefatis Rectori, Gardianis, fratribus et sororibus Fraternitatis sive Gilde supradicte, quod ipsi et successores sui terras, tenementa, redditus, possessiones quecumque, que tam de nobis in libero burgagio quam de aliis in socagio vel alio servicio quocumque tenentur, usque ad valorem quadraginta librarum per annum, tenendum eis et eorum successoribus imperpetuum, tam in sustentacionem certorum Capellanorum divina in honore prelibati Nominis Jesu, ubi predicta fraternitas, sive Gilda, fuerit stabilita, celebrancium, et in exhibicionem ceterorum Clericorum et Puerorum eis ibidem, juxta ordinaciones et statuta predicta, inde, ut predictum est, condenda serviturorum, quam pro supportacione et implesione quorundam aliorum onerum et pietatis operum per predictos Rectorem, Gardianos, fratres et sorores dicte Fraternitatis sive Gilde, et successores suos faciendum a quibuscumque personis ea eis dare, concedere, vel assignare volentibus, adquirere et recipere possint. Et hujusmodi personis quod ipsi terras, tenementa, redditus, et possessiones hujusmodi, usque ad annuum valorem supradictum eisdem Rectori, Gardianis, fratribus et sororibus, et eorum successoribus dare, concedere, et assignare valeant, habendum sibi et successoribus suis imperpetuum, in forma predicta, similiter, tenore presencium, licenciam dedimus specialem, statuto de terris et tenementis ad manum mortuam non ponendis edito, aut aliquibus aliis statutis sive ordinacionibus ante hec tempora editis, factis, sive ordinatis, non obstantibus; et hoc, absque fine seu feodo, ad usum nostrum capiendum seu solvendum, et absque aliquibus aliis Regeis literis, aut aliqua inquisicione super aliquo brevi de Ad quod dampnum, vel aliquo alio mandato regio in hac parte quovismodo habendum, prosequendum, seu capiendum. In cujus rei testimonium has litteras nostras fieri fecimus patentes. Teste meipso apud Westmonasterium, vicesimo quinto die Januarii, anno regni nostri tricesimo septimo.

[2.b] The confirmacion of kinge Harry the Seventhe

Henricus, Dei gracia Rex Anglie et Francie et Dominus Hibernie, omnibus ad quos presentes litere pervenerint, salutem. Inspeximus literas patentes recolende memorie domini Henrici Sexti nuper Regis, avunculi nostri precarissimi, factas in hec verba: Henricus, Dei gracia &c ut supra. Nos autem litteras predictas ac omnia et singula in eisdem contenta rata habentes et grata, ea pro nobis et heredibus nostris, quantum in nobis est, acceptamus et approbamus, ac dilectis nobis in Cristo Johanni Colett, clerico, nunc Rectori, Willielmo Bromwell et Johanni Monke, nunc Gardianis Fraternitatis sive Gilde sepe dicte, & fratribus et sororibus ejusdem Gilde, ac successoribus suis, tenore presencium ratificamus et confirmamus, prout littere predicte rationabiliter testantur. In cujus rei testimonium has literas nostras fieri fecimus patentes. Teste meipso apud Croydon, sexto decimo die Aprilis, Anno regni nostri vicesimo secundo.

f. 3r

[2.c] The foreseyde confirmacion drawene into Englisshe

Henry, by the grace of God king of Englonde and of Fraunce and lord of Irelande, to almaner people to whome this thise present lettres shalle comme, gretyng. We have seene and beholde the lettres patentes of the most excellent prince and oure entireliest beolved uncle Henry the Sixte, by the same grace of God kynge of Englonde and of Fraunce and lord of Irelande, oure predecessour, in thise wordes:

Henry, by the grace of God kyng of Englande and of Fraunce and lorde of Irelande, to alle people to whome thise present lettres shalle comme, Gretyng. Where, in the honoure of the most glorius Name of oure saviour Jhū Criste, many oure liege mene and faithful Cristen people, stired by devocioun, have heretofore right vertuosly begonne a Fraternite or Gilde amongest and of them self and of other parsones willyng to be of the same Fraternite and Gilde in a place called the crowdes of the cathedralle chirche of Seint Paule of London. Whiche Fraternite, so begonne as we undrestonde, hathe contenued peasibly and quietly tille now of late oure seid liegemene, dreding that the foreseide Fraternite and Gilde hathe not duely and laufully be founded and stablisshed after the sure and directe ordre of oure lawes, and yf it so benot than everything thereupone folowyng and dependyng shulde be voide and of none effecte. Wherfor they have made unto us humble request and supplicacion that, in the wey of charite and pite, we wolde vouchesauf to provide for the due, sure and laufulle fundacion and stabiliment of the same Fraternite or Gilde, and to take uppone us the name of the founder

45

and the charge of the righte and due fundacion as the onely founder of the same Fraternite or Gilde. Whereupone we, in consideracion of the premisses and to the humble peticioun of oure said loving subgettes, enclyned and agreed in this behalf, willing those thinges whiche be or may be to the laude and honoure of the seid most blissed Name of Jhū to be augmented and willing the same Fraternite or Gilde so devoutly as is aforeseid begonne after the due ordre of oure lawes, to be sure and parpetuelle, and takyng upon us the name of the foundour of the same Fraternite or Gilde and the charge of the fundacion of the same, to the laude honoure and glory of almyghtey God the Fader and the Sonne and the Holy Gost, and specially in the honour of the same Name of Jhū oure saviour, to whose honour the Fraternyte or Gilde aforesed as afore is rehercid is begonne. By tenoure of thise oure present lettres we make, fownde, ordeigne & stablisshe parpetuelly hereaftir to endure the same Fraternite or Gilde one Governour, a conveinent spiritualle mane, and of two Wardeyns, seculer parsones, and of othir parsones, mene and womene whatsoevir they be, admytted or hereafter forevirmore to be admytted brethrene and sistrene of the same Fraternite or Gilde in the foreseid place called the crowdes, unto the tyme by us or by the seide Govirnour, Wardeyns, bretherne and sustrene or their successours of a bettir, more profitable & more convenient place, with the licence, consent and assent of alle and everiche parsones having therin interest, shalbe in that behalf ordeigned and provided. And by thise presentz we make, create & ordeigne William Say,[5] professour of divinite, now deane of the chirche aforeseid, Governoure, and for the Govirnoure of the same brethirhede and Gilde, and Richard Forde, one of the remembrauncers of oure esthequer, and Henry Benet, one of the clerkes of the office of oure Prevy Sealle, Wardeyns and for Wardenis of the same Fraternite or Gilde, with the seid bretherne and sustrene now admyttede into the same Fraternite or Gilde as is aforeseid brotherne and sustrene and for bretherne & sustrene of the same Fraternite or Gilde as ys aforeseyde. And furthirmore, we wolle & graunte by thise presentes that the foreseid Fraternite or Gilde be called the Fraternite or Gilde of the Name of Jhesu in the cite of London forevirmore; and also that the forseid Govirnoure, Wardeyns, bretherne and sustrene of the same Fraternite or Gilde have parpetuelle successioun; and that also they and their successours forevirmore be called the Govirnoure, Wardeins, bretherne and sustrene of the Fraternite or Gilde of the Name of Jhū in the Cite of London; and that they be one body in themself and by & undre the name of the Govirnoure, Wardenis, bretherne and sustrene of the Fraternite or Gilde of the Name of Jhū in the cite of London they shalbe parsones parpetuelle, hable and have capacite in the lawe to receive and purchace landes, tenementis, rentes, services and emolumentes, rightes

---

5   William Say D.Th. (d. 1468), dean 1457–1468. *Fasti St Paul's 1300–1541*, 6.

and possessions whatsovir they be, spirituelle and temporelle, to holde to them and to their successours forevirmore. Ande moreovir, that they and their successours by the name aforeseide may enplede and be enpleded, and to pursue almaner causes, querelles and accions realle and parsonalle and mixt, of whatsoevir kynde or nature they shalbe, and also to answere and be answered and to defende them self undre the name aforeseide in the same causes, querelles and accions before alle juges, seculer and spirituelle, whatsoevir they be, yn in whatsoevir the courtis and places of us and of oure heires and in the courtes and places of alle othir parsones whatsoevir they be within oure roialme of Englonde, after the lawes and custumes of the same roialme; ande to doo and resteive alle othir thinges in like maner and fourme as othir oure liegemene, parsones able and capace, within the same oure roialme enplede and be

f. 3v

enpleded and myghte do in the courtis and places aforeseid after the lawes & custumes aforeseid. And that the same Govirnour, Wardeins, bretherne and sustrene & their successours forevirmore have a comon seale to serve to their besynes and actis to be done & sealede. And that they and their successours to guyde and governe the bretherede or Gilde aforeseid of them self and othir the brotherne and sustrene of othir parsones in the same Fraternite or Gilde from yere into yere. And whanne & as oftene as for the profitt & worshippe of the same Fraternite or Gilde it shalbe expedient, they may and shalle chese and make Wardeins; and the same Wardeins from their offices to remeve and expelle and othir Wardeins of them self into the offices aforeseid to chese and make; provided alwey that the foreseide deane of the cathedralle chirche of Seint Poule and everiche his successoure deane of the same chirche be alwey and contenuelly Governoure of the Fraternite or Gilde withoute enny eleccione thereof by the foreseid Wardeins, bretherne and sustrene in enny maner wise to be made. Ande that the foreseid Govirnour and Wardenis, brotherne and sustrene and their successours shalle make lefulle and honest congregacions and assembles of them self, and laufulle statutes and ordenaunces for the good governaunce of the Fraternite or Gilde aboveseid, as oftene and whanne as yt shalbe behovefulle or nedefulle, withoute enny punysshement, occasione, lette, parturbaunce or greving of us or of oure heires or of oure justices, escheatours, shirifes ore of othir the balifes or ministres, of us or of oure heires whatsoevir they be. And ovir that, of our more habundaunt grace we have graunted and givene licence for us and our heires by thise presentes to the foreseid Govirnoure, Wardeins, brotherne and sustrene of the Fraternite & Gilde aboveseide that they and their sucessours may purchace and resteive whatsoevir landes, tenementes, rentes and possessions whiche as welle of us in free burgages of othir in socage or by whatsovir service be holdene to the valour of £40 by yere, to holde to them and to their successours forevirmore aswelle to the sustentacone of certeine chapleins doing divine services in the honoure of the foreseid

47

Name of Jhū where the foreseid Fraternite or Gilde shalbe stablisshide, and to the exhibicion of certein clerkis and childrene there to serve, accordyng to the ordenances and statues aforeseide thereof to be made, as also for the supportacone and fulfilling of whatsomevir othir charges and werkes of pite to be made or done be the foreseid Govirnoure, Wardeins, bretherne and sustrene of the seid Fraternite or Gilde or their successours, that is to wite of whatsomevir parsones whiche to them wille give, graunte or assigne the premisses. And also by the tenour of thise presentis we have givene specialle licence to the same parsones that they may give, graunte and assigne the same landes, rentis, tenementes and possessions to the yerely value aboveseid to the same Govirnour, Wardeins, brotherne and sustrene and to their successours, to have to them and to their successours forevir in the fourme afore seide, the statutes of landes and tenementes not to be put to mortmayne or enny othir statutes or ordenaunces before this tyme made or ordeigned to the contrary notwithstondyng; and this to be hadde withoute fyne or fee to oure use to be takene or paide, and withoute enny othir oure lettres Inquisicone or writte de *Ad quod Dampnum*'[6] or enny othir oure commaundement in this behalf in ennywise to be hadde, pursued or takene. In witnesse wherof we have done to be made thise oure lettres patentes. Being witnesse oure self[7] at Westmynster the 25 day of January the 37 yere of our reigne [1459]. The forseide lettres and the contentes of the same we accept and approve and for us and our heires in asmuche as in us ys we afferme and stable and to oure welbeloved in Crist John Colet, clerke, now Governour, William Bromewelle and John Monke now Wardeins of the Fraternite or Gilde aforeseid, and to the brotherne and sustrene of the same Gilde and to their successours, by the tenour of thise presentes we ratifie and conferme as the forseide lettres resonably witnessethe. In witnesse whereof we have done to be made thise oure lettres patentes. Being witnesse oure self at Croydone the 26[the] day of Aprille in the 22th yere of oure reigne [1507].

[3] The actes and ordenaunces examened, approved and accept by the most reverend Fadere in God William, archebisshoppe of Caunterburry & chaunceller of Englonde,[8] Thomas Surrey, tresourer of Englonde,[9] John Fyneuxe, chief justice of the kinges benche,[10] and Robert Rede, chief justice of the comone place.[11]

---

6   *Ad quod damnum* (To what damage).
7   'self' is in the inner margin and appears to have been added subsequent to the main text, possibly in a different hand.
8   William Warham (d. 1532), Chancellor 1504–15. See *ODNB* 'Warham, William'.
9   Thomas Howard, 2nd duke of Norfolk (d. 1524), Treasurer 1501–22. See *ODNB* 'Howard, Thomas, second duke of Norfolk'.
10   Sir John Fyneux (d. 1525). See *ODNB* 'Fyneux [Fenex], Sir John'.
11   Sir Robert Rede (d. 1519). See *ODNB* 'Rede, Sir Robert'.

f. 4r

To alle true Cristein people to whome this present writing shalle comme, William, archebisshoppe of Caunterbury and chaunceller of Englonde, Thomas erle of Surrey, tresourer of Englonde, John Fyneuxe, knyghte, chief justice of the kynges benche, and Robert Rede, chief justice of the comone place of oure seid sovereigne lorde the kyng, send greting in oure Lorde everlastyng. Where in a certeine act in a parliament[12] of oure most dradde sovereigne lorde Henry the Seventhe, by the grace of God kyng of Englande & of Fraunce and lorde of Irelande, holdene at Westmynstre the 25 daie of January in the 19 yere of his most noble reigne, ordeigned and made for the wealle and profitte of his subjettes, it was among othir thinges ordeigned, establisshed and enacted that no maisters, wardeins and feliships of craftes or misteries nor enny of them, nor eny rulers of guildes or fraternites, shulde take uppon them to make enny actis or ordenaunces ne to execute eny actis or ordenaunces by them hertofore made in disheritaunce or dinumicione of the kingis prerogatif, nor of othir, nor against the comone profitte of his people, but yf the same actis and ordenaunces be examened and approved by the chaunceler, tresourer of Englonde, chief justices of either benche, or thre of them, or before bothe[13] the justices of assise in their circute or progresse in that shire. Where suche actis or ordenaunces be made uppone payne of forfaiture of £40 for every tyme that they do the contrary as in the seid acte more plainely it dothe appere. And where as the Rector, Wardeins and bretherne of the Fraternite or Gilde in the honoure of the most glorius Name of our Savyour Jhu, founded and establisshed by the prynce of reverende memory Kyng Harry the Sixt within the crowdes undir the cathedralle chirche of Seint Poule of London, willing and desiring the seid acte in alle thinges to be observed, have exhibit and presented afore us in the Starre Chambre at Westmynster the ten[the] day of February in the 22 yere of the reigne [1507] of oure seid sovereigne lorde a certeine booke of ordenaunces and statutes by the seid now Wardeins for good ordre and rule of the bretherne of the same fromhensforthe to be hadde and contenued, and theruppone by their peticioun have instantly desired us that we the seid ordenaunces and statutes in the seid booke conteyned wolde overse and examyne, and the same ordenaunces and statutes and every of them correct & amende aftir due fourme and conveinent maner and as the forseid act in the seid parliament made requirethe. We, welle parceiving their seid peticioun and desire to be good & resonable accordyng to their desires, and by auctorite of the seid act of parliament unto us commytted the actes and ordenaunces in the seid booke specified and every thyng in them conteignede have seene, redde and welle undrestonde, and every of the same actis and ordenaunces

---

12   Ordinances of Corporations Act 1503.
13   'bothe' written over erasure.

examyned, refourmed and amended. The tenours of whiche peticioun, actes and ordeneunces so by us seene, redde, examyned, refourmed and amended folowe and be thise: To the most Reverende Fadre in God William, archebisshope of Caunterbury, chaunceller of Englonde, and the righte honorable lorde the erle of Surrey, tresourer of Englonde, and the two chief justices of the kynges benche and common place. Mekely besechethe your good lordships the Rector, Wardeins and bretherne of the Fraternite or Guilde founded in the Name of Jĥu within the crowdes undre the cathedralle chirche of Seint Poule of London, that where by an acte of parliament holdene at Westmynster the 25 day of January the 19th yere of the reigne of oure sovereigne lorde kyng Harry the Seventhe it was enacted by auctorite of the same parliament that no maisters, wardeins and felishippe of craftes or misteries or enny of them, nor enny rulers of guildes or fraternitees, shulde take uppon theim to make enny actis or ordenaunces ne to execute any act or ordenaunces by them hereafore made in disheritaunce or dinumcion of the prerogatif of the kyng nor of othir, nor against the comon profiete of the people, but yf the same actes or ordenaunces be examened and approved by the chauncelor, tresourer of Englonde, and two chief justices of either benche, or thre of them, or before bothe the justices of assise in their circute or progresse in that shire where suche actis or ordenaunces be made, uppon peyne of forfeture of £40 for every tyme that they do the contrary. And ovir that, yt is enacted that none of the same bodies corporatt take uppon them to make enny actes or ordenaunces to restreyne eny parsone or parsones to sue to the kingis highenes or to enny of his courtis for due remedie to be had in their causes, ne putt ne execute enny penaltie or punysshement upponne enny of theym

f. 4v

for enny suche suyte to be made, uppon peyne of forfaiture of £40 for every tyme that they do the contrarie, and this acte to begynne and take effect at the fest of Pentecost thanne next commyng and fromthensforthe as by the same acte more plainely yt may appere. That it may like your good lordshippz or thre of you accordyng to the same acte of parliament to ovirse, examyne and approve a certeine booke conteynyng divers actis, statutes and ordenaunces devised and made for the good govirnaunce and poletique guidyng & mayntenyng of the same Fraternite, and the same actis, statutis and ordenaunces in the seid booke conteyned to be by you correctid and amended, and al suche as be good and resonable to be by you allowed & approved, and suche as benot resonable to be by youe cassed and and adnulled: And alle suche actes and ordenaunces by you so approved resonable and good to be putt yn writing and undre your sealles or signes to be deliverd to Maister John Colett, Doctour of Divinite, deane of the cathedralle chirche of Seint Paule, Rector, William Bromwelle and John Monke, citezeins of London, Wardeins of the seid Fraternite or Guilde, forto use & exercise the effecte of the same ordenaunces so by you approved accordyng to the seid Acte. Ande they shalle pray to almyghtey God for the preservacion of your good lordeshippes. The statutes and ordenaunces of the Fraternite founded in the honour of the Name of Jħu in the crowdes undre the cathedralle chuche of Seint Paule of London made by the Rector, Wardeins and bretherne of the seid Fraternite for the weale, poletique guidyng and maintenaunce of the same:

[4.a] The electioun of the Wardeins & 12 Assistentes to them

Fyrst it is agreede and ordeigned by the seid Rector, Wardeins and bretherne of the seid Fraternite of Jħu that every yere fromhensforthe parpetually a generalle assemble and congregacone of a convenient numbre of the brotherne of the seid Fraternite of Jħu be kept and holdene in the 26 daie of Marche yerely in a place competent and honest where as by the seid Rector and Wardeins shalle thynke most convenient, and their beyng assembled the seid Rectour and Wardeins, with the concent of the same bretherne, shalle name and chose two temparalle mene, able and honest and of good name, forto be Wardeins of the seid Fraternite for the yere folowyng. And ovir that shalle chose 12 honest and discrete parsones of the seid bretherne forto be Assistens to the seide Wardeins for the yere folowing. And in cas that enny of the seid Wardeyns or Assistences happene to deceace or avoide within the yere after they be chosene, thanne it is agreed and ordeigned that the seid Rector, Wardeins and Assistentes, or the more part of them, shalle assemble and procede to eleccioun of othir parsone or parsones in place of him or them so deceaced or avoidede.

[4.b] For the providyng and speding almaner of besines for the worshippe of the same Fraternite

Item it is agreed and ordeigned by the seid Rectour and Wardeins that they with their seid Assistens for the tyme being shalle provide, passe and spede almaner besynes for the weale and worshippe of the seid Fraternite or Guilde with as fulle power & auctorite as yf the hole numbre of the seid bretherne were therto called (or) present.

[4.c] Ther shalle no act passe withoute thassent of the Rectour and Wardeins & the most part of the Assistentes

Item it is ordeigned and agreed that none acte (or) ordenaunce shalbe made or cause to be made concernyng the seid Fraternite, except the seid Rectour, Wardeins and Assistentz, or the more part of them, therto be assenting and therto agree and give their advice and concent.

[4.d] For a common cheste to putt in their comon sealle & juelles with thre lokkes & thre keys, one key to remayne with the Rectour & the othir 2 keys with the Wardeins

f. 5r

Item it is agreed and ordeigned that a comon chest be had, wherin shalbe kept the comon sealle and alle the julles and comon tresoure belonging to the seid Fraternyte, uppon whiche chest shalle stonde thre severalle lokkis, one key therof to remayne in the custodie of the deane of Poules for the tyme beyng, parpetualle Rectoure of the seid Fraternite, and the othir two keys to remayne in the kepyng of either of the seid Wardens fo the tyme beinge.

[4.e] That the olde Wardeins shalle at a certeyne day rendre their accomptes

Item for asmuche as divers sommes of money belonging to the seid Fraternite have bene and be withholdene and kept in thandes of suche parsones as have bene Wardeins of the seid Fraternite, and of suche money wolle make none accomptes nor thereof make restitucione, by reasone whereof the the seid Fraternite is so impoverisshed and decaied that it is not able to bere the ordinary charges of prestis, clerkis, childrene and othir. Wherfor it is ordeigned and agreed that the Wardeyns of the said Fraternite fromhensforthe forevirmore shalle give up their accompt and rekenyng for the tyme of their office afore the Assistentis or afore suche auditours as by the seid Rector and Assistens shalbe named & appointed. And newe Wardeins chosene uppone the seid 26 daie of Marche or within two monethes next & inmediatly folowing the same daie. And also uppone the same daie or within two monethes folowing the seid olde Wardeins shalle deliver unto the newe Wardeins fully and holy alle the money and juelles remaynyng in their keping belonging to the seid Fraternite by indentures made betwene them, whereof the one partie of the same indentures shalle remayne with the Rector and the othir partie with the seid Wardeins. And also shalle delyver unto the newe Wardeins within the tyme afore lymytted the keys of the seid comon chest. And if the seid olde Wardeins make defaute and obserue not this ordenance in every poynt thane they shalle lose and forfeite their salarie whiche they shuld have for their labour. And yf yt fortune the Wardeins whiche have bene for the yere past to be chosene Wardeins for the yere folowing, it is ordeigned and agreed that they shalle yelde their accompt afore the seid Rector and assistens or the more part of them, or afore the seid auditours at the day or within two monethes afore specified. Providede alwey that every Wardeyne that shalbe fromhensforthe shalle stonde charged for his fellowe. And the seid Rector and Wardeyns shalbe bounde to kepe the seid Fraternite withoute enny losse or damage for almaner goodes and money remaynyng under their charge and keping as ferre as righte and good conctiens shalle require.

[4.f] For recovery of arreragis due unto the seid Fraternite in the kinges courtes

Item it is ordeigned and agreed that the seid Wardeins shalle aske, demaunde, levie and resteive almaner summes of money and goodis belonging to the seid Fraternite and alle arreragis restyng in thandes of enny brothir whiche hathe bene wardein of the same Fraternite, or in enny othir parsones handes whatsoeuir they be, and alle suche parsones for defaute of restitucone and payment of eny suche money to arrest and pursue in alle and everiche of the kinges courtes so farre as tille plenar restitucioun be made in that parte.

[4.g] For gownes to be givene to the Wardeins for their labours in their yere

Item it is ordeigned and agreed forasmuche as the Wardeins for the tyme being shalle do their voluntary labour and besines for the uppholdyng and maintenaunce of the seid Fraternite, and forto encorage them to be thereunto the more diligent and ententif, either of the same Wardeins shalle have for that yere that he shalle stonde wardeine a goune, clothe of suche coloure and price as the seid Rectour and Assistentes
f. 5v
shalle assigne, with two signes or conisaunces sownyng [i.e. sounding] to the Name of Jħu to be devised by the same Rectour and Assistentz. And moreovir, either of the seid wardeins shalle have in the name of rewarde suche a somme of money as the seid Rector and assistens shalle taxe and lymytte.

[4.h] For a potacioun to the bretherne at the charge of their boxe

Item it is agreed and ordeigned that at their assemble and daie of eleccion afore especified, a potacion be made to suche of the bretherne of the seid Fraternite as by the seid Rectour and Assistens shalbe thoughte convenient, and the cost thereof to be borne uppon the charge of the comon tresoure of the seid Fraternite so that they passe not 40s.

[4.i] That every proctour be sworne to answere his charge according to his covenauntes

Item it is ordeigned and agreed that no proctour or commissioner be admytted to restevie and gadre money for the seid Fraternite except he be sworne to bring into the seid Wardeins at the yeres ende withoute enny lenger delaie alle that somme of money that is specified in the covenauntes made theruppone betwene the seid wardeyns & him, withoute fraude or male ingigne. And moreovir, that he shalle truely present to the seid Wardeins at the seid yeres ende alle the names of the bretherne & sustrene within the procinct of his colleccone.

[4.j] That noo proxy be graunted above one yere and so signed by the handes of the Rectour and Wardenis

Item it is agreed and ordeigned that the Wardeins shalle deliver no proxi or comyssioun to enny parsone or parsones above one yere, and at the yeres ende every proctour or comyssioner shalle bring into the seid Wardeins his proxy or commissyoun, and that no newe lettres passe or be deliverd afore that the olde lettres be broughte inne and thane to be cancelled. Provided alwey that the seid lettres be signed withe thandes of the seid Rectour or Wardeins for the tyme beyng.

[4.k] That alle proxies graunted afore Michelmas last past be of none effect except suche as be in this booke amytted and those that by the lordes chaunceller, tresourer two chief justices or thre of them hereafter shalbe admyttede

And forasmuche as the comon sealle of the seid Fraternite hathe bene in keping of divers parsones many yeres past wherby gret harme myghte growe to the seid brothirhede by sealyng of writinges with the seid sealle. Wherfor it is agreed and ordeigned that almaner proxies or lesses or enny othir grauntes made wherunto standes the comon sealle of the seid Fraternite, that it stande as voide & adnulled, revoked and to none effecte, bering date before the fest of Seint Michelle Tharchangelle in the 22 yere of the reigne of king Harry the Seventhe [1506]; excepte proxies made and graunted to William Vowelle, gentilmane, and Roger Hyggyns, taillour, and al suche as shalbe approved and admytted by the chaunceler, tresourer and the two justices of either benche or thre of them. Provyded alwey that they that have enny suche sealle as is abovespecified shalle shewe their writing before the fest of Cristemas next commyng after the date hereof, orelles uttirly to be voide and of none effecte.

54

[5] The othe of the procuratour or commyssioner

f. 6r

Ye shalle swere that welle and truely ye shalle demeane your self to the Rectour and Wardeins of the Fraternite of Jħu for the tyme being, and in your office of procuratour to you commytted for as long as you shalle occupie the same, wele and truely shalle answer and delyver to the seid Rectour and Wardeins within the tyme of the yere of your occupieing or gaderyng alle suche sommes of money at suche place or places as shalbe specified in your covenauntes betwene them and you made or to be made to their use withoute delay, fraude or male engine [sic]. And within the same yere ye shalle also truely present, shewe and deliver to the seid Rector and Wardeyns at thende of the seid yere alle the names of the brotherne and sustrene within the procincte of your colleccioun, so God be your helpe and alle seintes.

Alle whiche statutis, actes and ordenances in maner & fourme afore specified at the request of the seid Rectour, Wardeins & brethirhede of Jħu aforeseide by auctorite of the seid Act of Parliament to us commytted, we the seid Chaunceller, Tresourer and Justices for good and laudable doo accept and admytte and by thise presentis asmuche as in us is ratefie and approve. In witnesse whereof to thise presentes we the seid Chaunceler, Tresourer and Justices have setto oure signes manuelles the 28 daie of Aprile and the 22th yere of the reigne of king Harry the Seventhe [1506].

f. 6v

[6.a] Othir ordenaunces enacted for divine service by the seid Rectour, Wardeins and brothers of the seid Fraternyte

Forasmoche as the honorable persone Maister John Colet, Doctour yn Theologie, deane of the cathedralle churche of Seint Poule in the cite of London and Rectour of the Fraternite founded and establisshed in the crowdes undre the seid chirche in the honour and in the Name of Jħū, William Bromwelle and John Monke, Wardeins of the same Fraternyte, with consent and assent of the more parte of the brotherne thereof, have ordeigned & establisshed that certeine obsequies and divine service shalbe yerely kept, holdene and observed in the seid crowdes forevirmore. And for maintenaunce of the same obsequies and service the seid Rectour, Wardeins & bretherne have ordeigned and establisshed for them and their successours asmuche as in them ys that certeine ordenary chargis and sommes of money shalbe levied and avaunced oute of the common tresoure of the seid Fraternite yerely to be givene and distributed to the ministres of the seid chirche in maner & fourme and under condicioun as folowithe.

55

[6.b] How the subdeane shalbe present at divine service in the fest of the Transfiguracion of oure Lorde & what he shalle have

First it is enacted, ordeyned and establisshed that in the vigile or evene of the fest named Transfiguracion of Oure Lorde at the first Evensong and also at matens & masse uppon the festivalle daie of Transfiguracone folowing, the subdeane of the seid cathedralle chirche of Seint Paule for the tyme being shalbe present parsonally, whiche shalle have & parceive aftir the seid masse done two shillinges.

[6.c] How the numbre is appointed to kepe the divine service there, & that a dirige shalbe kept with a masse of Requiem

Also, it is ordeigned an[d e]stablisshed[14] that yerely at the first Evensong, mateyns & masse of the seid fest of Transfiguracone of oure Lorde twelf petichanons if ther be somany, 8[15] chauntry preestis, six vicars and tenne queresters of the seid cathedralle chirche shalbe present in the seid crowdes, and there syng the divine service of Transfiguracion solemply by note after the divine service ordinary in the seid cathedralle chirche fully complet, at suche convienient tyme as the seid service be fulfillede. And in likewise it is ordeigned and establisshed that at Evensong uppon the seid daie of Transfiguracone, and also at matyns and hy masse uppon the daie next folowing whiche is named *festum de Nomine Jhū*, the seid numbre of petichanons, chauntry precestis, vicars and queresters shalbe present in the seid crowdes and there sing the divine service *de Nomine Jhū* solemply by note. And furthirmore, incontinently after the last Evensong evene uppon the same festivalle daie *de Nomine Jhu* the seid numbre of petichanons, chauntry preistes, vicaries & queresters, before their departure out of the crowdes, shalle syng a solmpne *Placebo & Dirige* by note for alle the brethrene and sustrene of the seid Fraternite, and on the morowe thane folowing a solmpne masse of Requiem by note. And the seid petichanons (shalhave) among them for their service as aboveseide twenty shillinges; the seid chauntry preestis to have amongist them eighte shillinges; and the seid vicaris to have amongist them nyne shillinges. Providede alwey that if enny of the seid persones that may conveniently be there and be absent and comme not to alle the divine service afore reherced, that than his part after the rate of his absence shalbe recomped of the seid summe and remayne to the common tresour aforeseide.

---

[14] Staining on the folio obscures occasional letters.
[15] Odd form of 'v' in viij and could be 'x', but eight chantry priests is the usual number in the accounts.

[6.d] For the processyone

Also, yt is ordeigned and establisshed that alle and singler highe chanons, pety

f. 7r

chanons, chauntry preistis, vicaries and queresters of the seid cathedralle churche that be present and bere a cope atte processions, aswelle uppone the seid festivalle daie of Transfiguracione as *de Nomine Jhū*, every of the seid parsones more and lesse there beyng and berying a cope to have and perceive [sic] for thos two processions 4d.

[6.e] For the hy masse and of the collacion

Item it is ordeigned that uppon the festivalle day *de Nomine Jhū* the subdene in absence of the dene, and in the absence of the subdeane one of the cardinalles of the seid cathedralle chirche, shalle syng the hy masse in a grey amys, parceiving for his service two shillynges. And if the deane of the seid chirche syng the seid masse and make a collacion at the same masse he shalle have six shillinges eighte pens. And if enny parsone othir thane the seid deane make a collacion, the same parsone to have thre shillinges foure pens, half of the seid six shillinges eighte pens; and the deane to have the residue yf he be present and doo the divine service aforeseid. And yn defaute of his presence the money to remayne to the comone tresoure aforeseyde.

[6.f] For the masse of Requiem

Also, yt is ordeigned that one of the petychanons shalle syng the masse of Requiem afore specifiede, and that two chauntry preestis of the seid numbre to be assigned by the subdeane shalle rede the Gospelles and Epistles at alle thre masses above rehercid, and every of them to have for their redyng beside their salary before extendide - 6d.

[6.g] The sextene

Also, yt is ordeigned that the sextene of the seid chirche, called keper of the vestry, for garnysshyng of the alters in the seid crowdes during the festivalle dais and divine service above especifiede, and for his labour in bering of bookis and othir ornamentes, shalle have thre shillinges foure pens.

[6.h] The vergers

Also, it is ordeigned that everiche of the 4 vergiers belonging to the seid chirche and attending duely alle the seid services in the seid festes shalle have 16d. And yf enny make defaute that thane the parte of him that so defautethe after the rate of his absence shalle remayne to the comon tresoure.

[6.i] The belle ryngers

Also, yt is ordeigned that two belle ryngers of the seid chirche shalle have for openyng, closyng and shitting the dores of the crowdes at al seasons whanne service shalbe, ore whane nede requirethe, aswelle in enny of the seid festis as Fridays and whanne *salves* shulde be songene or othir tymes convenient, so that the seid Fraternite benot hurte nor enpaired by their negligence. And also for rynging ryngers and tollyng of belles, blowyng organs, lighetyng & quenching of torches and tapers in maner & fourme as hathe bene accustumed, and for swepyng and making clene the seid crowdes - 33s. 4d. betwene them by the yere to be paide in fourme folowyng, that ys to sey in the fest *de Nomine Jhū* 13s. 4d. and 20s. to be payd quarterly.

[6.j] For Jhūs masse on the Fridays

Item it is ordeigned that the masse of Jħu be kept and songene solmpnely in the seid crowdes every Friday yerely as yt hathe bene accustumed. A cardenalle in his habite to syng the
f. 7v
masse and to praie for al the brothrene and sustrene of the seid Fraternite with certeine suffrages, rehercyng alle the names conteyned in the table in maner & fourme as beforetyme hathe bene accustumed, and he to have for his labour 4d. At everiche of the whiche masses beside the same preest that syngethe the masse shalbe present to syng the same by note solempnely pety chanons, vicars 7[16] in numbre, and tenne queresters, everiche of the same parsones to bere their habites and surplices, and everiche of the seid petichanons & vicaries to have for their labour - 2d.

[6.k] For the masse of Requiem on the Friday

Also, that incontinently after the seid masse of Jħu ended a masse of Requiem be songene by note every Friday yerely by one of the seid

---

[16]   'chanons vicars vij' is written over an illegible erasure.

petychanons in his habite, and to have for his laboure 4d. And yf a chauntry preest synge the masse he to have 2d. Of whiche masse six of the seid tenne queresters shalle syng the service accustumede.

[6.l] For thre *salves* to be songene daily

Also, it is ordeigned that after Complyne done in the seid cathedralle chirche thre *salves* shalbe songe solemply daily and yerely in the seid crowdes in places & dais accustumede, that is to sey before Jhu, oure Ladie & Seint Sebastiane.[17] Oone of the vicaries, maister of the seid queresters for the tyme being, to have for his labour yerely 26s. 8d. at 4 termes of the yere by evene porcions.

[6.m] For givinge gownes to the queresters

Also, yt is ordeigned that the Wardeins of the seid Fraternite of Jhū for the tyme being shalle paie and yerely deliver unto the maister of the amery of the seid chirche for the tyme beyng at the fest of Midsomer every yere £4, for and to thentent that the same maister shalle emploie and bestowe the same £4 uppone wollone clothe, and the same clothe he shalle distribute and do to be made in tenne gownes mete for the seid tenne queresters, to be worne at the festevalle daies aforeseide. And yf defaut be in the seid maister that enny of the seid queresters lakke his goune as is aforeseid, the same maister to pay for every goune so lakking not worne to the Wardeins of the seid Fraternite tene shillinges.

[7] Alle whiche ordenaunces beforeseid concernyng the ministres of Poules are ordeyned & establisshed by the seid deane, Rector, and Wardeins, with thassent and concent of the subdeane and mynystres aforeseid, to endure & contenue unto suche tyme as the Rectour and Wardeins hereaftere for the tyme beyng and othir havyng therin interest shalle thinke for a comone weale & profitt of the seid Fraternite more expedient to adnulle and repelle them or enny of them. And yn witnesse of the agrementis aforeseid the subdeane now being, in the name of alle the seid ministres by their assent and request, hathe subscribed here his name affermyng the seid ordenances to be good and stable and to be used likewise as (is) before rehercede.

---

17 A chantry at the altar of St Sebastian in the crypt was established by Alan de Hotham, a canon of St Paul's in 1352, and amalgamated with the chantry of 'Sancta Maria' in 1391; M-H. Rousseau, *Saving the Souls of Medieval London* (Farnham, 2011), 184. The images of the Blessed Virgin and St Sebastian presumably were associated with these pre-established altars.

Be me Ser John' Chyrche, subdene of þe sayde cathedral chyrche of seynt Paule . Ch'[18]

f. 8r

[8.a] For one that shalle attende to helpe preistis syng masse[19]

Also, it is ordeigned that an honest aged mane shalbe attendaunt at alle convenent tymes to helpe preestis to syng masse and to see the copes, vestimentis & othir ornamentes belongyng to the autres of the seid Fraternite be safly kept, ordred & lokked up in a chest, and to gif attendaunce and do suche othir neccssaries as by the seid Wardeins he shalbe appoyntede. For the whiche service he shalle have yerely 26s. 8d. to be paid quarterly.

[8.b] For the waites

Also, it is ordeigned that six waites yerely shalle goo in al the stretys of London and subbarbes of the same before the festis of the Transfiguracone of oure Lorde and *de Nomine Jhu* withe there instrumentes plaieng to gif warnyng and knowlege to the people of the seid festys. And they shalle have amongest them alle six for their laboure tene shillinges, provided alwey that yf ther wante enny of the same numbre of 6, that thane there shalbe abated of the same somme after the rate of the parsone or parsones so wantyng. And that the Wardeins or their deputie shalle deliver unto the seid six waites for every of them a banere pictured with the conusauns of Jhus, and also a liverey of Jhus browdred, alle the whiche baners & lyveries the seid waytys shalle redeliver unto the seid Wardeyns in the ende of the seide festis.

[8.c] For the bonefire

Also, it is ordeigned that yerely in the vigille of the fest *de Nomine Jhu*, a bonefire shalbe made in the chirche yerde of Seint Paule before the dore of the crowdes on the northesyde there, and that the proctour of London cause it to be done and to be allowed for the same 2s. 8d.

[8.d] For the payment of chargis on Fridais

---

[18]   Different script, presumably Church's own hand. John Church (d. 1509) was a minor canon of St Paul's. He may have had a personal connection with the Guild, and requested burial before the image of Jesus in the crypt chapel, TNA, PROB 11/16/190.

[19]   Main hand resumes.

Also, that the proctour of London or his deputie or enny othir by the Wardeyns assigned shalle yerely every Fridaie in the crowdes pay the preistis, clerkes & othir charges before none, and shalbe attendant & redie to do alle besynes whanne he ys commaunded by the seid Wardeins. And he to have for his laboure likewise as it shalbe covenauntede betwene the Wardeyns and him.

[8.e] For brede and ale to be exependede

Also, it is ordeigned that in the festis of the Transfiguracone of our Lorde and *de Nomine Jhu* shalbe brede and ale expended in the crowdes amongest the brothrene and sustrene. And the proctour aforeseid shalbe allowed for the same tene shillinges.

[8.f] For lyveryes

Also, it is ordeigned that against the seid fest of the Transfiguracone of our Lorde lyveries of golde and silver shalbe made and givene to the brothrene and sustrene after the olde custume by the proctour of London. And he to be allowed for the same 13s. and 4d. Except that the Wardeins, waites & Felishippe of Wexchaundelers shalle yerely have their conysaunces and lyveries ovir and beside the seid summe.

[8.g] For garnysshinge of the crowdys

Also, it is ordeigned that the seid proctoure shalle purveie and yerely ordeyne for the garnysshing of the crowdes with boughes and herbes after the old custume, and he to be allowed for that by the discretioun of the Wardeins for the tyme beynge.

f. 8v

[8.h] Rewarde to the prechours

Also, it is ordeigned that the seid proctour of London shalle every Sondaie pay to the prechours at Poules Cros and Seint Mary Spittelle, whiche in their bedys shalle remembre and praie for the brotherne and sustren of the seid Fraternite as yt hathe bene accustumed; every prechoure there 4d.

[8.i] For the accompte of the seid Proctour of London

Also, it is ordeigned that the seid Proctour shalle yerely make his accompte or as oftene and whanne the Wardeins for the tyme beyng shalle appointe, and that he be redie to do his duetie and to give warnyng to the bretherne & sustrene of the seyd Fraternyte to assemble at al tymes whanne as he shalbe commaunded by the seid Wardeins. And yf the seid proctour paie or axe to be allowed for ordynary charges othirwise and more thane is before lymytted, that thane he shalle not be allowed uppone his accompte for that surplusage of the seid Wardeins.

[Remaining two-thirds of this folio are blank]

f. 9r and f.9v – blank

f.10r[20]

[9] Here after folowithe the regestryng and entryng of diverse chartres, dedes and evidences belongyng to the Fraternite or Gilde of the Name of Jħu in the cite of London of alle suche londes and tenementes as they have apperteynnyng to the same Fraternite or Gilde, and the entryng of certene covenauntes and bondes betwene the Rector, Wardens, bretherne and susterne of the same Fraternite or Gilde and diverse other persones by indentures & other certene writtynges therof made, as by the same more playnly dothe appere. Alle the whiche forseide chartres, dedys, evidences, indentures & writtynges remayne in a grete comone chest belongyng to the seid Fraternire or Gilde of the Name of Jħu.

f. 10v

[10] Here ensuethe a conveyaunce by certene dedes of diverse londes & tenementes lying in Woxbrigge in the countie of Middlesex to the seid Fraternite or Gilde.

f. 10v – 11v [calendared deeds]

[10.a[21]] Grant by Ralph Botyller, knight, lord Sudeley, John Goode and John Latymer to Nicholas Lathelle, clerk of the pipe of the Exchequer, Sir John Barone and Sir John Gremstone, chaplains, of their two tenements in the vill of Uxbridge, one of which lies between the tenements of Sir Thomas Charleton, knight, and of William Dyer, and extends from the King's road of Uxbridge to the watercourse of the said Sir Thomas, and the other of which lies between the tenements of John Albrowe, citizen and mercer of London, and of Sir William Knyghtecote, chaplain, rector of the parish of Cowley, and extends from the said road to the lane called 'le blynde lane', with all their appurtenances in Middlesex. Also, grant of two fields called 'le Waterfeldes' lying between the lane called 'le Wodelane' and the

---

[20]   Different hand from Letters Patent and Ordinances.

[21]   I am grateful to Dr Hannes Kleineke for an early guide draft for this calendar of the Uxbridge deeds.

stream of water running there, and of five acres of arable land and half an acre of meadow lying separately in the counties of Middlesex and of Buckinghamshire, whereof one acre lies in Longridynge between the land formerly of William Waynfford, esquire, and now of Sir Thomas Borrughe, knight, and that of the heirs of Robert Manfilde, and another acre and a half of land lie in Lovelynche, and another acre of land lies in Cowleyfeld, and another acre of land in le Hale and half an acre of land lies in the field called 'Halfacrefelde', and the said half acre of meadow lies in Huntewik. Also grant of a close called 'Litill Rydynge' lying at the end of the said acre in Longrydynge. To have and to hold to themselves and their heirs and assigns forever, with warranty against all people.

Sealed by the grantors.

Witnesses: William Dyer and Stephen Clyfford, bailiffs of Uxbridge, Richard Curteys, John Oxstone, Richard Georges, Thomas Pese, John Walker, and many others.

Dated at Uxbridge, 7 March 7 Edward IV [1467].

f. 11 – 11v

[10.b] Grant by Nicholas Lathelle, clerk of the pipe of the Exchequer, Sir John Barone and Sir John Gremstone, chaplains, to John Hert of Uxbridge and Elizabeth his wife of the same properties [as in 10.a] to have and to hold to themselves and their executors and assigns for their lives in survivorship and for a year after the death of the longer living of them. Appointment of Martin Jolyff as attorney to deliver seisin.

Sealed by the grantors.

Witnesses as before.

Dated at Uxbridge, 7 April 7 Edward IV [1467].

f. 11v – 12r

[10.c] Grant and surrender reciting the terms of [10.b], by Elizabeth, late the wife of John Hert, deceased, formerly of Uxbridge, to Nicholas Lathelle, clerk of the pipe of the Exchequer, Sir John Barone and Sir John Gremstone, chaplains, of all her right and title in the above properties.

Sealed by the grantor.

Dated 16 February 49 Henry VI [1471].

f. 12v – 13r

[10.d] Grant by Nicholas Lathelle, clerk of the pipe of the Exchequer, Sir John Barone and Sir John Gremstone, chaplains, to Master Roger Radclyfe, dean of the Cathedral church of St Paul's and rector of the Fraternity or Guild of the Holy Name of Jesus in the city of London, and Richard Foorde, one of the remembrancers of the exchequer, and Henry Benet one of the clerks of the office of the Privy Seal, wardens of the said fraternity or guild, and to the brothers and sisters of the said guild, of the two properties and various lands **[as in 10.a]**.

To have and to hold to themselves and their successors forever for the support of the same fraternity or guild. Appointment of Martin Jolyff and John Hymsworthe, citizens of London, and William Chaunt, notary, as attornies to deliver seisin.

Sealed by the grantors.

Witnesses: Richard Curteys and John Bromer, bailiffs of Uxbridge, William Dyer, Richard George, John Walker, and others.

Dated at Uxbridge, 25 February 49 Henry VI [1471].

f.13v[22]

[11] Maister Alwyne: Torches to be kept by þe Wexchaundlers[23]}

Be it remembrede that Maister Nicholas Alwyne,[24] aldermane of London, bequethed to the Bretherhede of Jħu in London every yere duryng the space of 20 yere two newe torches of wex, either of them weying 8lb., to thentent that the same torches shalbe lighte at the levacione tyme every Fridaye at the masses of Jħu and of Requiem kept in the crowdes of Powles. The whiche torches the seid Maister and Felisshipe of Wexchaundelers in London be bounde to se them maynteined and kept yerely as by endenture betwene the same Maister Alwyne and them therof made more playnly apperethe.

[12] For the lighetes brennyng [sic] afore Jħu in þe crowdys to be yerely kept by the Felisshipe of Wexchaundelers etc }

It is condestendyde and aggreede betwene the Rector, Wardens bretherne and susterne of the Fraternite of Jħu in London onn the oone partie, and the Maister, Wardens and hole Felisshipe of the Crafte and Mistere of Wex Chaundelers in London onn the other partie, that the same Maister & Felisshipe shalle fynde certene lightes afore the awter of Jħu in the crowdys of Powles, and also pay certene money yerely to the same Fraternite, withe other certene covenauntes betwene the same Bretherhede and Crafte as by endenture beryng date the 20^{ti} day of January the 23th yere of kyng Henry the 7th [1508] therof betwene them made more playnly dothe appere, whiche indenture remaynethe in the comone chest belongyng to the seid Fraternite.

---

22   Possibly the same hand as Uxbridge deeds, and not the same as earlier ordnainces etc.
23   Headings of sections are in the left margin, sections enclosed by large bracket on the left.
24   Nicholas Ailwyn (d. 1506), mayor 1499–1500. C. M. Barron, *London in the Later Middle Ages* (Oxford, 2004), 348.

[13] For certene praiours to be seid & doone for the soules of Thomas Wyndeoute[25] & John Style by þe Bretherhode }

Memorandum that the 14th day of Aprille the yere of oure Lord Gode 1507 and the 22[the] yere of the reigne of kyng Henry the 7[the], Maister John Colet, Rector of the Fraternite of Jħu in London, William Brumwelle & John Munke, Wardens of the same Fraternite, covenaunte with William Broune, aldermane of London, Roger Bafforde, Thomas Baldry & John Kyme, Wardens of the Mercery, that for £10 sterlinges by thandes of the seid Thomas Baldry to the seid Rector & Wardens beforehande paide, that they shalle yerely dyryng the space of oone hundrethe yeres next after the seid 14 daie of Aprille cause the soules of Thomas Wyndeoute, aldermane, & John Style, mercer, to be praied for at every sermond at Powles Crosse and Seint Mary Spitelle yerely, and also at the masses of Jħu & of Requiem every Friday yerely duryng the seid space, upone payne to forfette to the seid Wardens of the Mercery and to theire successours at every tyme in makyng defaute of eny of the premisses 6d. withoute eny cause resonable lette it, as by endenture betwene them therof made more playnly dothe appere. Whiche indenture remanethe in the seid comone chest.

Memorandum[26] that for certeyn consyderacions it is aggreede betwene the parties expressede in the forsaid endenture that the forsaid Rectour and Wardeyns nor their successours in any wise shalbe charged to kepe and maynteyn the forsaid suffragis and preyers but frome the feast of Thannunacion of our Blessede Lady the Virgyne in the yere of oure lord Gode 1518[ten] unto thende and terme of twenty yeres than next ensuyng. And than and frome thensfourth alle the covenauntes conteyned in the said endentures to be voide and of none effecte.

By me Thomas Baldry[27]

f. 14r[28]

[14] The sale of the Bulhedde &c[29]

Memorandum that the 14[the] day of Novembre the 23[the] yere of the reigne of kyng Henry the 7[the] [1507], the Rector and Wardens of the Fraternite of Jħu, withe the consent of the bretherne & susterne of the same Fraternite, have solde alle that theire tenement or taverne called the Bullyshede at Seynt Martens Lane ende to oone John Pilbarough for a

---

25   Thomas Wyndout, (d. 1500) sheriff of London 1497–8. Barron, *London*, 348.
26   Different hand for this section.
27   Signature.
28   Same hand as main one in f.13v.
29   Small 'a' written in left margin at start of this and next three entries.

hundrethe pounde sterlinges.[30] Wherof, of £10 they holde them content & paide, and the fowre score & £10 residue to be paide at certen daies comprised in a dede indentede therof, made beryng date the first day of Decembre the 23th yere aforeseid, withe a clause of reentre for defaute of eny of the paymentes and other certen condicouns as more playnly apperethe in the same dede.

And it is condestendyde and aggreede by the seid Rector, Wardens bretherne and susterne of the same Fraternite that the seid hundrethe pounde shalle not be employed to noone other use but oonly to purchace oder londes therwith, to thentent that the gever of the same Bullyshede shulde be praied for accordyng to his last wille.[31]

[15] The lease made to Doctor Smythe of alle the devocions for terme of 7 yere

Memorandum that the Rectour & Wardens of the Fraternite of Jhu have lettene to ferme unto Maister Smythe, Doctor of Phesyke, alle the devocions of Englonde belongyng to the seid Fraternite from the fest of Cristmas in the yere of oure lord God 1506 unto thende & terme of 7 yere, for the summe of £28 sterling to be paide in fourme folowyng, that is to sey: every weke wekely in the crowdes onn the Friday alle the ordenary charges there, & every yere yerely also at the fest of Midsomer to the maister of the aumuepry for gownes for 10 queresters, £4. And the rest of the seid £28 to be paide yerely duryng the seid terme to the seid Rector & Wardens or to theire successours the first daie of Marche, as by endenture remaynyng in the seid comone chest more playnly dothe appere.

[16] The dette of Copwode

Memorandum that John Copwode,[32] gentilmane, owethe unto the seid Fraternite £17 10s., to be paide in fourme folowyng, that is to sey: at Mighelmas the yere of oure lord 1508, 50s.; & at Cristmas next after that, £5; and at Cristemas the yere of oure lord 1509, £5; and at Cristemas the yere of oure Lord 1510, £5, as by severalle obligacions remaynnyng in the seid grete comone chest more playnly dothe appere.

f. 14v

---

30 John Hatfeld alias Pilborough (d. 1520), a vintner and Assistant of the Guild.
31 The donor was Richard Ewen, a canon of St Paul's; see Introduction, p. 7.
32 Possibly a member of the Copwood family of Totteridge (Herts.) who in the sixteenth century held Copped Hall in that parish, 'Parishes: Totteridge', in *A History of the County of Hertford: Volume 3*, ed. William Page (London: Victoria County History, 1912), 148–50.

[17] Certene praiours to be seid for the soule of William Ipyswelle[33] }

Memorandum[34] that at the fest of Cristmas the yere of oure Lord God 1500 & 8[the] the Rector & Wardens of the Fraternite of Jħu in London covenaunted with the executours[35] of the testament of William Ipyswelle, mercer, that for £10 sterlinges by thandes of the same executours to the seid Rector & Wardens before hand paide, that they shalle yerely duryng the space of oone hundrethe yeres next after the seid fest of Cristmas cause the soule of the seid William to be praied for at every sermond at Powles Crosse & Seynt Mary Spytelle, and also at the masses of Jħu & of Requiem kept every Fryday in the crowdes of Pawlys duryng the seid space of oone hundrethe yere, as by endenture betwene them therof made more playnly apperethe.

[18] Certene praiours to be seid for the soule of Maister William Broune[36] }

Memorandum that at the fest of Ester the yere of oure lord God 1500 & 8[the] the Rector & Wardens of the Fraternite of Jħu in London covenauntede with the executours[37] of the testament of Maister William Broune, mercer & aldermane, decessyng maire of London, that for £13 6s. 8d. sterlinges by them to the seid Rector & Wardens before hand paide, that they shalle yerely duryng the space of oone hundrethe yeres next after the seid fest of Ester cause the soule of the seid Maister William Broune to be praied for at every sermond at Powles Crosse & Seint Mary Spytelle, and also at the masses of Jħu & of Requiem kept every Fryday in the crowdes of Powlys duryng the seid space of oone hundrethe yere, as by endenture betwene them therof made more playnly apperethe.

Memorandum[38] that for certeyne consyderacions it is agreede bitwene the parties expressede in the forsaide endenture, that the forsaide Rectour and Wardeyns nor their successours in any wise shalbe chargede to kepe and maynteyne the forsaide suffragis and preyers but frome the feast of

---

33 William Ipswell, mercer (d. 1508). A. Sutton, *The Mercery of London: Trade, Goods and People, 1130–1578* (Aldershot, 2005), 381n. Ipswell did not mention the Jesus Guild or a specific devotion to the Holy Name in his will, although he requested five trentals of masses of the Five Wounds, TNA, PROB 11/15/406.

34 Small 'pointer' mark in left margin at start of this and the next entry.

35 Simon Rice and James Gentle, both mercers. See Sutton, *Mercery*, 539, 466, 558.

36 William Browne (d. 1508), mercer, Mayor 1507–8. Barron, *London*, 349; see also Sutton, *Mercery*, 558.

37 Elizabeth his wife, William Browne his cousin, alderman of London, and Thomas Hynde, mercer, his son-in-law, Warden of the Jesus Guild 1520–2. TNA, PROB 11/16/13.

38 Different hand from previous section.

Thanuncacione of our Blessede Lady Seynt Mary the Virgyne in the yere of oure Lorde God 1518ten unto thende and terme of twenty yeres then nexte ensuyng. And than and frome thensforthe alle the covenauntes conteynede in the said endentures to be voied and of none effecte.

Per me Thomas Hynde.[39]

f. 15r[40]

[19] [Inspeximus of a writ of Privy Seal of Thomas Audley held in the files of Chancery]

Henricus Octavus, Dei gracia Anglie & Francie Rex, Fidei Defensor, Dominus Hibernie, et in terra Supremum Caput Anglicane Ecclesie, omnibus ad quos presentes litere peruenerint, salutem. Inspeximus quoddam breve nostrum de privato Sigillo dilecto et fideli Consilio nostro Thome Audeley, militi, Cancellario nostro Anglie, directum et in filaciis Cancellarie nostre residens in hec verba.

Henry the Eighte, by the grace of God kynge of Englonde & of Fraunce, Defensour of the Faith, Lorde of Irelonde, and in yerth Supreme Hed of the Churche of Englonde. To our trusty and right welbiloved Councellour Ser Thomas Audeley, knyghte, our Chauncellour of Englonde, greting. And where as we of late, upone greate & diverse urgent causes and consideracions us moving, have willed & comaundede you by our high and speciall comaundement that no lettres patentes of proteccion for religious houses, monasterys, hospitalles, chappelles, gildes and fraternities within this our realme to collecte and gather any almonse or other charitable devocions of our subjectes in eny citie, towne or borough for the same, for the supporting & maynteynyng of the said monasterys, hospitalles, gildes and fraternyties, shulde passe and be sealed[41] under our Greate Seale without our speciall lycence and comaundement by us gyven unto you for the sealyng and grauntyng of the same, as by our said comaundement ye have more perfecte knowledge. Knowe ye that, for asmuche as the Fraternitie of the Blessed and Holly Name of Jhus[42] kept within the cathedrall church of Seint Paule of London is of our fundacion and founded by our noble progenitor kyng Henry the Sixth, and moreover that the said Gilde and Fraternitie hath no previleges graunted

---

39 Different hand, clearly a signature.
40 Not the same hand as the 'Memoranda' on f. 14v.
41 Word written as 'seased' and corrected to 'sealed' by overwriting the second s.
42 Notation marks in left margin next to lines from 'of Jhus' to 'mayntenaunce & supportacionn'.

68

by the busshop of Rome nor his perredecessors,[43] nor yet landes and possessions, but only the charitable devocion, helpe and ayde of us & our subjectes for the mayntenaunce & supportacion of the said Gilde and Fraternitie. Wherfore we woll and comaunde you that ye do seale and cause to be sealed undre our Grete Seale from yere to yere at all tymes hereafter our lettres patentes of proteccone for the proctors and collectors of the said Fraternitie to collecte and gather the devocioun and charitable almes of our subiectes in all shires, cities, townes and borowes withyne this our realme and other places undre our obeysaunce, any statute, acte, provycion, ordynaunce, restraynt or comaundement heretofore by us to the contrary gyvene notwithstonding. And this our present warraunt shalbe at alle tymes a waraunt dormaunt for your discharge in this behalffe. Yovene undre our Pryvie Seale at our manour of Westminster the 9 day of June the 27[the] yere of our reigne [1535].

Nos tenorem brevis predicti ad requisicionem Willelmi Turke et Rogeri Barker, civium civitatis nostre Londoniensis et Gardianorem Fraternitatis siue Gilde predicte, duximus exemplificandum per presentes. In cuius rei testionium hac literas nostras fieri fec[imus] patentes . Teste me ipso apud Westmonistarium 24 die July anno regni nostri vicesimo septimo.

[Exemplificaiton of Letters Patent at the request of William Turke and Roger Barker, citizens of London and Wardens of the Fraternity aforesaid. Witnessed at Westminster 24 July 27 Henry VIII (1535).]

[f. 15v – blank]

f. 16r[44]
[20] Memorandum that, where as Sir Bartylmew Rede,[45] knyghte, by his testament and last wille gave and bequethed to thuse of the Fraternitie of Jhū founded in the crowdes under the cathedrall churche of Seint Paule of London the some of £6 13s. 4d. sterling, with the whiche was boughte a chalyce remaynyng in the said crowdes price £5. And £3 6s. 8d. was delyvered into thandes of William Bromwelle, mercer, and John Monke, wexchaundler, thene being Wardeins of the saide Fraternite towardes the makyng of a new paire of organs now remaynyng within the said crowdes. And sythene the decesse of the said Sir Bartholomew Rede, Dame Elizabethe Rede, wydow, late wif of the saide Sir Bartholomew, hath gyven and delyvered to thuse of the said Fraternitie £20 sterling, wherof Henry Dakers and Ellys Draper now Wardeyns of the said

43   Clear *per* abbreviation mark at start of word.
44   Different scribe from f. 15r.
45   Sir Bartholomew Rede (d. 1505), mayor of London 1502–3. Barron, *London*, 348.

69

Fraternitie knowlegene them selffes truely content and paide, satisfied. For the whiche said £30 by the saide Sir Bartholomew ande Dame Elizabethe to thuse aforesaid truely content and paide, at a generall assemble and courte holdene the 26 day of Marche in the yere of our Lorde God 1525 and in the 16th yere of the reigne of kyng Henry the VIII^{the} yt was enactede, stablisshede and grauntede by thassent (&) consent of Richarde Pace, deane of the cathedrall churche of Seint Paule of London and Rectour of the said Fraternitie, Henry Dakers and Ellys Draper Wardyns of the said Fraternitie, and by thassent, consent and aggrement of alle the Assistence of the said Fraternitie thane and there being present at the elleccione of new Wardeins, covenaunted and graunted with the said Dame Elizabethe and by thise presentes theme and their successours byndene, that they and their said successours from thensfourthe forever more shall cause to be hade in remembraunce every Sonday and other days whene and as often yt shall fortune any sermon or preching to be made at Poules Crosse or at Seint Mary Spyttell withoute Bisshoppesgate of London, the prechour or prechours that there shall shew, publysshe and declare the worde of almyghtie God, to reherse and say openly in their bede rolles and at their prayers there accustomed to be had and made thise wordes folowing, that is to saye: 'Of your charitie pray for the soules of Sir Bartholomew Rede, ł knyghte and late mayre of the citie of London, and Dame Elizabethe his wif, their frendes soules and all Cristene soules, onn whose soules Jhus have mercy'. And that the said Rectour and Wardeyns and their successours shall wekely frome thensfourthe every Frydaye accustomably forevermore cause the soules of the said Sir Bartholomew and Dame Elizabethe to be praid for in the chappell of Jhu' in the saide crowdes, or in any other place where the masse of Jhū shalbe kepte, amonges ande with other benefactours soules there accustomede to be praied for by name. And also every weke wekely forevermore at a masse of Requiem there to be had kepte, in lyke wise shall cause the names of the saide Sir Bartholomew and Dame Elizabethe to be remembrede by the preestes whiche shall synge or say the same masse of Requiem in his *memento* amonge and with other benefactours soules there to be remembred. Yovene the day and yere abovesaide.

The names of the Assistence being present at the premisses

Thomas Baldrye	Henry Hille	John Pyke	William Broket
John Browne	John Sandell	William Campyone	Richard Callarde
Henry Dakers	Richard Smythe	William Berde	Hughe Ac[to]ne
Ellys Draper	Stephene Warde	Thomas Nycolles	Richard Dowine
William Bromwell	Thomas Hynde	John Worsoppe	

John Monke   Stephene Lynne   William Pavyer[46]

William Botery

f. 16v[47]

[Letters of Protection]

[21.a] Henricus Octauvs, Dei gracia Anglie et Francie Rex, Fidei defensor, dominus Hibernie et in terra supremum capud [sic] Ecclesie Anglicane, universis et singulis archiepiscopis, episcopis, abbatibus, prioribus, archidiaconis, decanis et eorum officialibus rectoribus vicariis ac aliis personis ecclesiasticis quibuscumque necnon vicecomittibus maioribus balliuis constabulariis ministris et fidelibus legeis nostris quibuscumque tam infra libertates quam extra ad quos presentes litere pervenerint, salutem. Sciatis quod cum dilectus nobis Ricardus Pace,[48] decanus Ecclesis Cathedralis Sancti Pauli Londoniensis et ex hoc rector perpetuus fraternitatis siue Gilde glorisissimi Nominis Jhu' in criptis subtus ipsam Ecclesiam, Willielmus Turke et Rogerus Barker de London cives et gardiani pro tempore fraternitatis sive Gilde predicte licencia nostra fundente et erecte vbi hoc gloriosum nomen pre ceteris regni nostri Anglie locis maxime honoratum in redditibus et facultatibus ita insufficienter ac adeo exile existant. Quod bona eiusdem fraternitatis siue Gilde ad sustentacionem omnium et aliorum piorum operum tam in divinis serviciis eis multipliciter et necessarie incumbencium non sufficiunt nisi a Christi fidelibus et Deo devotis subueniatur eisdem ac providi idem rectour & gardiani, fratres et sorores fraternitatis sive Gilde predicte constituerunt, Henricum Hasylwod et substitutos suos nostros veros et legitimos collectores ac nostros generales et speciales nuncios in et per totam Diocesin Eboracensem cum Provincia eiusdem tam in locis exemptis quam non exemptis ad elimosinas pro sustenccione fraternitatis sive Gilde predicte a Christi fidelibus et Deo devotis petendum et colligendum nostra mediante licencia. Nos volentes securitati ipsius Henrici ac deputatorum suorum in hac parte gloriose providendum ob reverenciam et laudem ac cinceram devocionem quas penes ipsum gloriosum Nomen Jhu' preceteris in nostro scrinio pectoris gerimus et habemus suscepimus ipsum Henricum ad dictas elimosinas infra diocesin predictam petendum et colligendum ac deputatos homines et servientes suos. Necnon res et bona sua quecumque in protexcionem et defencionem nostras speciales, et ideo vos prelatas ac alias personas eccleiasticas precipimus et mandamus quatenus cum idem Henricus vel deputati sui ad ecclesias et loca vestra pro huiusmodi elimosinis ut prefertur a Christi

---

46   Paver's name is squashed in between Worsopp and Botery.
47   Different hand.
48   Richard Pace (d. 1536), dean 1519–36. *Fasti St Paul's 1300–1541*, 7.

71

fidelibus et Deo devotis petendum et colligendum accesserit vel accesserint ipsum vel ipsos in ecclesijs predictis et alibi benigne recipiatis et ipsum vel ispsos huiusmodi elimosinas libere querere et habere aceciam penes se retinere pro commodo fraternitatis sive Gilde predicte et absque impedimento aliquo permittatis. Necnon ipsum Henricum ac deputatos suos in dictis ecclesiis vertris et alijs benigniter admittatis ad agendum exponendum et declarandum clero et populo suffragia et benficia fraternitatis sive Gilde predicte. Aceciam omnia alia negocia dicte fraternitatis sive Gilde per literas nostras patentes gratuite recipere velitis vobisque vicecomitibus, majoribus, balliuis, constabulariis, ministris et aliis fidelibus nostris precipimus et firmiter mandamus quod ipsum Henricum ad dictas elimosinas in quibuscumque locis infra diocesim predictam petendum et colligendum ac omnes deputatos suos necnon res et bona sua predicta manuteneatis protegatis et defendatis. Necnon inferentes eis sue quantum in vobis est ab aliis inferri permittentes iniuriam molestiam dampnum impedimentum aliquod sue grauamen. Et si quid eis forisfactum sive iniuriatum fuerit id eis sine dilatione debite corrigi et reformari faciatis. In cuius rei testimonium hac literas nostras fieri fecimus patentes per unum annum duraturas. Teste me ipso apud Westmonasterium quarto die Aprilis anno regni nostri vicesimo septimo [1536].

Per ipsum regem &c   per Crumwelle

[21.b] [Calendered: Henry VIII, by the grace of God king of England and France etc., to all archbishops, bishops etc., in these present letters sends greetings.

Know that our beloved [in Christ] Richard Pace, dean of St Paul's Cathedral and perpetual Rector of the Fraternity or Guild of the most glorious Name of Jesus in the crypt of the said church, William Turke and Roger Barker, citizens of London and for the time being Wardens of the forsaid Fraternity or Guild, by our licence founded in our kingdom, [say that it] lacks rents and funds for the necessary maintainance of religious services and good works. To remedy this and to provide for the same Rector, Wardens, brothers and sisters of the foresaid Fraternity or Guild, Henry Hasylwode or his substitutes within the whole diocese and province of York, both areas exempt and not exempt, seeks through our licence to collect alms for the sustenance of the foresaid Guild or Fraternity from those faithful in Christ and in devotion to God. We are willing to provide security for Henry or his deputies in this respect for devotions given to him in honour of the glorious Name of Jesus, and issue our special protection for the same Henry and his deputies to gather the said alms, and command you to receive Henry or his deputies and allow without let or hindrance the collection of alms from all Christian faithful, clergy and people, for the support of the Fraternity or Guild aforesaid. And through these our Letters Patent we command all our sheriffs, mayors, bailiffs, constables and ministers to permit Henry and his deputies to seek and gather the said alms, goods or chattels, within all places within the diocese, and to protect them, and to make restitution for any harm or injury that may come to them for so doing.

In witness of which we make our letters patent for the duration of one year. By my witness at Westminster, 4 April in the 27 year of our reign [1536] By the king. By Cromwell.]

f. 27r[49]

[Second, incomplete, set of Ordinances of the Jesus Guild]

[22.a] Fraternitie as of alle other goodes as bokes, vestmentes, ornamentes, plate, jewelles, implementes ande other necessaries bilongyng to the saide Fraternitie, ande that in the same accompte the saide auditours shalle have sufficient power & auctoritie to make unto the said Wardens [and] accomptantes due and playne allowance of alle maner [of] sommes of money whiche shalbe paide spende & employede in their tymes for the conduct, mayntenaunce ande sustentacion off the saide Fraternitie in charges ordinarie, assisede ande put certene, that is to say: Wages, livereys, rewardes and potacions of the saide Wardens, wages ande rewardes of ministeres in divine service, & almes put certene by ordenaunces and statutes made by the said Rector, Wardens ande Assistentes accordyng to the same ordenaunces & statutes, and off alle other new werkes, emp[a]cions, provisions, reperacions & expences necessarie concernyng the same Fraternitie by discressions & resonable consideracions of the saide auditours for the tyme beyng. And that apone thende of every suche accompt, the saide auditours shalle see & recorde the delyverees, fulle contentacion and payment to be made by the saide accomptantes unto the saide newe Wardens, aswelle of alle suche sommes of money as shalbe founde due to the said Fraternitie by the saide accomptantes as of alle bokes, chalesses, vestmentes, ornamentes, plate, jewelles, implementes and alle other goodes and necessaries to the same Fraternitie bilongyng.

[22.b] Tresore chest[50]

Also that immediately after the said accoumptes, almaner [of] sommes

---

[49]   The manuscript is bound out of order; see codicological discussion in the Introduction. Different, neater hand to that of full ordinances and accounts of 1532–4, very professional-looking with hard-point ruling for whole text-block.

[50]   Heading for sections are in the left margin.

of redy money, plate and jewelles bilongyng to the saide Fraternitie shalle yerely be put in a tresore chest to the said Fraternitie bilonging, withe 3 lokkes & 3 kayes, wherof 2 kayes to remayne withe the saide Wardens for the tyme beyng ande the thridde [sic] kay withe oon of the saide assistentes which thene shalle have last ben Warden of the saide Fraternitie. Excepte that £20 of redy money shalle remayne in thandes of the said Wardens for the tyme beyng, therwithe to beyre, susteyne & mayntene alle suche charges as shalle growe and bilonge unto the saide Guilde and Fraternitie for the yere folowyng in their tyme, unto suche tyme as the yerely revenues, fermes of procuracies ande devocions may growe and come unto thandes of the saide Wardens for the same use: & that the same tresore chest

f.27v

shalle alwey remayne in the kepyng of the oldest Wardens of the saide Fraternitie for the tyme beyng, unto suche tyme as an hows shalbe parveide for the assembles of the saide Fraternitie and kepyng of their goodes ande tresore.

[22.c] Yeftes ande

Also that from hensforthe in every lesse of procuracies shalbe clerely except and reservede to the use of the saide Fraternitie almaner specialle yeftes, legacies and devocions grauntede ande made ande hereafter to be made biquethede ande grauntede by eny persone or persones withine this royalme to the use of the saide Guilde or Fraternitie. And that every procurator and fermer of procuracies of the saide Fraternitie shalle yerely and fro tyme to tyme accompt therof by othes ande unto the saide Rector ande Wardens make playne deliverye, contentacion ande payment of alle such specialle yiftes, legacies ande devocions over ande besides their yerely ferme, so that the saide p[ro]curatours ande fermers shalle no thyng have ne take to their owne use in ferme more then suche yerely devocions of the saide Fraternitie as have yerely bene accustumede to be paide, ande shalbe paid for the yerely accustumede pencion ande devocion of every breder and suster of the saide Fraternitie. Ande that every suche procurator shalle yerely duryng his procuracie and gederyng of devocions of the saide Fraternitie by his oth yelde a juste ande true accompte unto the saide Rector ande Wardens of alle maner sommes of money, plate, jewelles, bokes, vestmentes and ornamentes ande other goodes what so ever they shalbe, whiche shalbe grauntede and biquethede by every of the saide broders ande susters, ande to the use of the saide Fraternitie to the handes ande possessions of every suche procuratour or procuratours shalbe delyverede or causede to be delyverede, contentede & paide. Ande that for every suche somme or sommes of money or other goodes or catalles so grauntede or biquethede shalle come to thandes ande possessions of every suche procurator ande by

74

hym & his saide accoumpt omittede & concelede, the saide procurator shalle lose and forfett unto the saide Rectour and Wardens to the use of the said Guilde ande Fraternitie treble damages, that is to say 3 tymes the verrey value of alle suche somme or sommes of money and other goodes by them ande

f. 28r

every of them in their saide accomptes so wilfully omittede ande concelede ande that hereafter shalbe omittede ande concelede, as by indenture of every suche procuracie shalbe unto every suche procurator declarede ande expressede as parcelle of his covenauntes, where unto he shalbe boundene unto the said Rector ande Wardens by his writyng obligatory from tyme to tyme.

[22.d] The regestre of the names of the saide Fraternitie

Also that every suche procurator in like wise shalbe boundene yerely to bring in to the handes of the saide Wardens a boke or regestre whiche shalle contayne aswelle the names of alle bredren and susters of the said Fraternitie inhabitede or dwellyng withine the saide procint or cercuit of his procuracie & charge, as the names of almaner specialle benefactours of the saide Fraternitie, withe playn declaracion and expresse mencion ande certanty declarede, aswelle of almaner sommes of money ande other goodes by them grauntede, yevene and biquethede unto the saide use of the saide Fraternitie, as of the willes ande ententes of every suche benefactor, to thende they may be don ande prayed for in the saide Fraternitie accordyng to the same willis of the saide benefactors.

[22.e] Procuracies

Also that fro hensforthe no lesse or ferme of eny suche procuracie be grauntede to eny person or persons for eny longer tyme then for an hole yere, ande that apon sufficient suritie to pay unto the saide Wardens for the tyme beyng alle suche sommes of money as they shalle accorde for the saide ferme at 2 termes of the yere by even porcions. And in the ende of every yere to surrendre in to thandes ~~of the saide~~[51] of the said Wardens alle suche procuracies & indentures as they ande every of them shalle have of every suche lesse or ferme.

[22.f] Beyde men

Ferdermore it is enactede and establishede by the assent, agreament

---

[51] Deleted in manuscript by underlining.

ande consent aforsaide that 4 pore mene of goode and honest conversacion of the said Fraternitie, ande suche as can helpe to say masse ande can say matens, prime ande howres, evensong, and compleyne of Oure Lady, 7 psalmes ande Letaine *Placebo, Dirige* ande comendacion, whiche shalle yif dailly attendaunce in the saide chapelle of the saide Fraternitie

f. 28v

in the saide crowdes, helpyng preestes at masse ande praying for alle bredrene and susters of the saide Fraternitie, ande to kepe the saide crowdes ande to bryng enformacions at alle tymes when nede shall require of alle enormities, omissions ande defaultes of the ministres of the saide Fraternitie, aswelle in divine service to be omittede, abriggede ande withedrawen, as in other charges there to be conductede, don ande performede. Ande that alle the saide 4 pore mene shalle yif the saide attendaunce, that is to say: Fro the fest of Saynt Michelle Archaungelle unto the fest of Estre fro 7 of the clokk in the mornynge unto thende of all masses to be songene in the said crowdes for that day, and at 3 of the cloke at after none they shalle come ayene dailly and be at alle 3 *salves* to be kept in the saide crowdes. And fro the saide fest of Estre unto the saide fest of Saynt Michelle by alle the somer seasone fro 6 off the cloke in the mornyng unto alle masses shalbe done in the said crowdes for that day, and at 4 of the cloke at after none they shalle come ayen at after none in to the saide crowdes ande be present at alle the saide 3 *salves*. Also, every Friday when the belringer of the saide cathedralle churche shall toll to masse of Jħu the saide 4 beyde men shalbe redy there to helpe to ring the belle. Ande every of the saide poremene shalle have ande perceyve yerely of the devocions & profites growyng to the saide Fraternitie 40s. at 4 termes of the yere usuell by even porcions by thandes of the saide Wardens or their deputies or deputie for the tyme beyng. Ande that non of the saide 4 pore men shalle aske or crave almes, yiftes or rewardes by wey of beggyng or other wise apon the payne to lose 12d. at the first suche default, 2s. at the secunde default, ande to lose his roume for the 3de suche default. Ande that the saide Wardens, withe 3 or 4 of the saide Assistentes to be calde unto them, shalle aswelle elect ande take in pore men to fill the saide 4 roumes whene & as oft as they shall fortune to be voide, as fro tyme to tyme corect put them out of the same roumes for their offences ande trespasses, whene ande as oft as nede shalle require.

[22.g] Ande over this it is agreade ande ordeynede that the saide

f. 29r

24 Assistences or asmony of them as shalle have no lett but At (that) they may conveniently come to the saide crowdes in the festes of Transfigiracion ande Name of Jħu ande be present at alle divine service to be done there in the saide 2 festes, begynnyng at the first evensong

ande endyng withe the masse of Requiem to be don in the morowe next after the saide fest of the Name of Jħu, that is to say: The saide Aldermene Assistentes in gownes of skarlett, ande alle other Assistentes in gownes of violett clothe & hodes.

[22.h] Thies be the names of the Assistentes at the makyng of this ordenance:

Sir Stephan Jennyns, knyghte

Master Thomas Baldry, alderman

John Hosyer, marcer

William Bromwelle, marcer

John Mownke, wexchaundeler

Henry Hille, haberdassher

John Sandelle, vyntner

William Campione, grocer

Thomas Hynde, marcer

Stephan Lynne, haberdasher

Stephan Warde, wexchaundeler

John Catteby, grocer

John Hattfelde, vyntnier

Elis Draper, haberdassher

Hughe Fournesse, auditour

f. 29v – blank.[52]

---

[52]   F. 29v blank. Blank unfoliate sheet bound between folios 29 and 30.

ACCOUNTS OF THE JESUS GUILD
1514/15–1534/35

f. 30r[1]

[23] The 9th   accompt[2]
London[3]

Thaccompt of Henre Hille and John Sandelle, Wardens of the Fraternitie of the Name of Jħu in the crowdes of the cathedralle churche of Saynt Paule in London, fro the fest of Cristenmasse in the yere of our Lorde accomptede by the Churche of Englande 1514 and in the 6th yere of the reigne of kynge Henry the 8th unto the same fest then next ensuyng, that is to say by an hole yere.

[24] Arrerages

The same accomptantes be charged withe tharrerages of John Copwod by sundrie specialties, as in the fote of the last accompt of John Munke & Henre Hille, last Wardens of the said Fraternitie, more planely dothe appere } 53s. 4d.

Also withe tharrerages of William Goughe and Richard Vaughauin by like specialtes as in the last accompt in like wise dothe appere } 40s.

Also withe tharrerages of Davy John, fermer of the devocions of the diosis of Saynt Asse and Bangore in Wayles, for his ferme of the same as in the said last accompt in like wise dothe appere } 13s. 4d.

Also withe tharrerages due by John Munk and the said Henre Hille, late Wardens, there in their said last accompt, as in the fote of the same more playnely dothe appere } £56 17s. 1d.

Summa } £62 3s. 9d.

---

[1]   Pencil foliation resumes.
[2]   Header at top of folio.
[3]   All 'headings' in this account are in the left margin and centre-point of brackets for
       each section.

[25] Rentes & fermes }

Also withe the rentes ande fermes of 2 tenementes and certen landes in the town and feldes of Uxbrigge in the countie of Middlesex and Bukingham, lettene to ferme to William Baille and James Stansdale for 29s. 8d. by yere payable at the festes of Anunciacone of our Blessede [Lady] and Saynt Michelle Archaungelle by even porcions, that is to say for the same festes fallyng withein the tyme of this accompt[4] } 29s. 8d.

Summa – 29s. 8d.

f. 30v
Yet the[5]

Fermes of procuracies and devocions of the saide Fraternitie

Also withe the ferme of alle devocions to the saide Fraternite bilongyng in the diosis of Northewiche, Elie, Yorke, Durisme and Carlisle, lettene to Nicholas Smythe of Cambrigge for £20 for a yere withein the tyme of this accompt } £20

Also with the ferme of like devocions of part of the counties of Essex ande Hertforde lettene to Thomas Hethe as apperethe by obligacone withe condicone to pay 33s. 4d. at the festes of Estre, Midsomer, Michelmas ande Cristenmas by even porcions for the tyme of this accompt } 33s. 4d.

Also withe the other part of the counties of Essexe and Hertforde lettene to Thomas Norres for 33s. 4d. by yere for the tyme of this accompt } 33s. 4d.

Also withe the ferme of like devocions in the diosise of Cauntourbury ande Chechestre letten to Thomas Grey of Maydstone as apperethe by obligacone withe condicone to pay £4 10s. sterlinge at Cristenmasse fallyng withein the tyme of this accompt } £4 10s.

Also withe the ferme of like devocions in the diosise of Wynchestre and Sarum lettene to Roger Robyns as apperethe by obligacone with condicone to pay £4 sterlinge at the fest of Purificacone of our Blessed Lady fallyng withein the tyme of this accompt } £4

---

4   Traces of wax are visible on an indented square on the edge of the leaf next to this
     section, indicating the remains of applied seal, possibly on a 'wafer' of paper over the
     edge of the leaf. Traces of text can be seen on the verso of the leaf in same place.
5   From this point on there is a running header of 'Yet the' on the verso and '9th accompt'
     on the recto of each folio (i.e. reading 'Yet the 9th accompt' across an opening).

f. 31r

Yet fermes of procuracies ande other devocions of the saide Fraternitie

Also withe the ferme of like devocions in the diosise of Excestre lettene to John Lake, grocer of London, for 100s. by yere payable at Cristenmasse fallyng wethein the tyme of this accompt } 100s.

Also withe the ferme of like devocions in the diosise off Bathe and Wellis lettene to William Thomas for 53s. 4d. by yere payable at Midsomer and Cristenmasse fallynge wethein the tyme of this accompt, by even porcions } 53s. 4d.

Also withe the ferme of like devocions in the diosise off Worcestre, Chestre and Hereforde lettene to John Tyler & Richarde Stilfelde for £10 by yere payable at the fest of Estre, as apperethe by obligacone dated the 24th day of Decembre in the 7th yere of the reigne of kyng Henry the 8th wethein the tyme of this accompt } £10

Also withe the ferme of like devocions in the diosise of Saynt Davy and Bangore in Wales letton to John Davye for 20s. by yere for the tyme of this accompt } 20s.

f. 31v

[26] Fermes of procuracies and devocions of the saide Fraternitie

Also receyvede of Thomas Holmes, apprower of the devocions in the kynges court, the citie of London and the Innes of Court and Chauncerie, by the othe of the saide Thomas withe 20s. in redy money, that is to say: Fro the fest of Cristenmasse in the said yere of our Lorde 1514 unto the fest of Annunciacone of our Lady then next ensuyng, 75s. 6½d. Also fro the same fest of Annunciacone unto Midsomer then next ensuyng, 76s. Also fro the same Midsomer unto Michelmas thene next ensuyng, £17 8d. Ande fro the same Michelmasse unto Cristenmasse then next ensuyng, £4 11s. ½d. In alle, as by 4 billis of parcelles of thaccompt of the said Thomas more playnely dothe appere. Ande 20s. of the Wexchaundelers } £30 3s. 3d.

Summa } £80 13s. 3d.

Somme of alle the saide receiptes } £144 6s. 8d.

Wheroff

81

[27] Divine service

The saide accomptauntes accompt in paymentes ordinarie made in the said cathedralle churche to sundrie ministres of the same churche beyng present & kepyng divine service of & in the festes off Transfiguracone & Name of Jhu this yere, withe *Placebo* ande *Dirige* withe note inmediatly after the last evensong of the saide fest of the Name of Jhu, ande masse of Jhu in like wise in the morowe thene next after for the Fraternitie, that is to say: To the subdeane }

f. 32r

Yet divine service ande other wages & rewardes ordinare

beyng present in alle the premisses & synging highe masse in the saide festes of Transfiguracone & Name of Jhu 4s. Also to every of 12 peticanons 3s. 4d., <u>40s.</u> Also to 2 vicars beyringe copes in the saide festes in place of the chauntrie prestes, in reward <u>18d.</u>[6] And to every of 6 vicars 2s. 8d., in alle <u>16s.</u> Also to highe canons, peticanons, chauntrie prestes, vicars ande choresters beynge present & beyringe copes in the processions in the saide festes off Transfiguracion & Name of Jhu, to every of them 4d., in alle <u>31s.</u> Also a peticanon singynge the saide masse of Requiem 6d. & to 2 chauntrie prestes redyng the Pistelle & Gospelle at alle 3 masses afore expressede, eithur of them 12d., in alle <u>2s. 6d.</u> Also for the collacone made there at the highe masse in the said festes of the Name of Jhu <u>6s. 8d.</u> Also to the sacristene for garnishing of aulters ande beyring of bokes & other ornamentes <u>4s.,</u> withe <u>8d.</u> of rewarde this yere onely. Also to 4 vergers there beyng attendant, to every of them 20d. withe <u>20d.</u> off rewarde this yere onely, <u>6s. 8d.</u> And to the belringers for their labours in the said festes besides 20s. to them payde quarterly for kepyng off the dores of the saide crowdes, withe 12d. of rewarde this yere onely, <u>14s. 4.d.</u> In alle, by the Rector of the said Fraternitie and by the Assistentes of the same it is ordeyned & enactede deducted therof 3s. 4d. for the saide collacone made in the absence of the ~~ab~~ said (deane). And so allowances to the said accomptauntes } £6 3s. 4d.

Also for the masse of Jhu by note solempnely kept in the saide crowdes every Friday by a cardinalle singinge the saide masse, 6 vicars & 10 choresters of the said cathedralle churche in their

f. 32v

---

[6] Some but not all individual sums for expenditure have been underlined in this account. Since this may relate to the accounting process this has been replicated precisely.

Yet divine service & other wages & rewardes ordinarie

habites & surplices, that is to say: To the cardinalle synginge the saide highe masse of Jhū ande prayinge for alle bredrene ande susters of the saide Fraternitie, & specially for certene names by him there redde in a table. And a masse of Requiem by note in like wise every Fryday inmediatly after the saide masse of Jhu by a peti canon or a chauntrie prest and 6 choresters of the said cathedrale churche in their surpluces & habites accordynge to the saide ordenances, that is to say for 44 suche Fridayes fallynge witthein the tyme of this accompt £6 12s., & 8s. 4d. of rewarde afore the makyng of this ordenances. In alle as by 4 billes of thaccompt of the saide Thomas Holmes more play nely doth appere } £7 4d.

Also to oon of the vicars, maister of the saide choresters, kepyng 3 *salves* dailly in the saide crowdes after Compleyn don in the same cathedralle churche afore the images of Jhu, our Blessed Lady ande Saynt Sebastian, & takyng for his labor 26s. 8d. at 4 termes of the yere usuels by even porcions, that is to say for the same 4 termes witthein the tyme of this accompt accordynge to the aforsaide ordenances } 26s. 8d.

Also to the belringers of the said cathedralle churche for their labours ande dailly attendances; openyng, closynge & shotyng of dores of the saide crowdes; rynging & tollynge of bellis; blowynge of organs; lightynge & quinchynge of torches & other lighetes; swepynge & makyng clene of the saide crowdes; at 20s. by yere payable quarterly, besides 14s. 4d. for them allowede for the saide festes of Transfiguracone & Name of Jhū this yere acordynge to the aforesaid ordenances } 20s.

f. 33r

Yet divine service ande other wages ande rewardes ordinare

[28] Also for the rewarde of the saide Wardens this yere, limited & taxede by the saide Rectour ande Assistentes accordynge to the said ordenaunces £4. And over that, the saide Henre Hille in rewarde for his attendaunce this yere 20s., in alle } 100s.

Also for theire lyverees of clothyng for the Wardens witthe cognisaunces of the Name of Jhu, limitede in like wise by the saide Rectour ande Assistentes accordynge to the saide ordenances } £4

Also to Hughe Fournesse, oon of the auditours of this accompt, for the ingrosynge of the same } 20s.

[29] Also to Thomas Holmes, assigned proctour, to gayder & receyve almaner of devocions of the saide Fraternitie in the kynges court, the citie & suburbes of London, Innes of Court & Chauncerie by way of enproment, that is to say: For the receipt of £29 3s. 3d. after 3s. 4d. of every 20s. } £4 17s. 2½d.

Also to the saide Thomas attendyng dailly in the said crowdes and helpyng prestes at masse, kepyng the vestmentes & other ornamentes of the saide Fraternitie, withe other neccessary attendaunces by hym yevene apone the said Wardens there at 26s. 8d. by yere payable quarterly } 26s. 8d.

[30] Also to the prechours at Paules Crosse and Saynt Marie Spitelle remembrynge and prayinge for the sawles of alle the bredrene ande susterene of the saide Fraternitie, for every sermonde 4d. accordyng to the saide ordenaunces, that is to say for 47 Sondayes ande }

f. 33v

Yet divine service ande other wages ande rewardes ordinarie

ande [word repeated] Goode Friday at Paules Crosse [and] 3 daies in Estre Weke at Saynt Marie Spitelle, as by a bille of parcelles made by the saide Thomas Holmes more playnely dothe appere } 17s.

Also to 6 waytes withe baners payntede, cognisaunces enbrowdrede withe Jhus, goynge alle the stretes ande suburbs of London playing withe their instrumentes to yif warnynge & knowlegge to the people of the saide Fraternitie of the saide festes of Transfiguracone & Name of Jhu, accordynge to the aforesaide ordenances 10s., [and] in rewarde by cause of their attendaunce at the dyner & for their garlondes, 4s. In alle, withein the tyme of this accompt } 14s.

[31] Also to the proctour of the saide Fraternitie in London for the bonefire made afore the northe dore of the saide crowdes yerely in the even of the said fest of the Name of Jhū 2s. 8d. Also, by thandes of the saide Henre Hille to John Munke for 8 dozen lyverees (of Jhus 12d., & to John Baxter for like lyverees) 6s. 8d., in alle 10s. 4d. Also by thandes of the said Thomas Holmes for like lyverees of Jhus, that is to say: The first quarter of this yere 4s. 2½d.; in Midsomer quarter 3s. 9½d.; in Michelmas quarter 40s. 5d.; and in Cristenmasse quarter 3s. 4d. In alle, 51s. 9d. Also for garlandes, bowes & herbis parveide & spent in garnishinge of the said crowdes in the said festes 5s. In alle, withein the tyme of this accompt as by 4 billes of parcellis of thaccompt of the saide Thomas more playnely dothe appere } 67s. 1d.

Also for wex spent in the said crowdes, besides the wex there found by by the Wexchaundelers this yere, as by a boke of parcellis therof remayninge withe this accompt more playnely dothe appere withein the tyme of this accompt } 33s. 9d.

Summa } £38 6s. ½d.

f. 34r

[32] Almes[7] }

Also to the almonyner of the said cathedralle churche for 10 gownes for 10 choresters of the saide cathedralle churche servyng Gode in the said crowdes, aswelle in the saide festes of Transfiguracone and of the Name of Jhū, as every Friday at masses of Jhū & Requiem, and also at the *salvees* [sic] there kept by the saide Fraternitie £4, & in rewarde by thandes of Thomas Holmes to the saide choresters 12d. In alle } £4 12d.

Also to John Wallis, John Wyminghaum, William Russelle & William Bamene, pore mene appoyntede to the almes of the saide Fraternitie, kepyng the crowdes, helpynge prestes at masse & praying for alle bredrene & sustrene of the saide Fraternitie, every of them after 26s. 8d. by yere for the first half yere endet at Midsomer 53s. 4d., and every of them after 40s. by yere for the other half yere endet at Cristenmasse, accordynge to the forsaide ordenaunces, £4. In alle withein the tyme of this accompt } £6 13s. 4d.

Also by thandes of Thomas Holmes to 4 mene helpyng in the crowdes in the said festes of Transfiguracone & Name of Jhu 6s., [and] to the porter, 2d. Also, by thandes of ~~Thomas~~ Maister Hille to pore folkes in the saide festes, 3s. 2d. Ande to prestes synginge masse on the day of comemoracone of Alle Sawles 4s. In alle } 13s. 4d.

Summa – £11 7s. 8d.

[33] Empacions }

Also for sundrie ornamentes & neccesaries parveide & boughte to the use of the saide Fraternitie by thandes of the said Henre Hille, that is to say: In ernest, for a paire of organs 3s. 4d., [and] for a cushene of verdeire stuffede withe fedders that was lost on Jhūs day 6s. 8d. In alle, 10s. Also by thandes of the saide Holmes for prikyng of 25 anthemps of Jhu }

7   Small 'a' to right of word before bracket here and for next two sections.

f. 34v

Yet Empacions

& our Lady & Saynt Sebastiane <u>12s. 10d.</u>, & coverynge of a boke off the same anthemps <u>20d</u>. An aube of bresselle clothe <u>2s. 9d</u>. 4 deskes for anthemps bokes <u>2s</u>. A candelstike of latene <u>5d</u>. A scons <u>6d</u>. Irne for the scons to stand in 4d. 25 skynns of velome <u>8s.</u> 6 ellis of holonde clothe spent in a surplece <u>3s. 6d.</u> A spade <u>6d</u>. A ladder <u>17d</u>. 5 mattes <u>12½d.</u> 2 half portuos pryntede in papur <u>2s. 8d.</u> A boke withe lessons <u>12d</u>. In alle, as by 4 billis of thaccompt of the saide Thomas Holmes more playnely dothe appere, <u>38s. 7½d.</u> } 48s. 7½d.

Summa } 48s. 7½d.

[34] Reperacions }

Also in sundrie reperacions by thandes of Master Hille, that is to say: To a carpenter for removyng of the particone in the saide crowdes for enlargynge of the churche <u>23s. 4d.</u> Payintynge of the same particone <u>40s</u>. Amendyng of the glasse wyndows in the crowdes <u>18d</u>. Makyng of the dores in the crowdes <u>5s</u>. Cariage of the tresore chest & settyng it up <u>3d</u>. Lymnynge of the corporacone <u>16d</u>. Garnettes & boltes for the quere dore <u>4s. 8d.</u> 2 cases for the wyndows of the crowdes <u>5s. 4d.</u> Paynting of 9 Jhus in the crowdes <u>5d</u>. To Robert Nelsone, glasier, as apperethe by his bille <u>30s. 2d.</u> Makyng of the parclose about the organs <u>10s.</u> Makynge of a sete for Maister Deane <u>2s. 3d.</u> Tenter hokes <u>2d</u>. Also, in ernest for amendynge of the organs there at 2 tymes <u>6s. 8d.</u> In alle, £6 11s. 1d. Also, by thandes of Thomas Holmes, that is to say: For amendynge of the organs 2s. Bromis 2d. Amendyng of the masse boke 2d. Bayring of a ladder to mende the belle at 2 tymes 2d. Amendyng of the belle whele <u>10d</u>. Also, in Midsomer quarter amendynge of a payr of garnettes 2d. 4 quarters of tymbre spent in makynge of fete for fourmes 8d. A lode & 4 sakkes of lyme <u>20d</u>. A carpenter half a day <u>4d</u>. A plasterer & his laborer 5 dayes in the crowdes workynge <u>5s. 5d.</u> A pece of tymbre spent
f. 35r

Yet reperacions

there <u>9d</u>. Amendyng of the pavement in the crowdes <u>16d</u>. 3 candelstikes of irene for the priksong boke <u>8d</u>. A kay for the maires sete in the crowdes <u>3d.</u> 200 of gilt nayles for the same <u>8d</u>. Also, in Michelmas quarter for payntynge of 140 Names of Jhus 4s 6d. A ladder <u>17d</u>. Bromys <u>3d</u>. Nayles & sprigges <u>23½d</u>. To a carpenter for his labour & for a quarter borde &

12 fote of formes 20d. Amendyng of the pavement in the crowdes 16d. A bawdrike for the grete belle 2s. A sterop of irne for the same belle 8d. Takyng down & cariage of a belle to the founders 7d. Chaungyng of a belle at Jhus dore 9s. 10d. And to the organe maker in fulle payment of amendynge of the organs 10s. Ande in Cristenmasse quarter, a stock & a whele for the belle at Jhūs dore 5s. 2 sheris, a calkene, a sterop, a bolt & a stay for the same belle & amendyng of the clapper therof 12d. Ande for stapuls & hokes for the dore of the organs 4d. In alle by thandes of the saide Thomas Holmes, as by 4 billes of the parcelles of his accompt dothe appere, 55s. 8½d. In alle, in reperacions withein the tyme of this accompt } £9 6s. 9½d.

Summa } £9 6s. 9½d.

[35] Expenses neccesarie

Also, by thandes of Maister Hille for sundrie expenses neccesarie, that is to say: For botehire to Lambethe to speke withe my Lorde Chauncelere for oon off the proctours 3d. For 4 copies writyng & translatynge of the ordenances for the bretherede 12d. For washynge of clothes that were fowlede at the festes off Jhūs 8d. Also to attourney of the Comene Place to warne Greys wiff[8] to pay har duety that she owethe to the Fraternitie 4d. Also for an hogges hede of wyne yevene to Maister Deane of Paules, Rector off the saide Fraternitie, by concideracone of the saide Wardens and Assistentes of the saide Fraternitie 30s. In alle, by thandes of Maister Hille, 32s. 3d. Also, by thandes of Thomas Holmes, the first quarter for synging brede & wyne 3s. 11d. Ande for washing of aubis & towelles 2d. Also the seconde quarter for synging brede & wyne 3s. 6d. Portage of a chest fro

f. 35v

Yet expenses neccesarie[9]

Maister Munkes[10] hows unto the crowdes 1d. A baskett for holy brede 2d. Also the thridde quarter, for synginge [brede] & wyne 4s. 6½d. 6lb. tallowe candelle 9½d. Brede for haly brede 2d. Cariage of 2 lode of dust 4d. Wyne to the maisters of Paules 3d. Inke & papar 3d. & for an hamar & hokes 5d. Scorynge off basens, cruettes & candelstekes 6d. Grese for the belle & tappis for ale 3½d. Makynge clene of the crowdes 6d. 2 burdene rishus 4d. 6 blake candelstikes 4d. Grete pynnis for hangyng of

---

8   Probably the wife of Thomas Grey of Maidstone.
9   Small letter 'a' to right of heading before bracket.
10   John Monk, waxchandler and past warden of the Guild.

the crowdes 1 ½ d. Ande the 4th quarter, for synginge [brede] & wyne 4s. 7d. Bromes 1d. 3 kayes 9d. Portage of a ladder 2d. tallowe candelle 3 ½ d. Ande for 2 gallons *dimidium* [half] of lampe oyle <u>3s. 4d.</u> In alle, by thandes of the said Thomas Holmes, <u>25s. 9 ½ d.</u> } 58s. ½d.

Summa } 58s. ½d.

[36] Potacions

Also, by thandes of Maister Hille for sundrie expenses neccesarie, that is to say: At the electone of the Wardens in drynke for the Assistentes <u>2s.</u> 3d. Also, for expenses at the first audit of John Munke & Henry Hille, late Wardens, at Maister Munkes hows, <u>11s. 11d.</u> Also at the Miter when the Assistentes assemblede there for makyng of the ordenances <u>20s. 10d.</u> Also for the dyner in the festes of Transfiguracone & Name of Jhu <u>65s. 5½d.</u> Ande for potacions at dyverse other assembles of the said Wardens & Assistentes this yere <u>40s.</u> In alle, £7 5½d.

Also spent in the saide festes of Transfiguracone & Name of Jhū in meit & drynke apone the bredrene & sustrene comyng in there by thandes of the said Thomas Holmes, that is to say: In meit & drynk <u>5s. 11d.</u> Also for goode ale 5 barelles <u>18s. 4d.</u> In alle, <u>24s. 3d.</u>

In alle, withein the tyme of this accompt as by the saide 4 billes off parcelles of the said Holmes dothe appere } £8 4s. 8½d.

Summa } £8 4s. 8½d.

f. 36r

Somme of alle the

saide paymentes } £72 11s. 10½d.

And so remaynethe due to the

saide Fraternitie } £71 14s. 9½d.

Wherof

Allowede for a pair of organes new boughte } £10

Also for Hughe Fournesse for his labour in drawynge and engrossynge alle the newe ordenances concernyng the Fraternitie, aswelle for the ministres of Paules as for theleccone of the Wardens, Assistentes & Auditours & for procuracies &c, by concideracione of the auditours of this accompt } 26s. 8d.

Ande so remaynethe } £60 8s. 1½d.

[37] Remaynethe apon

John Copwode by sundrie specialties } 53s. 4d.

William Goughe and Richard Vaughan by like specialties } 20s.

Davy John, late proctor of the diosise of Saynt Asse & Bangeore } 13s. 4d.

The Feliship of Waxchaundelers of London } 6s. 8d.

Ande apon the saide accomptantes } £55 14s. 9½d.

Wheroff deliverde in to the tresorye of the olde money there remayninge } £ 46 17s. 1d.

And so remayneth } £8 17s. 8½d.

Whiche money is delyverde to thandes of John Sandelle & John Mathewe nowe Wardens for the yere begyniynge at Cristenmasse in the yere of our Lorde 1515 & in the yere 7th yere of kyng Henre the 8th *Et eqz.*

Memorandum that aswelle the aforseide somme of £46 17s. 2d. remayning in the said tresore chest, as the aforesaide somme of £8 17s. 8½d., and also the 3 obligacions of Copwode, every of them of 100s. wherof is no more due but 53s. 4d., and the obligacone of William Goughe & William [sic] Vaughane of 40s., wheroff 20s. is due, be alle delverde by the said accomptantes unto thandes of John Sandelle & John Mathewe, now Wardens of the saide Fraternitie, in presence of the auditours of this accompt the 24th day of Aprille in the 8th yere of the reigne of kyng Henre the 8th [1516].

f. 36v

[38] Also the obligacions of the fermers of the proxies that be chargede for this yere, that is to say:

The obligacione of Thomas Wellis & John Coke for Somersett shire for } 53s. 4d.

The obligacone of Henry Thorntone & William Marke for Cornwaile & Devone } £6 13s. 4d.

Item of Richard Stilfelde & John Tyler & John Halle for £15 wherof is due } £10

Item of Thomas Hethe & Rauff Shirwode for 100s. wherof is due } 40s.

Item of Roger Robyns & Robert Warenne for £10 wherof is due } 100s.

Item of Rice ap Howelle & Richard Lyne for 40s. wherof is due } 26s. 8d.

Item of Thomas Norres & Thomas Higheam for 100s. wherof is due } 40s.

Item of Robert Oliver, William Meyde & Robert Semensone for £10 wherof is due } 100s.

Item of Nicholas Smythe, besides £10 paid afore hande } £10

Auditours of this accompt {

11

.

.

.

Per me Hugonem Fournesse[12]

f. 37r

[39] London[13]

Thaccompt of John Sandelle and John Mathewe, Wardens of the Fraternitiee of the Name off Jħu in the crowdes of the cathedralle churche off Saynt Paule in London, fro the fest off Cristenmasse in the yere off oure Lorde accomptede by the Churche off England 1515 ande the 7^the yere of the reigne of kynge Henry the 8^the unto the same fest thene next ensuynge, that is to say by oone hole yere.

Arrerages

The same accomptantes be chargede withe tharrerages off John Copwode by sundrie specialties as in the fote off the last accompt of Henry Hille & John Sandelle, last Wardens off the saide Fraternitie, more playnely dothe appere } 53s. 4d.

Also withe tharrerages of William Goughe and Richard Vaughehaun by lyke specialties as in the last accompt (in) like wise dothe appere } 20s.

Also withe tharrerages of Davy John, fermer of the devocions of the diosise of Saynte Asse & Bangore in Wales, for his ferme of the same as in the last accompt in like wise dothe appere } 13s. 4d. *Renutt[in]do quod disperaut'*[14]

---

11   Large brackets with four dots but no names above Fourness's name.
12   Elaborate flourish similar to notarial mark after Fourness's name.
13   All headings for this account are in the left margin with large brackets indicating the
     section concerned.
14   Addition, possibly in a different hand.

Also withe tharrerages of the Feliship of Wexechaundelers in London } 6s. 8d.

Also withe tharrerages due by Henre Hille and the saide John Sandelle, late Wardens, there in theire last accompt, as in the fote of the same more playnely dothe appere } £55 14s. 9½d.

Summa } £60 8s 1½d.

[40] Rentes & fermes

Also withe the renttes and fermes of 2 tenementes & certene landes in the towne & feldes of Uxebrigge in the countie off Middlesex & Bukingham lettene to William Baylly & James Standale for 29s. 8d. by yere, payable at the festes off Annunciacone off oure Blessede Lady & Saynte Michelle the Archaungelle by evine porcions, that is to say for the same festes fallynge wit hein the tyme of thys accompt } 29s. 8d.

Summa } 29s. 8d.

Also withe the ferme of alle the devocions in [sic] the said Fraternitie bilonginge in the diosise off Northewiche, Elie, Yorke, Durisme & Carlesle lettene to Nicholas Smythe of Chambrigge for £20 for a yere wit hein the tyme off thys accompt } £20

f. 37v
Yet the[15]

Fermes off procuracies and other devocions of the saide Fraternitie

Also withe the ferme off like devocions off part of the counties off Essexe ande Hertforde lettene to Thomas Hethe as apperethe by obligacone withe condicone to pay 40s. at the festes of Ester, Midsomer, Michelmas, (&) Cristenmasse by evin porcions for the tyme of this accompt } 40s.

Also withe the other part off the counties off Essex and Hertforde lettene to Thomas Norres for 40s. by yere for the tyme off this accompt } 40s.

Also withe the ferme off like devocions in the diosise off Cantorbury & Chechestre lettene unto Robert Olyver off London, masone, as apperethe by obligacone withe condicone to pay 100s. sterlinge at Cristenmasse falling wit hein the tyme off thys accompt } 100s.

Also withe the ferme off like devocions in the diosise of Wynchestre & Sarum lettene to Roger Robyns as apperethe by obligacone withe

---

[15] Running header of 'yet the' on all verso folios and '10th accompt' on the recto folios of this account (i.e. reading 'Yet the 10th accompt' across an opening).

condicone to pay 100s. sterlinges at the fest off Purificacone of oure Lady falling wethein the tyme of thys accompt } 100s.

Also wethe the ferme off like devocions off the diosise of Excestre lettene to John ~~Lake Grocere of London~~ (Thornetone, sergeaunt of armes, & William Marke of Liskarde in the countie of Cornewaille)[16] for ~~100s.~~ (13s.) by yere payable at Cristenmasse fallinge wethein the tyme of thys accompt } ~~100s.~~ £6 13s. 4d.

Also wethe the ferme of like devocions in the deosise off Bathe & Welles lettene to William Thomas for 53s. 4d. by yere payable at Midsomer & Cristenmasse fallinge wethein the tyme of this accompt } 53s. 4d.

Also wethe the ferme off like devocions in the diosise of Worcestre, (Chestre) & Hereforde lettene to John Tyler & Richard Stilfelde for £10 by yere}

f. 38r
Yet fermes of proxies &c }

payable at the fest off Estre as apperethe by obligacone datede the [blank] day of Decembre in the 8[the] yere of the reigne of kyng Henry the 8[the] [1516] } £10

Also wethe the ferme off like devocions in the diosise of Sainte Davy & Bangore in Wales lettene to John Davy for [errasure] by yere for the tyme of this accompt } [erasure17]

Also receyvede of Thomas Holmes, apprower off the devocions in the kynges court, the citie off London and the Innes off Court and Chauncerie by the othe of the said Thomas } £29 15s. 3½d.

Also receyvede of the Wardens & Feleship of Wexchundelers off London for ann annualle rent at 20s. by yere as in the ~~presed~~ (saide) precedent for the said tyme } 20s.

Summa } ~~£83 8s. 7½d.~~ ~~£85 23½d.~~ 8s. 7½d.

Somme off alle the saide receiptes – ~~£146~~[18] ~~6s. 5d~~ (~~19s 9d~~ £147 6s. 5d.)

Whereoff

[41] Divine service }

---

[16] 'countie of Cornewaille' written in inner margin in same hand, with a notation mark in the main text.
[17] Erased figure includes £ s d.
[18] Corrected from £145 to £146 by the addition of 'j' in lighter ink.

The saide accomptantes accompt in paymentes ordinarie to be made in the crowdes off the said cathedralle churche' to sundrie ministres off the same churche beynge present and kepynge divine service there, off & in the festes of Transfiguracone & Name off Jħu thys yere, withe *Placebo & Dirige* withe note inmediately after the last eviensonge of the said fest off the Name of Jhu' ande masse off Requiem in like wise in the morowe thene next after for the Fraternitie, that is to say: To the Subdeane beyng present at alle the premisses and singing the highe masse in the said festes, for eithere day 2s., in alle 4s.[19] Also to 2 chauntrie prestes bayrynge copes in the saide festes in rewarde 3s. 4d. (Also to 11 peticanions 36s. 8d. & to 6 vicars 14s.) Also to every highe canone, peticanone, chauntrie prest, vicars ande choresters beyng present & bayringe copes in the saide

f. 38v

Yet divine service, wages & rewardes & other ordinare charges}

festes off[20] Transfiguracone & Name off Jħu 4d., in alle 34s. Also to a peticanone singinge the masse of Requiem 6d. & to 2 chauntrie prestes redyng the Pystelle & Gospelle at 3 masses afore expressede 2s. Also for the collacone made there at the highe masse in the saide festes of the Name off Jħu 6s. 8d. Also to the sacristene for garnishyng off the aulters and bayring of bokes & other ornamentes 3s. 10d. Also to 4 vergers there beyng attendant, to every of theme 16d. withe 20d. in rewarde thys yere, 6s. 8d. And to the belringers for ther labours in the saide festes, besyde 20s. to theme paide quarterly for kepyng of the dores of the saide crowdes, 13s. 4d. In alle, as by (the) Rector of the saide Fraternitie & by the Wardens & Assistentes off the same, it is ordeynede & enactede deductede theroff 3s. 4d. for the saide collacone made in the absence off the said deane, and so allowance to the saide accomptantes } £6 20d.[21]

Also for the masse of Jħu by note solempnly kept in the saide crowdes every Friday by a cardinalle, 7 peticanones & [blank] vicars, 10 choresters of the saide cathedralle churche in their habites & surplices, that is to say: To the saide cardinalle singing the said masse of Jħu & prayinge for alle bredrene & susters of the saide Fraternitie and in specially for certene names by hym there rede in a table, & a masse off Requiem by note in like wise every Friday inmediatly after the said masse off

---

[19]   In this account, most but not all of the individual sums for expenditure have been underlined. Since this may have been associated with the accounting process this has been replicated precisely in the edition.

[20]   'festes off' written over erasure.

[21]   Two lines of text (illegible) erased in left margin next to this section.

Jhu by a peticanone or a chauntrie prest & 6 choresters of the saide cathedralle churche in their surplices & habites for 45 suche Fridayes fallynge withein the tyme of thys accompt } £7 9s. 6d.

Also to oone of the vicars, maister of the saide choresters, kepyng 3 *salves* daily in the saide crowdes, after Complayne done in the same cathedralle churche, afore the images of Jhu, oure Blessed Lady &

f. 39r
Saint Sebastiane, & takinge for his labor 26s. 8d. at 4 termes off the yere by evin porcions accordyng to the saide ordenances } 26s. 8d.

[42] Yet divine service wages &c }

Also to the belringers of the saide cathedralle churche for their labours and daily attendances, openynge, closynge & shotynge of dores of the said crowdes, ryngynge & tollynge of belles, bloynge of organs, lighteynge & quinchynge off torches & other lighetes, swepynge & makynge clene of the said crowdes, at 20s. by yere payable quarterley, besydes 13s. 4d. for them allowede for the saide festes of Transfiguracone & Name of Jhu accordynge to the forsaid ordenances } 20s.

Also for the rewarde off the saide Wardens thys [yere], limitede and taxede by the said Rector & Assistentes accordinge to the saide ordenaunces, £4. And over that for the saide John Sandelle in rewarde thys yere 20s. In alle } 100s.[22]

Also for their liveryes of clothynge for the saide Wardens withe cognisaunces off the name of Jhu, limitede in like wise by the said Rector & Assistentes accordynge to the saide ordenances } £4

Also to Hughe Fournesse, oone of the said auditours off this accompt, for the engrossynge of the same } 20s.

Also to Thomas Holmes, assignede proctor to geder and receyve almaner off devocions of the saide Fraternitie in the kynges court, the citie & suburbes of London, Innes of Court & Chauncerie by way off enproment, that is to say for the recept of £29 15s. 3½d. after 3s. 4d. of every 20s. } £4 19s. 2d.[23]

---

[22] 'ioos.' erased below the legible text.
[23] 'Yet divine service & other charges …. rewardes …….' erased in left margin next to this entry.

Also to the saide Thomas Holmes, attendynge daylly in the said crowdes & helpyng prestes at masse, kepynge the ɫ vestmentes & other ornamentes of the saide Fraternitie, withe other neccessarie attaendaunces by hym yevine apone the said Wardens there, at 26s. 8d. by yere payable quarterly } 26s. 8d.

f. 39v

Yet divine service & other charges &c

Also to the prechers at Paules Crosse & Saint Marie Spitelle remembringe & prayinge for the saules off alle bredrene & sustrene of the saide Fraternitie accordynge to the said ordenance, that is to say: For 43 Sondayes and Goode Friday at Paules Crosse & 3 dayes in Ester Weke at Saynte Marie Spitelle, as by a bylle off parcelles of the saide Wardens more playnely dothe appere } 15s. 8d.

Also to 6 waytes withe baners payntede, cognisaunces enbrodrede withe Jħu, goinge alle the stretes & suburbs of London playinge withe their instrumentes to yiff warnynge & knowlegge to the people of the said Fraternitie of the forsaide festes off Transfiguracone & Name off Jħu, accordynge to the forsaide ordenaunce 10s., & in rewarde 3s. In alle withein the tyme off thys accompt, as by the saide boke off parcelles of the saide Wardens playnely dothe appere } 13s.

Also to the proctor off the saide Fraternitie off London for the bonefire afor the northe dore of the crowdes yerely in the evin off the said fest off the Name off Jħu 4s. 8d. Also for lyvereys off Jhus off golde for the Assistentes & other worshipfulle mene & their wifes and for the Wexchaundelers at sundrie tymes, that ys to say: At oone tyme for 9 grosse & 4 dozen[24] off Jhus 15s. 7d. For 13 dozen roses 5s. 5d. For 400 of smale Jħus 16d. Another tyme for 1000 & a dozen (an half) of smale Jħus 3s. 8d. Also the first quarter of thys yere for 3 grose of Jħus & 2 dozen of roses 8s. 4d. & for 17 dozen smale Jħus 3s. 4d. The secunde quarter for 12 dozen roses 4s. 6d. & for 80 dozen smale Jħus 12s. 6d. The 4[the] quarter for 4 dozen roses 16d. & for 30 dozen smale Jħus 4s. 2d. Also for bowes & herbes pro parveide & spent in garnishynge of the saide crowdes 4s., & for 2 burdene } 69s. 1d 67s. 1d.

f. 40r

rishus 4d. In alle, withein the tyme of thys accompt }[25]

---

[24] 'dozen' expanded by editor from dd' for this entry.
[25] End of bracket from section on previous folio.

Yet divine service

Also for synginge brede 2s. 5½d., wine 19s. 10d. (6d.) boughte for prestes synginge masse in the saide crowdes, & for brede to make haly brede 3s. 11½d. In alle withein the tyme off thys accompt, as by the boke off parcelles of the saide Wardens playnely dothe appere } 25s. 11d.

Also for wexe spent in the saide crowdes beside the wexe there founde by the Wexchaundelers thys yere, as by a boke off percelles ther of remaynige with thys accompt more playnely dothe appere withein the tyme of thys accompt } £39 19s. (31s. 4d.)

Summa } £39 19s. 18s. 16s. 8d.

[43] Empacions[26]

Also for sundrie ornamentes & neccessaries parveide & boughte to the use off the saide Fraternitie, that is to say: For 2 corporasse clothes 2s.; for 4 surplices 12s.; ande for 4 sakering belles & 4 stokys 2s. 4d. In alle } 16s. 4d.

Summa } 16s. 4d.

Reperacions

Also in sundrie reperacions, that is say: For makynge of a pewe for the aldermene 46s. 8d. And for mendyng off the belfrey and makynge of the clapers £8 7s. 10d. For paying pavynge of the crowdes 8d. For mendynge of a bawdrike for the belles 4d. For nailles 2d. For 34 fote of planke bordes & for nailles 17d. In alle, as by the saide boke of parcelles theroff remaynynge withe thys accompt planely dothe appere } £10 17s. 1d.

Summa } £10 7s. 1d.

[44] Expenses necessarie

Also for sundrie expences neccessarie, that is to say: To 6 mene for their attendance in kepynge of bokes & drawyng off drinke in the saide

---

26 'Empacions' and 'Reperacions' have been erased slightly above current marginal words, and the 'side lines' have been redrawn on this folio, suggesting last minute changes to layout.

festes <u>9s. 8d.</u> Also for a hogges hede of wine yevene to Master Deane of Paules, Rector of the saide Fraternitie, by concideracone of the Wardens ande Assistentes of the same Fraternitie <u>25s.</u> And for a froshe

f. 40v
Expences neccessarie

samone yevene to my lorde of London[27] to have tymbre & scafalde for the belfrey, <u>20s.</u> To the wexchaundeler <u>6s. 8d.</u> To Master Monkes mane for cariage of bokys <u>8d.</u> To the glasier at oone tyme for mendynge of the windowes <u>18d.</u>, at a nother tyme <u>12d.</u> For cariage off the tresore chest <u>8d.</u> Also yevine to 6 childrene of the Kynges Chapelle for singinge of Jħus masse <u>12d.</u> For mendynge of a chalesse <u>4d.</u> For mendynge of a loke 2 tymes <u>2d.</u> For halywater stike <u>1½d.</u> For entringe of a playnte <u>2d.</u> For mendynge & beyringe of the organs <u>18d.</u> For bromes <u>2d.</u> For ~~mendyof~~ mendynge of 3 vestmenstes [sic] <u>4d.</u> For (3) skynes of parchement to cover bokes <u>19d.</u> For scorynge of basons and candelstikes <u>8d.</u> For nailes & [erased letter] hokes <u>5d.</u> For water to make halywater <u>2½d.</u> For grese for the belles & the newe stoke <u>4½d.</u> For bromis & tappis <u>4d.</u> For mendyng of the olde pewe & a loke & 3 kayes <u>3s. 10d.</u> For lavander & roses for the clothes <u>1d.</u> For 6lb tallowe candelle <u>7d.</u> For haliwater strinkylles <u>3d.</u> For grete pynnes <u>1½ d.</u> For makyng clene off the balfrey & cariage of 5 lodes of robishe <u>23d.</u> For 13lb tallowe candelle <u>15d.</u> For removynge of the brasse over the peue <u>18d.</u> For 2 payre of garnettes & 2 lokes & 5 kayes ande irone for the sakeringe belles <u>6s. 5d.</u> For 5 mattes & 5 hassokes <u>12d.</u> For removynge of the Scripture <u>7d.</u> For nailles <u>3½d.</u> For drinke for the joyner <u>2d.</u> For a rope of 9(lb) weighte <u>9d.</u> For a lyne for the sakeringe belle <u>1d.</u> For bromis <u>1d.</u> For writynge of a bille for Stisfelde <u>2d.</u> Ande for 11 quarters [sic] off lampe oyle <u>3s. 8d.</u> In alle, as by the saide boke off parcelles remayninge withe thys accompt playnly dothe appere } £4 15s. 3½d.

Summa } £4 15s. 3½d.

[45] Almes

Also to the almoyner of Paules for 10 gownes for 10 choresters off the saide cathedralle churche servyng Gode in the saide crowdes
f. 41r

yet Almes[28]

---

27   Richard FitzJames, bishop of London (elected 1506, d. 1522), see *ODNB*, 'FitzJames, Richard'.
28   'Almes' erased in left margin by first paragraph.

aswelle in the saide festes of Transfiguracone & off the Name off Jħu, as every Fridaye at masses off Jħu & Requiem, and also ~~all~~ at alle the *salvies* [sic] there kept by the saide Fraternitie £4 ~~3s. 4d.~~ & in rewarde thys yere ~~12d.~~ (4s.), in alle } £4 4s. 4d.

~~Yet expenses necessarie~~

Also to John Walles, John Wynnygham, William Russelle & William Bamene, poremene appoyntede to the almes of the said Fraternitie, kepynge the saide crowdes, helpyng prestes at masse & prayinge for alle bredrene and susters of the saide Fraternitie, every off theme at <u>40s.</u> by yere payable quarterly accordynge to the saide ordenance, <u>£8</u>. And over that, in the saide festes off Transfiguracone & Name of Jħu <u>16d.</u> Also, to 19 prestes and poremene onn Alle Saule day in almes <u>2s. 6d.</u> In alle withein the tyme of thys accompt, as by the saide boke off parcelles remaynyng withein thys accompt playnely dothe appere } ~~£12 7s. 2d.~~ £8 3s. 10d.

Summa } £12 ~~7s. 2 d.~~ 8s. 2d.

[46] Potacions[29]

Also in sundrie potacions ande expences necessarie in the festes off Transfiguracone & Name off Jħu apone the bredrene & susters comynge in there, that is to say: For brede to drinke withe 4½d. (for) 6 barelles of ale 22s. Also for brede & mete for Thomas Holmes & othere mene for 3 dayes <u>10s. 5d.</u> Also for the dyner onn Jħus day <u>66s. 5d.</u> Also spent at eleccone of the Wardens <u>4s.</u> Also at the audit off Henre Hille and John Sandelle, late Wardens <u>15s. 6d.</u> Also spent att divers other assimbles of the saide Wardens[30] & Assistentes thys yere <u>40s.</u> In alle, as by the saide boke of percelles remayninge withe thys accompt playnely dothe appere } £7 18s. 8½d.

Summa } £7 18s. 8½d.

f. 41v

Some of alle the said paymentes } £76 12s. 4d.

And so remaynethe due to the said Fraternitie } £70 14s. 1d.

---

[29] Second 'potacions' erased next to this section.
[30] End of word written over erasure.

[47] Remayne apone

John Copwode by sundrie specialities } 53s. 4d.

William Goughe & Richard Vaughan by like specialities } 20s.

Davy John, late proctor of the diosise of Sainte Asse & Bangore } 13s. 4d. *Renuttiando &c.*

The Feliship of Wexchaundelers off London } 6s. 8d.

Henry Thorntone, sergeaunt of armes, and William Marke off Liskarde in [the] countie off Cornewaile, yomane, by obligacione } £6 13s. 4d.

John Davy for the diosise of Saint in Bangore [sic] at ~~20s~~ (26s. 8d.) by yere, that is to say for a yere withein the tyme off thys accompt } ~~20s.~~ (26s. 8d.)

And upone the saide accomptes } £58 9d.

Alle whiche money the said accomptauntes have deliverde to the handes of John Mathewe & John Broune, Wardens of the saide Fraternitie for the yere ~~endede~~ next ensuyng, thende of this accompt in presence off the auditours off the same accompt under writtene, that is to say:[31]

Per me Hary Hylle'
Per me William Bromwelle
Stevyne Warde
Henricus Dakers
Per me Johannem Worsoppe
Per me Hugo Fournesse

f. 42r[32]

[48] Obligacions deliverde by the said accomptauntes unto thandes of John Mathewe & John Browne, Wardens for the yere next ensuynge, the fest off Cristenmasse in the yere off oure Lorde 1516 and in the 8the yere of the reigne of kyng Henre the 8the.

First the obligacone of Nicholas Smythe of Cambrigge, fermer of the proxies in the counties & diose of Norwiche, Elie, Yorke, (Duresme) & Carlisle, conteyning } £20

Item another obligacone of Thomas Rocheforde, fermer off part off Essexe, conteyning } 40s.

---

31   This paragraph is in a very similar but probably different hand from the main account. The names are signatures, with small pointer marks next to Worsopp and Fourness. Fournesse's signature is followed by an elaborate flourish similar to a notarial mark as he used in the previous account.

32   Text starts half way down the page, and same hand as 'All which money...'.

Item an obligacone of Thomas Norreys, fermer off another part off Essexe (conteyning) } 40s.

Item an obligacone off Robert Oliver, fermer of the diosise off Cantorbury ande Chichestre cot conteyning } 100s.

Item an obligacone off Roger Robyns, fermer of the diosis of Wyncsestre & Sarum, conteyning } 100s.

Item an obligacone off John Thorntone, sergeaunt off armes, & William Marke, fermers off Cornewaille (for the last yere) conteyning } £6 13s. 4d.

Item an obligacone of William Thomas for Bathe & Welles } 53s. 4d.

Item an obligacone of Richard Stilfelde & John Tiler for the diosise off Worcestore, Chestre & Hereford } £10

And an obligacone of Rice ap Howelle for Saint Davyes in Wales conteyning } 26s. 8d.

f. 42v - blank

f. 43r[33]

[49][34] Thaccompte off John Mathew and John Browne, Wardeyns of the Fraternitie of the Name of Jhu' in the crowdes of the cathedralle churche of Seint Paule in London, frome the fest of Christemas in the yere off oure Lorde accoumpted by the Churche of Englonde a thowsande, fyve hundrethe and sixtene, and the 8the yere of the reigne of king Henry the 8th, that ys to say by one hole yere.

The same accomptaunces ben charged with tharrerages of John Copwoode by sundry specialties, as in the fote of the last accompt of John Sandelle and John Mathew, late Wardeyns of the said Fraternitie, more pleynly dothe appere } 53s. 4d.

Also with tharrerages of William Gowghe and Richarde Vaughan by like specialties, as in the said last accompt in like wise dothe appere } 20s.

Also withe tharrerages of Henry Thornetone by obligacion } £6 13s. 4d.

Also withe tharrerages of the Felisshippe of Wexchaundelers in London } 6s. 8d.

Also with tharrerages due by John Mathew and John Broune, late Wardeyns, there in their last accompt as in the fote of the same more pleynly dothe appere } £58 9d.

Summa – £68 14s. 1d.

[50] Also with the rentes and fermes of two tenementes and certeyne landes in the towne and feldes of Uxbridge in the counties of Middlesex and Buckingham lettene to William Baily and James Standale for 29s. 8d. by yere, payable at the feastes of Thannunciacion of oure Blessed Lady

---

33 Very different hand and layout to previous accounts.
34 In the lower right margin there are clear traces of wax from a round applied seal.

and Seint Mighelle Tharchaungelle by evene porcions, that ys to say for the same feast[s] falling within the tyme of this accompt } 29s. 8d.

Also withe the ferme of alle the devocions in the saide Fraternitie belongging in the diocese of Norwiche, Elie, Yorke, Durisme and Carleslie, lettene to Nicholas Smythe of Cambrige for £20 for a yere within the tyme of this accompte } £20

f. 43v
Also withe the ferme of like devocions of parte of the counties of Essexe and Hertforde lettene to Thomas Hethe, as appereth by an obligacione with condicione to pay 40s. at the festes of Ester, Midsomer, Mighelmas and Christemas by evene porcions for the tyme of this accompt } 40s.

Also with the other parte of the counties of Essexe and Hertforde lettene to Thomas Norys for 40s. by yere for the tyme off this accompt } 40s.

Also with the ferme of like devosyons in the diocese off Caunterbury and Chechestre lettene to Robert Olyver off London, masone, as apperithe by obligacone with condicione to pay 100s. sterlinges at Cristmas falling within the tyme of this accompt } 100s.

Also withe the ferme off like devocions in the Diocese off of [sic35] Winchestre and Sarum lettene to Roger Robyns as apperithe by obligacions with condicione to pay 100s. sterlinges at the feast of the Purificacion of oure Lady falling within the tyme of this accompt } 100s.

Also with the ferme of like devocions of the diocese of Excester lettene to ~~John~~ (Henry) Thornetone, sergeaunt of armes, and to William Marke of Liskarde in the countie of Cornewalle for £6 13s. 4d. by yere payable at Christemas falling within the tyme of this accompt } £6 13s. 4d.

Also resceved of Ryce ap Howelle for the devosion of Seint Daves by the handes of Richarde Lynde, wexchaundeler } 26s. 8d.

Also with the ferme of like devocions in the diocese of Bathe and Welles lettene to William Thomas for 53s. 4d. by yere paiable at Midsomer and Christemas falling within the tyme of this accompt } 53s. 4d.

---

35   Line-break separates the repeated words.

Also with the ferme of like devocions in the diocese of Worcester, (Chestre), and Herfforde lettene to John Tyler and Richarde Styfelde for £10 by yere payable at the feast of Ester, as apperithe by obligacione dated the [blank] day of [blank] in the 9^{the} yere of the reigne of king Henry the 8th } £10

f. 44r

Also with the the ferme of like devocions in the diocese of Seint Davy and Bangore in Wales lettene to John Davy for 20s. by yere for the tyme of this accompt } 20s.

Also reseyved of Thomas Holmes, apprower of the devocions in the kinges courte and Chauncere, by the othe of the saide Thomas } £26 14s. 1d.

Also reseyved of the Wardeyns and Felisshipe of Wexchaundelers of London for an annuelle rent at 20s. by yere, as in the saide president for the saide tyme shewithe } 20s.
Also reseyved of the bequest of Sir Richarde Haddone,[36] knight and alderman of London, the 8th day of May in the 9th yere of the reigne of king Henry the 8th } 40s.
Also reseyved of Maister Hosyers[37] gift the 29 day of July in the saide 9th yere of oure sovereyne lorde the king } 20s.
Also reseyved of Thomas Holmes for a paire of organs by hyme solde } 42s.

**Summa* of alle the saide receiptes[38] } £158 14s. 2d.*

Wheroff

[51] The said accomptaunces accompt in paymentes ordinary to be made in the crowdes of the said cathedralle churche to sundry ministres of the same churche beyng present and keping divine service there, of and in the feastes off Transfiguracione and Name of Jhu' this yere, withe *Placebo* and *Dirige* with note inmediatly after the last evensong of the saide feast of the Name of Jhu', and masse of Requiem in like wise in the morow thane next after, for the Fraternitie, that ys to say: To the subdeane beyng present at alle the premisses and singing the highe masse in the saide feastes, for eyther day 2s., in alle 4s. Also to

---

36 Richard Haddon (d. 1517) mercer, sheriff 1496–7 and mayor of London 1506–7, 1513–14. Barron, *London*, 348–9.
37 Probably John Hosier (d. 1521), mercer. Sutton, *Mercery*, 381n, 382n, 526n, 558.
38 Two erased words to the left of this entry.

8 chauntry prestes bering coopes

f. 44v

in the saide festes, in rewarde 10s.[39] Also to 12 peticanons 40s., and to
6 vicars 16s. Also to every highe canone, peticanone, chauntry preest,
vicars and choresters beyng present and bering copes in the saide
feastes of Transfiguracone and Name of Jhu' 4d., in alle 32s. 6d. Also
to a petie chanone singing the masse of Requiem 6d., and 2 to two
chauntry preestes reding the Pistelle and Gospelle at 3 masses afore
expressede 2s. Also to Maister Bisshoppe[40] for seying of *Deprofundes*
2d., and to the maister of the amery for his childrene, 12d. Also for
the collacone made there at the high masse in the saide festes of the
Name of Jhu' 6s. 8d. Also to the sacristene for garnysshing of the
aulters and bering bokes and other ornamentes 3s. 10d. Also to 4
vergers there beyng attendaunt, to every of theyme 12d. with 20d. in
rewarde this yere, 6s. 8d. And to the belle ringers for their laboures in
the said feastes besides 20s. to theyme paide quarterly for keping of
the dores of the saide crowdes, 13s. 4d. In alle, by the Rectour of the
saide Fraternitie and by the Wardeyns and Assistens of the same, yt ys
ordeyned and enacted deducted theroff 3s. 4d. for the saide collacone
made in the absentes of the saide deane, and so allowaunce to the
saide accomptaunces } £6 13s. 4d.

Also for the masses of Jhu' solempnely by note kept in the said crowdes
by the subdeane, a cardinalle or peticanon and by 6 vicars and 10
choresters of the saide cathedralle churche in their abbettes and surplices,
and to a chauntry preest singing the masse of Requiem by note every
Fryday ynmediatly after the saide masse of Jhu' with 6 of the saide
choresters, that ys to say: To the subdeane beyng present 4d. To the
peticanone singing the saide masse of Jhu' 8d. And to the chauntry prest
singing the masse of Requiem 4d. And to every of the saide 6 vicars 4d.
Summa } £7 15s. 4d.

Also to one of the vicars, maister of the saide choresters, keping 3 *salves*
daily in the saide crowdes after Complyne done in the saide cathedralle
churche, afore the ymage of Jhu', oure Blessed Lady and Seint Sebastiane,
and taking for his laboure 26s. 8d. at 4 termes of the yere by evene
porcions according to the said ordenaunces } 26s. 8d.

Also to the belle ringers of the saide cathedralle churche for their

---

[39] Most but not all of the individual sums for expenditure have been underlined in this
      account. Since such underlining may relate to the accounting process this has been
      replicated exactly in this edition.

[40] It is uncertain whether this is the bishop of London or a priest named Bishop.

laboures and daily attendaunces, openyng, closing and shetting of dores of the saide crowdes, ringing and tolling of belles, blowing of orgeyns, lyghting and quenching of torches and other lightes, sweping and making clene of the saide crowdes, at 20s. by yere payable quarterly

f. 45r

besides 13s. 4d. for theyme allowede for the saide feastes of Transfiguracion and Name of Jhu' according to the saide ordenances } 20s.

Also for the rewarde of the saide Wardeyns this yere, lymytted and taxede by the saide Rectour and Assistentes according to the saide ordenaunces £4, and overthat the saide John Mathew in rewarde this yere 20s., in alle } £5

Also for their lyveres of clothing for the said Wardeyns with cognisaunces of the name of Jhu', lymyted in lyke wise by the said Rectour and Assistentes according to the saide ordenaunce } £4

Also to John Worsoppe, one of the awdytours of this accompt, and for thengrosing of the same } 20s.

Also to Thomas Holme, assigned prouctour to gather and reseyve alle maner of devocions of the said Fraternitie in the kinges courte, the cite of London and subbarbes of the same, the Innes of Courte and Chauncery by wey off emproment, that ys to say for the reseit of £26 13s. 1d. after 3s. 4d. of every 20s. } £4 8s. 4d.

Also to the saide Thomas Holme entending daily in the saide crowdes and helping preestes at masse, keping the vestmentes and other ornamentes of the saide Fraternitie, 26s. 8d. by yere paiable quarterly } 26s. 8d.

Also to the prechers at Paules Crosse and Seint Mary Spitelle, remembring and praying for the sowles of alle bretherne and susterne of the saide Fraternitie according to the saide ordenaunce, that is to say: For 48 Sondaies and Good Fryday at Paules Crosse and 3 daies in Ester Weke at Seint Mary Spitelle, as by a bille of parcelles of the saide Wardeyns more pleynly dothe appere ~~24s.~~ } 24s. 4d.

Also to 6 waites with baners payntede, cognisaunces enbroderede with Jhu', goyng alle the stretes and subbers [sic] of London playing with their instrumentes to gif warnyng and knowledge to the people of the saidd Fraternitie of the forsaidd feastes of Transfiguracione and Name of Jhu', according to the forsaide ordenaunce 10s., and in rewarde 3s.

f. 45v

In alle within the tyme of this accompt, as by the saide boke of parcelles of the saide Wardeyns pleynly dothe appere } 13s.

[52] Also to the proctour of the saide Fraternitie of London for the bonfire before the north dore of the crowdes yerely in the evene of the saide fest of the Name of Jhu' 2s. 8d. Also for 6 Jhūs gevene to the king, the quene and other grete estates 2s. 5d. Also for lyveres of Jhūs of golde for the Assistentes and other worshipfulle mene and their wifes, 24 dossene 8s. 4d. Also for 21 grosse smale Jhūs 33s. Also for 1000 of smalle Jhūs for childrene 3s. 2d. Also for bowes and yerbes purveyede and spent in garnysshing of the saide crowdes 4s. 8d., and 2 burdeyne of russhes 4d. In alle within the tyme of this accompt } 54s. 7d.

Also for singingbrede 2s. 8d. Also for wyne 18s. 4d. Also brede for halybrede 4s. 3d. In alle within the tyme of this accompt } 25s. 3d.

Also for wexe spent in the saide crowdes beside the wexe there founde by the Wexchaundelers this yere, as by a boke of parcelles therof remaynyng with this accompte more pleynly dothe appere, within the tyme of this accoumpt } 29s. 10d.

[53] Also for sundry ornamentes and necessaryes purveyede and bought to the use of the saide Fraternitie, that ys to say: For a pece of bokeram for the awters 4s. Also for 21 elles of Normandie clothe for 4 albes and for making of theyme 12s. Also for a botelle of tynne for singing wyne 10d. A basket for halybrede 1d. Also for a dossene of quyssions for people to knele onn 2s. 4d. Also for 20 hassokes for pewes 22d. Also for a boke of the feast of Jhu' of [sic] Transfiguracione 2s. Also for 4 stoppes of irone for the organs 20d. Also for a padlok for the belfrey 5d. Also for a Scripture pece and 7 quarrelles of glasse 10d. Also for roses and lavendure for clothes 3d. Also for an yrone for the deske of the organs 4d. And for 4 snuffers and fyve pykkers for torches 9d. In alle } 27s. 4d.

Also in sundry reperacions, that ys to say: For making of 10 new pewes for the Assistens and gilding of the scochyns, £12 20d.

f. 46r

Also paide to a marbeler for cutting of 2 pillers for setting of the pewes 8d. Also for the pewes 200 of 5d. naile 8d.; 200 of 4d. nayle 6d.; 200 *dimidium* [half] of 3d. naile 5d.; a 100 of 2d. nayle 1d.; and a quarter of a 1000 of sprygges 1½d. Also hokes grete and smalle 1d. Also a 100 of grete pynnes 1½d. Also for mending of a lantrone 2½d. For mending of 2 crewettes 1d. Also for changing of a candelstyk 2d. Also for paving of Jhūs dore 2d. Also for mending of the orgeyns 4d. Also for sawing of planckes for awters 15d. In alle } £12 6s. 7½d.

[54] Also in sundry expensys neccessarie, that ys to say: For a hoggeshed of wyne to Master Deane, Rectour of the saide Fraternitie, 23s. 4d., and for cariage 8d. Also for a side and a cheyne of fresshe salmone gevene to my lorde of London to have his good wille for the purchasing of *Scala Cely,*[41] 9s. 4d. Also paide for bote hyre whane Master Genyns[42] and dyvers of the Assistens went to Fullam and for drynking whane they came home, 2s. 9d.[43] Also spent upone Master Potkyne for his counseille to be had for *Scala Cely* 2s., and for writing of a boke of Jhūs 12d. Also for a potacione made to the Assistens whane they assemblede at the Horsse Hed for reformacione of dyvers maters conserning the saide Fraternitie 3s. 6d. Also for a pike gevene to Master Genyns 2s. Also paide to Master Shelley for his counseille to be had for the gift of a tenement which he promyses to geve to the saide Fraternitie 3s. 4d. Also spent upone Master Fairefox[44] and other of the Kinges Chapelle 13d. Also spent uppone the deane of Seint Daves 10d. Also for brede, ale and bere that was gevene to the joynours whane they set upp the pewes 2d. Also for bromes 2d. Also for scoring of basons, ewers and candelstikes 6d. Also for paper, penne and ynke 4d. Also for gresying of belles 2d. Also for a lok and a key for the seet of the proctour and for 2 staies of irone for the deske 10d. Item to a plasterer ande his laborer ande for 2 sakkes of lyme to wasshe the wyndowes 17d. Also for a box for singing brede 1d. Also for trussing of the grete belle and for mending of the whele of the seconde belle 18s. Also for steling of 2 gogeons and mending of staies and keys for the grete belle and for a steroppe of irone for the new whele of the same belle weying 6lb, 12d. Also for a quarter of coles and an erthene pane for the bedemene 6d. Also paide for a proxe for the proctour of London 6d. Also for mending of 2 vestmentes, one blak and the other rede, and for sylk of the same 12d. Also for the mending of a surples 4d. Also for the wryting of 2 supplicacions, one to the bisshop of London and the other to the deane of Paules, 8d. Also for the hyre of a horsse for to desire a lettre frome the bisshop of London to the

---

41 The *Scala Coeli* indulgence. See N. Morgan, 'The Scala Coeli Indulgence and the Royal Chapels', in *The Reign of Henry VII: Proceedings of the 1993 Harlaxton Symposium,* ed. B. Thompson (Stamford,1995), 82–103.

42 Sir Stephen Jenyns (d. 1523), Mayor of London 1508–09, assistant of the Jesus Guild 1507–23.

43 The number is ambivalent, and could be 10 corrected from 9 (i.e. jx)

44 Dr Robert Fairfax (d. 1521) composer and Gentleman of the Chapel Royal. See *ODNB* 'Fayrfax [Fairfax], Robert'.

bisshope of Exetour for the proctour of that diocese 3s. 2d., and for 3 grene geesse and *dimedium* [half] a dossene of pegeons gevene at that tyme to the saide bisshoppe of London 2s. 5d. Also

f. 46v

for 16lb of talughe candelle 18½ d. Also for 3 galons and a potelle of lampe oyle 4s. 8d. Also for wasshing of awter clothes, awbes, surplices and alle other lynene 4s. 8d. Also gevene to the queresters 1d. And for white threde ½d. Also paide to two mene bering the ladder for mendyng of the belle at Jhūs dore 2d. In alle } £4 9s. 11d.

[55] Almes[45]

Also to the almoyner of Paules for 10 gownes for tenne choresters of the said cathedralle churche servyng God in the saide crowdes, aswelle in the saide feastes of Transfiguracone and of the Name of Jhu' as every Fryday at masses off Jhūs ande Requiem, ande also at alle the *salves* there kept by the saide Fraternitie £4. Ande in reward this yere 3s. 4d. In alle } £4 3s. 4d.

Also to John Walles, John Wynnyngham, William Russelle and William Bavene, poremene appoynted to the almes of the saide Fraternitie, keping the saide crowdes, helping preestes at masse, ande praying for alle bretherne and susterne of the saide Fraternitie, every of theyme at 40s. by yere payable quarterly according to the saide ordenance £8. Ande over that, in the saide feastes of Transfiguracione and Name of Jhu' 16d. Also to 32 preestes ande 4 pore mene onn Alle Sole Day in almes 3s. In alle within the tyme of this accompt as by the saide boke of parcelles remaynyng within this accompt pleynly doth appere } £8 4s. 4d.

[56] Potacions

Also in sundry potacions and expensys necessary in the feastes of Transfiguracion and Name of Jhu' upone the bretherne and susters commyng to the crowdes, that ys to say; For brede to drynk with 3d. Also for barelles and a kylder of ale 16s. 6d. Also for brede and mete for Thomas Holmes and other mene for 3 daies 4s. 5d. Also gevene to 4 porters to 2 mene to kepe the awters and bokes and for drawing of ale 11s. 4d. Also for the dynner on Jhūs Day £4. Also spent at the elleccione of the Wardeyns 5s. 2d. Also spent at the awdyt of John Sandelle and John Mathew, late Wardeyns of the saide Fraternitie, 24s. 10d. Also

---

45   This and following sub-heading are in the left margin.

spent at dyvers other assembles of the saide Wardeyns and Assistence 40s. In alle } £9 2s. 6d.

Summa of alle the said paymentes } £79 11s. 2½d.

f.47r

And so remaynethe due to the saide Fraternitie } £79 2s. 11½d.

Wheroff

[57] John Copwode by bille – 53s. 4d.

William Goughe and Richarde Vaughan by specialtie } 20s.[46]

The Felissipe of Wexchaundelers } 6s. 8d.

Henry Thornetone, sergeant of armes, and William Marke of Lyskarde in the countie of Cornewalle, by obligacione withe condicione for 2 yeres } £13 6s. ~~1d.~~ 8d.

John Davie of Brekenocke by obligacione } 26s. 8d.

The same John owethe for this yere } 10s.

Robert Olyver of London, masone, by obligacione } 50s.

Item [blank] abatede of the payment allowede to Thomas Holmes } 33s.

Rest delyverede to John Broune and Richard Smyth, the resevers of this accompt } £59 2s. 7d.

Memorandum the saide John Broune have reseyvede the saide some of £59 2s. 7d. of John Mathew, accomptaunt, and alle specialties in this accompt specified and conteynede.

[58] Obligacions delyvered by the handes of John Mathewe, accomptaunt, unto thandes of John Broune and Richarde Smythe, Wardeyns for the yere next ensuyng, that ys to say frome the feast of Cristmas in the 8th yere of the reigne of king Henry the 8the unto the feast of Cristmas thane next ensuyng in the 9th yere of oure saide soveraigne lorde the king.

f.47v

First an obligacione of Nicholas Smythe of London } £15

Item an obligacione of Thomas Rocheforde of London, yomane, and of Raufe Shirwode, citezene and bruer of London } 40s.

Item an obligacione of Roger Robyns, citezeine ande haberdassher of London } £5

Item an obligacione of Henry Story of Welles in the countie of Somerset,

---

46   *Nichille* ('nothing') written in left margin against this entry, and also by the entry for John Davie.

yomane, ande of William Graunthaum, citezene ande merchaunttaillour of London } £5

Item an obligacione of Richarde Styfelde of Worcester ande of John Tyler of the cite of Coverntre, yomane, and John [blank], citezene and grocer of London } £10

Item an obligacione of Thomas Norres of Belerica in the countie of Essexe and of Thomas Highaum of London, gurdeler } £5

Item an obligacione of Robert Olyver, fremasone, William Mede, bruer, Thomas Turnour, citezeine and shermane of London } £6

Item an obligacione of Henry Thornetone, one of the sergauntes of armes of oure soverayne lorde the king, and William Markes of Lyskarde } 20 marces.

Item John Davie of Brekenock } 40s.

Item an obligacione of William Goughe of Tawger } 40s.

Per[47] me William Bromwelle

Per me Thomas Hynde, mercer

Per me Johannem Jossone[48]

Per me Johannem Worsoppe

f. 48 - blank

f. 48v

[59][49] This is the accoumpte of John Browne ande Richarde Smythe, Wardeyns of the Fraternitie of the Name of Jhū in the crowdes of the cathedralle churche of Seint Paule in London, frome the feast of Christemas in the yere of oure lorde God accompted by the Churche of Englonde 1517th and in the 9th yere of the reigne of kyng Henry the 8th, that is to say by one hole yere.

Arreagis[50]

The same accomptaunces ben charged with tharrerages of John Copwoode by sundry specialties, as in the fote of the last accompt of John Mathew and John Browne, late Wardeyns of the saide Fraternitie, more pleynly apperith } 53s. 4d.

Also withe tharrerages of William Goughe ande Richarde Vaughan by

---

47   The abbreviation for Bromwelle and Josson is an odd combination of the marks for *per* and *pro*. For evidence that Bromwell signed the account in person, see [47].

48   Sign-manual 'X' appears to the right of Josson's and Worsopp's names.

49   Traces of sealing wax can be seen near the outer edge of leaf two-thirds of the way down, matching traces on recto.

50   All headings in this account are in the left margin with large brackets enclosing text unless otherwise indicated.

like specialties, as in the said laste accompt in likewise dothe appere, *summa* } 20s.
Also with tharrerages of John Davy as apperithe in the remayne of the forsaide laste accompte } 10s.
Also with tharrerages of Henry Thornetone as apperithe in the remayne of the saide last accompt } £13 6s. 8d.
Also withe tharrerages of the Felishippe of Wexchaundelers of London, *summa* } 6s. 8d.
Also withe tharrerages of Robert Olyver, fremasone, as apperithe in the remayne of the last accompt *summa* } 50s.
Also withe tharrerages due by the said John Browne and Richarde Smythe in their last accompt, as in the fote of the same accompte more pleynly dothe appere } £59 2s. 7d.

Summa } £79 9s. 3d.

f. 49r

[60] Rentes & fermes

Also withe the rentes and fermes of two tenements and certeyn londes in the townes and feldes of Uxbrige in the counties of Middlesex and Bukingham lettene to William Baily and James Standale for 29s. 8d. by yere paiable at the festes of Seint Mighelle Tharchaungelle and Thannunciacione of oure Blessed Lady by evene porcions, that is to say for the same festes falling within the tyme of this accompt, *summa* } 29s. 8d.

Also with the ferme of alle the devocions to the saide Fraternitie belonging in the diocese of Norwiche, Elie, Durham and Carlile letten to Nicholas Smyth of Cambrige for £20 for a yere within the tyme of this accompt } £20
Also withe the ferme of like devocione of parte of the counties of Essexe and Hertforde lettene to Thomas Rocheforde as apperithe by obligacione, to pay 40s. for the tyme of this accompt, *summa* } 40s.
Also with the ferme of lyke devocione of the other parte of the counties of Essexe and Hertforde lettene to Thomas Norrys for 40s. by yere for the tyme of this accompt, *summa* } 40s.
Also with the ferme of like devocione in the diocese of Kent and Chichestre lettene to Robert Olyver, fremasone, for this present yere of accompt *summa* } £5
Also with the ferme of like devocione in the diocese of Winchestre and Sarum lettene to Roger Robyns as apperith by obligacione, to pay £5 sterlinges within the tyme of this accompt, *summa* } £5
Also with the ferme of like devocions of the diocese of Exetour lettene to Henry Thornetone, sergeaunt of armes, and to William Mark of Lyskarde

in the countie of Cornewalle for £6 13s. 4d. payable at Christemas within the tyme of this accompt, *summa* } £6 13s. 4d.

Also with the ferme of like devocions of the diocese of Bathe and Welles lettene to Henry Story and William Grauntham for £5 to pay 53s. 4d. within the tyme of this accompte, *summa* } 53s. 4d.

f.49v
Fermes of procuares

Also withe the ferme of like devocions of the diocese of Worcestre, Chester and Herforde lettene to Nich[ol]is Styfelde, John Tyler and John Halle, grocer, for £10 within the tyme of thys accompte, *summa* } £10

Also receyved of John Tyler, clerk, clerk of Jhūs, for the devocions gatherede in London for 3 quarter } £17 12s. 1d.

Also receyved of the wardeyns and Felisshippe of Wexchaundlers of London for an annuelle rent of 20s. by yere } 20s.

Also receyved of Maister Nicolles,[51] fisshemonger, towardes the makyng of Jhūs shoes, *summa* } 3s. 4d.

Also receyved of the parsone[52] of Mary Magdalens in Olde Fisshe Strete of London to thuse of Jhus, *summa* } 10s.

Also receyved of John Sandelle, vyntener, to like use, *summa* } 3s. 4d.

Also receyvede of Sir Edmonde Massey, preest, for devocions gevene to Jhūs, *summa* } 2s.

Summa *totalis* of alle the receites } £153 16s. 4d.

Wherof

f. 50r
[61] Divine services

The said accomptaunces accompt in paymentes ordinary to be made in the crowdes of the said cathedralle churche to sundery ministres of the same churche beyng present ande kepyng divine service there, of and in the festes of Transfiguracione and Name of Jhu', and masse of Requiem in like wise on the morow than next after for the said Fraternitie, that is to say: To the subdeane beyng present at alle the premysses and syngyng

---

51 Thomas Nicolles, fishmonger.
52 The incumbent at the time was William Osbourne. C. Hennessy, *Novum Repertorium Ecciesiasticum Parochiale Londinense; or London Diocesan Clergy Succession from the Earliest Time to the year 1898* (London, 1898), 319.

the highemas in the saide festes, for either day 2s., in alle, 4s. Also to 8 chauntery prestes beryng coopes in the saide festes, in reward 10s. Also to to [sic[53]] 12 peticanons 40s.; and to 6 vicars 16s.; also to every highe canon, petycanone, chauntery preest, vicars and choresters beyng present ande beryng coopes in the said festes of Transfiguracione and Name of Jhu' 4d. In alle, 32s. Also to a petycanone synging the masse of Requiem and reding the Pistelle and Gospelle at the 3 masses a fore expressede and for saying of *Deprofundis* 2s. 4d. Also to the maister of the almery for his childrene 12s. Also for the collacion made there at the highe masse in the said festes of Name of Jhu' 3s. 4d. Also to the sacristene for garnysshing of alters and for beryng of bokes and other ornamentes 4s. Also to 4 vergers there beyng attendaunt, to every of theme 16d. withe 20d. in rewarde this yere, 6s. 8d. Also to belle ryngers for their labours in the saide festes besides 20s. to theme paide quarterly for kepyng of the dores of the saide crowdes, 13s. 4d. In alle, *summa* } £7 3s. 8d.

Also for the masses of Jhū solempnely by note kept in the saide crowdes by the subdeane, a cardinalle or peticanone and by 6 vicars and 10 choresters off the saide cathedralle churche in their abbettes and surplices, and to a chauntery preest singing the masse of Requiem by note every Fryday ynmediatly after the said masse of Jhu' withe 6 of the saide choresters, that is to say to the subdeane beyng present 4d. To the peticanone synging the saide masse of Jhu' 8d. Ande to the chauntery preest singyng the masse of Requiem 4d. And to every of the saide (6) vicars 4d. *Summa* } £8 13s. 6d.

Also to one of the vicars, maister of the saide choresters, kepyng 3 *salves* daily in the saide crowdes after Complyne done in the same cathedralle churche, before the ymage of Jhu', oure Blessede Lady and Seint Sebastiane, ande takyng for his laboure 26s. 8d. at 4 termes of the yere according to the saide ordenaunce } 26s. 8d.

f.50v
[62] Yet divine services ande other charges

Also to the belle ryngers of the saide cathedralle churche for their labours and daily attendauntes, openyng, closing and shetting of dores of the saide crowdes, rynging and tollyng of belles, blowing of orgeyns, lightyng ande quenching of torches and other lightes, swepyng and makyng clene of the saide crowdes, at 20s. by yere payable quarterly, besides 13s. 4d. for them allowede for the saide festes of Transfiguracione and Name of Jhū according to the saide ordenaunce } 20s.

---

53   Line break between repeated word.

Also for the rewarde of the saide Wardeyns this yere, lymyted and taxed by the saide Rectour and Assistens according to the said ordenaunce, £4. Ande over that to the said John Browne in rewarde this yere 20s. In alle } £5

Also for their lyveres of clothing for the saide Wardens with cognisaunces of the name of Jhu', lymyted in lyke wise by the said Rectour and Assistentes according to the saide ordenaunce, *summa* } £4

Also to John Worsoppe, one of the awdytours of this accompt, for thengrosing and making of the same accompte, *summa* } 20s.

Also to John Burges, sexten, entendyng daily in the saide crowdes and helpyng preestes and [sic] masse, kepyng the vestementes ande other ornamentes of the saide Fraternitie, for a yere and a quarter ended at oure Lady Day the Annunciacione, *summa* } 33s. 4d.

Also to the prechers at Poules Crosse and Seint Mary Spitelle remembryng and prayying for the soules of alle the bretherne and sustrene of the saide Fraternitie accordyng to the saide ordenaunce, that ys to say: For 43 Sondaies and Goode Fryday at Poules Cros and 3 daies in Esterwyke at Seint Mary Spitelle, *summa* } 24s. 4d.

Also to the 6 waites with baners paynted, cognisaunces enbroderede with Jhūs, goyng alle the stretes ande subberbes of London playing with their instrumentes to gife warnyng and knowlage to the people of the saide

f. 51r
Yet divine services

Fraternitie for the saide festes of Transfiguracione (& Name) of Jhu according to the foresaide ordenaunce 10s., and in rewarde 3s. 4d. In alle withine the tyme of this accompt, *summa* } 13s. 4d.

Also to the prouctour of the said Fraternitie for the bonefire before the northe dore of the said crowdes yerely in the evene of the saide feast of the Name of Jhu' 2s. 8d. Also for lyveres gevene to the kyng and the quene and to other grete estates, and for goldene lyveres for the Assistentes and their wifes, and for other smalle lyveres for comone people, servauntes and childrene 51s. 10d. In alle, *summa* } 54s. 6d.

Also paide for synging brede, for brede for haly brede, and for wyne, in alle within the tyme of this accompt, *summa* } 30s. 8d.

Also for wexe spent in the saide crowdes besides the wexe there founde by the Wexchaundelers this yere, as apperithe by a bille of parcelles within the tyme of this accompte, *summa* } 34s. 3d.

[63] Expences neccarie

Also in sundry potac[...] expences necessary, that is to say: To a pore preest for writing of parcelles that was received of Master Belamy and of Maister Belle 2d. Also, to Thomas Holmes for money by hyme paide as apperithe by his bille 17s. 2d. Also for 2 kayes, one for the pewes and the other for Jhūs boxe, 8d. Also for lyme and to 2 men to wasshe and white lyme the crowdes 16d. Also for 2 dossene and 9lb. of talughe candelle 3s. 5d. Also for 8 quartes of oyle at 4d. *le* quarte 2s. 8d. Also for a new lampe 1d. Also for bromes, nedille and threde 10d. Also for wasshing of corpores clothes, for wasshing of surplices, awterclothes and other lynene 5s. 2d. Also for a rope of 12lb. for the belles at 1d. quarter *le* lb., 4s. 4½d. Also for setting on the same rope 4d. Also for 8 fadome of corde for the lampe 2d. Also for mendyng of mas bokes 6d. Also for an accione takyne ayenst Thomas Holmes, for the arrest of the same, and for the amercyerament 22d. Also for a citacione for one John Savage[54] 2s. 6d. Also for a copee of the declaracion of Jhūs 12d. Also for Jhus shoes of sylver 19s. 4d., ande for burnysshing of Jhus 4s. Also for scoring of the candelstykes, the lampe, the braunche and the basons 8d. Also for talughe

f. 51v

candelle at the fest of Transfiguracione of Jhūs 5d. Also for 2 burdone of russhes 4d. Also for bromes and gresyng off belles 6d. Also for 2 tapers for angelles on the alter of Jhūs 2d. Also for flowres, bowes and garlondes in the fest of Transfiguracione of Jhūs 4s. 4d. Also spent in my lord of Canterbures courte upon John Savage for slaundring of Jhūs Brotherhode 11s. 6d. Also gevene in a present to my lorde of London this yere by the Wardeyns and certene of the Assistens 6s. 8d. Also paide for a hoggished of wyne gevene to maister deane 24s. In alle } £5 14s. 1½d.

[64] Yet expences necessary and almes

Also to the almoyner of Poules for 10 gounes for 10 choresters of the saide cathedralle churche servyng God in the saide crowdes, aswelle in the saide festes of Transfiguracione and Name off Jhu' as at every Fryday at masse

---

54   Possibly Sir John Savage VII, (d. 1528). See *ODNB* 'Savage family (per. *c.* 1369–1528)'.

of Jhu' ande Requiem, and also at alle the *salves* there kept by the saide Fraternitie £4. And in rewarde this yere 3s. 4d. In alle } £4 3s. 4d.

Almes

Also to John Wales, John Wynnynghaum, William Russelle and William Banene, poremene appoynted to the almes of the saide Fraternitie, kepyng the crowdes, helpyng preestes at masse and praying for alle the bretherne and susterne of the saide Fraternitie, every of theme 40s. by yere payable quarterly according to the saide ordenaunce, £8. And over that in the saide festes of Transfiguracione and Name of Jhu' 16d. Also to 32 preestes and 4 pore mene onn Alle Salowene Day in almes 3s. 10d., and for devocione pence 2s. 3d. In alle, *summa* } £8 7s. 5d.

[65] Potacions

Also in sundry potacions neccary, that is to say: For a potacone hade the 29 day of January *anno* 9° [1518] at the Hors Hede 2s. 5d. Also for a drynkyng made at the Hors Hede at the vewyng of Master Jenyns londes 8d. Also for apotacione [sic] the 26 day of Marche at the elleccione of Master Smythe 4s. 2d. Also for a potacione for the Assistens at assembly made for the declaracione of Jhūs 12d.[55] Also for the dyner on Jhūs day £4. Also spent at the awdite of John Mathew and John Browne, late Wardeyns of the saide Fraternitie, 20s. Also for a potacione made to the Assistens at the elleccione of a new clerk 12d. Also for a potacione made to the Assistens for vewyng of the fundacione of the crowdes 12d. Also for 5 barrelles and a kylderkyne of ale in the fest of Jhūs 22s. Also for brede and mete for John Tyler ande other mene for 5 daies 4s. 6d. Also gevene to 4 porters and to 2 mene that kept the awters and bokes ande for drawing of ale 11s. 4d. Also spent at certeyne tymes upone the Assistens and other straungers commyng to Jhūs masse, and upone proctours, 40s. In alle } £9 8s. 1d.

f. 52r

Summa of alle the saide paymentes } £65 7s. 2½d.

And so remaynethe due to the saide Fraternitie } £88 9s. 1½d.

Wheroff

---

55   This is an ambiguous reference, but could relate to the terms of the indulgence offered by the Jesus Guild (see Introduction, p. 11).

[66] Remayne uppon

John Copwode by bille } 53s. 4d.

William Gowghe and Richarde Vaughaun by specialtie } 20s.[56]

The Felisshipe of Wexchaundelers - 6s. 8d.

Henry Thornetone, sergeant of armes, and William Mark of Lyskarde in the countie of Cornewalle, by obligacione with condicione for 2 yeres £13 6s. 8d., and for this present yere without obligacion £6 13s. 4d. *Summa* } £20

Rest delyverede to Richarde Smythe and William Bromewelle, the receyuers of this accompte

} £64 9s. 1½d.

Memorandum the saide Richarde Smythe hathe receyvede the saide some of £64 9s. 1½d. [sic] and alle the specialties in this accompt specified and conteynede }

Per me Johannem Mathew[57]

Per me *Stephaunum* Warde

Per me Elys Draper

Per me Johannem Worsoppe

f. 52v

[67] Obligacions delyverede

Obligacions delyvered by thandes of John Browne, accomptaunt, unto the handes of Richarde Smythe and William Bromewelle, Wardeyns for this yere next ensuyng, that ys to say frome the fest of Christemas in the 9th yere of the reigne of kyng Henry the 8th [1517] unto the fest of Christemas than next ensuyng in the 10th yere of oure saide soveraigne lorde the kyng [1518].

First an obligacioun of Nicholas Smythe of London of £15 to pay £10, *summa* } £10

Item an obligacione of Thomas Rocheforde of London, yoman, and Rauf Shirwoode, citezeine and bruer of London, of £5 to pay 40s. *Summa* } 40s.

---

56   *Nichill'* (nothing) written in the margin between Copwoode and Gowgh in a different hand.

57   All four names appear to be signatures, but there is a mark consisting of a cross and capital A next to the entries for John Matthew and Stephen Warde, suggesting that one of them made his mark in place of or as well as signing.

Item an obligacion of Roger Robyns, citezein and haberdassher of London, *summa* } £5

Item an obligacione of Henry Story of Welles in the countie of Somerset, yoman, and William Graunthaum, citezein and merchaunttaillour of London, of £5 to pay } 53s. 4d.

Item an obligacione of Nicholas Styfelde of Worcestre, John Tyler of Coventre, yomane, and John Halle citezeine and grocer of London of } £10

Item an obligacione of Thomas Norrys of Belerica in the countie of Essexe, yomane, and Thomas Highaum of London, girdeler, of £5 to pay } 40s.

Item an obligacione of Richarde Inskype of the cite of Chichestre in the countie of Sussexe, proctour, and Robert Olyver, citezeine and fremasone of London, of £3 6s. 8d. to pay 33s. 4d. *Summa* } 33s. 4d.

Item an obligacione of Williame Mynskypp of the Caunterbury yomane, John Foster citezeine ande sherman of London, and John Baker of Suthwerk in the countie of Surrey, inneholder, in £6 to pay £5. *Summa* } £5

Item an obligacione of Nicholas ~~Adams~~ Williams of Chepstow in the marche of Wales and Edmonde Turnour of London, gentilmane, in 40s. to pay } 30s.

f. 53r

Item an obligacioun of John Prendregast, pryour of the monastery of Seint Peter and Poule of Sellisker in Irelonde,[58] and Philipp Nele, citezein and merchaunt taillour of London, of £4 to pay 40s. *Summa* } 40s.

Item 3 obligacions and a bille of John Copwoode for the payment of } 53s. 4d.[59]

Item an obligcaione of Henry Thornetone and William Mark of Lyskarde of } £13 6s. 8d.

f. 53v

[68] This is the accoumpte of Richarde Smythe ande William Bromewelle, Wardeynes of the Fraternitie of the Name of Jhu in the crowdes of the cathedralle churche of Seint Paule of London, frome the feast of Christemas in the yere of oure lorde Gode accompted by the Churche' of Englonde 1518 and in the 10th yere of the reigne of king Henry the 8th, that is to say by one hole yere.

The saide accomptaunce ben chargede with tharrerages of John Copwoode by sundry specialties, as in the fote of the last accoumpt of John Broune ande the said Richarde Smyth, late Wardeyns of the saide Fraternitie, more pleynly appereth } 53s. 4d.

---

58   Selskar Abbey, Co. Wexford.
59   The final two entries are in same hand as main account but not as neat, possibly as though added slightly later.

Also with the arrerages of the Felisshippe of Wexchaundeleres of London } 6s. 8d.

Also with the arrerages of Henry Thornetone as apperethe in the remayne of the laste accompte, *summa* } £20

Also with the arrerages due by the saide Richarde Smythe and William Bromewelle in the last accompte, as in the fote of the same accompte more pleynly dothe appere } £64 9s. 1d.

Summa } £87 9s. 1d.

[69] Also with the rentes and fermes of two tenementes and certeyne landes in the townes and feldes of Woxbridge in the counties of Middlesex and Bukingham lettene to William Baily and James Standale for [erasure] 29s. 8d. by yere paible at the feastes of Seynt Mighell Tharchaungelle and the Annunciacione of our Blessede Lady by evyne porcions, that is to say for the same festes falling within the tyme of this accompte } 29s. 8d.

Also with the ferme of alle the devocions of the saide Fraternitie belonging in the diocese of Norwiche, Elie, Durham and Carlile lettene to Nicholas Smyth of Cambridge by indenture for a yere within the tyme of this accompte } £20

Also with the ferme of like devocions of the dioces of Worcetour, Chester and Herforde lettene to John Tyler of Coventre for £10 within the tyme of this accompte } £10

f. 54r

Also with the ferme of like devocione of parte of the counties of Essex and Hertforde letten to Thomas Rocheforde as apperethe by obligacion to pay 40s. for the tyme of this accompte } 40s.

Also with the ferme of like devocione of the other part of the saide counties of Essexe and Hertforde lettene to Thomas Norrys for 40s. by yere for the tyme of this accoumpt } 40s.

Also with the ferme of lyke devocione of the diocese of Canterbury and Chichestre lettene to Richarde Inskype of the citie of Chichestre and Robert Olyver, citezein ande fremasone off London, due for the tyme of this accompt } 33s. 4d.

Also with the ferme of like devocions of the diocese off Kanterbury lettene to William Mynskype of Canterbury, yoman, duie in the tyme of this accompte } £5

Also with the ferme of like devocions of the diocese of Bathe ande Welles letten to Henry Story of Welles in the countie of Somerset and

William Graunthaum, citezein and merchaunt taillour of London, due in the tyme of this accompte } 53s. 4d.[60]

Also with the ferme of like devocions for the ferme of Irelande lettene to John Predregast, priour of the monastery of Seint Peter and Paule of Sellisker in Irelonde, due in the tyme of this accompt } 40s.

Also with the ferme of like devocione in the diocese of Wintone and Sarum lettene to Roger Robyns, citezeine and haberdassher of London, within the tyme of this accompt } £5

Also with the ferme of like devocions in the dioces of Seint Asse lettene to John Tailour for 13s. 4d. } 13s. 4d.

Also with the ferme of like devocions of the diocese of Exetour letten to Henry Thornetone ~~John Tyler for £4 by yere as apperith by an abligacion with condicion~~ } £6 13s. 4d.

f. 54v

Also with the ferme of like devocions of the citie of London lettene to ferme by indenture for one yere to Walter Sheffelde, proctour, for £21 10s. for the tyme of this accompte } £21 10s.

Also receyvede of John Tyler for the arrerages of the devocions of London by hym due for the tyme of his occupying of the prouctorship of the same, £3 19s. 4d. in fulle payment of his saide arrerages } £3 19s. 4d.

Also receyved of the wardeyns of the Felisshipe of Wexchaundelers of London for an anuelle rent of 20s. by yere } 20s.

Also of Nicholas Williams of Chepstow in the Marches of Wales and Edmonde Turnour of London, gentilmane } 30s.

Summa } £92 2s. 4d.

Summa totalis of alle the receites } £178 11s. 5d.

Wherof

[70] The saide accomptauntes accoumpt in paymentes ordinary to be made in the crowdes of the saide cathedralle churche to sundry ministers of the same church beyng present and kepyng divine service there, of and in the saide festes of Transfiguracione and Name of Jhu', and masse of Requiem in likewise on the morow than next after for the saide Fraternitie, that is to say: To the subdeane beyng present at alle the premisses and synging the high mas in the saide feastes, for eyther day 2s., in alle 4s. Also to 8 chauntery preestes bering copes in the saide festes of Transfiguracione and Name of Jhu' in rewarde 13s. 4d.[61] Also to 12

---

60   53s. written over an erasure.
61   13s. written over an erasure.

peticanons 40s. And to 6 vicars 16s. 8d. Also to every high canon, peticanone, chauntery

f. 55r

preestes, vicars and choresters beyng present and berying copes in the saide feastes 4d., in alle 25s. 8d. Also to a petycanone synging the masse of Requiem ande redyng the Pistelle and Gospelle at the 3 masses afore expressede and for saying of *De profundes* [sic] 2s. 10d. Also for the collacion made there at the highmas in the said feast of Name of Jħu 3s. 4d. Also to the sacristen for garnysshing of auters and for beryng of bokes and other ornamentes 3s. 10d. Also to 4 vergers there beyng attendaunt, to every of theyme 16d. with 20d. in rewarde this yere, 6s. 8d. Also to the belle ringers for their labours in the saide feastes, besides 20s. to theym paide quarterly for kepyng of the dores of the saide crowdes 12s. 8d. In all } £6 9s.

Also for the masses of Jhu' solempnely by note kept in the saide crowdes by the subdeane, a cardinalle, a peticanone and by 10[62] choresters and 6 vicars of the saide cathedralle churche in their abbettes and surplices, and to a chaunttery preest synging the masse of Requiem by note every Fryday ynmediatly after the saide masse of Jhu' with 6 of the saide choresters, that is to say: To the subdeane beyng present 4d. To the peticanone synging the saide masse of Jhu' 8d. And to the chauntery prest synging the said masse of Requiem 4d. And to every of the saide 6 choresters 4d. In alle, for 46 Frydaies within the tyme of this accompt } £7 13s. 4d.

Also to one of the vicars, maister of the saide choresters, kepyng 3 *salves* daily in the saide crowdes after Complyn done in the same cathedralle churche, before the ymages of Jhu', our Blessede Lady and Seynt Sebastian, and takyng for his labour 26s. 8d. at 4 termes of the yere according to the saide ordenaunce } 26s. 8d.

Also to the belle ringers of the saide cathedralle churche for their labours and daily attendaunces in openyng, closyng and shetting of dores of the saide crowdes, rynging of belles, blowing of organs, lyghting and quenchyng of torches and other lighetes, sweping and makyng clene of the saide crowdes at 20s. by yere paiable quarterly, besides 12s. 8d. for them allowede in the saide feastes } 20s.

f. 55v

Also for the rewarde of the saide Wardeyns this yere, lymytede and taxed

---

[62]   The figure looks as though it was corrected from 5.

by the saide Rectour and Assistence accordyng to the said ordenaunces
£4 ~~and over that to the said Richard Smythe in rewarde this yere~~ } £4

Also for their lyveres of clothing for the saide Wardeyns withe
conysaunces of the Name of Jħu, lymytede in likewise by the saide
Rectour and Assistantes } £4

Also to John Worsoppe for the engrosing and makyng of this accompt } 20s.

Also to John Onehande [erasure], sexten, entending daily in the saide
crowdes, kepyng the vestmentes and other ornamentes of the saide
Fraternitie, for thre quarters of a yere and an halff within the tyme of
this accompt, takyng 40s. by yere } 35s

Also to the prechers at Poules Crosse and Seint Mary Spitelle, remembryng
and preying for the soules of alle the bretherne and susterne of the saide
Fraternitie according to the saide ordenaunces, that is to say: For 46
Sondaies and Goode Fryday at Paules Crosse and 3 daies in Ester Weke
at Seint Mary Spitelle Summa } 16s. 8d.

Also to the 6 weites with baners payntede, conisaunces enbrowderede
with Jħūs, goyng alle the stretes and subbarbes of London pleying with
theire instrumentes to gif warnyng and knowledge to the people of the
saide Fraternitie for the saide festes of Transfiguracione and Name of
Jħu', according to the saide ordenaunce 10s., and in rewarde 3s. In alle
within the tyme of this accompte } 13s.

Also to the prouctour of the saide Fraternitie for the bonefire before the
northe dore of the saide crowdes yerely in the evyne of the saide feast
of the Name of Jħu' 2s. 8d. Also for lyveres gevyne to the king and the
quene and other grete
f. 56r
estates and for the Assistentes and their wifes, and for other smale
lyveres for the bretherne and susterne of the saide Fraternitie 58s. 2d.
In alle, *summa* } £3 10d.

Also paide for synging brede, for brede for haly brede, and for wyne
spent in the saide crowdes in the tyme of this accompt } 28s. 4d.

Also for wexe spent in the saide crowdes besides the wexe there founde
by the Wexechaundelers this yere, as apperith by abille of parcelles in
the tyme of this accompt } 43s.

[71] Also in sundry expences necessary, that is to say: For 2 cordes for a belle and the lampe in the crowdes 6d. Also for scoring of lampes, candelstikkes and cruettes 15d. Also for 2 kaies and mending of a lok 7d. Also for mending of the belle 6d. Also for mending of the pue in the crowdes and for nailes and lyme and for the workemanship of the same 8s. 8d. Also for russhis and garlondes on Jhūs day 3s. Also for gresing of belles 10d. Also for punysshing of falce proctours 2s. Also for mending of bookes belonging to the saide crowdes 15s. Also for wasshing of clothes, that is to say awter clothes, corpores, surplices ande other lynene 4s. 6d. Also for 16 quartes oile at 4d. the quart, and for 4 dossene candelle at 12d. the dossene, 9s. 4d. Also for costes to Knolle[63] to get lysaunce of my lorde of Canterbury for proctours, for a man and a horsse for 2 daies, 5s. 4d. Also to John Tyler for the labour he toke at the said feastes 20s. Also to Maister Buttry[64] for a doblet cloth of satyne gevyne to Master Potkyne 25s. 8d. Also to 3 porters for kepyng of the dores in the said feastes 3s. Also paide to John Worsoppe for a paire of endentures made for Walter Sheffelde of the ferme of the devocions of London 3s. 4d. Also for the writing of 2 tables of Jhūs 2s. Also paide to the said John Worsoppe for the hire of his servant and hors for 4 daies to get the pardone seallede at Canterbury by the Lorde Legat,[65] and for the writing of the saide pardone 10s. Also paid to his servaunt for the seale of the Legat, and his expences in ryding to Canterbury, as by abille of parcelles dothe appere 15s. 4d. In alle, *summa* } £6 10s. 10d.

f. 56v

[72] Also to the almoyner of Poules for 10 gownes for 10 choresters of the saide cathedralle churche servyng God in the saide crowdes, aswelle in the saide feastes of Transfiguracione and Name of Jhu' as at every Fryday at masse of Jhu' and Requiem, and also at the *salves* there kept by the saide Fraternitie, £4. And in rewarde this yere 3s. 4d. In alle } £4 3s. 4d.

Also to John Wales, John Wynnynghaum, William Russelle and William Banene, poremene appoyntede to the almes of the saide Fraternitie, kepyng the crowdes, helpyng preestes at masse and preying for alle the bretherne and susterne of the saide Fraternitie, every of theyme 40s. by yere paiable quarterly according to the saide ordenaunce, £8. And over that in the feastes of Transfiguracione and Name of Jhu' 20d. Also to preestes ande pore men on Alle Solowene Day in almes 7s. 6d. In alle } £8 9s. 2d.

---

63   Knole House (Kent), a residence of the archbishop of Canterbury.
64   Possibly William Botry, mercer, future warden of the Jesus Guild.
65   Thomas Wolsey, (d. 1529) cardinal archbishop of York and papal legate.

Also paide to Maister Worsoppes servaunt for his labour in writyng of this accompt } 3s. 4d.

[73] Also in sundry potacions necessary, that is to say: For a portacione had at the Myghter for dyvers of the Assistentes 17d. Also for a portacione at the chosing of the Wardeyns 7s. 3d. Also spent at the audite of John Broune 20s. Also for the dyner onn Jhūs day £4. Also for 5 barrelles and a kylderkene of ale and a nother of beer in the said feastes 22s. Also to a womane for servyng of ale 8d. Also for mete and drynke for 5 daies for them that kept the crowdes 4s. 6d. Also spent at the Starr in Chepe 10d. Also for glasing in the crowdes 8s. Also spent at certyne tymes upone the Assistentes and other straungers commyng to Jhus masse and upone the proctours 40s. In alle } £9 4s. 8d.

f. 57r

Summa of alle the saide paymentes } £63 17s. 2d.

And so remaynethe due to the saide Fraternitie } £114 14s. 3d.

Wherof

[74] John Copwoode by bille } 53s. 4d.

The Felisshippe of Wexchaundelers } 6s. 8d.

Henry Thornetone, sergeant of armes, and William Mark of Liscarde in the countie of Cornewalle, by obligacione for 2 yeres (£)13 s̶ (6s.) 4̶d̶. (8d.), and for the devocions of the diocese of Exetour for one hole yere in the accompt of John Broune and Richarde Smythe without obligacone, £6 13s. 4d. *Summa* } £26 13s. 4d.

John Tailour of the diocese of Seint Asse by obligacione } 6s. 8d.

Henry Story of Welles by obligacione } £3

Walter Sheffelde proctour of London } 40s.

Nicholas S̶m̶y̶t̶h̶ (Williams) of Chepstow in the Marches of Wales and Edmonde Turnour of London, gentilman } 30s.

Summa } £36 10s.

Rest delyverede to William Bromewelle and Stevene Warde the receyours of this accompte } £78 4s. 3d.

The whiche some of £78 4s. 4̶ 3d. the saide Richarde Smythe hath delyverede unto William Bromewelle (and Stevyne Warde) before the awditours according to the saide ordenaunce, the whiche ys put in to the chest belonging to the saide Fraternitie, except £20 remaynenyng in the handes of the said William according to the ordenaunce aforemade.

Per me John Munk
Per me Hary Hylle
Per me Thomas Hynde
Per me Thomas Nyccolles } Audytoures[66]

f. 57v

[75] Obligacions deliverede by thandes of Richard Smyth, accomptaunt, unto thandes of William Bromewelle and Stevyne Warde, Wardens for this yere next ensuyng, that is to say frome Christemas in the 10th yere of the reigne of kyng Henry the 8th unto the feast of Christemas thane next ensuyng [1518].

First an obligacione of Nicholas Smythe of Cambridge of } £10

Item an obligacione and an endenture of the same Nicholas for the ferme of the diocese of Elie, Durham, Norwiche and Carlile } [No amount]
Item an obligacione of John Tyler of Coventre, yomane of } £10
Item an obligacione of Richard Ynskype and Robert Olyver of 5 marces, to pay 33s. 4d.} 33s. 4d.
Item an obligacione of Henry Story and William Graunthaum of £5, to pay 4 marces } 4 marces
Item an obligacione of William Mynskype, John Ferster and John Baker of £6, to pay £5 } £5
Item an obligacione of Thomas Norrys and Thomas Highaum of £4, to pay 40s. } 40s.
Item an obligacione of Thomas Rocheforde and Raufe Sherwode of 5 marces, to pay 40s. } 40s.
Item an obligacione of Roger Robyns of £5, to pay } £5
Item an obligacione of Hamnet Holbroke of } 20s.
Item an endenture made to John Tyler of alle the devocions of Worcetour, Herforde, Coventre and Lychfelde } [No amount]
Item an endenture of Hughe Hattone made for the archedeconry of Chestre } [No amount]
Item an obligacione of Henry Story and John Tyler of £4, wherof receyved 20s., so restith due } £3
f. 58r
Item an obligacione of John Tailour of 13s. 4d., wherof receyvede 6s. 8d. and so restith due } 6s. 8d.
Item an obligacion of Nicholas Williams of 40s., to pay 30s., wherof receyvede *nichille* [nothing]} 30s.
Item an endenture and an obligacione of Walter Sheffelde for the

---

[66] Monk, Hylle, and Nyccolles are signatures; Hynde is close to the hand of the main scribe, but could also be a signature. 'Audytours' in hand of main scribe.

devocions of London lettene to hyme for a yere for £21 10s., wherof receyvede £19 10s. and so resteth due } 40s.

Item an obligacione of Henry Thornetone of 20 marces, to pay 10 marces } 10 marces

Item a bille of John Copwoode of 53s. 4d. } 53s. 4d.

f. 58v

[76] This is the accompte of William Bromwelle and Stephen Warde, Wardeynes of the Fraternitie of the Name of Jĥu in the crowdes of the cathedrall churche of Seynt Paule of London, frome the feast of Christemas in the yere of our lorde Gode accomptede by the churche of England 1519, and in the 11ᵗʰ yere of the reigne of kyng Henry the 8ᵗʰ, that is to say by one hole yere.

Fyrst the said accomptauntes bene chargede with tharrerages due by the said William Bromwell and Stephene Warde in the last accompte, as in the fote of the same accompte more playnly doth appere } £78 4s. 3d.

Also with tharrerages of John Copwood as apperith by dyverse specialties delyverede to the said accomptauntes } 53s. 4d.

Also with tharrerages of the Wexchaundlers of London for a quyssyone by theime lost } 6s. 8d.

[77] Also with the rentes and fermes of two tenementes and certeyne londes in the townys and feldes of Uxbridge in the counties of Middlesex and Bukingham lettene to William Bayly and Jamys Standale for 29s. 8d. by yere, payable at the feastes of Seynt Mighelle Tharchaungell and Thannunciacione of our Blessede Lady by evyne porcions, that is to say for the same feastes falling within the tyme of this accompte } 29s. 8d.

Also with the ferme of alle the devocions of the said Fraternytie belonging in the dioces of Norwitche, Elie, Durham and Carlile lettene to Nicholas Smyth of Cambridge by indenture for a yere within the tyme of this accompte } £20

Also with the ferme of like devocions of the dioces of Worcetour, Chester and Herfforde lettene to John Tyler of Coventre for £10 within the tyme of this accompte } £10

Also with the ferme of like devocions of parte of the counties of Essexe and Hertfforde lettene to Thomas Rocheforde as apperith by obligacione to pay 40s. for the tyme of this accompte } 40s.

f. 59

Also with the ferme of like devocions of the other parte of the said counties of Essexe and Hertfford lettene to Thomas Norrys for 40s. by yere for the tyme of this accompte } 40s.

Also with the ferme of like devocions of the dioces of Canterbury and

Chechestre lettene to Richard Inskippe of the citie off Chechestre and Robert Olyver, citezeine and fremasone of London, due for the tyme of this accompte } 33s. 4d.

Also with the ferme of like devocyons of the diocese of Kanterbury lettene to William Mynskippe of Canturbury, yoman, due in the tyme of this accompte } £5

Also with the ferme of like devocions of the diocese of Bathe and Welles lettene to Henry Story of Welles in the countie off Somerset and William Graunthaum, citezeine and merchaunte taylour of London, due in the tyme of this accompte } 53s. 4d.

Also with the ferme of like devocions in the diocese of Wintone and Sarum lettene to Roger Robyns, citezeine and haberdassher of London, within the tyme of this accompt } £5

Also with the ferme of like devocyons in the diocese of Seynt Asse lettene to John Taylour for 6s. 8d. } 6s. 8d.

Also with the ferme of like devocions of the diocese of Exetour lettene to Henry Story and John Tyler for £4 by yere as apperith by an obligacyone with condicione } £4

Also with the ferme of like devocyons of the citie of London lettene to ferme by indenture for one yere to Walter Sheffelde, prouctour, for £20 10s. for the tyme off this accompte } £20 10s.

Also with the devocions of the dioces of Exetour lettene to William Marke of Lyscard and Henry Thorntone as apperith by obligacione } £6 13s. 4d.

Also receyvede of the Wardeyns of the Felisshippe offe Wexchaundlers of London for an annuelle rent of 20s. by yere } 20s.

Also of Nicholas Williams of Chepstow in the Marches of Wales and Edmond Turnour of London, gentilmane } 30s.

f. 59v

Also of the bequest of Robert Berelle, grocer } 3s. 4d.

Also gevyne by William Stathum,[67] mercer } 3s. 4d.

Also of the bequest of Robert Serle,[68] brewer } 6s. 8d.

Summa totalis of alle the charges and receites } £164 13s. 11d.

Wheroff

[78] The said accomptauntes accoumpte in paymentes ordynary to be made in the crowdes of the said cathedrall churche to sundry ministers of the same churche being present and keping divyne service there, and in the said feastes of Transfiguracione and Name of Jhu' and masse

---

[67] William Statham, d. 1525. See Sutton, *Mercery*, esp. 215, 46in., 54in.
[68] TNA, PCC PROB 11/20/56.

of Requiem in like wise onn the morow thane next after for the said Fraternitie, that is to say: To the subdeane being present at alle the premysses and synging the highmas in the said feastes, for eyther day 2s., in alle, 4s. To 8 chauntry prestes bering coopes in the said feastes of Transfiguracone and Name of Jhu', in rewarde 13s. 4d. To 12 peticanons 40s. To 6 vicars 16s. 8d. To every highe canone, peticanone, chauntry prestes, vicars and choresters being present and bering copes in the said feastes 4d., in alle 26s. To a peticanone synging the masse of Requiem and reding the Pistille and Gospelle at the 3 masses afore expressede and for saying of *De profundis* 2s. 10d. Also for the collacione made there at the highmas in the said feast of Name of Jhu' 3s. 4d. To the sacristene for garnisshing of awters and for bering of bookes and other ornamentes 3s. 10d. To 4 vergers there being attendaunt, to every of theime 16d. with 20d. in rewarde this yere, 6s. 8d. Also to the bell ryngers for their labour in the said feastes besides 20s. to theime paid quarterly for keping of the dores of the saide crowdes, 12s. In alle } £6 8s. 8d.

f. 60r

Also for the masses of Jhu solemply by note kept in the saide crowdes by the subdeane, a cardenalle, a petycanone and by 10 choresters and 6 vicars of the said cathedralle churche in their habittes and surplices, and to a chauntry preest synging the masse of Requiem by note every Fryday immediatly after the said masse of Jhu' with 6 of the said choresters, that is to say: To the subdeane being present 4d. To the petycanone singing the saide masse of Jhu' 8d. And to every of the saide 6 choresters 4d. And to the chantry prest singing the said masse of Requiem 4d. In alle, for 45 Frydays within the tyme of this accompt } £7 10s.

Also to one of the vycars, maister of the saide choresters, kepyng 3 *salves* daily in the said crowdes, after Compleyne done in the same cathedralle churche, bifore the images of Jhu', our Blessed Lady and Seynt Sebastyane, and taking for his labour 26s. 8d. at 4 termes of the yere according to the said ordenaunce } 26s. 8d.

Also to the belle ryngers of the said cathedralle churche for their labour and daily attendaunces in openyng, closyng and shettyng of dores of the said crowdes, ringing of belles, blowing of organs, lighting and quenching of torches and other lightes, sweping and making clene of the said crowdes, at 20s. by yere payable quarterly besides 12s. 8d. for theime allowede in the said feastes } 20s.

[79] Also for the rewarde of the said Wardeyns that [sic] yere, lymittede and taxede by the said Rectour and Assistence according to the said ordenaunce £4 } £4

Also for their lyveres of clothing for the said Wardeyns with conysaunces of the name of Jhu', limyttede in like wise by the said Rectour and Assistaunces } £4

Also to John Worsoppe for thengrossing and making of this accompte } 20s.

Also to the prechers at Poules Crosse and Seynt Mary Spytelle remenlbring [sic] and praying for the soules of alle the bretherne and susterne of the saide Fraternitie according to the saide ordenaunce, that is to say for 44 Sondays and Good Fryday at Poules Crosse and 3 dayes in Ester Weke at Seynt Mary Spitelle at 8d. every Sonday. *Summa* } 32s.

f. 60v
Also to John Onehande, sextene, entending daily in the said crowdes, keping the vestmentes and other ornamentes of the said Fraternitie for a hole yere within the tyme of this accompt, taking 40s. by yere } 40s.

Also to the 6 weites with banars payntede, conysaunces enbrowderede with Jħus, going alle the stretes and subbarbes of London pleying with their instrumentes to gyfe warnyng & knowlege to the people of the said Fraternitie for the said feastes of Transfiguracone and Name of Jhu', according to the said ordenaunce 10s., and in rewarde 3s. In alle within the tyme of this accompt } 13s.

Also to the proctour of the said Fraternitie for the bonfyre before the north dore of the said crowdes yerely in the evyne of the said feast of the Name of Jhu' 2s. 8d.; and for cressytt light for the same bonfyre 2d.; and for lyveres gyvene to the worshipfulle persones of the Assistence & to the Wexchaundlers at 4d. the pece; and for lyveres delyverede to the proctour of London from Christemas to Middesomer } 36s.

Also paid for singing brede, for brede for holy brede, and for 43 galons of wyne spent in the said crowdes in the tyme of this accompte } 38s. 3d.

Also for wexe spent in the said crowdes besides the wexe founde there by the Wexchaundlers this yere, as apperith by a bille of parcelles in the tyme of this accompte } 54s. 11d.

Also to the almoyner of Poules for 10 gownes for 10 choresters of the said cathedralle churche servyng Gode in the saide crowdes, aswell in the said feastes of Transfiguracione and Name of Jhu' as at every Fryday at masse of Jhu' and Requiem, and also at the *salves* there kept by the said Fraternitie, £4. And in rewarde this yere 3s. 4d. In alle } £4 3s. 4d.

Also to John Marchaunt, John Smyth, John Bayntone and John Mussedge, poremene appoyntede to the almes of the said Fraternitie, keping the crowdes, helping prestes at masse and praying for alle the bretherne and susterne of the saide Fraternitie, every of theime 40s. by yere payable quarterly according to the saide ordenaunce, £8; and over that in the feastes of Transfiguracone and Name of Jhu' 20d. Also to preestes and pore mene onn Jhus day in almes 6s. 8d. In alle } £8 8s. 4d.

f. 61r

[80] Also in sundry expences necessary, that is to say: To Onehande for mendyng of 4 surplices, for turnyng and making of ann awter cloth of white damaske for Jhus awter, for scoryng of 8 candelstikes, 4 basons, the great braunche, the lampe, and for coles, bromes, holy, ive, pacthrede, pynnys [and] nayles spent in the hanging of the crowdes, 7s. 1d. For wasshing of alle the lynnene clothes belonging to the said crowdes and setting onn the parawbes onn the vestmentes 10s. Paid for botehyre at dyverse tymes 6d. Paid to Bamen by the comaundement of the Assistence at the discharging hym of his servyce of the said Fraternitie 10s. Also the same day in brede and wyne amonge the Assistence 18d. In expences going to Uxbridge to vew the londes and tenementes belonging to the saide Fraternitie, whiche was vewede by William Bromwelle, John Mathew and Thomas Hynde at the desyre of the Assistence, that is to say; for horse hyre, the charges of theime selffe, and their servantes 19s. 8d., [and] to Water Sheffelde which rode bifore to Uxbridge 2s. 4d., *summa* 22s. In expences for the sute of William Marke of Lyscarde and Henry Thorntone for tharrages of the dioces of Exetour, 12s. 3d. For 3 hengis, a lokke, a key and for mendyng of a chest in the crowdes, with a key for the Wardeyns pew dore, with other necessaryes 3s. 3d. For stuff and making of 4 quyssions of sarcenet of the colours of violet and blew whiche the Wardeyns were wont to were 8s. For mendyng of the belle at the crowdes dore with a new rope 16d. For 3 galowns and a quarte of lampe oyle 3s. 10d. For 5 doseine *dimidium* of tallow candelle 6s. 10d. For mendyng of a clapper for the great belle 6s. 8d. For a hoggehedde of wyne gyvene to maister deane[69] in rewarde for making and directing of dyverse letters unto dyverse bissoppes to suffre the proctours to gather in their dioces 25s. For 5 barrelles of ale, a kilderkyne of bere and for brede spent at the feast of Jhus 21s. 6d. To 4 porters kepyng the dores [at] the saide feastes 4s. For 2 womene taking the charge of the masars and drawing of ale 2s. 4d. To the 4

---

69   Either John Colet (d. 1519) or Richard Pace (d. 1536).

pore mene for their attendaunce 16d. To Onehande for watching and gevyng attendaunce 3 nyghtes 16d. For 2 stone pottes 2d. For flowers and garlandes at the said feast 3s. 4d. For russhes and bowes 7d. For mete for mene gevyng attendaunce by the space of 3 days 4s. 3d. To the choresters brekefastes at 2 severell tymes 16d. To the pore mene at dyverse tymes 2s. 6d. Also to John Worsoppe for a peire of endentures made bitwene the saide accomptauntes and Walter Sheffelde 3s. 4d. For an inventory of the goodes, juelles and ornamentes of Jhūs 3s. 4d. For wyne gyvene to Maister Meryng spent at the Sonne in Fletestrete onn certeyne of the Assistence 14d. For taking downe and setting uppe of the claper ~~of the great~~ of the great belle [and] tallowing and dressing of the belles 20d. For a pully of brasse and a rope for the lampe 5s. } £8 15s. 5d.

[81] Also in sundry potacions necessary, that is to say: At the electione of the Wardeyns 4s. 11d. Also at the awdytt
f. 61v
of Maister Smyth 20s. Also for the dynner on Jhūs day £4. Also the said accomptauntes axene allowaunce for charges spent uppone the Assistence and other straungers comyng to Jhus masse and uponn the proctours, as byfore tyme hath bene allowede, 40s. Spent at the Horsehedde in Chepe amonge certeyne of the Assistence at the graunting of the lease of John Tyler 16d. } £7 6s. 3d.

Also in ornamentes and other stuff bought to thuse of the said Fraternitie, that is to say: 2 vestmentes of white tewke for Lent without awbes 16s. Paid by the comaundment of the Aldermene and of alle the Assistence for 55 yerdes 3 quarter of blacke sarcenett for 24 hoddes at 8s. the yerde, *summa* £22 6s. For makyng and lynyng of the said hoddes 26s. For a shete to ley the hoddes in 12d. } £24 9s.

Summa totalis of alle the said paymentes } £89 22d.

And so remaynith due to the said Fraternytie } £75 12s. 1d.

Wheroff

John Copwoode by bille } 53s. 4d.
The Felisshippe of Wexchaundlers } 6s. 8d.
John Tyler and Henry Storige } 40s.
Hamlett Holbroke } 20s.
William Marke and Henry Thornetone } £6 13s. 4d.
John Taylour } 6s. 8d.
Nicholas Willyams } 10s.

Richard Inskyppe } 6s. 8d.
William Mynskippe } 50s.
Walter Sheffeld } £3 10s.

Summa } £19 16s. 8d.

f. 62r
Rest delyverde to Stephene Warde and Thomas Hynde, the receyvours of this accompte } £55 15s. 5d.

The whiche said somme of £55 15s. 5d. the saide William Bromwell hath delyverede unto the said Stephene Warde and Thomas Hynde bifore the awdytours accordyng to the said ordenaunce. The whiche is putte into the chest belonging to the said Fraternitie, except £20 remaynyng in thandes of the said Stephene, whiche the saide Stephene hath receyved in golde at the gevyng upp of this accompt.

And so restith in the chest of the tresory } £35 15s. 5d.

Per me John Sandelle[70]
Per me Johannem Mathew
Per me Johannem Browne[71]
Per me Elys Draper

f. 62v
[82] Obligacions delyverede by thandes of Willam Bromwelle, accomptaunt, unto thandes of Stephene Warde and Thomas Hynde, Wardeyns for this yere next ensuyng, that is to say frome Christemas in the 12th yere of the reigne of king Henry the 8the [1520] unto the feast of Christemas thane next ensuyng.

Fyrst an obligacone of Nicholas Smyth of Cambridge of - £10, and £10 in money by the said Nicholas to the said Stephene paide.
Iteme, an obligacone with an indenture of the same Nicholas of 40 marces to fulfille covenaunttes }
Item an obligacone of Thomas Rochefforde and Rauffe Sherwoode of 5 marces, to pay 40s. } 40s.
Item ann obligacone of Roger Robyns of £5, to pay } £5
Item ann obligacone of Walter Sheffelde and Thomas Lamb of £40, to pay £20 10s. with an endenture } £20 10s.

---

70   Signatures.
71   Large Tau cross drawn before Browne's name, which appears to be a signature.

131

Item an obligacone of William Marke of Lyscarde with two sewrties of £20, to pay 10 marces } 10 marces

Item ann obligacone of Henry Storige of Welles for sewertie of Willyam Marke of 10 marces }

Item ann obligacone of John Tyler of Coventre and Richarde Harrys of London of £10, with an endenture of the same John Tyler }

Item ann obligacone of Hugh Hattone, brewer, and William Danyelle with an endenture of 33s. 4d. whiche they pay for John Tyler } 33s. 4d. Also, the said John Tyler hath paid to Stephene Warde } 6s. 8d.

Item ann obligacone of John Taylour of 26s. 8d., due } 6s. 8s.

Item ann obligacone of Richarde Inskippe and Robert Olyver of 5 marces, to pay 36s. 8d. } 36s. 8d.

Item ann endenture of the same Richarde Inskippe, with an obligacone of £20 to fulfille coveneuntes }

f. 63r

Item ann obligacone of John Tyler and Henry Storyge of £6, to pay £4, due } 40s.

Item ann obligacone of Henry Storyge and Walter Andrew of £6, to pay £4 } £4

Item ann obligacone of William Mynskipp of Caunturbury, John Foster and John Baker of £6, to pay £5, due } 50s.

Item ann obligacone of Hamlett Holbroke of Waryngtone of 40s., to pay 20s. } 20s.

Item ann obligacone of Thomas Norrys and Thomas Highaum of £4, to pay 40s. } 40s.

Item ann obligacone of Henry Storige of Welles of 40s.

f. 63v

[83] This is the accompte of Stephen Warde and Thomas Hynde, Wardeyns of the Fraternitie of the Name of Jhū in the crowdes of the cathedrall churche of Seint Paule of London, frome the feast of Christemas in the yere of oure lorde God accompted by the churche of Englonde 1520 and in the 12 yere of the reigne of kyng Henry the 8the, that is to say by the space of one hole yere.[72]

First the said accomptauntes bene charged with tharrerages due by the saide Stephene Warde and Thomas Hynde in the last accompte, as in the foote of the same accompte more playnly dothe appere } £55 15s. 5d. Also with therrerages of John Copwode } 53s. 4d.

[84] Also with the rentes and fermes of two tenementes and certeyne

---

[72] 'and in the 12 yere...hole year' appears to have been added after the preceding text and is written in a lighter ink and less formal hand.

londes in the townes and feldes of Uxbridge in the countie [sic] of Middlesex and Bukingham lettene to William Baily and Jamys Standalle for 29s. 8d. by yere, payable at the feastes of Seint Mighelle Tharchaungell and Thannunciacione of oure Blessede Lady by evyne porcyons, that ys to say for the same feastes falling withein the tyme of this accompte } 29s. 8d.

Also with the ferme of alle the devocions of the sayde Fraternitie belongyng in the dioces of Norwiche, Elie, Durham and Carlyle lettene to Nicholas Smythe of Cambridge by indenture for a yere within the tyme of this accompte } £20

Also with the ferme of like devocyons of the dioces of Worcetour, Chestour ande Herfforde lettene to John Tyler of Coventre for £10 within the tyme of this accompte } £10 6s. 8d.

Also with the ferme of lyke devocyons of parte of the counties of Essexe and Hertfforde lettene to Thomas Rochefforde as apperithe by obligacyone to pay 40s. for the tyme of this accompte } 40s.

f. 64r

Also with the ferme of lyke devocyons of the other parte of the saide counties of Essexe and Hertfforde lettene to Thomas Norrys for 40s. by yere for the tyme of this accompte } 40s.

Also with the ferme of lyke devocyons of the dyoces of Kent lettene to John Fooster, shermane, for £5 by yere for the tyme of this accompte } £5

Also with the ferme of lyke devocyons of the dyoces of Bathe and Welles lettene to Henry Storige of Welles in the countie of Somerset and William Graunthaum, citezeine and merchaunt taylour of London, due in the tyme of this accompte } 53s. 4d.

Also with the ferme of like devocions of the dioces of Wintone and Sarum lettene to Roger Robyns, citezeine ande haberdassher of London, within the tyme of this accompte } £5

Also with the ferme of like devocyons of the dyoces of Seint Asse lettene to John Taylour for 6s. 8d. } 6s. 8d.

Also with the ferme of like devocyons off the dioces of Kanter[bury] and Chichester lettene to Rycharde ~~Myn~~ Ynskyppe of the citie of Chichester and Robert Olyver, citezein and free masone of London, due for the tyme off this accompt } 33s. 4d.

Also with the ferme of like devocyons of the dioces of Exetour lettene to Henry Story and John Tyler for £4 by yere as apperithe by obligacyone with condicon } £4

Also with the ferme of like devocyons of the citie of London lettene by endenture to Water Shefelde, proctour, for £21 by yere for the tyme of this accompte } £21

f. 64v

Also with the ferme of like devocyons of the dioces off Exetour lettene to

133

William Marke of Lyscarde and Henry Thornetone by yere as apperithe by obligacyone } £6 13s. 4d.

Also of Hughe Hattone, citezeine and brewer of London, for the archedeconry of Chester and the Yle of Mane } 33s. 4d.

Also of Hamblet Holbroke of a duetie of 20s. by hyme due in the last accompte } 10s.

Also of the said John Fooster of a duetie of 50s. that was due by one Minskyppe of Caunturbury, as apperithe in the saide last accompte } 50s.

Also of the wardens of the Felysshyppe of Wexchaundelers of London for ann annuelle rente of 20s. by yere } 20s.

Also of the said wardeyns of Wexchaundelers for the rerage for a quyssyone by theyme loste } 6s. 8d.

Also of the bequest of one John Badbe } 12d.

Also for 2 lyverreys of golde } 38s.

Summa totalis of alle the charges and receiptes } £148 10s. 9d.

Wheroff

f. 65r

[85] The said accomptauntes accompte in paymentes ordinary to be made in the crowdes of the said cathedrall churche to sundrye ministres of the same churche being present and keping divine service there, and in the feastes of the Transfiguracione and Name of Jhū, and masse of Requiem in like wise onn the morow thane nexte after for the saide Fraternitie, that ys to say: To the subdeane being present at alle the premisses and singing the highemas in the saide feastes, for either day 2s., in alle 4s. To 8 chauntrye preestes beryng cooppes in the saide feastes of Transfiguracyone and Name of Jhū in rewarde 13s. 4d. To 12 petycanons 40s. To 6 vycars 16s. 8d. To every highe canone, petycanone, chauntry preestes, vycars and choresters being present and bering coopes in the said feastes 4d., in all 26s. To a petycanone singing the masse of Requiem and reding the Pystell and Gospell at the 3 masses bifore expressede ande for saying of *De profundis* 2s. 10d. Also for the collacyone made there at the highmas in the saide feast of Name of Jhū 3s. 4d. To the sacristene for garnysshing of awlters and for bering of bookes and other ornamentes 3s. 10d. To 4 vergers there being attendaunte, to every of theyme 16d. with 20d. in rewarde this yere, in alle 7s. And to the bell ryngers for their labour in the saide feastes besides 20s. to theime paid quarterly for keping of the dowres of the saide crowdes 10s. 4d. *Summa* } £6 7s. 4d.

Also for masses of Jhū solempnely by note kepte in the said crowdes by the subdeane, a cardenalle, a petycanone and by 10 choresters and 6 vycars of the said cathedrall churche in their habettes ande surplices, and to a chauntrie preest syngyng the masse of Requiem by note every Fryday ymmediatly after the saide masse of Jhū with 6 of the saide choresters, that ys to say: To the subdeane being present 4d. To the petycanone singyng the saide masse of Jhu 8d. And to the chauntrie preest singyng the masse of Requiem 4d. And to every of the saide choresters 4d. In alle for 45 Frydayes within the tyme of this accompte } £7 10s.

f. 65v

Also to one of the vycars, maister of the said choresters, kepying three *salves* dayly in the said crowdes after Compleyne done in the same cathedrall churche, bifore the ymages of Jhū, oure Blessede Ladye and Seint Sebastyane, and taking for his labour 26s. 8d. at 4 termes of the yere according to the said ordenaunce } 26s. 8d.

Also to the bell ryngers of the saide cathedrall churche for their labour and daily attendaunces in openyng, closyng and shittyng of dores of the saide crowdes, rynging of belles, blowing of organs, lighting and quenching of torches and other lightes, swepyng and making clene of the said crowdes, at 20s. by yere payable quarterly, besides 10s. 4d. for theyme allowede in the saide feastes, with 20d. in rewarde thys yere } 21s. 8d.

[86] Also for the rewarde of the said Wardeyns thys yere, lymyttede ande taxede by the said Rectour and Assistence accordyng to the saide ordenaunce £4, *summa* } £4

Also for their lyveres of clothing for the said Wardeyns with conysaunces of the Name of Jhū, lymytted in lyke wise by the saide Rectour and Assistence } £4

Also to John Worsoppe for thengrossing and makyng of this accompte } 20s.

Also to Onehande and Thomas Holmes entendyng dayly in the saide crowdes, kepyng the vestmentes ande other ornamentes of the saide Fraternitie for a hole yere within the tyme of this accompte, taking by yere 40s. } 40s.

Also to prechers at Poules Crosse and Seint Marye Spytell remembring and praying for the soules of alle the bretherne and susterne of the said

Fraternitie according to the said ordenaunce, that ys to say 44 Sonnedayes and Good Frydaye at Poules Crosse and thre dayes in Ester Weke at Seint Marye Spytell at 8d. every Sonnedaye, *summa* } 32s.

f. 66r

Also to the 6 weightes with baners payntede, conysaunces enbroderde with Jhūs, going alle the stretes and subarbes of London pleying with their instrumentes to gyve warnyng and knowlege to the people of the saide Fraternitie for the said feastes of Transfiguracyone and Name off Jhū, according to the saide ordenaunce 10s. and in rewarde 3s. In alle within the tyme of this accompte } 13s.

Also to the proctour of the said Fraternitie for the bonfyre bifore the northe doore of the said crowdes yerelye in the evyne of the said feast of the Name of Jhū 2s. 8d., and for cressytt light for the same bonfyre 2d. And for lyveres gyvene to the worshipfull persones off the Assistence ande to the Wexchaundelers at 4d. the pece } 17s. 8d.

Also paide for singing brede, for brede for haly brede, and for 39 galons of malmesseye spent in the said crowdes within the tyme of this accompte } 36s.

Also for wexe spente in the said crowdes besides the wexe foundede by the Wexchaundelers thys yere, as apperithe in a boke of parcelles in the tyme of this accompte } 43s. 10½d.

Also to [the] almoyner of Poules for 10 gownes for 10 choresters of the saide cathedralle churche servyng Gode in the saide crowdes, aswell in the saide feastes of Transfiguracyone and Name of Jhū as at every Frydaye at the masse of Jhū and Requiem, and also at the *salves* there kepte by the saide Fraternitie } £4 3s. 4d.

Also to John Merchaunte, John Smythe, John Bayntone and John Mussedge, pooremene appoyntede to the almes of the saide Fraternitie, keping the crowdes, helping preestes at masse and praying for alle the bretherne and susterne of the saide Fraternitie, to every of theime 40s. by yere payable quarterly according to the saide ordenaunce, £8. Also to preestes and poore mene onn Jhūs day in almes 8s. 4d. } £8 8s. 4d.

f. 66v

[87] Also in sundrye exspences necessarye, that ys to saye: First for wasshing of alle the lynnene clothes belonging to the saide crowdes, for

setting onn of the parawbys onn the vestementes, ande for mending of the awbys 12s. 6d. For scowering of the canstykes [sic], basons, lampe and braynches, and for nayles, pynnes, bromes, coles, a fyer panne, russhes and 2 hoopes for 2 garlondes, 4s. 6d. For 3 galons and a quarte of lampe oyle 3s. 2d. For a dozeine of tallowe candell 12d. For lyme and workemanshipp for whiting of the said crowdes 13s. 4d. For 1 100 *dimidium* of planke borde for the awlters and for 15 legges for the same 5s. 10½d. For 2 carpenters to leye the same plankes 16d. For brykk, lyme, sande ande for paving of the pavementes 11½d. For a lode of lyme for the awlters and the vawte 10d. For a plastorer ande his laborer by the space of 5 days 5s. 5d. For hanging uppe of a lytell belle 4d. For a rope and a key for the organs 5d. For pytche for the superalteryes, for a sconse and for mending of Jhus dore 5d. For making of a claper for the gret belle ande for tallowing of belles 18s. 4d. For payntyng of 18 Jhūs uppone pyllers 18d. For 4 vestement gurdelles ande for a snoffer for torches 6d. For 5 barelles of ale and a kylderkyne of bere, and for brede spent at the saide feast of Jhūs 21s. 4d. To 3 porters keping the doores of the saide crowdes in the said feastes 3s. To 2 womene taking the charge of the masers and drawing of ale 2s. To the 4 poore mene for their attendaunce 16d. For flowres and garlondes at the said feaste 3s. 4d. To Thomas Holmes for watching 3 nyghtes 16d. For meete for the mene gyving their attendaunce the space of 3 dayes 2s. 8d. For the choresters brekefast at 2 severell tymes 2s. To a choresters for prycking of Jhūs masse 2s. 4d. For makyng of 5 new surplices 5s. And to Wa[l]ter Sheffelde in rewarde this yere 12d. *Summa* } £5 16s. 9d.

[88] Also in sundrye potacyons necessary, that ys to say: At the eleccyone of the Wardeyns 4s. 6d. Also at the awdytt of Maister Bromwelle 20s. Also for the dynner onn Jhūs day £4. Also the saide accomptauntes axene allowaunce for charges spent uppone the Assistence and other straungers commyng to Jhūs masse and uppone the proctours as byfore tyme hath bene allowede 40s. *Summa* } £7 4s. 6d.

f. 67r

Also in ornamentes and other stuff boughte to thuse of the said Fraternitie, that ys to saye: For 37 elles of lynnene clothe price the elle 6d., *summa* 18s. 9d. For the chaunging of 4 chaleseys, of the whiche 4 were made 3 new chaleseys, £5 7s. 2d., and for halowing of the same chaleseys 12d. *Summa* } £6 6s. 11d.

Summa totalis of alle the paymentes ys } £66 8s. ½d.

And soo remaynethe due to the said Fraternitie } £82 2s. 8½d.

Wherof

[89] John Copwood } 53s. 4d.
John Taylour } 6s. 8d.
Richard Inskyppe } 33s. 4d.
William Mark and Henrye Thornetone } £6 13s. 4d.

Summa } £11 6s. 8d.

Rest delyverede to Thomas Hynde and Stephene Lynne, the receyours
of this accompte } £70 16s. ½d.

The whiche said some of £70 16s. ½d. the saide Stephene Warde hathe
delyverede unto the said Thomas Hynde ande Stephene Lynne bifore
the awdytours according to the saide ordenaunce, the whiche ys put
into the chest belonging to the said Fraternitie excepte £20 remaynyng
in thandes of the said Thomas Hynde, whiche the saide Thomas Hynde
hathe receyvede at the geving upp of this accompte.

And so restithe in the chest of the tresory } £50 16s. ½d.

Per me John Munk
Per me Harry Hylle
Per me William Botery
Per me Herry Dakrs } Awdytours[73]

f. 67v

[90] Obligacions delyverede by thandes of the saide Stephene Warde,
accomptaunt, unto thandes of Thomas Hynde ande Stephene Lynne,
Wardeyns for this yere nexte ensuyng, that ys to say frome Christemas
in the 13[74] yere of the reigne of king Henrye the 8th [1521] unto the feast
of Christemas thane nexte ensuyng.

Fyrst ann endenture of Nicholas Smythe of Cambridge, with ann obligacyone
of 40 marces to fulfyll covenauntes.
Item ann obligacyone of Roger Robyns of £5 sterling, to pay } £5
Item ann endenture of Walter Sheffelde and Thomas Lambe with an
obligacyone of £40 to fulfyll covenauntes.
Item ann obligacyone of William Mark with two sewerties of £20, to
pay 10 marces } 10 marces
Item ann obligacyone of Henry Storyge of Welles for sewertie of
William Mark aforesaid of 10 marces, to pay } 10 marces
Item ann obligacyone of John Tyler of Coventre and Robert Kechyne,

---

73   Signatures. 'Awdytours' in hand of main scribe.
74   'xiij' in faint, shaky hand, possibly over an erasure.

citezene and talughchundeler of London, of £10 6s. 8d., to pay } £10 6s. 8d.

Item ann endenture of Hughe Hattone, citezeine and brewer of London, of 33s. 4d. sterlinges, whiche he payeth for John Tyler } 33s. 4d.

Item ann obligacyone of John Taylour of 26s. 8d. to pay 6s. 8d. } 6s. 8d.

Item ann ~~ann~~ obligacyone with ann endenture of John Foster, citezeine and shermane of London, with two sewerties of £10 to fullfyll covenaunntes } £10

Item ann endenture of John Tyler of Coventre [no ammount].

f. 68r

Item ann endenture of Rycharde Ynskyppe of the citie of Chichester in the countie of Sussexe, with ann obligacione of £20 to fulfyll covenauntes.

Item ann obligacyone of John Tyler and Henry Storige of £6, to pay £4 } £4

Item 2 obligacyons of Hammet Holbroke of 40s. a pece, to pay 20s. apece } 40s.

Item ann obligacyone of Thomas Norrys and Robert Nycolsone of £4, to pay 40s. } 40s.

Item ann obligacyone of Henry Storige of 40s., to pay } 40s.

Item ann obligacyone of Thomas Rochefforde of 5 marces, to pay 40s. *Summa* } 40s.

f. 68v[75]

[91] This is the accompte of Thomas Hynde and Stephene Lynne, Wardeyns of the Fraternitie or Guilde of the Name of Jhū in the crowdes of the cathedralle churche of Seint Paule of London, frome the feast of Christemas in the yere of oure lorde God accomptede by the Churche of Englonde 1521 and in the 13th yere of the reigne of king Henry the 8th, that ys to saye by the space of one hole yere.

First the said accomptauntes bene chargede with the arrerages due by the saide Thomas Hynde and Stephene Lynne in the last accompte, as in the foote of the same accompte more playnly dothe appere } £70 16s. ½d.

Also with the arrerages of John Copwoode } 53s. 4d.

[92] Also with the rentes and fermes of two tenementes and certene londes in the towne and feldes of Uxbridge in the countie [sic] of Middlesex and Bukingham lettene to William Baily and Jamys Standall for 29s. 8d. by yere payable at the feastes of Seint Mighell Tharchaungell

---

[75] Many of the section headings have an elaborate pen-flourished initial with a small guide-letter.

and Thannunciacione of oure Blessede Lady by evyne porcyons, that ys to say for the same feastes falling within the tyme of this accompte } 29s. 8d.

Also with the ferme of alle the devocyons of the saide Fraternitie belonging in the diocesses of Durham, Carlyle, Norwiche and Ely lettene to Nicholas Smyth of Cambridge by indenture for a yere within the tyme of this accompte } £20

Also with the ferme of like devocyons of the diocese of Worcetour, Chester and H Herfforde lettene to John Tyler of Coventre for £10 6s. 8d. within the tyme of this accompte } £10 6s. 8d.

Also with the ferme of parte of the counties of Essexe and Herfford [sic] lettene to Thomas Norrys for 40s. by yere for the tyme of this accompte } 40s.

f. 69r

Also with the ferme of like devocyons of the other parte of the said counties of Essexe and Herfford [sic] lettene to Thomas Rochefforde as apperithe by ann obligacione to pay 40s. for the tyme of this accompte } 40s.

Also with the ferme of like devocyons of the dioces of Kanter[bury] lettene to John Fooster for £5 by yere for the tyme of this accompte } £5

Also with the ferme of like devocyons of the dioces of Canter[bury] and Chichester lettene to Richard Ynskyppe of the citie of Chechester due for the tyme of this accompte } 33s. 4d.

Also with the ferme of like devocyons of the dioces of Bathe and Welles lettene to Henry Storyge of Welles in the countie of Somerset and William Graunthaum, citezeine and marchaunt taylour of London, due within the tyme of this accompte } 53s. 4d.

Also with the ferme of like devocyons of the dioces of Wintone and Sarum lettene to Roger Robyns, citezeine and haberdassher of London, within the tyme of this accompte } £5

Also with the ferme of like devocyons of the diocese of Exetour lettene to Henry Storige and John Tyler for £4 by yere as apperithe by ann obligacione with condicione } £4

Also with the ferme of like devocyons of the citie of London lettene by indenture to Walter Sheffelde, proctour, for £20 10s. for the tyme of this accompte } £20 10s.

Also with the ferme of like devocyons of the diocese of Exetour lettene to William Marke of Lyscarde and Henry Thornetone as apperithe by obligacione } £6 13s. 4d.

f. 69v

Also with the ferme of like devocyone of the dioces of Seint Asse lettene to Hamlett Holbroke for 20s. by yere due within the tyme of this accompte } 20s.

Also of Hughe Hattone, brewer, whiche he payeth for John Tyler } 33s. 4d.

Also of the Wardeyns of the Felysshippe of Wexchaundelers of London for ann annuell rente of 20s. by yere } 20s.

Also of Richarde Ynskypp of Chichester by thandes of Maister Stephene Warde of tharrerages due by the said Richarde, as in the fote of the last accompte more playnly shewithe } 20s.

***Summa totalis* of alle the charges and reyscytes ys }** £159 9s. ½d.

Wheroff

[93] The said accomptauntes accompte in paymentes ordinary to be made in the crowdes of the said cathedrall churche to sundry ministres of the same churche being present and keping dyvyne service there and in the said feastes of Transfiguracione and Name of Jhu, and masse of Requiem in lyke wise onn the morow thane nexte after for the said Fraternitie, that ys to say: To the subdeane being present at alle the permisses and singing highemas in the said feastes, for either day 2s., in alle 4s. To 8 chauntry preestes bering coopes in the said feastes of Transfiguracione and Name of Jhu' in rewarde 13s. 4d. To 12 petycanons 40s. To 6 vycars 16s. 8d. To every highe canone, petycanone, chauntry prestes, vycars and choresters bering [sic] present and bering coopes in the saide feastes 4d., in alle 24s. 8d. To a petycanone singing the masse of Requiem and reding the Pistell and Gospell at the 3 masses bifore exsspressede and for saying of *Deprofundis* 2s. 10d. Also for the collacione made there at the highmas in the said feast of Name of Jhu' 3s. 4d. To the sacristene for garnisshing of awlters and for bering of bokes & other ornamentes 3s. 10d. To 4 vergers there being attendaunt, to every of theme 16d., with 20d. in rewarde this yere, in alle 7s. And to the belle ringers for their labour in the said feastes besides 20s. to theme paide quarterly for keping of the doores of the saide crowdes, 11s. 8d. } £6 7s. 4d.

f. 70r

Also for the masses of Jhūs solempnely by note kepte in the said crowdes by the subdeane, a cardenall, a petycanone and by 10 choresters and 6 vycars of the said cathedrall churche in their habettes and surplyces, and to a chauntry preest singing the masse of Requiem by note every Frydaye ymmediately after the masse of Jhu' with 6 of the choresters, that ys to say: To the subdeane being present 4d.; to the petycanone singing the masse of Jhu' 8d.; and to a chauntry preest singing the masse of Requiem 4d.; and to every of the choresters 4d. In alle for 45 Frydays within the tyme of this accompte } £7 10s.

Also to one of the vycars, maister of the saide choresters, keping three *salves* daily in the saide crowdes after Complayne done in the same cathedrall churche, bifore the images of Jhū, oure Blessede Lady and Seint Sebastiane, taking for his labour 26s. 8d. at foure termes of the yere according to the saide ordenaunce } 26s. 8d.

Also to the belle ryngers of the said cathedrall churche for their labour and daily attendaunces in openynge, closing and shitting of the doores of the said crowdes, ryngyng of belles, blowing of orgayns, lighting and quenching of torches and other lightes, sweping and making clene of the said crowdes, at 20s. by yere payable quarterly besyde 11s. 8d. for theime allowed in the said feastes, with 20d. in rewarde this yere } 21s. 8d.

[94] Also for the rewarde of the Wardeyns this yere, lymittede and taxede by the saide Rectour and Assistence according to the saide ordenaunce £4 } £4

Also for their lyvereys of clothing for the saide Wardeyns with conysaunces of the Name of Jhū, lymittede in likewise by the saide Rectour and Assistence } £4

f. 70v
Also to John Worsoppe for making of this accompte } 20s.

Also to Thomas Holmes, sextene, entending daily in the saide crowdes, keping the vestmentes and other ornamentes of the said Fraternitie for a hole yere within the tyme of this accompte, taking by yere 40s. } 40s.

Also to prechers at Poules Crosse and Seint Mary Spyttell remembring and praying for the soules of alle the bretherne and susterne of the saide Fraternitie according to the saide ordenaunce, that is to say 44 Sondays and Good Fryday at Poules Crosse and 3 days in Ester Weke att Seint Mary Spyttelle at 8d. every Sonday } 32s.

Also to the 6 weightes with baners payntede, conysaunces enbroderd with Jhūs, going alle the stretes and subarbes of London pleying with their instrumentes to gyve warnyng and knowlage to the people of the said Fraternitie for the saide feastes of Transfiguracione and Name of Jhū, according to the said ordenaunce 10s. and in rewarde 3s. In alle within the tyme of this accompte } 13s.

Also to the proctour of the said Fraternitie for the bonfyre bifore the northe doore of the said crowdes yerely in the evyne of the saide feast of the Name of Jhū 2s. 8d., and for cressitt light for the same bonefyre 2d. And for lyveres gyvene to worshipfull persones of the Assistence and to the Wexchaundlers 11s. 8d. } 14s. 6d.

[95] Also paide for singing brede, for brede for holy brede, ande for 36 galons of malmesey spent in the saide crowdes in the tyme of this accompte } 34s. ½d.

Also for wex spent in the saide crowdes bysyde the wexe foundede by the Wexchaundlers this yere, as apperithe in a boke of parcelles in the tyme of this accompte } 50s. 8d.

f. 71r

Also to the almoyner of Poules for 10 gownes for 10 choresters of the said cathedrall churche servyng God in the said crowdes, aswell in the said feastes of Transfiguracione and Name of Jhu' as at every Fryday at masse of Jhū and Requiem,and at the *salves* there kepte by the said Fraternitie } £4 3s. 4d.

Also to John Marchaunt, John Smythe, John Bayntone and John Mussedge, poore mene appoyntede to the almes of the said Fraternitie, keping the crowdes, helping preestes at masse and praying for alle the bretherne and susterne of the saide Fraternitie, every of theime 40s. by yere payable quarterly according to the said ordenaunce £8. Also to preestes and poore mene onn Jhus day in almes 10s. 8d. } £8 10s. 8d.

Also to Maister Worsoppes servant for his labour in thengrossing uppe of this accompte } 3s. 4d.

[96] Also in sundry expences necessary, that ys to say: First for wasshing of alle the lynnene clothes belonging to the said crowdes, for setting onn of the parawbys onn the vestmentes and for mending of the awbys and vestementes 12s. 10d. For scowring of the candellstykkes, basons, lampe ande braunches, and for nayles, pynnes, bromes and coles and for russhes, 7s. 7½d. For 2 galons of lampe oyle 3s. 2d. For 2 dozeine of tallow candell 2s. 6d. For flowres, garlondes and erbys onn Jhūs day 3s. 4d. To a plastorer ande his laborer for whiting of the pillers and wyndowes in the churcheyarde by the space of 3 days 3s. 4d. Paide for 6 sackes of lyme 12d. For 5 barrelles of ale, a kilderkyne of bere, ande for brede spent in the said feast 21s. 4d. To 4 porters keping the doores of the crowdes 4s. To 2 womene taking the charge of the masers and

143

drawing of ale 2s. To Thomas Holmes for 3 nyghtes attendaunce 16d. To the 4 poore mene for their attendaunce 16d. For mete for the mene gyving their attendaunce 3 days 2s. 8d. For correcting of 6 quayres of playne songe 16d. And to Wa[l]ter Sheffeld in rewarde this yere 12d. } £3 8s. 10d.

f. 71v

[97] Also in ornamentes and other stuff bought to the use of the said Fraternitie, that is to say: First 2 vestmentes of white tewke with droppes for Lent 14s. Paide for 20 elles of white clothe for 4 albes at 6d. the elle, 10s. Paide for 13 yerdes *dimidium* [half] of bokeram to lyne the 4 vestmentes 5s. For 4 masse bookes printede in partechement £7. Paide for 21 yerdes of russet clothe for gownes for the poore mene £3 10s. Paide for a gret cheste to lay in the vestmentes 10s. And for the holowing of the vestmentes and 3 corperases and for the making of the 4 albes 20d. } £12 10s. 8d.

Also in sundry potacions necessary, that is to say: At the eleccione of the Wardeyns 5s. 6d.; at the awdytt of Maister Warde 20s.; also for the dyner onn Jhūs day £4. Also the said accomptauntes axene allowaunce for charges spent uppone the proctours, Assistence and other straungers commyng to Jhūs masse as bifore tyme hathe bene allowede 40s. In alle } £7 5s. 6d.

Summa totalis **of alle the paymentes is** } £70 11s. 10½d.

And so remaynethe due to the said Fraternitie } £88 17s. 2d.

Wherof

John Copwoode } 53s. 4d.
Henry Storige and William Graunthaum } 53s. 4d.
Henry Storige and John Tyler } £4
William Marke and Henry Thornetone } £6 13s. 4d.
Hamlett Holbroke } 20s.
Richarde Ynskyppe of Chichestere[76] } 13s. 4d.

Summa } £17 13s. 4d.

f. 72r

[98] Rest delyverede to Stephene Lynne and Henry Dakers, the recyvours of ths accompte } £71 17s. 2d.

---

76 'Chichestre' written over erasure.

The whiche saide some of £71 17s. 2d. the said Thomas Hynde hathe delyverede unto the said Stephene Lynne and Henry Dakers bifore the awdytours according to the saide ordenaunce. The whiche ys putt into the cheste belonging to the saide Fraternitie, excepte £20 remaynyng in the handes of the saide Stephene Lynne whiche the saide Stephene Lynne hathe receyvede att the gevyng uppe of this accompte.

And soo restith in the chest of the tresory } £51 17s. 2d.

Per me William Bromwelle[77]
Per me William Campyon
Per me Stephaunus Warde
Per me John Jossone

f. 72v

[99] Obligacions delyverede by thandes of the saide Thomas Hynde, accomptaunt, unto the handes of the saide Stephene Lynne and Henry Dakers, Wardeyns for this yere nexte ensuyng, that ys to say frome Christemas in the 14th yere of the reigne of king Henry the 8the [1522] unto the feast of Christemas thane nexte folowing.

First ann endenture of Nicholas Smythe of Cambridge with ann obligacione of 40 marces sterlinges to perfourme the covenauntes.
Item ann endenture of Walter Sheffelde with ann obligacione of the same Walter and one Thomas Lambe of £40 sterling to perfourme the covenauntes.
Item ann endenture of Richarde Ynskippe of the citie of Chechester within the countie of Sussexe with ann obligacione } [no amount]
Item ann endenture of Hughe Hattone, citezeine and brewer of London, of 33s. 4d. sterlinges whiche he paieth for John Tyler } 33s. 4d.
Item ann endenture of John Tyler of Coventre [no amount]
Item ann obligacione of John Tyler and Robert Kechyne, citezeine and talughchaundler of London, of £10 6s. 8d. } £10 6s. 8d.
Item ann obligacione of John Tyler of Coventre and Henry Storige of Welles, yomene, of £6, to pay £3 } £3
Item ann obligacione of Henry Storige of Welles of 40s., to pay } 40s.
Item ann obligacione of Henry Storige of Welles for sewertie of William Mark of Lyscarde of £6 13s. 4d., to pay £6 13s. 4d. } £6 13s. 4d.
f. 73r
Item ann obligacione of William Marke of Lyscarde with 2 sewerties of £20, to pay £6 13s. 4d. } £6 13s. 4d.

---

77   Signatures.

Item ann obligacione of Roger Robyns of London, haberdassher, of £5, to pay } £5
Item ann obligacione of Thomas Rochefforde and Rauff Sherwoode of 5 marces, to pay 40s. } 40s.
Item ann obligacione of Thomas Norreys and Robert Nicolsone of £4, to pay 40s. } 40s.
Item ann obligacione of Robert Bristow and Balthazar Guercii[78] of £10, to pay £5 } £5
Item ann obligacione of John Taylour of 26s. 8d. sterlinges, to pay 6s. 8d. } 6s. 8d.
Item 2 obligacions of Hamblet Holbroke of 40s. apece, to pay 20s. a pece } 40s.

f. 73v[79]

[100] This is thaccompte of Stephen Lynne and Henry Dakers, Wardeyns of the Fraternitie or Guylde of the Name of Jhū foundede in the crowdes in the cathedrall churche of Seint Paule of London, frome the feast of Christemas in the yere of oure lord God a thousaunde fyve hundrede twenty ande two, and in the 14th yere of the reigne of kyng Henry the 8the, that ys to say by the space of one hole yere.

First the said accomptauntes beene charged with tharrerages due by the said Stephen Lynne and Henry Dakers in the last accompte, as in the foote of the same accompte more playnly dothe appere } £71 17s. 2d.
Also with tharrerages of Henry Thornetone } £6 13s. 4d.
Also with tharrerages of John Coopwoode } 53s. 4d.
Also with tharrerages of Henry Storyge of Welles by obligacione £3, and for a yeres ferme of the dioces of Exetour lettene to the said Henry and John Tyler for £4 by yere £4 } £7
Also with tharrerages of Henry Storyge and William Graunthaum as apperith in the last accompte } 53s. 4d.
Also with tharrerages of Hamlett Holbroke as apperithe in the laste accompte } 20s.
Also with tharrerages of Rycharde Ynskypp of Chichester } 13s. 4d.

Summa totalis of alle tharrerages – £92 10s. 6d.

[101] Also with the fermes and rentes of two tenementes & certene londes lyng in the townes and feldes of Uxbrydges in the countie [sic]

---

78 Balthasar Guersie d. 1551, physician, surgeon to Katherine of Aragon and Henry VIII. See Margaret Pelling and Frances White, 'GUERSIE, Balthasar', in Physicians and Irregular Medical Practitioners in London 1550–1640 Database (London, 2004), on British History Online.
79 Large pen-flourished initial with guide-letter at start of account.

of Middlesex and Bukingham lettene to William Bayly and Jamys Standell for 29s. 8d. by yere, payable at the feastes of Seint Mighell and Thannunciacone of our Lady by evyne porcyons, that ys to say for the same feastes falling within the tyme of this accompte } 29s. 8d.

f. 74r

Also with the ferme of alle the devocyons to the said Fraternitie belonging of the dioces of Durhaum, Carlyle, Norwiche and Ely lettene to Nicholas Smythe of Cambridge by indenture for a yere within the tyme of this accompte } £20

Also with the ferme of lyke devocyons of the dioces of Worcetour, Chestour and Herfforde lettene to John Tyler of Coventre for £10 6s. 8d. within the tyme of this accompte } £10 6s. 8d.

Also with the ferme of parte of the counties of Essexe and Hertfford lettene to Thomas Norrys for 40s. by yere for the tyme of this accompte } 40s.

Also with the ferme of the other parte of the counties of Essexe and Hertfford lettene to Thomas Rochefforde for 40s. by yere } 40s.

Also with the ferme of lyke devocyons of the dioces of Kanter[bury] lettene to Robert Bryscowe for £5 by yere for the tyme of this accompte } £5

Also with the ferme of lyke devocyons of the dioces of Kanter[bury] and Chichester lettene to Rycharde Ynskypp of Chichester due for the tyme of this accompte } 33s. 4d.

Also with the ferme of lyke devocyons of the dioces of Wintone and Sarum lettene to Roger Robyns, haberdassher of London, for £5 by yere } £5

Also with the ferme of lyke devocyons of the citie of London lettene by indenture to Walter Sheffelde, proctour, for £20 10s. by yere } £20 10s.

Also with the ferme of the archedeconry of Chester and the Ile of Mane lettene to John Herfforde for 33s. 4d. } 33s. 4d.

Also of the same John Herfforde for a new leasse to hym made of the said archedeconry and Ile } 20s.

f. 74v

Also with the ferme of lyke devocyons of the dioces of Bathe and Welles lettene to Henry Storyge of Welles and William Graunthaum, merchaunt taylour of London, within the tyme of this accompte } 53s. 4d.

Also with the ferme of lyke devocyones of the dioces of Exetour lettene ł to Henry Storyge and John Tyler for £4 } £4

Also with the ferme of Seint Asse and Bangor lettene to Davyd Johnesone of Wrexhaum by yere 10s. } 10s.

Also of the Wardeyns of the Felysshippe of Wexchaundlers of London for ann annuell rent of 20s. by yere } 20s.

Also of the gifte of one Sir Thomas Rogers, preest of Welles } 6s. 8d.

Also of the gifte of Richard Forthingfolde, fysshemonger } 20d.

Also of the gifte of Henry Ogell of Uxbridge } 6s. 8d.

Also for waxe offreede before Jhūs } 21s. 4d.

Summa totalis of alle the charges and reseyttes is } £173 3s. 2d.

Wherof

[102] The said accomptauntes accompte in paymentes ordinary to be made in the crowdes of the said cathedrall churche to sundry ministers of the same churche being present and keping dyvyne service there and in the saide feastes of Transfiguracione and Name of J~~h~~u, and masse of Requiem onn the morow ~~in lyke wise~~ than nexte after for the said Fraternitie, that ys to say: To the subdeane being present at alle the premisses and singing highe mas in the said feastes, for either day 2s., in alle 4s. To 8 chauntry preestes bering coopes in the said feastes of Transfiguracioun and Name of Jhu' in rewarde 13s.

f. 75r

4d. To 12 petycanons 40s. To 6 vycars 16s. 8d. To every high canone, petycanon, chauntery preest, vycars ande choresters being present and bering coopes in the saide feastes 4d., in alle 29s. 8d. To a petycanon synging the masse of Requiem and reding the Pystell and Gospell at the 3 masses before expressede and for saying of *Deprofundis* 2s. 10d. Also for the collacione made there at the highmas in the saide feast of Name of Jhū 3s. 4d. To the sacristene for garnysshing of awlters and for bering of bookes and other ornamentes 3s. 10d. To 4 vergers there being attendaunt, to every of theme 16d. with 20d. in rewarde this yere, in all 7s. And to the bell ryngers for their labour in the said feastes besydes 20s. to them paide quarterly for keping of the doowres of the said crowdes 12s. } £6 12s. 8d.

Also for the masses of Jhūs solempnely by noote kepte in the said crowdes by the subdeane, a cardynalle, a petycanon and by [blank] choresters and 6 vycars of the said cathedrall churche in their habettes and surplices, and to a chauntery preest synging the masse of Requiem by noote every Fryday ymmediatly after the masse of Jhū with 6 of the choresters, that is to say: To the subdeane being present 4d. To the petycanon synging the masse of Jhū 8d. And to a chauntery preest synging the masse of Requiem ande to every of the vycars 4d. In alle for 46 Frydays within the tyme of this accompte } £7 13s. 4d.

Also to one of the vycars, maister of the saide choresters, keping 3 *salves* daily in the saide crowdes after Complayne done in the same cathedrall churche, before thimages of Jhū, oure Blessed Lady and Seint Sebastyane, takyng for his labour 26s. 8d. at 4 termes of the yere according to the saide ordennce } 26s. 8d.

Also to the bell ryngars of the saide cathedrall churche for their labour and dayly attendaunces in openyng, closyng and shittyng of the doowres of the crowdes, ryngyng of belles, blowing of orgaynes, lighting and quenching of torches and other lyghtes, sweping ande makying clene of the said crowdes, at 20s. by yere payable quarterly besydes 12s. for them allowede in the said feastes } 20s.

f. 75v

[103] Also for the rewarde of the Wardeyns this yere, lymyttede and taxed by the said Recour and Assistence according to to [sic] the said ordenaunce £4 } £4

Also for their lyvereys of clothing for the saide Wardeyns, with conysaunces of the name of Jhū, lymyttede in lyke wise by the said Rectour and Assistence £4 } £4

Also to John Worsoppe for making of this accompte } 20s.

Also to Thomas Holmes, sextene, entending daily in the saide crowdes, keping the vestmentes and other ornamentes of the saide Fraternitie, for a hole yere within the tyme of this accompte taking by yere 40s. } 40s.

Also to the prechers at Poules Crosse and Seint Mary Spytell remembring and praying for the soules of alle the bretherne and susterne of the said Fraternitie according to the said ordenaunce, that ys to say 44 Sondays and Good Fryday at Poules Crosse and 3 days in Esterweke at Seint Mary Spytell at 8d. every Sonday } 32s.

Also to the 6 waightes with baners payntede, conysaunces enbroderede with Jhūs, going alle the stretes and subarbes of London playing with their instrumentes to gyve warnyng and knowlege to the people of the said Fraternitie for the saide feastes of Transfiguracione and Name of Jhu, according to the said ordenaunce 10s., and in rewarde 3s. In all within the tyme of this accompte } 13s.

Also to the proctour of the said Fraternitie for the bonfyre before the north dowre of the said crowdes yerely in the evyne of the said feaste of the Name of Jhū 2s. 8d., for cressytt lyght for the same bonfyre 2d. And for lyverys gyvene to worshipfull persones of the Assystence and to the Wexchaundlers 11s. 8d. } 14s. 6d.

f. 76r

[104] Also for singing brede, for brede for holy brede, and for 43 galons and a pottell of malmesey spent in the said crowdes in the tyme of this accompte } 51s. 9d.

Also for waxe spent in the said crowdes besydes the waxe foundede by the Wexchaundlers this yere, as appreithe in a booke of parcelles in the tyme of this accompte } £3 6½d.

Also to the almoyner of Poules for 10 gownes for 10 choresters of the said cathedrall churche servyng God in their habettes in the said crowdes, aswell in the saide feastes of Transfiguracione and Name of Jhū as onn every Fryday at masse of Jhū and Requiem, and at the *salves* there kepte by the said Fraternitie } £4 3s. 4d.

Also to John Marchaunt, John Smythe, John Bayntone and John Mussedge, powre mene appoynted to the almes of the said Fraternitie, keping the crowdes, helping preestes at masse and praying for alle the bretherne and susterne of the said Fraternitie, every of them 40s. by yere payable quarterly according to the said ordenaunce, £8. Also to preestes and powre mene onn Jhūs Day and onn Alle Soules Day in almes 14s. } £8 14s.

[105] Also in sundry expences necessary, that ys to saye: First for wasshing of alle the lynnen clothes belonging to the said crowdes, for setting onn of parawbys onn the vestmentes and for mending of awbys and vestmentes 11s. 4d. For scowring of candellstykes, basons, lampes and braynches, and for nayles, pynnes, pacthrede, bromes, cooles and russhes 11s. 5d. For 2 galons *dimidium* [half] of lampe oyle and for 2 dozeine of tallowe candell 6½d. 6s. ½d. For flowres, garlondes ande

f. 76v

erbys onn Jhūs day 3s. 4d. To a glasyer for mending, taking downe, settyng upp and clensing of alle the glasse wyndowes in the crowdes 30s. For 5 barelles of ale, a kylderkyn of bere and for brede spent in the saide feastes 21s. 4d. For asshen cuppes and tappes 8d. To 4 porters keping the dowres of the said crowdes 4s. To 2 women taking the charge of the masers and drawing of ale 2s. To Thomas Holmes for 3 nyghtes attendaunce 16d. (To the 4 poore mene for their attendaunce 16d.) For meete for the mene gyving their attendaunce 2s. 8d. For 8 stays of ~~yrone~~ yrone for 8 fourmes, for lede, a masone and a joyner to mende the same fourmes 3s. 6d. For writing of 9 lessons of the servyce of Jhūs 3s. To the choresters in rewarde this yere 2s. To Sir Rychard Gate, preest of Paules, for a hole yeres ferme for the waxe offerede before Jhūs ended at Myghelmas within the tyme of this accompte 13s. 4d. To Walter Sheffelde, proctour, in rewarde this yere 2s. And to Maister Woorsoppes servaunt in rewarde this yere for the engrossing upp of this accompte 3s. 4d. In alle } £6 2s. 7½d.

[106] Also in ornamentes and other stuff bought to thuse of the said Fraternitie, that is to say: First 4 yerdes of blake satene of bridges for vestmentes at 2s. 2d. *le* yarde, 8s. 8d. For 30 elles of rau[..] clothe for 4 albes at 7d. *le* elle, 11s. 8d. For mending and repayring of 4 albes, for makyng of new forpartes of 3 vestmentes, for makyng of 12 chales clothes, and for a yarde of grene bokeram 10s. 4d. In alle } 30s. 8d.

Also in sundry potacyons necessary, that ys to say: At the eleccyone of the Wardeyns 5s. 8d. At the eleccioun of Maister Browne, alderman, into the rome of Sir Stephene Jenyns[80] 7s. 6d. At the awdytt of Maister Thomas Hynde 20s. For the dynner on Jhūs day £4. Also the saide accomptauntes axene allowance for charges spent uppone the proctours, Assystence and other straungers commyng to Jhūs masse as before tyme hathe bene allowed 40s. } £7 13s. 2d.

f. 77r

***Summa totalis* of alle the paymentes and discharges ys } £64 8s. 3d.**

And so remaynith due to the said Fraternitie } £108 14s. 11d.

Wheroff

John Coopwood } 53s. 4d.
Henry Storyge and William Graunthaum } £5 6s. 8d.
Henry Storyge and John Tyler } £11
Henry Thornetone } £6 13s. 4d.
Hamlet Holbroke } 20s.
Davyd Johnesone } 3s. 4d.
Richarde Ynskypp of Chichester } 13s. 4d.

Summa } £27 10s.

---

80   Sir Stephen Jenyns (d. 1523), merchant taylor, sherrif and mayor of London (Barron, *London*, 348, 350). It is unknown where this room was located, or indeed whether this should be read as Jenyn's place or space, perhaps in relation to seating for the Guild officers.

Rest delyvered to Henry Dakers and Ellys Draper, reseyvours of this accompte } £81 4s. 11d.

[107] The whiche said some of £81 4s. 11d. the said Stephene Lynne hathe delyverede unto the said Henry Dakers and Ellys Draper before the audytours according to the said ordenaunce. The whiche ys put into a cheste belonging to the saide Fraternitie, excepte £20 remaynyng in thandes of the said Henry Dakers whiche the said Henry Dakers hath reseyved at the geving upp of this accompte, wherof the same Henry knowlegithe hymselff wele and truely satisfiede.

And so restithe in the chest of tresory } £61 4s. 11d.

Wherof remaynithe in thandes of Maister John Browne, aldermane, upone ann obligacione, £40 parcell of the said £61 4s. 11d.[81]

f. 77v

[108] Obligacions delyverede by thandes of the said Stephen Lynne, accomptaunte, unto the handes of the saide Henry Dakers and Ellys Draper, Wardeyns for this yere nexte ensuyng, that is to say frome Christemas in the 15 yere of the reigne of King Henry the 8[the] [1523] unto the feast of Christemas thane nexte folowing.

First ann endenture of Nicholas Smythe of Cambridge with ann obligacione of 40 marcces [sic] to perfourme the covenauntes of the endenture.
Item ann endenture of Walter Sheffelde with ann obligacione of the same Walter and one Thomas Lambe of £40 to perfourme the covenauntes of the endenture.
Item ann endenture of Rycharde Ynskypp of Chichester in the countie of Sussexe with ann obligacione of the same Richarde of £20 to perfourme the covenauntes of the endenture.
Item ann endenture of Thomas Lecetour and John Herfforde of Budworthe in the Hante in the countie of Chester, with ann obligacione of the same Thomas and John of £10 to perfourme the covenauntes of the endenture.
Item ann obligacione of Robert Briscow and Balthasar Guercii of £10 to pay £5 } £5
Item ann endenture of John Tyler of Coventre [no amount]
Item ann obligacioun of John Tyler and Robert Kechyne of London, talughchaundler, of £10 6s. 8d., to pay } £10 6s. 8d.

---

[81] Smaller, possibly rushed version of main hand.

Item ann obligacione of John Tyler and Henry Storyge of Welles of £6, to pay £3 } £3

Item ann obligacione of William Marke of Lyscarde with 2 sewertys of £20, to pay £6 13s. 4d. } £6 13s. 4d.

f. 78r

Item ann obligacioun of Henry Storyge of 40s., to pay } 40s.

Item ann obligacione of Henry Storige for the sewertie of William Marke of Lyscarde of £6 13s. 4d. to pay } £6 13 4d.

Item ann obligacioun of Roger Robyns of £5, to pay } £5

Item ann obligacione of Thomas Rochefforde and Rauff Sherwood of 5 marcces, [sic] to pay 40s. } 40s.

Item ann obligacione of Thomas Norrys and Robert Nycolsone of £4, to pay 40s. } 40s.

Item ann obligacione of John Taylour of 26s. 8d., to pay 6s. 8d. } 6s. 8d.

Item ann obligacione of Hamlet Holbroke of 40s., to pay } 20s.

Item ann obligacione of the same Hamlet of 40s., to pay } 10s.

Item a bill of Davide Johnesone of 3s. 4d., to pay } 3s. 4d.

Per me Thomas Hynde[82]

Per me John Sandelle

Per me William Broket

Per me Ricadus [sic] Calarde

f. 78v[83]

[**109**] This is thaccompte of Henry Dakers and Ellys Draper, Wardeins of the Fraternitie or Gilde of the Name of Jhū founded in the crowdes under the cathedrall churche of Seint Paule of London, frome the feast of Christemas in the yere of oure lord Gode a thousaunde, fyve hundred, twentie and foure and in the fyftene yere of the reigne of kyng Henry the Eight unto the feaste of Christemas thane nexte ensuyng,[84] that is to say by the space of one hole yere.

Arreragies

First the said accomptauntes ben charged with the arrerages due by the said Henry Dakers and Ellys Draper in the last accompte, as in the foote of the same accompte more playnely dothe appere } £81 4s. 11d.

Also with tharrerages of John Copwood } 53s. 4d.

---

82 Signatures.

83 For this account there are headings in the left margin and large brackets framing sections. Guide-letter within ornate pen-flourished T at start of account.

84 This is in fact the account for 1523/24.

Also with tharrerages of Henry Thournetone } £6 13s. 4d.

Also with tharrerages of Hamlet Holbroke as apperith by obligacions } 20s.

Also with tharrerages of David Johneson as apperith by bylle } 3s. 4d.

Also with tharrerages of Henry Storige of Welles as apperith by obligacion } 40s.

Also with tharrerages of the same Henry Storige as apperith in the foote of the last accompte } £8

Also with tharrerages of the same Henry Storige as apperith in the foote of the last accompte } £5 6s. 8d.

Also with tharrerages of Rychard Ynskyppe of the citie of Chichester } 13s. 4d.

Summa } £107 14s. 11d.

f. 79r

[110] Fermes of procuares

Also with the fermes and rentes of two tenementes and certene londes lying in the towne and feldes of Uxbridge in the counties of Middlesex and Bukingham lettene to William Baily and Jamys Standelle for 29s. 8d. by yere, payable at the feastes of Seint Mighell and Thannuncciacione of oure Blessed Lady by evyne porcyons, that is to say for the same feastes within the tyme of this accompte } 29s. 8d.

Also with the ferme of alle the devocyons to the said Fraternitie belonging of the province of Yorke and the diocises of Lincolne, Ely and Norwiche letten to Nicholas Smythe of Cambridge by indenture for a yere within the tyme of this accompte } £20

Also with the ferme of like devocyons of the diocises of Worcetour, Chestour and Herfforde lettene to John Tyler of Coventre for £10 6s. 8d. within the tyme of this accompte } £10 6s. 8d.

Also with the ferme of parte of the ~~diocese~~ counties of Essexe and Hertfforde lettene to Thomas Norrys for 40s. by yere for the tyme of this accompte } 40s.

Also with the ferme of the other parte of the counties of Essexe and Hertfford lettene to Thomas Rochefforde for 40s. by yere within the tyme of this accompte } 40s.

Also with the ferme of like devocyons of the dioces of Canter[bury] lettene to Robert Bristow for £5 by yere within the tyme of this accompte } £5

Also with the ferme of like devocions of the dioces of Chichester lettene to Rychard Ynskippe of Chichester for 33s. 4d. by yere for the tyme of this accompte } 33s. 4d.

Summa } £42 9s. 8d.

f. 79v

Fermes of procuares

Also with the ferme of like devocions of the dioces of Wintone and Sarum lettene to Roger Robyns for £5 by yere for the tyme of this accompte } £5

Also with the ferme of like devocions of the citie of London lettene by indenture to Wa[l]ter Sheffelde for £20 10s. by yere for the tyme of this accompte } £20 10s.

Also with the ferme of like devocions of the archedeconry of Chester and the Yle of Mane letten to John Herfford for 33s. 4d. by yere for the tyme of this accompte } 33s. 4d.

Also with the ferme of like devocions of the dioces of Bathe and Welles lettene to Henry Storige off Welles for 53s. 4d. by yere for the tyme of this accompte } 53s. 4d.

Also with the ferme of like devocions of the dioces of Exetour lettene to Henry Storige for £4 by yere } £4

Also with the ferme of like devocions of the dioces of Seint Asshe [sic] and Bangor lettene to Davide Johneson for 10s. by yere } 10s.

Also of the Wardeins of the Felisshipp of Wexchaundlers of London for an annuell rent of 20s. by yere } 20s.

Also of the gifte of my Lady Reede[85] to be praid for forevermore within the said crowdes } £20

Also of the gifte of Nicholas Smyethes wiff of Cambridge towardes the making of the new pews in the crowdes } 10s.

Summa } £55 16s. 8d.

f. 80r

Also of the bequest of John Mathew,[86] late citezeine and baker of London, decessed } 40s.

Also of the bequeste of John Jossone, late citezein and skynnere of London, decessed } 6s. 8d.

Also for wexe offered before Jhūs } 21s. 4d.

Summa } £3 8s.

***Summa totalis* of alle the charges and reiseittes** } £209 9s. 3d.

Wherof paid oute

---

[85] Dame Elizabeth Rede (d. 1523), widow of Sir Bartholomew Rede (d. 1505), mayor of London. Barron, *London*, 348.

[86] Warden of the Jesus Guild, 1515–17.

[111] Divine service

The saide accomptauntes accompte in paymentes ordinary to be made in the crowdes of the said cathedral churche being present and keping dyvyne service there, and in the feastes of Transfiguracion and Name of Jhū and masse of Requiem onn the morow thane nexte after for the said Fraternitie, that ys: To the ~~deane~~ subdeane being present at all the premisses and syngyng highmas in the said feastes, for either day 2s., in all 4s. To 8 chauntery preestes bering copes in the said feastes of Transfiguracione and Name of Jhu' in rewarde 13s. 4d. To 12 petycanons 40s. To 6 vykars 16s. 8d. To every highe canone, petycanon, chauntry preest, vykars and choresteres being present and bering coopes in the said feastes 4d., in alle 29s. 8d. To a petycanon synging the masse of Requiem and reding the Pistell and Gospell at the 3 masses before expressed and for saying of *Deprofundis* 2s. 10d. For the collacion made there at the highemas in the said feast of Name of Jhū 3s. 4d. To the sextene for garnisshing of aultars and for bering of bookes and other ornamentes 3s. 10d. To 4 vergers there being attendaunt, to every of theime 16d. with 20d. in rewarde this yere, in all 7s. And to the bell ryngars for their labour in the said feastes besides 20s. to them paid quarterly for keeping of the dowres of the said crowdes, 12s. } £6 12s. 8d.

Summa patent

f. 80v

[112] Yett divine service and other charges[87]

Also for the masses of Jhū solempnely by note kepte in the said crowdes by the subdeane, a cardynall, a petycanone, 6 vykars and by 10 choresters of the said cathedrall churche in their habettes and surplices, and to a chauntrye preest synging the masse of Requiem by noote every Fryday ymmediatly after Jhūs masse with 6 of the choresters, that is to say: To the subdeane being present 4d. To the petycanon synging the masse of Jhu' 8d. And to a chauntry preest synging the masse of Requiem and to every of the vykars 4d. In all for 46 Frydais within the tyme of this accompte } £7 13s. 4d.

Also to one of the vykars, maister of the said choresters, keeping three *salves* daily in the said crowdes after Complayne done in the same cathedrall churche, before thimages of Jhū, our Blessed Lady and Seint

---

[87] 'and other charges' in smaller and less formal script and lighter ink in this and the next sub-heading.

Sebastyan, taking for his labour 26s. 8d. at foure termes of the yere according to the ordenaunce } 26s. 8d.

Also to the belle ryngers of the said cathedrall churche for their labour and daily attendaunce in opening and shetting of the dowres of the crowdes, rynging of belles, blowing of organs, lighting and quenching of torches and other lighetes, sweping and making clene of the said crowdes, at 20s. by yere payable quarterly besides 12s. to them allowed in the said feastes } 20s.

Also for the rewarde of the Wardeins this yere, lymytted and taxed by the Rectour, ~~and~~ Wardeyns and Assistence according to the said ordenaunce £4 } £4

Also for the lyvereis of clothing for the said Wardeins, with conysaunces of the Name of Jhū, lymitted in like wise by the said Rectour and Assistence £4 } £4

Also to John Worsopp for the making of this accompte } 20s.

Also to Thomas Holme, sextene, entending daily in the said crowdes, keeping the vestments and other ornamentes of the said Fraternitie for a hole yere within the tyme of this accompte, taking by yere 40s. } 40s.

Summa } £21

f. 81r

[113] **Yet divine service** and other charges[88]

Also to prechers at Poules Crosse and Seint Mary Spyttell remembring and praying for the soules of alle the bretherne and susterne of the said Fraternitie according to the said ordenaunce, that ys to say for 44 Sondais and Good Fryday at Poules Crosse and thre days in Ester Weke at Seint Mary Spyttell at 8d. every Sonday } 32s.

Also to the 6 waighties with baners paynted, conysaunces enbrowderd with Jhūs, going alle the stretes and subarbes of London playing with their instrumentes to gyve warnyng and knowledge to the people of the said Fraternitie for the said feastes of Transfiguracion and Name of Jhū, according to the said ordenaunce 10s. and in rewarde this yere 3s. 4d.

---

[88] 'and other charges' added in a less formal hand and lighter ink.

In alle within the tyme of this accompte } 13s. 4d.

Also to the proctour of the said Fraternitie for the bonefyre before the northe dowre of the said crowdes yerely in the evyne of the saide feast of the Name of Jhū 2s. 8d. For cressitt light for the same bonfyre 2d. And for lyvereys given to the worshipfull persones of the Assistence and to the Wexchaundlers 11s. 8d. } 14s. 6d.

Also for syngyng brede, for brede for holybrede, and for 42 galons and a pottell of malmesey spent in the said crowdes in the tyme of this accompte } 48s. 6d.

Also for waxe spent in the said crowdes besides the waxe founded by the Wexchaundlers this yere as appreith in a boke of parcelles delyvered to the awdytours of this present accompte } 59s.

Also to the almoyner of Poules for 10 gownes for 10 choresters of the said cathedrall churche servyng God in their habettes in the said crowdes, aswell in the said feastes of Transfiguracion and Name of Jhū as onn every Frydaye at masse of Jhū and Requiem and at the three *salves* there kepte daily by the said Fraternitie } £4 3s. 4d.

Summa } £12 10s. 8d.

f. 81v
[114] Almes

Also to John Mussedge, John Smyth, Thomas Batone and Richard Eve, poore men appoynted to the almes of the said Fraternitie, keeping the crowdes, helping preestes at masse and praying for alle the bretherne and susterne of the saide Fraternitie, every of theime 40s. by yere payable quarterly according to the said ordenaunce, £8. Also to preestes ande powre men onn Jhūs Day and onn Alle Soules Day in almes 14s. 4d. } £8 14s. 4d.

[115] Exspences neccessarie

Also in sundry exspences necessary, that is to say: First for wasshing of alle the lynnene clothes belonging to the said crowdes, for setting onn of parawbys onn the vestmentes, and for mending of awbys, surplices and vestmentes, 14s. 6d. For scowring of candellstykkes, basons, lampes and braunchises and for pynnes, pacthrede, bromes, colys and russhes 8s. 10d. For flowres, garlondes and erbys onn Jhūs Day 3s. 4d. For the mending of the whele of the gret bell ande for mending of the whele of the bell hanging over the dowre of the saide crowdes 3s. For ropes and for gresing of alle the belles 14d. For a lok and a kay for the dowre of the house wherin the ale lyeth at Jhūs tyde 10d. For plankes, planche bourdes, quarters and for nayles, and to carpenters for the making of the new pews in the crowdes £4 10s. For lengthing of the stall in the quyer 20d. For the carving of ann image of Seint John 3s. For 2 elles of brysell cloth for towelles 18d. For a canstyke [sic] of yrone ande for a paring shovell of yrone 12d. For 3 new belle candellstykes and for the chaunging of ann olde candelstike 2s. 2d. To the glasyer for mending and clensyng of the glasse wyndowes 3s. To a plasterer and his servaunt for the whiting of the crowdes by the space of a day 13d. For 2 sakkes of lyme 4d. For paynting of 16 Jhūs onn the pyllers 2s. 2d. For the sute of certene specialties of dyverse of the proctours as particulerly doth appere in a bille delyvered to the awdytourus of this present accompte 43s. To the choresters in rewarde this yere 20d. To Sir Richard Gate, preest of Poules, for a hole yeres ferme for waxe offered before Jhūs ended at Mighelmas within the tyme of this accompte 13s. 4d. For correcting of 8 bookes of the service of Jhūs 16s. For 5 barelles of ale, a kylderkyne of bere and for brede spent in the said feastes 21s. 4d. For asshene cuppes, tappes and trays 8d. For 4 porters keeping the dowres of the said crowdes 4s. To the two women taking the charge of masers and for drawing of ale 2s. To Thomas Holme for 3 nyghtes attendaunce 16d. To the 4 poore men for their attendaunce 16d. For meete for men gyving their attendaunce 2s. 8d. For 3 galons of lampe oyle and for 3 dozeine *dimidium* [half] of tallow candell 7s. 2½d. To Walter Sheffelde in rewarde this yere 2s. To John Baynton the almes mane for a hole yere of the almes of 5d. by the weke to hyme graunted by alle the Assistence, 21s. 4d. And to Maister Worsoppes servaunt for the making and engrossing uppe of this accompte 3s. 4d. } £13 4s. 1½d.

Summa } £21 18s. 5½d.

f. 82r

[116] Potacions

Also in sundry potacyons necessary, that ys to saye: At the elleccion of the new Wardeins 7s. 8d. At severalle tymes spent uppone certene of the Assistence 5s. 6d. At the awdytt of Stephene Lynne 20s. For the dynner onn Jhūs Day £4. Also the said accomptauntes axene allowaunce for charges spent upon the proctours and other straungers comyng to Jhus masse as before tyme hath byn allowed 40s. In alle } £7 13s. 2d.

Summa patent

Summa totalis **of alle the charges and reseittes }** £209 9s. 3d.

Summa totalis **of alle the payments & discharges }** £69 14s. 11½d.

And so remayneth due to the said Fraternitie } £139 14s. 3½d.

Wheroff

[117] First the said accomptauntes axene allowaunce for the arrerages of John Copwood } 53s. 4d.

Item for tharrerages of Henry Storige as apperithe by obligacione } 40s.

Item for tharrerages of the same Henry of £8, and for the yerely ferme of £4 for the dioces of Exetour as apperith by obligacione } £12

Item for tharrerages of the same Henry of £5 6s. 8d., and for the yerely ferme of 53s. 4d. for the dioces of Bath and Welles, late in the tenour of the same Henry } £8

Item for tharrerages of Henry Thornetone } £6 13s. 4d.

Item for tharrerages of Hamlet Holbroke as apperithe by obligacions } 20s.

Item for tharrerages of Daveide Johnesone of 3s. 4d., and for the yerely ferme of 10s. for the dioces of Seint Asse and Bangor } 13s. 4d.

Item for tharrerages of Richarde Ynskippe of 13s. 4d., and for the yerely ferme of 33s. 4d. for the dioces of Chichester } 46s. 8d.

Item for the yerely ferme of 40s. of parte of the counties of Essexe and Hertfff[ord] lettene to Thomas Norrys as apperith by obligacione } 40s.

Summa } £37 6s. 8d.

f.82v

Rest delyvered to Ellys Draper and John Pyke, reseyvours of this accompte } £102 7s. 7½d.

The whiche saide some of £102 7s. 7½d. the said Henry Dakers hathe delyverd unto the said Ellys Draper and John Pyke before the awdytours according to the said ordenaunce. The whiche is putt into a cheste belonging to the said Fraternitie excepte £20 remaynyng in the handes of the said Ellys Draper, whiche Ellys resyvede at the giving uppe of this accompte, wherof the same Ellys knowlegithe hymselff wele and truely satisfied. And £40 parcell of the said £102 7s. 7½d. remaynethe in thandes of Master John Browne, alderman, as apperithe by obligacione remaynyng in the chest of the treasury.[89]

---

[89] The final sentence is not as neatly written and quite cramped, suggesting it was a later addition.

And soo restyth in the chest of tresory } £82 7s. 7½d.

[118] Obligacions delyverede by thandes of the said Henry Dakers, accomptaunte, unto thandes of the said Ellys Draper and John Pyke, Wardeins for this yere nexte ensuing, that is to say frome Christemas in the 16 yere of the reigne of king Henry the 8ᵗʰᵉ [1524] unto the feast of Christemas thane nexte folowing.

First ann indenture of Robert Shethar, citezeine and merchaunt taylour of London, and Richard Piersone of Cambridge, with an obligacione of £40 to perfourme the covenauntes of the indenture.
Item ann indenture of Walter Sheffeld with ann obligacion of the same Walter and one Thomas (Lambe) of £40 to perfourme the covenauntes of the indenture.
Item an indenture of John Tyler of Coventre [no ammount]
Item ann obligacione of Robert Briscow and Baltharsar Guercii of £10, to pay } £5

f. 83r
Item ann obligacione of John Tyler of £10 6s. 8d., to pay } £10 6s. 8d.
Item ann other obligacione of the same John Tyler of £4, to paye } £3
Item ann indenture of Richard Ynskipp of Chichester with ann obligacione of the same Richard of £20 to perfourme the covenauntes of the indenture.
Item an indenture of Thomas Leicetour and John Herfforde of Budwourth in the Haute in the countie of Chester, with ann obligacion of the same Thomas and John of £10 to perfourme the covenntes of the indenture.
Item ann obligacione of William ~~ty~~ Marke of Lyskarde with 2 sewerties of £20, to pay } £6 13s. 4d.
Item ann obligacione of Henry Storige of Welles for the sewertie of the same William Marke of £6 13s. 4d., to paye } £6 13s. 4d.
Item ann obligacione of the same Henry of £20, to pay } £12
Item ann obligacion of the same Henry of 40s., to pay } 40s.
Item ann obligacion of John Taylour of 20s., to pay } 6s. 8d.
Item ann obligacione of Roger Robyns of £5, to pay } £5
Item ann obligacione of Thomas Norrys and Robert Nicolsone of £4, to pay } 40s.
Item ann obligacion of Hamlet Holbroke of 40s., to pay } 20s.
Item ann obligacion of the same Hamlet of 40s., to pay } 10s.
Item a bille of David Johnesone of 3s. 4d., to pay } 3s. 4d.

Per me John Munk[90]

90   Signatures.

Per me Stephen Lynne

Per me William Broket

Per me Richard Calarde

f. 83v[91]

[119] This is thaccompte of Ellys Draper and John Pyke, Wardeins of the Fraternitie or Gylde of the most glorious Name of Jhū founded in the crowdes under the cathedralle churche of Seint Paule of London, frome the feast of Christemas in the yere of our Lorde God a thousaunde, fyve hundrede, twenty and foure, ande in the 16 yere of the reigne of kyng Henry the Eight unto the feast of Christemas thane nexte ensuyng, that ys to say by the space of one hoole yere .

Firste the said accomptauntes ben charged with tharreragies due by the saide Ellys Draper and John Pyke in the last accompte, as in the foote of the same accompte more playnely dothe appere } £102 7s. 7½d.

Also with tharreragies of John Copwoode as apperithe by bille } 53s. 4d.

Also with tharreragies of Henry Storige as apperithe by severelle obligacions } £14

Also with ann obligacione of the same Henry Storige of £6 13s. 4d. to pay £6 13s. 4d. } £6 13s. 4d.

Also with tharreragies of Hamnet Holbroke as apperithe by two severelle obligacions } 30s.

Also with tharreragies of David Johnsone as aperithe by bille } 3s. 4d.

Also with tharreragies of John Taylour as apperithe by obligacione } 6s. 8d.

Also with tharreragies of Rycharde Ynskyppe off Chichester as apperithe in the foote of the last accompte } 46s. 8d.

Also with tharreragies of Thomas Norrys as apperithe by obligacione } 40s.

Also with tharreragies of William Marke of Lyskarde, whiche was callede tharreragies of Henry Thournetone, as aperithe by obligacion } £6 13s. 4d.

Also with ann obligacione of John Tyler of Coventre as aperithe by obligacion } £3

Summa } £141 14s. 3½d.

f. 84r

[120] Also with the fermes of two tenementes and certene londes lying in the towne and feldes of Uxbridge in the counties off Middlesex and

91   A less elaborate layout to that of 1522/23.

Bukingham lettene to William Baily and Jamys Standelle for 29s. 8d. by yere, payable at the feastes of Seint Mighell ande Thannunciacion of our Blessede (Lady) by evyne porcyons, that is to say for the same feastes within the tyme of this accompte } 29s. 8d.

Also with the ferme of all the devocyons belongyng to the saide Fraternitie of the province of Yorke and the dioces of Ely, Lincolne and Norwiche lettene to Richarde Piersone of Cambridge ande to Robart [sic] Shethar, citezein ande merchaunt tailour of London, by indenture for a yere within the tyme of this accompte } £24

Also with the ferme of like devocyons of the dioces of Worcetour, Chestour and Hertfford [sic] lettene to John Tyler of Coventre for £10 6s. 8d. by indenture within the tyme of this accompte } £10 6s. 8d.

Also with the ferme of like devocyons of parte of the counties of Essexe and Hertfford lettene to Thomas Norrys for 40s. by yere, this yere voide } 40s.

Also with the ferme of like devocyons of the other parte of the counties of Essexe and Hertfford lettene to Thomas Rochefforde for 40s. by yere, this yere voide ande not lettene } 40s.

Also with the ferme of like devocions of the dioces of Canterbury lettene to Robert Briscow for £5 by yere as apperithe by obligacione within the tyme of this accompte } £5

Also with the ferme of like devocyons of the dioces of Chichester lettene to Richarde Ynskyppe of Chichester for 33s. 4d. by yere as apperithe by indenture, this yere voide } 33s. 4d.

Also with the ferme of like devocions of the dioces of Wintone and Sarum lettene to Rogier Robyns for £5 by yere as apperithe by obligacione } £5

Also with the ferme of like devocyons of the citie of London lettene by indenture to Walter Sheffelde for £20 10s. by yere for the tyme of this accompte } £20 10s.

Summa } £71 19 s 8d.

f. 84v

Also with the ferme of like devocyons of the arche deconry of Chester and the Yle of Mane lettene by indenture to John Herfforde for 33s. 4d. by yere for the tyme of this accompte } 33s. 4d.

Also with the ferme of like devocyons of the dioces of Seint Asse and Bangour lettene to David Johnesone for 10s. by yere, thys yere voide } 10s.

Also of the Wardeins of the Felisshippe off Wexe chaundlers of London for ann annuelle rent of 20s. by yere } 20s.

Also of Walter Sheffelde for a leasse to be made unto hym of parte of the counties of Essexe and Middlesex } 20s.
Also for waxe offred before Jhūs } 25s. 3d.
Also for the hyer of 5 hoddes of blak satene } 5s.

Summa } £5 13s. 7d.

Summa *totalis* of alle the charges ande rescittes is } £219 7s. 6½d.

Wherof paide oute

[121] The said accomptauntes accompte in paymentes ordinary to be made in the crowdes of the said cathedralle churche being present and keping dyvyne service there, and in the feastes of Transfiguracione and Name of Jhu' ande masse of Requieme [sic] onn the morow than nexte and ymmediatly folowing, that is to say for the said Fraternitie. First, to the subdeane being present at alle the premisses and syngyng highemas in the saide feastes, for either day 2s., in all 4s. To eight chauntery preestes bering coopes in the saide feastes of Transfiguracione ande Name of Jhū in rewarde 13s. 4d. To 12 perycanons 40s. To 6 vykars 16s. 8d. To every highe canone, petycanon, chauntry preest, *vyk* vykars and choresters being [present]

f. 85r

and bering coopes in the said feastes 4d., in alle 29s. 8d. To a petycanone syngyng the masse of Requiem and reding the Pistell and Gospelle at the 3 masses before expresside and for saying of *Deprofundis* 2s. 10d. For the collacione there made at the highemas in the fest of the Name of Jhū 3s. 4d. To the sextene for garnisshing of aulters and for bering of bookes and other ornamentes 3s. 10d. To 4 vergers ther being attendaunt to every of theim 16d. with 20d. in rewarde this yere, in all 7s. And to the bell ryngers for their labour in the said feastes besydes 20s. to theim paide quarterly for keping of the dowres of the saide crowdes 12s. } £6 12s.

Also for the masses of Jhūs solempnely by noote kepte in the said crowdes by the subdeane, a cardinalle, a petycanone, 6 vykars and tenne choresters of the said cathedralle churche in their habettes and surplices, and to a chauntry preest syngyng the masse of Requiem by noote every Frydaye ymmediatly after Jhus masse with 6 of the choresters, that ys to say: To the subdeane being present 4d. To the petycanone syngyng the masse of Jhū 8d. And to a chauntery preest syngyng the masse of Requiem and to every of the vykars 4d. In all for 40 Frydays within the tyme of this accompte } £6 13s. 4d.

Also to one of the vykars, maister of the saide 10 choresters, keping three *salves* daily in the said crowdes after complayne donne in the same Cathedral churche, before the ymages of Jhū, oure Blesside Lady and Seint Sebastyane, takyng for his labour 26s. 8d. at foure termes of the yere according to the ordynaunce } 26s. 8d.

Also to the bell ryngers of the said cathedralle churche for their labour and daily attendaunce in openyng and shitting of the doores of the said crowdes, rynging of belles, blowing of orgaynes, lighting & quenching of torches and other lightes, sweping and making clene of the said crowdes, at 20s. by yere payable quarterly besydes 12s. to theim allowed in the saide feastes } 20s.

[122] Also for the rewarde of the Wardeins this yere, lymyttede and taxede by the Rectour and Wardeins and Assistence according to the saide ordenunce } £4

Summa } £19 12s.

f.85v
Also for lyverys of clothing for the said Wardeins withe conysaunces of the name of Jhu', lymyttede in like wise by the said Rectour and Wardeins and Assistence } £4

Also to John Worsoppe for the makyng of this accompte } 20s.

Also to the prechers at Poules and Seint Mary Spyttelle remembring and praying for the soules of all the brethrene and sustrene of the said Fraternitie acording to the said ordenaunce, that ys to say for 44 Sondays and Good Fryday at Poules Crosse ande three days in Ester Weke at Seint Mary Spytelle, at 8d. every Sondaye } 32s.

Also to the 6 weightes with banners payntede, conysaunces enbrowderde with Jhūs, going all the stretes and subarbes of London playing with their instrumentes to gyve warnyng and knowledge to the people of the said Fraternitie for the said feastes of Transfiguracone and Name of Jhū, according to the said ordenaunce 10s., and in rewarde this yere 3s. 4d. In alle, within the tyme of this accompte } 13s. 4d.

Also to the proctour of the said Fraternitie for the bonfyre before the northe doore of the said crowdes yerely in the eveyne of the said feaste of the Name of Jhu 2s. 8d. For cressit light for the same bonfyre 2d. And for lyverys gyvene to the Wexchaundlers and to the worshipfullist persones of thassistence 11s. 8d. } 14s. 6d.

Also for syngyng brede, for brede for holybrede, and for 38 galons of malmesey spent in the said crowdes within the tyme of this accompte } 45s. 10½d.

Also for wex spent in the said crowdes besyde the wex founde by the Wexchaundlers this yere for the tyme of this accompte } 44s. 11d.

Also to the almoyner of Poules for 10 gownes for 10 choresters of the said cathedralle churche servyng God in their habittes in the said crowdes, aswell in the said feastes of Transfiguracione and Name of Jhū as onn every Fryday at masse of Requiem and Jhū and at the three *salves* there kepte daily by the said Fraternitie } £4 3s. 4d.

Summa } £16 13s. 11½d.

f. 86r

Also to Thomas Holme, sextene, attending daily in the said crowdes, keping the vestmentes and other ornamentes of the said Fraternitie, for a hole yere within the tyme of this accompte } 40s.

Also to John Mussedge, John Smythe, Thomas Batone and Richard Eve, poore mene appoynted to the almes of the saide Fraternitie, keping the crowdes, helping preestes at masse and praying for all the bretherne and sustrene of the said Fraternitie, every of theim 40s. by yere payable quarterly according to the said ordenaunce, £8. Also to preestes ande poore mene onn Jhūs day and onn Alle Soules Day in almes 13s. 4d. } £8 13s. 4d.

[123] Also in sundry exspences necessary, that is to say: First for wasshing of all the lynnene clothes belongyng to the said crowdes, for setting onn of parawbys onn the vestmentes, and for mending of awbys & vestmentes and for makyng of 5 new surplices, 18s. 10d. For scowring of candylstykes, basons, lampes, ande brayncheses; for pynnes, pakthrede, bromys, cooles, russhes and nayles; for mending of lokkes; and for 8 fathome of roope for the gret braynche: 9s. 6d. For flowers, garlondes and erbys on Jhūs day 3s. 4d. For making of a belle clapper that was brokene 6s. 8d. For 2 new bawldrykes for 2 gret belles 6s. For a ryng for the gret bawldryk 6d. For trussing of belles and for gresse for the belles 12d. To the glasyer for mending & clensing of the glasse wyndowes in the crowdes 5s. 6d. To a plasterer ande his servaunt for whyting of the crowdes by the space of 2 days 2s. 2d. For 4 sakkes of lyme 8d.

To Sir Richarde Gates, preest of Poules, for a hole yeres ferme for wexe offryde before Jhūs, ended at Mighelmas within the tyme of this accompte 13s. 4d. For 5 barelles of ale, a kylderkyne of bere and for brede spent in the saide feastes 21s. 4d. For asshene cuppes, tappes and trayes 8d. To 4 porters keping the doores of the crowdes 4s. To two ~~wek~~ womene taking the charge of the masers and for drawing of ale 2s. To Thomas Holme for 3 nyghtes attendaunce 16d. To the same Thomas for watching in the crowdes whene the new seyttes were made in the crowdes, whiche sholde have bene paide by Master Dacres late Wardeine,[92] 5s. Paide for 2 lettres of lycense under my Lorde Cardynalle[93] seale whene all the pardones were disadnullyde 46s. 8d. Gyvene in rewarde to my Lord Cardynalles servaunt 3s. 4d. For botehyer and in other necessary exspences at dyverse tymes spent for the suett of the saide 2 lettres of lycense 2s. 2d. To the 4 poore mene gyvyng

Summa } £10 13s. 4d.

f.86v

their attendaunce 16d. For meete for mene g for for [sic[94]] gyvyng their attendaunce 2s. 8d. For 3 galons and a pottell of lampe oyle and for 2 dozein *dimidium* [half] of tallow candelle 7s. 6d. To Walter Sheffelde in reward this yere 2s. To John Bayntone the almes mane for a quarter and 8 wekes of the almes of 5d. the weke to hym graunted by alle the Assistence, 8s. 4d. To Master Worsoppes servaunt for thengrossing upp of this accompte and for making of ann inventory of the ornamentes belonging to the crowdes 5s. And to the Gray Fryer that prechede in the crowdes onn Jhūs day by the commaundment of all the Assistens, towardes his exhibicion 3s. 4d. In alle } £9 4s. 2d.

[124] Also in sundry potacyons necessary, that ys to say: At the elleccione of the new Wardeine 7s. 8d. Spent at the makyng of ann inventory of the ornamentes belonging to the crowdes 2s. 8d. At severelle tymes spent upone certene of thassistence 6s. 8d. At the awdytt of Master Dacres 20s. For the dynner onn Jhūs day £4. Also the said accomptauntes axene allowaunces for charges spent uppone the proctours and other straungiers commyng to Jhūs masse as before tyme hathe bene allowede 40s. In alle } £7 17s.

Also in ornamentes and other stuff bought to thuse of the said Fraternitie, that ys to say: First for 21 yardes of russett clothe for gownes for the poore mene £3 10s. For 24 yerdes of *ynkylle* for awbe gurdelles 11d.

---

92 Henry Dacres, d. 1537.
93 Thomas Wolsey (d. 1530), cardinal archbishop of York.
94 Word repeated across a line-break.

And for holowing of the gyrdelles and of corporases 12d. } £3 11s. 11d.

Summa } £20 13s. 1d.

Summa totalis of alle the charges and reseittes is } £219 7s. 6½d.

Summa totalis of the payments and discharges is } £67 12s. 4½d.

And so restith due to the said Fraternitie } £151 15s. 2d.

Wheroff

[125] The said accomptauntes axene allowaunce for the arreragies of John Copwood by bille } 53s. 4d.

f.87r

Item Rogier Robyns as apperithe by obligacione } £4

Item Richarde Ynskyppe of Chichester for tharrerages of olde 13s. 4d., and for the ferme of the dioces of Chichester lettene to the same Richarde for 33s. 4d. by yere, this yere void by reasone of the Jubyly at Rome[95] } 46s. 8d.

Item Robert Shethar and Richarde Pyersone of Cambridge } £15

Item Robert Bristow for Kent } 20s.

Item John Tyler of Coventre } 40s.

Item Thomas Norrys for parte of the ~~dioces~~ counties of Essexe and Hertfford lettene to the same Thomas for 40s. by yere, this yere void and not occupyede } 40s.

Item Thomas Rochefforde for the other parte of the said counties of Essexe and Hertfforde lettene to the said Thomas for 40s. by yere, this yere voide and not occupyede } 40s.

Item David Johnesone for the ferme of the dioces of Bangor and Seint Asse lettene to the said Davide for 10s. by yere, this yere voide and not occupyed; and for tharreragies of the same Davide as apperithe by bille 3s. 4d. } 13s. 4d.

Item with tharreragies of Hamlet Holbroke as apperithe by obligacions } 30s.

Item for tharreragies of Henry Storige of Welles as apperithe by obligacions } £20 13s. 4d.

Item for tharrerages of Williame Marke of Lyskarde, whiche was namede therrerages of Henry Thornetone, as aperithe by obligacion } £6 13s. 4d.

Item John Tyler of Coventre as apperithe by obligacion, whose day of payment ys not yet comme } 40s.

Summa } £62 10s.

---

[95]   The 64th Papal Jubilee. See Introduction, p. 26.

Rest delyverede to John Pyke and William Campyone, reseyvours of this accompte } £89 5s. 2d.

f.87v

The whiche somme of £89 5s. 2d. the saide Ellys Draper hathe delyverede unto the saide John Pyke and William Campyone before the auditours according to the ordenaunce. The whiche ys putt into a chest ~~Remay~~ belongyng to the saide Fraternitie except £20 remaynyng in thandes of the said John Pyke, whiche the same John Pyke reseyved at the gyving upp of this accompte, wherof the said John Pyke knowlegithe hymself wele and truely satisfiede. And £40 parcell of the saide £89 5s. 2d. remaynithe in thandes of Master Browne, aldermane, as apperithe by obligacione remaynyng in the chest of tresory.

And so restithe in the chest of tresory } £69 5s. 2d.

[126] Obligacions delyverede by thandes of the saide Elys Draper, accomptaunt, unto the handes of the said John Pyke and William Campyone, Wardeins for this yere nexte ensuyng, that is frome Christemas in the 17 yere of the reigne of kyng Henry the Eighte [1525] unto the feast of Christemas thane next folowing.

First ann indenture of Robert Shethar, citezeine and merchaunt tailour of London, and Richarde Pyersone of Cambridg with ann obligacione of £40 to perfourme the covenauntes of the indenture.
Item ann indenture of Walter Sheffelde, with ann obligacion of the same Walter and Thomas Lambe of £40 to perfourme the covenauntes of the indenture.
Item ann indenture of John Tyler of Coventre [no amount].
Item ann obligacione of John Tyler of £4 to pay 40s. } 40s.
Item ann obligacione of the same John of £10 6s. 8d., rest due of the same obligacion } 40s.
Item ann obligacion of the same John Tyler & one Robert Hunt of £10 6s. 8d.
f.88r
Item an indenture of Richarde Ynskyppe of Chichester, with ann obligacione of £20 to perfourme the covenauntes of the indenture.
Item an indenture of Thomas Leicetour and John Herfforde of Budwourthe in the Hante in the countie of Chester, with ann obligacione of the same Thomas and John of £10 to perfourme the covenauntes of the indenture.
Item ann obligacione of Henry Storige of 40s. to pay } 40s.[96]

---

[96] Small letter 'a' in left margin next to the three entries for Henry Storige, for William Marke and John Philippe, and for the two entries for Hamlet Holbroke.

Item an obligacion of the same Henry of £20 to pay } £12
Item ann obligacion of the same Henry of £6 13s. 4d. to pay – £6 13s. 4d., whiche is made for the sewerty of William Merke.
Item ann obligacione of William Marke, John Philippe and John Marke of £20 ,to pay } £6 13s. 4d.
Item ann obligacione of John Taylour of 20s., to pay } 6s. 8d.
Item ann obligacione of Robert Briscow of £5, rest due } 20s.
Item ann obligacione of Rogier Robyns of £5, rest due } £4
Item an obligacione of the same Rogier of £5, to pay } £5
Item ann bille of David Johnesone of 3s. 4d. } 3s. 4d.
Item ann obligacion of Hamlet Holbroke of 40s., to pay } 10s.
Item ann obligacion of the same Hamlett of 40s,. to pay } 20s.
Item 3 obligacions of John Coopwoode, every obligacione of £5.
Item a bille of the same John Copwoode [no amount].
Item ann indenture of Walter Sheffelde for Middlesex with ann obligacion of the same Walter of £5 to perfourme the covenauntes of the indenture.
Item ann obligacion Richarde Gates and Robert Ray of [blank] to pay } 33s. 4d.
Item ann obligacion of Thomas Norrys of £4, to pay } 40s.

Per me Henry Dacres[97]
Be me Thomas Pargette
Be me William Bromwelle
Per me Hugonem Actone

f. 88v

[127] This is thaccompte of John Pyke and William Campyone, Wardeins of the Fraternitie or Gilde of the most glorious Name of Jhū founded in the crowdes of the cathedralle churche of Seint Paule of London, frome the feast of Christemas in the yere of oure lord God 1525 and in the yere 17ᵗʰ yere off the reigne of our soverayne lorde kyng Henry the Eight that is to say frome (unto) the feast of Christemas thene nexte ensuyng, that is to say by the space of one hole yere.

First the said accomptauntes bene chargede with tharreragies due by the saide John Pyke and William Campyone in the last accompte, as in the foote of the same accompte more playnly dothe appere } £89 5s. 2d.
Also with tharreragies of John Copwoode as apperithe by bille } 53s. 4d.
Also with tharreragies of Rogier Robyns as apperithe by obligacione £4; Hamlett Holbroke by obligacione 30s.; Henry Storige by obligacione £20 13s. 4d.; William Marke and other by obligacione £6 13s. 4d.; and John Tyler by obligacione 40s. In alle } £34 16s. 8d.

97   Signatures.

Also with tharreragies of the province of Yorke, the dioces of Ely, Lincolne and Norwiche lettene to Richarde Piersone and Robert Shethar £15; the dioces of Canterbury lettene to Robert Briscowe 20s.; the dioces of Chichester lettene to Richarde Ynskippe 46s. 8d.; the dioces of Worcetour, Chestour and Hertfford [sic] lettene to John Tyler of Coventrie 40s.; the dioces of Seint Asse and Bangour lettene to Davide Johnesone 13s. 4d.; the counties of Essexe and Hertfford lettene to Thomas Norrys 40s.; and the countie of Middlesex lettene to Thomas Rochefforde 40s. } £25

[128] Also with the fermes of two tenementes and certene londes lying in the towne and feldes of Uxbridge in the counties of Middlesex and Bukingham lettene to William Baily and Jamys Standelle for 29s. 8d. by yere payable at the feastes of Seint Mighelle Tharchaungelle ande Thannunciacione of oure Blessede Lady by evyne procyons, that is to say for the same feastes within the ~~tyme of~~ tyme of this accompte } 29s. 8d.

Summa } £153 4s. 10d.

f. 89r

Also with the ferme of all the devocyons belongyng to the said Fraternitie of the province of Yorke and the dioces of Ely, Lincolne and Norwiche lettene to Robert Shethar, citezeine and merchaunt taylour of London, and to Richarde Piersone of Cambridge by indenture for a yere within the tyme of this accompte } £24

Also with the ferme of like devocyons of the dioces of Worcetour, Chestour and Hertfford [sic] letten to John Tyler of Coventre for £10 6s. 8d. within the tyme of this accompte } £10 6s. 8d.

Also with the ferme of like devocyons of parte of the countie of Essexe lettene to Thomas Norrys for 40s. by yere as apperithe by obligacione for the tyme of this accompte } 40s.

Also with the ferme of like devocyons of the countie of Middlesex ande of parte of the countie of Essexe lettene to Walter Sheffelde by yere, as apperithe by indenture for the tyme of this accompte } 40s.

Also with the ferme of like devocyons of the citie of London letterne to the saide Walter by indenture for ~~40s.~~ £20 10s. by yere for the tyme of this accompte } £20 10s.

Also with the ferme of like devocyons of the dioces of Canterbury lettene to Robert Briscow for £5 by yere as apperithe by obligacione for the tyme of this accompte } £5

Also with the ferme of like devocyons of the dioces of Chichester lettene to Richarde Ynskippe of Chichester by indenture for 33s. 4d. by yere for the tyme of this accompte } 33s. 4d.

Also with the ferme of like devocyons of the dioces of Wintone and Sarum lettene to Rogier Robyns for £5 by yere as apperithe by obligacione for the tyme of this accompte } £5

Summa } £70 10s.

f. 89v

Also with the ferme of like devocyons of the archedeconry of Chestour and the Yle of Mane lettene by indenture to John Herfforde for 33s. 4d. by yere for the tyme of this accompte } 33s. 4d.

Also with the ferme of like devocyons of the dioces off Seint Asse ~~and~~, Bangour and Menevene[98] lettene to Evane Fermouce by indenture for half a yere within the tyme of this accompte } 33s. 4d.

Also with the ferme of like devocyons of the dioces of Exetour, Bathe and Welles lettene to Henry Thornetone for a halff yere within the tyme of this accompte } £3 10s.

Also with the ferme of like devocyons of the dioces of Dyvelyne and Armicane[99] lettene to John Mastok of Deyvelyne aforesaide as apperithe by obligacione for the tyme of this accompte } 33s. 4d.

Also for waxe offrede before Jhūs } 22s. 4d.

Also of the Wardeins of the Felisshippe of Wexchaundlers of London for ann annuelle rent of 20s. by yere } 20s.

Also for the hyer of 6 hoodes of blak sattene } 8s.

Also of the bequest of John Felde, fisshemongre } 6s. 8d.

Summa } £11 7s.

Summa totalis of alle the charges and reiceittes } £235 22d.

Wheroff paid oute

f. 90r

[129] The said accomptauntes accompte in paymentes ordinary to be made in the crowdes of the said cathedralle churche being present and keping dyvyne service in the feastes of Transfiguracion and Name of Jhū and masse of Requiem onn the morow thene nexte and ynnmediatly folowing, that is to say for the said Fraternitie. Firste, to the subdeane being present at all the premisses and syngyng highe mas in the said feastes, for either day 2s., in all 4s. To 8 chauntry preestes bering coopes in the said feastes in rewarde 13s. 4d. To 12 petycanons 40s. To 6 vykars 16 s 8d. To every highe canone, petycanone, chauntry preest, vykar and chorester being present and bering copes in the said feastes of Transfiguracione and Name of Jhū 4d., in alle 27s. 6d. To a pety canone synging masse of Requiem and reding the Pistelle and Gospelle at the

---

98 Menevia, i.e. St David's.
99 Dublin and Armagh, both metropolitans of their respective provinces.

said 3 masses and for saying of *Deprofundis* 2s. 10d. For the collacione there made at the highemas in the feast of the Name of Jhū 3s. 4d. To the sextone for garnishing of the aulters and for bering of bookes and other ornamentes 3s. 10d. To 4 vergiers there being attendaunt, to every of theim 16d. with 20d. in rewarde this yere, 7s. And to the belle ryngars for their labour in the said feastes besides 20s. to theime paid quarterly for keping of the doores of the saide crowdes, 12s. In alle } £6 10s. 6d.

Also for the masses of Jhū solempnely by noote kepte in the saide crowdes by the subdeane, a cardinalle, a petycanone, 6 vykars and tenne choresters of the said cathedralle churche in their habettes and surplices, and to a chauntry preest syngyng the masse of Requiem by note every Fryday ymmediatly after Jhūs masse with 6 of the coresters, that is to say: To the subdeane being present 4d. To the petycanone syngyng the masse of Jhu' 8d. To the chauntry preest syngyng the masse of Requiem and to every of the vykars 4d. In alle, for 40 Frydays within the tyme of this accompte } £6 13s. 4d.

Also to one of the vykars, maister of the saide tenne choresters, keping 3 *salves* daily in the said crowdes, after Complayne donne in the said cathedralle churche, before the ymages of Jhu' oure Blessed Lady and Seint Sebastyane, taking for his labour 26s. 8d. at foure termes of the yere according to the ordenaunce } 26s. 8d.

Summa } £14 10s. 6d.

f. 90v

Also to the belle ryngars of the said cathedralle churche for their labour and daily attendaunce in openyng, closing and shetting of the doores of the said crowdes, for rynging of belles, blowing of orgaynes, lighting and quenchinge of torches and other lightes and for sweping ande makying clene of the saide crowdes at 20s. by yere payable quarterly, besides 12s. to theim allowede in the said feastes } 20s.

[130] Also for the rewarde of the Wardeins this yere, lymyttede and taxede by the Rector, Wardeins and Assistence of the said Fraternitie according to the ordenaunce } £4

Also for the lyvereys of clothing for the said Wardeins with conysaunces of the Name of Jhū, lymytted in like wise by the said Rectour, Wardeins and Assistence } £4

Also to John Worsoppe for the makyng and engrosing uppe of this accompte } 20s.

Also to the prechers at Poules Crosse and Seint Mary Spittelle remembryng and praying for the soules of alle the bretherne and susterne of the said Fraternitie according to the said ordenaunce, that is to say for 43 Sondais and Good Fryday at Poules Crosse and 3 days in Ester Weke at Seint Mary Spittelle at 8d. every Sonday } 31s. 4d.

Also to the 6 waightes with banners payntede, conysaunces enbrowderede with Jħus, going all the stretes and suburbes of London ge playing with their instrumentes to gyve warnyng and knowledge to the people of the said Fraternitie for the said feastes of Transfiguracion and Name of Jħū, according to the said ordeunce 10s., and in reward this yere 3s. 4d. for the tyme of this accompte } 13s. 4d.

Also to the proctour of the said Fraternitie for the bonfyre before the northe doore of the said crowdes yerely in the evenyng of the said feast of the Name of Jħu 2s. 8d. For cressit lighte for the same bonfyre 2d. And for lyveres gyvene to the Wexchaundlers ande to the worshipfulle persones of thassistence 11s. } 13s. 10d.

Summa } £12 18s. 6d.

f. 91r

Also for syngyng brede, for brede for holy brede, and for 31 galons and a pottelle of malmesay spent in the said crowdes within the tyme of this accompte } 39s. 1d.

Also for waxe spent in the said crowdes beside the waxe foundede by the Wexchaundlers this yere for the tyme of this accompte } 45s. 8d.

Also to [the] almoyner of Poules for 10 gownes for 10 choresters of the said cathedralle churche servyng God in their habettes in the saide crowdes, aswelle in the said feastes of Transfiguracione and Name of Jħū as every Fryday at the masse of Requieme and at the 3 *salves* there kept daily by the saide Fraternitie } £4 3s. 4d.

Also to Thomas Holme, sextene, attending daily in the said crowdes, keping the vestmentes and other ornamentes belongyng to the said Fraternitie for a hole yere within the tyme of this accompte } 40s.

Also to John Mussedge, John Smythe, Thomas Batone and Richarde Eve, poore mene appoyntede to the almes of the said Fraternitie, keping the crowdes and helping preestes at masse and praying for alle the bretherne and susterne of the said Fraternitie, every of theim 40s.

by yere payable quarterly according to the said ordenaunce £8. Also to preestes and poore mene on Jhus day and onn All Soules Day in almes 10s. 8d. } £8 10s. 8d.

[131] Also in sundry exspences necessary, that is to say: First, for wasshing of alle the lynnene clothes belongyng to the said crowdes, for setting onn of the parawbes onn the vestmentes, for mending of awbes, vestmentes and surplices, 12s. 8d. For scowring of candelstikes, basons, lampes and braynchises, }

Summa } £18 18s. 9d.

f.91v

for pynnes, pakthrede, bromes, cooles, russhes and nayles, and for mending of the roope at the doore of the said crowdes, and of lokkes, 7s. 3d. For flowres, garlondes and herbes onn Jhus day 3s. 4d. For mending of a grett belle, for furlokkes, plates, bolts, nayles and staples for the same belle 9s. 8d. For tymbre, work manshippe and mending of the frame of the same belle 16s. To the glasyer for mending and clensing of the glasse wyndowes 4s. 6d. For brik, lyme, sande and workemanshippe for whiting of the crowdes and for planche bourde and quarters for mending of the seyttes and fourmes of the said crowdes 11s. 3d. To Sir Richard Gates, preest of Poules, for a hole yeres freme for wexe offrede before Jhus ended at Mighelmas within the tyme of this accompte 13s. 4d. For 5 barelles of ale, a kilderkyne of bere and for brede spent in the crowdes in the said feastes 21s. 4d. For asshene cuppes, tappes and trayes 8d. To 4 porters keping the doores of the said crowdes 4s. To two womene takyng the charge of the masers and for drawing of ale 2s. To Thomas Holme for 3 nyghtes attendaunce 16d. To the 4 poore mene gyvyng their attendaunce 16d. For meete for the mene gyvyng their attendaunce 2s. 8d. For 4 gallons and a pottell of lampe oyle and for 4 dozeine of tallow candelle 9s. 1d. To Walter S Sheffelde in reward this yere 2s. 2s. To the chorestars in rewarde this yere 16d. Spent for the sewte of certene proctours at Westminster as apperithe by bille 12s. 6d. Paid to Master Worsoppe for certene writynges made bytwene the said accomptauntes, Wa[l]ter Sheffelde and a preest of Wales for the dioces of Bangour, Seint Davys and Seint Asse and the countie of Middlesex, 6s. 8d. And to Master Worsoppes servaunt for the writing of this accompte 3s. 4d. In alle } £7 5s. 7d.

Also in sundry potacyons necessary, that is to say: At the eleccyoun of the new Wardein 8s. 10d. Spent uppone certene of thassistences at assembles at severelle tymes 7s. 3½d. At the awdytt of Master Draper 20s. sterling. For the dynner onn Jhus day £4. Also the said accomptauntes axene allowaunce for charges spent upone the proctours and other straungiers comyng to Jhūs masse as before tyme hathe byne allowed 40s. In alle } £7 16s. 1½d.

Summa } £15 20½d.

f. 92r

Summa *totallis* of alle the charges and receittes } £235 22d.

Summa *totalis* of alle the paymentes and dischargies is } £61 9s. 5½d.

Rest due to the said Fraternitie is } £173 12s. 4½d.

Wheroff

[132] The said accomptauntes axene allowaunce for tharreragis of John Copwood ~~bill~~ by bille } 53s. 4d.
Richard Ynskyppe of Chichester for tharreragis in the last accompte, and for this yere ferme of the dioces of Chichester } £4
Robert Shethar and Richard Piersone of Cambridge } £8
Walter Sheffelde for Middlesex } 40s.
Robert Briscow for Kent } 26s.
Thomas Norrys for tharrerages in the last accompte } 40s.
Thomas Rocheford for tharrerages in the last accompte } 40s.
David Johnesone for tharrerages in the last accompte } 13s. 4d.
Hamlett Holbroke by obligaciouns } 30s.
Henry Storige by obligacions } £20 13s. 4d.
William Marke of Lyskard by obligacione } £6 13s. 4d.
John Tyler by obligacione whose day of payment is not yet comme 20s., and for the arrerages of his ferme in the last accompte 40s. } £3
John Mastok for the dioces of Dyvelyne by obligacion } 33s. 4d.

Summa } £56 2s. 8d.

Rest delyvered to William Campyon and John Worsoppe, receyvours of this accompte } £117 9s. 8½d.

f. 92v

The whiche said some of £117 9s. 8½d. the said John Pyke hathe delyvered unto the said William Campyon and John Worsoppe before the awdytours according to the ordenaunce, wherof is putt into a chest belongyng to the said Fraternitie £53 9s. 8½d. Remaynyng in thandes of the said William Campyone £20, whiche the same William receyved at the gyving uppe of this accompte, and 3 goblettes withoute covers of silver parcell gilt weying 22 onzes, whiche 3 goblettes lyene to pledge for £4 due by Rogier Robyns in the last accompte. And £40 parcell of the said some of £117 9s. 8½d. remaynithe in thandes of Master John Browne, late aldermane, as apperithe by obligacioun remaynyng in the chest of tresory belongyng to the said Fraternitie.

Memorandum[100] that the £40 remaynyng in the handes of the saide John Browne was delyvered unto hym in angelles nobles after 6s. 8d. the noble, whiche amountithe to £45 after the rate as the money now goithe. And £29 remaynyng within the said chest in the last accompte was in like wise in angelles nobles after 6s. 8d. the nobille, thencrease wheriof amunt to £3 12s. 6d. Ande so thencrease of the saide golde amunt to £8 12s. 6d. over a[n]d above the saide somme of £117 9s. 8½d.

[133] Obligacions delyvered by thandes of the said John Pyke, accomtaunt, unto thandes of the said William Campyone and John Worsoppe, Wardeins for this yere nexte ensuyng, that is to say frome Christemas in the 18th yere of the reigne of kyng Henry the 8th [1526] unto the feastes of Christemas thene nexte folowing.

First ann indenture of Robert Shethar, citezeine and merchaunt tailour of London, and Richard Piersone of Cambridge, with ann obligacione of £40 to perfourme the covenauntes of the indenture.
Item ann indenture of John Tyler of Coventre [no amount].
Item an obligacione of the same John Tyler of £4, to pay 20s. } 20s.
Item ann obligacione of the same John of £10 6s. 8d. Rest due of the same obligacionn 40s. } 40s.
Item an obligacione of the same John Tyler and one Robert Hunte of £10 6s. 8d. to pay } £10 6s. 8d.
Item ann indenture of Richard Ynskippe of Chichester, with an obligacione of £20 to perfourme the covenauntes of the indenture.
f. 93r
Item an indenture of Walter Sheffelde with ann obligacioun of ~~£20~~ £40 to perfourme the covenauntes of the indenture.
Item ann other indenture of the same Walter with ann obligacione of £5 to perfourme the covenntes of the same indenture.
Item an indenture of Thomas Leycetour and John Herfforde of Budworthe in the Haute in the countie of Chester with ann obligacione of £10 to perfourme the covenauntes of the same indenture.
Item ann obligacione of Henry Storige of 40s. to pay } 40s.
Item ann obligacione of the same Henry of £20, to pay } £12

---

[100] Paragraph in smaller, cramped hand but probably same scribe.

Item ann obligacione of the same Henry of £6 13s. 4d., to pay £6 13s.
4d. whiche was made for sewurtye of William Marke } £6 13s. 4d.
Item ann obligacione of William Marke, John Philippe and John Marke
of £6 13s. 4d. to pay } £6 13s. 4d.
Item ann obligacione of John Taylour of 20s. to pay } 6s. 8d.
Item ann obligacione of Rogier Robyns of £5 to pay } £5
Item a bille of David Johnesone of 3s. 4d. } 3s. 4d.
Item an obligacione of Hamlet Holbroke of 40s. to pay } 10s.
Item ann obligacione of the same Hamlet of 40s. to pay } 20s.
Item 3 obligacions of John Copwoode, every obligacione of £5, and a
bille of the same John Copwoode.
Item ann obligacione of th Thomas Norrys of £4 to pay } 40s.
Item ann obligacione of Richarde Gates and Robert Ray of } 33s. 4d.

Per me Johannem Browne
Thomas Hynde
Per me John Nychelles
Be me Wyllyam Brothurs } Awdytours[101]

f.93v[102]

[134] This is thaccompte of William Campyon and John Worsoppe,
Wardeins of the Fraternitie or Gilde of the most glorious Name of Jhū
foundede in the crowdes of the cathedrall churche of Seint Paule of
London, from the feast of Christemas in the yere of oure lord God 1526
and in the 18the yere of the reigne of oure soverayne lord king Henry
the 8th unto the feast of Christemas thene nexte ensuyng, that ys to say
by the space of one hole yere.

First the said accomptauntes been chargede withe tharreragies due by
the said William Campyone and John Worsoppe in the last accompte,
as in the fote of the same accompte more playnely dothe apere } £117
9s. 8½d.

Also with tharreragis of John Copwoode as apperethe by bylle } 53s.
4d.
Also with tharrerages of Wa[l]ter Sheffelde for Middlesex } 40s.
Also with tharreragies of Richarde Ynskipe for the dioces of Chichester
} £4
Also with tharreragies of Rychard Piersone of Cambridge and Robert
Shethar of the province of York the dioces of Ele, Lincolne and
Norwiche } £8

---

101 Signatures, with 'Awdytours' in hand of main scribe.
102 Account partly ruled in crayon, almost certainly a different scribe.

Also with tharreragies of Robert Bristow for Kent } 26s.
Also with tharreragies of Thomas Norrys [for] the counties of Essexe
and Hartfford } 40s.
Also with tharreragies of Thomas Rocheforde for the countie of
Middlesex } 40s.
Also with tharreragies of Davide Johnesone for the dioses of Seint Asse
and Bangour } 13s. 4d.
Also with tharreragies of Wylliam Marke of Lyskar[d] by obligacyone
} £6 13s. 4d.
Also with tharreragies of Hamblett Holbroke by obligacions } 30s.
Also with tharreragies of of Henry Storige by obligacyons } £20 13s. 4d.
Also with tharreragies of John Tyler by obligacione } £3
Also with tharreragies of John Mastoke for the dioses of Dyvelyne }
33s. 4d.

Summa } £173 12s. 4½d.

f.94r

[135] Also with fermes of two tenenementes and certeyne londes lying
in the towne and feldes of Uxbridge in the counties of Middlesex and
Bukkingham lettene to William Baily and James Standelle for 29s. 8d.
by yere payable at the feastes of Seint Mighelle Tharchaungelle ande
Thannunciacione of oure Blyssyde Lady by evyne porcyons, that is to
say for the same feastes within the tyme of this accompte } 29s. 8d.

Also with the ferme of alle the devocyons belonging to the said Fraternitie
of the province of Yorke and the dioces of Ely, Lyncolne and Norwiche
lettene to Robert Shethare, citezeine and merchant taylour of London,
and to Richarde Piersone of Cambridge by indenture for a yere within
the tyme of this accompte } £24
Also with the ferme of of [sic] lyke devocyons of the dioces of Worcetour,
Chestour and Hertfford [sic] lettene to John Tyler of Coventre for £10
6s. 8d. within the tyme of this accompte } £10 6s. 8d.
Also with the ferme of lyke devocyons of parte of the countie of Essexe
lettene to Thomas Norrys for 40s. as aperethe by obligacione for the
tyme of this accompte } 40s.
Also with the ferme of lyke devocyons of the countie of Middlesex and
parte of the countie of Essexe lettene to Wa[l]ter Sheffelde by yere as
aperethe by indenture for the tyme of this accompte } 40s.
Also with the ferme of like devocyons of the citie of London lettene to
the said Walter by indenture for £20 10s. by yere for the tyme of this
accompte } £20 10s.
Also with the ferme of like devocyons of the dioces of Canterbury
lettene to Robert Bristowe for £5 by yere as aperethe by obligacione
for the tyme of this accompte } £5

Also with the ferme of like devocyons of the dioces of Chichester lettene to John Sestone of Lewes by indenture for 33s. 4d. by yere for the tyme of this accompte } 33s. 4d.

Also with the ferme of like devocyons of the dioces of Wintone ande Sarum lettene to Roger Robyns for £5 by yere as aperethe by obligacione for the tyme of this accompte } £5

f. 94v

Also with the Freme of lyke devocyones of [the] archedeconry of Chestour and the Yle (of) Mane lettene by indenture to John Hertfforde for 33s. 4d. for the tyme of this accompte } 33s. 4d.

Also with the ferme of lyke devocyons of the dioces of Seint Asse and Bangour and Seint Daves lettene to Evane Fermoue by indenture for halff a yere within the tyme of this ~~acom~~ accompte } 33s. 4d.

Also with the ferme of lyke devocyons of the dioces of Exetour, Bathe and Welles lettene to Henry Thornetone by yere within the tyme of this accompte } £7

Also with the ferme of lyke devocyons of the dioces of Dyvelyne and Armicane[103] lettene to John Mastoke of Dyvelyne aforesaide as aperithe by obligacyone for the tyme of this accompte } 33s. 4d.

Also for waxe offrede before Jhūs } 17s. 5d.

Also of the wardeins of the Felisshippe of Wexchaundlers of London for an annuell rent of 20s. by yere } 20s.

Also of the bequest of Thomas Michell, ier[n]monger } 3s. 4d.

Summa } £86 5d.

Summa totalis of alle the chargis and receytis } £259 12s. 9d.

Wherof paied

f.95r

[136] The said accomptauntes accompte in paymentes ordenary to be made in the crowdes of the said cathedralle churche being present and keping dyvyne service in the feastes of Transfiguracione and Name of Jhū and masse of Requiem onn the morow thene nexte and ymmedyatly folowing, that is to say: First to the subdeane being present at all the premisses and synging highmas in the said feastes, for eyther day 2s., in all 4s. To 8 chauntrey prestes bering copies in the saide feastes in rewarde 13s. 4d. To 12 petycanons 40s. To 6 wykars [sic] 16s. 8d. To every highe canone, petycanone, chauntry prest, vykar ande chorestar

---

[103] Dublin and Armagh (although the second placename looks rather more like Antrim, it was not a diocese in medieval Ireland).

being present and bering copies in the said feastes of Transfiguracione and Name of Jhū 4d., in all 26s. 8d. To a petycanone singing masse of Requiem and reding the Pystell and Gospelle at the said 3 masses and for saying of *Deprofundis*, 2s. 10d. For the collacione there made at the highemas in the feastes of the Name of Jhū 3s. 4d. To the sextone for garnisshing of the aulters and bering of bokes and other ornamentes 3s. 10d. To 4 vergiers there being attendaunt, to every of theme 16d. with 20d. in rewarde this yere, 7s. And to the bell ryngers for their labour in the saide feastes besydes 20s. to theym paiede quarterly for keping of the dores of the saide crowdes 13s. 8d. In all } £6 11s. 4d.

Also for the masses of Jhū solempinely by note kepte in the saide crowdes by the subdeane, a cardinall, a petycanone, 6 vykers and tenne choresters of the said cathedrall churche in their habettes and surplices [and] to a chauntrey prest synging masse of ~~masse~~ Requiem by note every Fryday ymmedyatly after Jhūs masse with 6 of the choresters, that ys to saye: To the subdeane being present 4d. To the petycanone synging the masse of Jhū 8d. To the chauntrey prest synging the masse of Requiem and every of the vykers 4d. In all, for 44 Frydayes within the tyme of this accompte } £7 6s. 8d.

Also to the maister of the saide tenne choresters keping 3 *salves* dayly in the saide crowdes, after Complayne donne in the said cathedrall churche, byfore the ymages of Jhū, oure Blessyde Lady and Seint Sebestyane, taking for his labour 26s. 8d. at foure termes of the yere according to the ordenaunce } 26s. 8d.

Also to the bell ryngers of the saide cathedralle churche for their labour and dayly attendaunce in openyng, closing and shetting of the dores of the said crowdes, for rynging of belles, blowing of orgaynes, lighting and quenching of torches and other lightes, and for sweping and making clene of the said crowdes, at 20s. by yere payable quarterly besydes 13s. 8d. to them allowede in the saide feastes } 20s.

f. 95v

[137] Also for the rewarde of the Wardeins this yere, lymyttede and taxede by the Rector, Wardeins and Assistence of the said Fraternitie according to the ordenaunce } £4

Also for lyveres of clothing for the said Wardeins with conysaunces of the Name of Jħu, lymyttede in like wyse by the said Rector, Wardeines and Assistence } £4

Also to John Worsoppe for the making and engrosing uppe of this accompte } 20s.

Also to the prechers at Poulys Crosse and Seint Mary Spitell, remenbring and praying for alle the soules of alle the bretherne and sustrene of the saide Fraternitie according to the said ordenaunce, that ys to say for 43 Sondayes ande Goodfrydaye at Poules Crosse and 3 dayes in Ester Weke at Seint Mary Spyttell, at 8d. every Sondaye } 27s. 4d.

Also to the 6 waighetes with banners payntede, conysaunces enbroderede with Jhūs, going all the stretes and suburbes of London playing with their instrumentes to gyve warnyng and knowlege to the people of the saide Fraternitie for the saide feastes of Transfiguracione and Name of Jhū, according to the saide ordenaunce 10s., and in rewarde this yere 3s. 4d. for the tyme of this accompte } 13s. 4d.

Also to the procter of the said Fraternitie for the bonfyre before the northe doore of the said crowdes yerely in the saide evenyng of the said feast of the Name of Jhu 2s. 8d. For the cressett lighte for the same bontefyre 2d. And for lyveres gyvene to the Wexchaundlers and to the worshipfull persones of thassistence 5s. } 7s. 10d.

Also for singing brede, for brede for holy brede, and for 34 gallons and a pottell of malmesey spent in the saide crowdes within the tyme of this accompte } 42s. 9½d.

Also for waxe spent in the said crowdes besyde the waxe foundede by the Wexchaundlers this yere for tyme of this accompte } 53s. 8d.

f. 96r

Also to the almoyner of Poulys for 10 choresters of the saide cathedrall churche servyng God in their habettes in the saide crowdes, aswell in the said feastes of Transfiguracione ande Name of Jhu as every Frydaye at the masse of Requiem and at the 3 *salves* there kept dayly by the said Fraternitie } £4 3s. 4d.

Also to Thomas Holmes, sextene, attending dayly in the said crowdes [and] keping the westmentes [sic] and other ornamentes belonging to the said Fraternitie for a hole yere within the tyme of this accompte } 40s.

Also to John Mussedge, Thomas Batone, Richarde Eve ande William [erasure] Missylbroke, pouremene appoyntede to the almes of the said

Fraternitie, keping the crowdes and helping prestes to [sic] masse and praying for alle the bretherne and sustrene of the said Fraternitie, every of them 40s. by yere payable quarterly according to the said ordenaunce £8. Also to the prestes and pore mene onn Jhūs daye and Alle Soules Daye in almes 10s. 8d. } £8 10s. 8d.

[138] Also in sundry exspences necessaries, that is to saye: First for wasshing of alle the lynnene clothes belonging to the saide ~~Fraternitie~~ crowdes, for setting onn of the par awbes onn the westmentes [sic] and surplices, for mending of awbes, westmentes and surplices, and for a pece of gurdyll rybonde, 12s. 11d. For scowering of candelstikkes, basons, lampes & braynches, cruettes [and] the holy water stokke 20d. For pynnes, bromes, [and] lampe oyle 5s. 6½d. For water for holy water, for a lader for the palys, for colys, for cariage of dunge from Jhus dore, for clensing and making clene of the stayers of the crowdes, for mending of lokkes and stapulles for the pewes, and for a lawpe, 22d. To the glasyer for mending of glasse wyndowes & for clensing of the same wyndowes 4s. 6d. For 3 dozeine of talow candelle 3s. 9d. For 2 paxis for 2 aulters 6d. For russhis, for mending of a paring yrone, for mending of a fourme, for entring of Master Jenyns name, for gresse for belles, for a claspe for a bell and for nayles for the same, 22d. To the herbe wyff for garlondes, roses, jelyfors, herbis, [and] flowers onn Jhus day 3s. 6d. For 5 barelles of ale and for bere 21s. 4d. For tappes [and] trayes 8d. To 4 porters 4s. To 2 womene to drawe ale 2s. To Thomas Holmes for watching 16d. To 4 poure mene for watching 16d. For mete for them 2 dayes 2s. 8d. Item to Wa[l]ter Sheffeld for his rewarde 2s. Item to the choresters for their rewarde 12d. Item to Sir Richarde Gates, prest, for a hole yeres freme for waxe offred before Jhūs, endyde at Mighelmas within the tyme of this accompte 13s. 4d. Item for the hyer of clothe onn Jhūs daye and for hanging upp of them 2s. Item gyvene to John Monke[104] in almoys by the assent of the Assistence 10s. }

f. 96v

Item for 3 letters conweying to Storige and Tyler, and for bote hyer to Westemynster 4½d. Item paiede to Master Cleybroke[105] for 2 letters of lycense for the province of York, the dioces of Lincolne, Norwiche and Ele, 26s. 8d. Item paiede for ropis for the belles 5s. 8d. For the new making of a claper to the 3ᵈᵉ bell 7s. Item paiede for a quarter of a hundrede of paving tyle to a mende the flower[106] in the crowdes whiche was brokene 7d. For lyme and sande 2d. For a tyler and his mane for *dimidium* [half] a daye 6½d. Item gyvene to the prestes that saide masse

---

104 Warden of the Jesus Guild, 1506/6, 1513/14.
105 Possibly William Clayburgh (Claybroke), prothonotary of Chancery. H. A. Kelly, *The Matrimonial Trials of Henry VIII* (Stanford, 1976), 9–10, 75.
106 That is, the floor. See New, 'Jesus Chapel', 118 n.37.

in Jhus Chapell onn Jhūs daye 3s. 5d. Gyvene to the pore folke onn the morow after the masse of Requiem donne 3s. 4d. Item gyvene to 29 prestes that sange masse uppone All Soule Daye 3s. 4d. Delte to pore folkes the same day 3s. 4d. Item for 38 ellis & a half of bresell clothe for 8 awbes at 6½d. the elle, 20s. 8d. For making of the said 8 awbes 2s. 8d. Item paiede to Rauff Candewell, attourney in the Comane Place, as aperethe by his byll 28s. 8d. Item paiede to Master Worsoppes servaut for the writing upp of this accompte 3s. 4d. } £10 7s. 4½d.

[139] Also in sundry potacyons necessary, that ys to say: At the eleccione of the new wardene 7s. 7d. Spent at the awdyte of Master Pyke 20s. For the dynner onn Jhus day £4. For a potacione to the Assistence at the admyssione of one of the poure mene 4s. 6d. Spent at certeyne assembles upone the Assistence 3s. 1d. Also the saide accomptauntes axene allowaunce for charges spent upone the procters and other ~~charges~~ st(r)aynegers comyng to Jhūs masse as before tyme hath byne alowede 40s. *Summa* } £7 15s. 2d.

Summa } £65 6s. 2d.

Summa totalis off all the charges and receytis } £259 12s. 9½d.

Summa totalis of alle the paymentes and discharges } £65 6s. ~~10d.~~ 2d.

Rest due to the said Fraternitie } £194 6s. 7½d.

Wheroff

f.97r

[140] The said accomptauntes axene alowaunce for tharreragis of John Copwoode } 53s. 4d.

Item[107] for tharreragis of Rycharde Ynskype for the dioces of Chichester } £4

Item for tharreragis of John Sestone for this yere ferme for the dioces of Chichester } 33s. 4d.

Item for tharreragis of Rycharde Peiersone and Robert Shethar for the province of Yorke, the dioses of Ely, Lincolne and Norwiche of the last accompt £4, and of this yeres ferme £12, *summa* } £16

Item for tharreragis of Thomas Norres of the last accompt } 40s.

Item for tharreragis of Thomas Rocheforde of the last accompt } 40s.

Item for tharreragis of Davy Johnsone of the last accompt } 13s. 4d.

Item for tharreragis of Hamblett Holbroke } 30s.

---

[107] There is a small 'x' written in left margin next to the entries for Ynskyppe, Sestone, Norres, Rocheforde, Johnsone, Holbroke and Bristow.

Item for tharreragis of Henry Storige of the last accompt by obligacione } £20 13s. 4d.
Item for tharreragis of William Marke of the last accompt } £6 13s. 4d.
Item for tharreragis of John Tyler as aperethe in the foote of the last accompte } £3
Item for tharreragis of John Mastoke as aperethe in the foote of the last accompte 33s. 4d., and of this yeres ferme 33s. 4d. } £3 6s. 8d.
Item for tharreragis of Walter Sheffelde for parte of the countie of Essexe and for the countie of Middlesex of the yeres ferme of this accompt } 40s.
Item for tharreragis of Roger Robyns of the yeres ferme of this accompt } 40s.
Item of tharreragis of Robert Bristow of the last accompte for Kent } 26s.

Summa } £69 9s. 4d.

Rest delyverede to John Worsopp and William Brothers, receyvours of this accompte } £124 17s. 3½d.[108]

f. 97v

The whiche said somme of £124 17s. (3d.) [sic] the said William Campyone hathe delyverede unto the said John Worsoppe and William Brothers before the awdytours according to the ordenaunce, wherof is put into a chest belonging to the said fraternitie £64 17s. 3d.; remaynyng in thandes of the said John Worsoppe £20, whiche the same John receyvede at the gyving upp of this accompt. And 3 goblettes without covers of silver parcell gilte weying 22 onzes, whiche 3 goblettes lyene to pledge for £4 due by Roger Robyns, and £40 parcelle of the said somme of £124 9s. 1d. [sic] remaynethe in thandes of Maister John Browne, late aldermane, as aperethe by obligacione remaynyng in thandes of the said John Worsoppe.

Memorandum that the said £40 remaynyng in thandes of the said John Browne was delyverede unto hym in angell nobles after 6s. 8d. the noble, whiche amountithe to £45 after the rate as the money now goith.

[141] Obligacions delyverede by thandes of the said William Campyone, accomptaunt, unto thandes of the said John Worsoppe and William Brothers, Wardeins for this yere nexte ensuyng, that ys to say from Christemas in the 19th yere of the reigne of king Henry the 8th [1527] unto the feast of Christemas thene next folowing.

---

108   The sum 3½d. added in lighter ink and slightly smaller script but same scribe.

First an indenture of Robert Shethar, citezeine and merchaunt taylour of London, and Richarde Piersone of Cambridge with an obligacione of £40 to perfourme the covenauntes of the indenture.

Item an indenture of John Tyler of Coventre [no amount].

Item an obligacione of the same John Tyler of £4, to paye 20s. } 20s.

Item an obligacione of the same John of £10 6s. 8d., rest due of the same obligacione, 40s. } 40s.

Item an obligacione of the same John Tyler and one Robert Hunte of £10 6s. 8d., to pay } £10 6s. 8d.

Item an indenture of Rycharde Ynskipe of Chichester with an obligacion of £20 to perfourme the covenauntes of the indenture }

Item an indenture of Walter Sheffeld with an obligacione of £40 to perfourme the covenauntes of the indenture.

Item ann other indenture of same Walter with an obligacione of £5 to perfourme the covenauntes of the same indenture.

Item an indenture of Thomas Leycetour and John Herfforde of Budworthe in the Haute in the countie of Chester with an obligacione of £10 to perfourme the covenauntes of the same indenture.

f. 98r

Item an obligacione of Henry Storige of 40s., to pay } 40s.

Item an obligacione of the same Henry of £20, to pay } £12

Item an obligacione of the same Henry of £6 13s. 4d., to pay £6 13s. 4d., whiche was made for sewertie of William Marke } £6 13s. 4d.

Item an obligacione of William Marke, John Philippe and John Marke of £6 13s. 4d., to paye } £6 13s. 4d.

Item an obligacione of John Taylour of 20s., to pay } 6s. 8d.

Item an obligacione of Roger Robyns of £5, to pay } £5

Item a bill of Davide Johnsone of 3s. 4d. } 3s. 4d.

Item an obligacione of Hamblett Holbrok of 40s., to pay } 10s.

Item an obligacione of the same Hamblett of 40s., to pay } 20s.

Item 3 obligacions of John Copwoode, every obligacione of £5, and a bill of the same John Copwoode }

Item an obligacione of Thomas Norrys of £4, to pay } 40s.

Item an obligacione of Richarde Gates and Robert Ray of [blank] } 33s. 4d.

f. 98v

[142] This is thaccompte of John Worsoppe and William Brothers, Wardeins of the Fraternitie or Gilde of the most gloryous Name of Jhū foundede in the crowdes of the cathedrall churche of Seyint Paule of London, from the feast of Christemas in the yere of our lord God 1527ti and in the 19th yere of the reigne of our soverayne lord kyng Henry the 8th unto the feast of Christemas then next ensuyng, that is to saye by the space of one hole yere.

First the said accomptauntes chargene them selves with tharrerages in the fote of the last accompte } £124 17s. 3½d.

Also with tharrerages of John Copwoode in the fote of the last accompte, *summa* } 53s. 4d.

Also with tharrerages of Richarde Ynskippe for the diose of Chichester in the fote of the last accompte } £4

Also with tharrerages of John Sestone for the dioses of Chichester } 33s. 4d.

Also for tharrerages of Richard Peiersone and Robert Shether for the provynce of York, the dioses of Ely, Lincolne and Norwiche, as more playnely aperethe in the foote of the last accompte } £16

Also with tharrerages of Thomas Norres as apperethe in the foote of the last accompte } 40s.

Also with tharrerages of Thomas Rochefforde, as aperethe in the foote of the last accompte } 40s.

Also with tharrerages of Davyde Johnesone of the last accompte } 13s. 4d.

Also with tharrerages of Hamlett Holbroke } 30s.

Also with tharrerages of Henry Storige of the last accompte by obligacyone } £20 13s. 4d.

Also with tharrerages of William Marke of Lyskar[d] of the last accompte } £6 13s. 4d.

Also with tharrerages of John Tyler as aperethe in the fote of the last accompte } £3

Also with tharrerages of John Mastok as aperethe in the fote of the last accompte } £3 6s. 8d.

f.99r

Also with tharrerages of Wa[l]ter Sheffeld of the countie [sic] of Essexe and Middlesex, as aperethe in the last accompte } 40s.

Also with tharrerages of Roger Robyns [as] aperethe in the last accompte } 40s.

Also with tharrerages of Robert Bristow of the last accompte for Kent } 26s.

Also with the bequest of John Clerke of Norwiche } 3s. 4d.

Also with the bequest of John Paynter of Plummouthe } 20s.

Also resceived of William Campyone, for that he was twyse alowede for the almes gevene upone Alholowene Daye and All Sollene Daye } 10s. 8d.

Also of thencrease of the £40 whiche remaynethe in the handes of John Browne, whiche £40 the same John reseyvede in angell nobles after the rate of 6s. 8d. the noble, whiche amounntethe to the somme of £45 sterlinges after the rate as the money now goithe, *summa* } £5

Summa } £201 7½d.

[143] Also with the ferme of two tenementes and certeyne londes lying in the towne and feldes of Uxbridge in the counties of Middlesex

and Bukkingham lettene to William Baily and James Standell for 29s. 8d. by yere payable at the feastes of Seynt Mighell Tharchaungell and Thannunciacione of our Blessede Lady by evyn porcyons, that is to saye for the same feastes within the tyme of this accompte } 29s. 8d.

Also with the ferme of alle the devocyons belonging to the said Fraternitie of the provynce of York, the dioces of Ely, Lincolne and Norwiche lettene to Robert Shether, citezeine and merchaunt taylour of London, and to Richard Peiersone of Cambridge by indenture for a yere within the tyme of this accompte } £24

Also with the ferme of lyke devocyons of the dioses of Worcetour, Chester and Herfforde lettene to John Tyler of Coventre for £10 6s. 8d. within the tyme of this accompte } £10 6s. 8d.

f. 99v

Also with the ferme of lyke devocyons of parte of the countie of Essexe lettene to Thomas Norres for 40s. by yere, as aperethe by obligacione for the tyme of this accompte } 40s.

Also with the ferme of lyke devocyons of the countie of Middlesex and parte of the countie of Essexe lettene to Wa[l]ter Sheffelde by yere, [as] aperethe by indenture for the tyme of this accompte } 40s.

Also with the ferme of lyke devocyons of the citie of London lettene to the said Walter by indenture for £20 10s. by yere for the tyme of this accompte } £20 10s.

Also with the ferme of lyke of lyke [sic] devocyons of the dioces of Canterbury lettene to Robert Bristow for £5 by yere, as aperethe by obligacione for the tyme of this accompte } £5

Also with the ferme of lyke devocyons of the dioces of Chichester lettene to John Sestone of Lewes by indenture for to 33s. 4d. by yere for the tyme of this accompte } 33s. 4d.

Also with the ferme of lyke devocyons of the dioces of Wyntone and Sarum lettene to Roger Robyns for £5 by yere, as aperethe by obligacione for the tyme of this accompte } £5

Also with the ferme of lyke devocyons of the archedeconry of Chestour and the Yle (of) Mane lettene by indenture to John Harfford for 33s. 4d. for the tyme of this accompte } 33s. 4d.

Also with the ferme of lyke devocyons of the dioces of Seint Asse, Bangour and Seint Daves letten to Evan Fermoue by indenture for a half a yere within the tyme of this accompte } 33s. 4d.

Also with the ferme of lyke devocyons of the dioces of Exetour, Bathe and Welles lettene to Henry Thornetone by yere within the tyme of this accompte } £7

Also with the ferme of lyke devocyons of the dioces of Develyne and

Armicane[109] lettene to John Mastoke of Develyne aforsaide as aperethe by obligacione for the tyme of this accompte } 33s. 4d.

f. 100r
Also for Waxe offrede before Jħus } 15s. 1d.
Also of the Wardeins of the Felisshippe of Wexchaundlers of London for an annuell rent of 20s. by yere } 20s.

Summa } £85 14s. 9d.

Summa totalis of alle the charges and reseytes } £286 15s. 4½d.

Wheroff paied

f. 100v
[144] The said accomptauntes accompte in payment ordenary to be made in the crowdes of the said cathedrall churche being present and keping dyvyne service in the feastes of Transfiguracione and Name of Jħū and masse of Requiem onn the morow thene next and ymmediatly folowing, that is to saye: First to the subdeane being present at alle the premisses and syngyng highe masse in the said feastes, for eyther daye 2s., in all 4s. To 8 chauntrey prestes bering copes in the said feastes in rewarde 13s. 4d. To 12 petycanons 40s. To 6 vykars 16s. 8d. To every highe canone, petycanone, chauntrey prestes, vykar and chorester being present and bering copies in the said feastes of Transfiguracione and Name of Jħū 4d., in all 26s. 8d. To a petycanon synging masse of Requiem and reding the Pystell and Gospell at the said 3 masses and for saying of *Deprofundis* 2s. 10d. For the collacione there made at the highemasse in the feastes of the Name of Jħū 3s. 4d. To the sextone for garnisshing of the aulters and bering of bokes and other ornamentes 3s. 10d. To 4 veirgiers their being attendaunt, to every of them 16d. with 20d. in reward this yere, 7s. And to the bell ryngers for their labour in the said feastes besydes 20s. to them paied quarterly for keping of the dores of the said crowdes 13s. 8d. } £6 11s. 4d.

Also for the masses of Jħu solempnely by note kepte in the said crowdes by the subdeane, a cardinalle, a petycanone, 6 vykers and 10 choresters of the said cathedrall churche in their habettes and surplices, [and] to a chauntrey prest synging masse of Requiem by note every Frydaye ymmediatly after Jħūs masse with 6 of the choresters, that ys to saye: To the subdeane being present 4d. To the petycanone synging the masse of Jħu 8d. To the chauntrey pest syngyng the masse of Requiem and

---

109   Dublin and Armagh.

every of the vykers[110] 4d. In all for 47^ti Frydays within the tyme of this accompte } £7 16s. 8d.

Also to the maister of the said tenne choresters keping 3 *salves* daily in the said crowdes, after Complayne done in the said cathedrall churche, before the images of Jhu, our Blessed Lady and Seyint Sebestyan, takyng for his labour 26s. 8d. at foure termes of the yere according to the ordenaunce } 26s. 8d.

f. 101r

Also to the bell ryngers of the saide cathedrall churche for their labour and daily attendaunce in openyng, closyng and shetting of the dores of the said crowdes, for rynging of belles, blowing of orgaynes, lighting and queniching of torches and other lightes, and for sweping and making clene of the said crowdes at 20s. by yere payable quarterly, besydes 13s. 8d. to them alowed in the said feastes } 20s.

[145] Also for the rewarde of the Wardeins this yere, lymittede and taxede by the Rectour, Wardeins and Assistence of the said Fraternitie according to the ordenaunce } £4

Also for lyvers of clothing for the said Wardeins withe conysaunces of the name of Jhu, lymittede in lyke wyse by the said Rectour, Wardeins and Assistence } £4

Also to John Worsoppe for the making and engrossing uppe of this accompte } 20s.

Also to the precherses at Poulys Crosse and Seint Mary Spitell remenbring and praying for all the soules of alle the bretherne and sustrene of the said Fraternitie according to the said ordenaunce, that is to saye for 39^ti Sondayes and Good Frydaye at Poulys Crosse and 3 dayes in Ester Weke at Seint Mary Spytelle at 8d. every of the said dayes } 27s. 4d.

Also to the 6 weightes with banners payntede, conysaunces enbroderede with Jhus, going alle the stretes and suburbes of London playing with their instrumentes to gyve warnyng and knowlege to the people of the said Fraternitie for the said feastes of Transfiguracione and Name of Jhū, according to the said ordenaunce 10s. and in rewarde this yere this yere 3s. 3d. [sic] for the tyme of this accompte } 13s. 4d.

---

110 'and every of the vykers' possibly written over erasure.

Also to the proctour of the said Fraternitie for the bonfyre before the northe dore of the said crowdes yerely in the saide evenyng of the said feast of the Name of Jhu 2s. 8d. For the cressett lighte for the same bonfyre 2d. } 2s. 10d.

f. 101v

Also for synging brede, for brede for holybrede, and for 39ti galons and a potell of malmesey spent in the said crowdes within the tyme of this accompte } 48s. 8d.

Also for waxe spent in the said crowdes besyde the waxe foundede by the Wexchaundlers this yere for the tyme of this accompte } 49s. 6d.

Also to the almoyner of Poulys for 10 choresters of the said cathedrall churche servyng God in their habettes in the said crowdes, aswell in the said feastes of Transfiguracione and Name of Jhu as every Frydaye at the masse of Requiem and at the 3 *salves* there kepte dayly by the said Fraternitie } £4 3s. 4d.

Also to Thomas Holme, sextene, attending daily in the said crowdes, keping the vestmentes and other ornamentes belonging to the said Fraternitie for a hole yere within the tyme of this accompte } 40s.

Also to Thomas Batone, Richarde Eve, John Loryng and William Myssilbroke, poure mene appoyntede to the almes of the said Fraternitie, keping the crowdes and helpyng prestes to masse and praying for alle the bretherne and sustrene of the said Fraternitie, every of them 40s. by yere payable quarterly according to the said ordenaunce } £8

Summa } £46 19s. 8d.

f. 102r

[146] Also in sundrey exspences necessary, that is to saye: First for wasshing of alle the lynnene belonging to the crowdes 10s. For settyng onn of the awbes, for mending of awbes, vestmentes & surplices 3s. 4½d. For scowring of candestykkes, basons, lampes and branches 18d. For bromes, pynnes, russhes, reedes to swepe copwebbes downe, nayles, hookes, lavendre, nedulles, pakthrede, 19½d. For a lantorne with a wyer, a perser with 5 irons for mending of the steyere & paving in the crowdes, for mending 4 lokkes of the pewes, 2s. 4d. Paied to the glasyer for this yeres fee and for scowering of glasse 4s. 6d. Item for redemyng of the holy water stokkes that was stollene, for a staye of irone to fastene the same holy water stokke to the pelour, for sowdre, workemanshippe, for

a lok and a key for the same, and for 2 holywater sprynkelles, 2s. 10d. For mending [and] regestring of two masse bokes of paper 20d. For colys, brede and ale for pouremene, starche for corporas kerchers, for scowring of (a) pewter pott for water, for a baskett to cary out dust, for a boxe for synging brede, for a pece of lether hungrey for the organs, for carying of a lode of rubbusshe, 20½d. For 5 galons of lampe oyle and for 2 dozeine of taloughe candell 9s. 2d. To the erbe wiff for garlondes, roseys, jelofers, erbes [and] flowers spent in the crowdes onn Jhūs daye 3s. 4d. For 5 barelles of ale and a kylderkyne of bere 21s. For tappes and trayes 8d. Paiede to 4 porters 4s. To 2 womene to drawe ale 2s. To Thomas Holmes for watching 16d. To 4 pouremene for waching 16d. For mete for them 2 dayes 2s. 8d. Item to Walter Sheffelde for his rewarde 2s. To the queresters for their rewarde 12d. To Ser Richarde Gates, prest, for wex offerede before Jhus 13s. 4d. For the hyre of clothe onn Jhūs daye 2s. 8d. Item paied to Yugo Carpenter for makyng of a new frame and a whele for the secunde bell and for hanging upp of the same bell 26s. 8d. Item paiede to Conwey Smythe for yrone werk for the said frame and bell as aperethe by his bill 24s. Item paied for the levery of Thomas Holmes, Walter Sheffelde and of the 4 poure mene £3 10s. Item paiede to the precher for the collacyone made onn Jhūs daye 3s. 4d. Item paiede to Walter Sheffeld whiche the Assistence grauntede hym in rewarde 30s. Item paied to Eve for a rewarde grauntede by the Assistence towardes the making of a patene of a chalys whiche was stollene from his awlter onn Cristmas Daye 6s. 8d. Item for the hyre of a hourse for Thomas Holmes to ryde to the busshoppe of Ely with a lettre of instaunce from my lorde of London[III] to suffre the proctours to gadre within the dioces of the said busshoppe of Ely, and for his costes, and in rewarde gevene to the same bussoppes officers 7s. 6½d. Item paiede for lyveres gevene to the Wexchaundlers and to the worshipfulle [persons] of the Assistence and other of the bretherne & sustrene of the f.102v

said Fraternitie 8s. 6d. Item gevene to the prestes that saide masse in Jhūs Chappell onn Jhūs daye 3s. 9d. Gevene to the ~~prestes~~ powre folke onn the morow after the masse of Requiem 3s. 4d. Item gevene to the prestes that sang masse in the crowdes upone All Soullene Daye 3s. 7d., and delt to the poure people the same daye 3d. 4d. Item paide to Rauff Caldewell, attourney in the Comene Place, as aperethe by his bill 12s. 4d. Paide to John Worsoppes servaunt for thengrossing up of this accompte 3s. 4d. Paide for the kinges lettres patentes undre his brode seale[112] to gadre in the dioces of Seint Asse, Bangour and Seyint Davies 10s. Item for costes and chargis to vew the landes at Woxbrige whiche

---

[III] Cuthbert Tunstall, bishop of London.
[112] Presumably the Great Seal, although possibly a deputed version of it.

bene now lettene to ferme for 40s. by yere, and for meting and bowding of the same londes, 9s. 4d. }

Summa } £15 19s. 9d.

[147] Also in sundry potacyons necessary, that is to saye at the eleccione of the new Wardeins 11s. 9d. Spent at the awdite of Master Campyone 20s. For the dynner onn Jhus day £4. For a potacyone to the Assistence at the admissione of Master Spenser[113] to be one of the Aldermene of the said Fraternitie, [and] Bengemyne Dygby, mercer, and Thomas Croppes to be of the Assistence, 8s. 3d. Also the said accomptauntes axene allowaunce for charges spent upone the proctours and other straungers comyng to Jhūs masse as before tyme hathe bene allowed 40s. } £8

Summa totalis **of alle the charges and reseytes** } £286 15s. 4½d.

Summa totalis **of alle the paymentes and discharges** } £70 19s. 5d.

Rest due to the said Fraternitie } £215 15s. 11½d.

Wheroff

f. 103

[148] Also the said accomptauntes axene allowaunce for tharrerages of Richarde Piersone and Robert Shether of the last accompte } £8
Item for tharrerages of Henry Storige as aperethe by obligacione } £12
Item for tharrerages of William Marke by obligacyone as aperethe in the last accompte } £6 13s. 4d.
Item for tharrerages of Walter Sheffelde as aperethe by obligacione in the last accompte } 40s.
Item for tharrerages of Roger Robyns due in the last accompte 40s., and of this yeres ferme £5, *summa* } £7
Item for tharrerages of Robert Bristow } 46s. 8d.
Item for tharrerages of this yeres ferme of the dioces of Seint Asse, Banger and Seint Davies lettene to Hughe Rogers and other } £3 6s. 8d.

Summa } £41 6s. 8d.

The said accomptauntes axene allowaunce of thise sommes hereafter ensuyng, whiche sommes the hole Assistence, consyderinge the yere of Jubely[114] and for other consyderacyons them moving, have pardonede,

---

113 Probably Sir James Spencer (d. 1544), vintner, mayor of London 1527/8. Barron, *London*, 351, 352. Spencer bequeathed £5 to the Jesus Guild in his notably Catholic will, TNA, PROB 11/30/139.
114 The year 1527 was the final year of the 64th Jubilee.

for gevene and releasede the persons here undre namede of the arrerages of the last accompte, that is to saye: Of the arrerages of John Copwoode 26s. 8d. Item tharrerages of Richarde Ynskyppe for that he dyede in prysone and in povertie, £4. Item John Sestone for the yere of Jubely 33s. 4d. Item of tharrerages of Richarde Peiersone & Robert Shethare, £4. Item tharrerages of Thomas Norres 40s. Item tharrerages of Thomas Rocheforde 40s. Item tharrerages of Davy Johnsone 13s. 4d. Item of the tharrerages of Hamlett Holbroke 30s. Item of the arrerages of Henry Storige £8 13s. 4d., for asmoche as he aggreede to paye £12 for his arrerages for payment, of the whiche £12 the same Henry hathe bounde hym selff by obligacione to paye yerely 40s. Item of the arrerages of John Tyler 20s. for asmoche as it is evydently founde that he hathe paide the same 20s. in the tyme of Elys Draper, as in the accompt of the same Elys playnly shewethe. Item the arrerages of Robert Bristow 26s. Item for tharrerages of John Mastok for asmoche as the busshoppes in Irelande in no wyse wolde suffre hym to levy nor gader in their dioses the charitie and devocyons of well disposede people, £5. *Summa* } £33 2s. 8d.

f.103v

Rest delyverede to William Broders and William Botery, reseyvours of this accompt } £141 6s. 7½d.

The whiche said somme of £141 6s. 7½d. the said John Worsoppe hath delyverede unto the said William Broders and William Botery before the awdytours according to the ordenaunce, wherof ys put into a chest belonging to the said Fraternitie £71 18s. 5½d. Remaynyng in the handes of the saide William Broders £20 8s. 2s., whiche the same William reseyved at the gyving up of this accompt, and 3 goblettes without covers of silver parcell gilte weying 22 onzes, whiche 3 goblettes lyene to pledge for £4 parcell of the said somme of £141 6s. 7½d., due by Roger Robyns. And £45 parcell of the said somme of £141 6s. 7½d. remaynethe in thandes of Maister John Browne, late Aldermane, as aperethe by obligacione remaynyng in the said chest.

[149] Oblygacyons delyverede by thandes of the said John Worsoppe, accomptaunt, unto thandes of the said William Broders and William Botery, Wardeins for this yere nexte ensuyng, that is to saye from Christemas in the 20ti yere of the reigne of kyng Henry the 8the [1528] unto the feast of Christemas then next folowing.

First an indenture of Robert Shethere, citezeine and merchaunt taylour of London, and Richard Peirsone of Cambridge with an obligacione of £40 to perfourme the covenauntes of the said indenture }

Item an indenture of John Tyler of Coventre of the leasse of the dioces of Worcetour, Herfford, Coventre and Lychefelde } [no amount]

Item an obligacione of the same John and of John Tyler his sonne of the towne of Yatte in the countie of Glowcestre, yoman, of £10 6s. 8d. }

f. 104

Item an indenture of Wa[l]ter Sheffeld of the lease of the citie of London and subberbes of the same and the house of our soverayne lorde the kyng, with an obligacione of £40 to perfourme the covenauntes of the said indenture }

Item an indenture of the said Walter of the lease of Middlesex and the fyve hundredes within the countie of Essexe, and an obligacione with condicione of £5 to perfourme the covenauntes of the said indenture }

Item an obligacione of the same Walter of £4 to pay 40s. at Cristmas next commyng }

Item an indenture of Thomas Leycetour and John Herfforde of the lease of the archedeconry of Chestre and the Yle of Mane, and an obligacione with condicione of 40 £ to perfo[r]me the covenauntes of the same indenture }

Item an obligacione with condicione of Henry Storige of £20, to paye £12 }

Item an obligacione with condicione of William Marke, John Philippe and John Marke of Lyskar[d] of £20, to pay £6 13s. 4d. }

Item an obligacione of Roger Robyns of £5, to pay } £5

Item an other obligacione of the said Roger of £5, to pay } £5

Item an other obligacione with condicone of 5 marke, to pay } 40s.

Item an obligacione with condicione of Thomas Norres of £4, to pay } 40s.

Item an obligacione with condicione of Henry Thornetone and James Alysaunder of £10, to pay } £7

Item an obligacione of Robert Briscow of £5.

Item an obligacione with condicione of Hughe Rogers, Richarde Downe and Roger Ferne of 5 marke, to paye £3 6s. 8d. for the dioces of Seyint Daveys, Seynt Asse and Bangour }

Item an indenture of Lawrence Andertone of the leasse of the archedeconry of Chestre and the Ile (of) Mane and an obligacione of £10 with condicione to perfourme the covenauntes of the said indentures.

f. 104v

Item an indenture of John Sestone of Lewes of the leasse of the dioces of Chichester, with an obligacione of £5 to perfourme the covenauntes of the said indentures.

Item an obligacione with condicione wherin the said John Sestone ys bounde in £20 to delyver unto the Wardeins alle maner of bookes, regesters, scrippes, scrowes or munymentes consernyng the names of the bretherne and sustrene of the said Fraternitie.

Item an inventory of the juelles, goodes and ornamentes belongying to the said Fraternitie.

f. 105r

[**150**] This is thaccompte of William Brothers and William Botery, Wardeins of the Fraternytie or Gilde of the most gloryous Name of Jhū foundede in the crowdes of the cathedralle churche of Seynt Paule of London, form the fest of Christemas in the yere of our lord 1 [sic] God 1528^{ti} and in the 20^{ti} yere of the reigne of kyng Henry the 8th unto the fest of Christemas thene next ensuyng, that is to say by the space of one hole yere.

First the said accomptauntes chargene them selves with therrerages in the foote of the last accompte } £141 6s. 7½d.

Also with therrerages of Richarde Peirsone and Robert Shether of the last accompte } £8

Also with therrerages of Henry Storige as a perethe by obligacione } £12

Also with tharrerages of William Marke by obligacione, as aperethe in the last accompte } £6 13s. 4d.

Also with therrerages of Wa[l]ter Sheffelde as apereth by obligacione in the last accompte } 40s.

Also with therrerages of Roger Robyns due in the last accompte } £7

Also with therrerages of Robert Bristow } 46s. 8d.

Also with therrerages of this yeres ferme of the dioces of Seynt Asse, Banger and Seynt Davyes lettyne to Hughe Rogers and other } £3 6s. 8d.

Summa } £182 13s. 3½d.

f. 105v

[**151**] Also with the ferme of two tenementes and certeyne londes lying in the towne and feldes of Uxbridge in the counties of Middlesex and Bukkingham lettyne to William Bayly and James Standelle for 40s. by yere payable at the festes of Seynt Mighelle Tharchaungelle and Thannunciaacione [sic] of our Blessed Lady by evyne porcions, that is to say for the same festes within the tyme of this accompte } 40s.

Also with the ferme of alle the devocions belongyng to the said Fraternitie of the provynce of York, the dioces of Ely, Lincolne and Norwiche lettyne to Robert Shether, citizeine and merchaunt taylour of London, and to Richarde Peirsone of Cambridge by endenture for a yere within the tyme of this accompte } £24

Also with the ferme of lyke devocyons of the dioces of Worcetour, Chester and Herfforde lettyne to John Tyler of Coventre for £10 6s. 8d. within the tyme of this accompte } £10 6s. 8d.

Also with the ferme of lyke devocyons of parte of the countie of Essexe lettene to Thomas Norres for 40s. by yere as apereth by obligacione for the tyme of this accompte } 40s.

Also with ferme of lyke devocions of the countie of Middlesex and parte of the countie of Essexe lettene to Wa[l]ter Sheffelde by yere as apereth by indenture for the tyme of this accompte } 40s.

Also with the ferme of lyke devocyons of the citie of London lettene to the said Wa[l]ter by indenture for £20 10s. by yere for the tyme of this accompte } £20 10s.

f.106r

Also with the ferme of lyke devocyons of the dioces off Canterbury lettyne to Robert Bristow for £5 by yere as apereth by obligacione for the tyme of this accompte } £5

Also with the ferme of lyke devocyons of the dioces of Chichestre lettyne to John Sestone of Lewes by indenture for 33s. 4d. by yere for the tyme of this accompte } 33s. 4d.

Also with the ferme of lyke devocyons of the dioces of Wyntone and Sarum lettyne to Thomas Holme for £5 by yere as aperethe by obligacione for the tyme of this accompte } £5

Also with the ferme of lyke devocyons of the archedeconry of Chestour and the Yle of Mane lettyne by indenture to John Herfforde for 33s. 4d. for the tyme of this accompte } 33s. 4d.

Also with the ferme of lyke devocyons of the dioces of Seynt Asse, Bangour and Seynt Davyes lettyne to Evane Formoue by indenture for half a yere within the tyme of this accompte } 33s. 4d.

Also with the ferme of lyke devocyons of the dioces of Exetour, Bathe and Welles[115] lettyne to Henry Thornetone by yere within the tyme of this accompte } £7

Also for waxe offerede before Jħus – 17s.

Also of the Wardeyns of the Phelisshipe of Wexchaundlers of London for an annualle rent of 20s. by yere } 20s.

Also for the hyer of 7 blak ho sattene hoodes } 9s. 4d.

Summa } £85 3s.

f. 106v

Summa *totales* of alle the charges and reseytes } £267 16s. 3½d.

Wherof paid

[152] The said accomptauntes accompte in payment ordenary to be made in the crowdes of the said crowdes cathedrall churche being present and kepyng dyvyne service in the festes of Transfiguracione and Name of Jħu and masse of Requiem onn the morowe thene next and ymmedyatly

---

[115] 'Exetour, Bathe and Welles' written over erasure.

folowing, that is to saye: First, to the subdeane being present at all the premysses and synging high masse in the said festes, for eyther day 2s., in all 4d. To 8 chauntrey prestes be(r)ing copies in the said feastes, in rewarde 13s. 4d. To 12 petycanons 40s. To 6 vykers 16s. 8d. To every highe canone, petycanone, chauntrey prestes, vyker and chorester being present and bering copies in the said feastes of Transfiguracione and Name of Jhu 4d., in all 27s. 2d. To a petycanone synging masse of Requiem and reding the Pystelle and Gospelle at the said 3 masses and for saying of *Deprofundis* 2s. 10d. For the collacione there made at the highe masse in the festes and Name of Jhu 3s. 4d. To the sextone for garnysshing of the aulters and bering of bokes and other ornamentes 3s. 10d. To 4 veirgers their being attendaunt, to every of them 16d. with 20d. in rewarde this yere, 7s. And to the belle ryngers for their labour in the said festes besydes 20s. to them paide quarterly for keping of the dores of the said crowdes 13s. 8d. } £6 11s. 10d.

Also for the masses of Jhu solempnely by note kepte in the said crowdes by the subdeane, a cardynalle, a petycanone, 6 vykers and 10 choresters ~~that is to say~~ of the said cathedralle churche in their habeittes and surplices, [and] to a chauntrey prest syngyng masse of Requiem by note every Fryday ymmediatly aftre Jhūs masse with 6 of the choresters, that is to say: To the subdeane being present 4d. To the petycanone synging the masse of Jhū 8d. To the chauntrey prest synging the masse of Requiem and every of the vykers 4d. In alle, for 47te Frydayes within the tyme of this accompte } £7 16s. 8d.

f. 107r

Also to the maister of the said tene choresters, kepyng 3 *salves* daily in the said crowdes, aftre Complayne done in the said cathedrall churche, before the ymages of Jhu, our Blessed Lady and Seynt Sebastiane, takyng for his labour 26s. 8d. at 4 termes of the yere according to the ordenaunce } 26s. 8d.

Also to the belle ryngers of the said cathedralle churche for their labour and day[ly][116] attendaunce in openyng, closyng and shetting of the dores of the said crowdes, for ryngyng of belles, blowing of orgaynes, lighting and quenching of torches and other lightes, and for swepyng and makyng clene of the said crowdes at 20s. by yere payable quarterly, besydes 13s. 8d. to them alowede in the saide feastes } 20s.

[153] Also for the rewarde of the Wardeins this yere, lymyttede and taxede by the Rectour, Wardeins and Assistence of the said Fraternitie

---

[116]   Mark on manuscript, possibly wax.

according to the ordenaunce } £4

Also for lyvers of clothing for the said Wardeins with conysaunces of the name of Jħu, lymyttede in lyke wyse by the saide Rectour, Wardeins and Assistence } £4

Also to John Worsoppe for the makyng and engrossing up of this accompte } 20s.

Also to the prechers at Poulys Crosse and Seynt Mary Spytelle remenbring and praying for all the soules of all the bretherne and sustrene of the said Fraternitie according to the said ordenaunce, that is to say for 40 Sondayes and Good Fryday at Poulys Crosse and 3 dayes in Ester Weke at Seynt Mary Spytelle at 8d. every of the said dayes } 29s.

Also to the 6 weightes with banners paynetede, conysaunces enbrowderede with Jħūs, going all the stretes and subburbes of London playing with their instrumentes to gyve warnyng and knowlege to the peopylle of the said Fraternitie for the said festes of Transfyguracione and Name of Jħu, according to the said ordenaunce 10s., and in rewarde this yere 3s. 4d. for the tyme of this accompte } 13s. 4d.

f. 107v
Also to the proctour of the said Fraternitie for the bonfyre before the northe dore of the said crowdes yerely in the said evenyng of the fest of the Name of Jħu 2s. 8d. For the cressett light for the tyme of this accompte [no amount] } 2s. 10d.

Also for syngyng brede, for brede for holy brede, and for 44ᵗⁱ gallownes of malvynsey at 12d. the gallone, *summa* – 44s. Spent in the said crowdes within the tyme of this accompte } 53s. ½d.

Also for waxe spent in the said crowdes besyde the waxe foundede by the Wexchaundlers this yere for the tyme of this accompte } 53s. 9d.

Also to the almoyner of Poulys for 10 choresters of the said cathedrall churche servyng God in their habeittes in the said crowdes, aswelle in the said festes of Transfiguracione and Name of Jħu as every Fryday at the masse of Requiem and at the 3 *salves* kepte dayly by the said Fraternitie } £4 3s. 4d.

Also to Thomas Holme, sextone, attending dayly in the said crowdes, kepyng the vestmentes and other ornamentes belonging to the said Fraternitie for a hole yere within the tyme of this accompte } 40s.

Also to Thomas Batone, Richarde Eve, John Loryng and William Myssilbroke, powremene appoynetede to the almes of the said Fraternitie, keping the crowdes and helping prestes to masse and praying for alle the bretherne and susterne of the said Fraternitie, every of them 40s. by yere payable quarterly according to the said ordenaunce } £8

f. 108r

[154] Also in sundry exspences necessary, that ys to say: For wasshing of all the lynnene clothes belonging to the crowdes 10s. For setting onn of awbes, mendyng of vestmentes, awter clothes, surplices and towelles 3s. 2d. For 40 elles of lynnene cloth for awbes 33s. 4d. For makyng of the same awbes 2s. 2d. For 2 halywater stykkes [and] 4 snoffers to put out lynkes 6d. For 4 velome skynnes, mending of 5 masse bokes, and for prykkyng of a masse whiche Docter Fayrefaxe[117] gave to Jħus Chapell, 5s. 6d. For entring of an accione [against] Robyns and for resting of hym, and for a mercement paid for hym to the sh[e]ryffes, 22d. For hokes, pynnes, pakthrede, russhes, bromes, nayles, and for pavyng in Jħus Chapelle, mending of lokkes, and carying awey of russhes, 2s. 1d. For 2 dozeine of new hassokkes 2s. For a rope weying 19lb. and for teying of a rope at Jħūs Dore 2s. 11d. For scowring of candelstykes, basons, lampes and braunches 11d. For makyng clene of glasse wyndowes and for 4 quarelles for the same wyndowes 2s. For mending and gresyng of belles, for a lampe, mending of a key and the lokk of the halywater stokke, for 2 stayes and a hoke of irone for the deske, and for gl[o]wing of the dyadane onn Jħus hede, 11d. For mending [and] turnyng of the orgaynes, and for a stay, 2 payre garnettes, 2 lopes, 2 hokes, nayles, ledges, and 2 dayes work of a carpenter for the same orgaynes, 9s. For hanging of Jħus Chapell 5s. For purchesing of my Lorde Cardenalles[118] seale for one of the proctours, 10s. For coles, brede [and] ale at sondry tymes to the pouremene 19d. For 5 galondes of lampe oyle and 2 dozeine of taloughe candelle 8s. To the erbe wyffe for garlondes, roses, jelofers, erbys and flowers spent in the crowdes onn Jħus Day 3s. 4d. For 5 barelles of ale 20s. For tappes [and] trayes 8d. To 4 porters kepyng the dores 4s. To 2 women to draw ale 2s. To Thomas Holme for whatching 16d. To 4 pouremene for watching 16d. For mete for them 2 dayes 8d. To Wa[l]ter Sheffelde for his rewarde 2s. To the queresters for their rewarde 12d. To Ser Richarde Gates, prest

---

[117] Dr Robert Fayrfax (d. 1521). For his association with the Jesus Guild, see D. Mateer and E. A. New, '"In nomine Jesu": Robert Fayrfax and the Guild of the Holy Name in St Paul's Cathedral', *Music and Letters* 81 (2000), 507–20.

[118] Thomas Wolsey (d. 1530), cardinal archbishop of York.

of Poules, for wex offerede before Jħus 13s. 4d. For lyveres gvene to the Wexchaundlers and to the Assistence and other, the bretheren and sustrene of the same Fraternitie, 7s. 9d. To the prestes that said masse in Jħus Chapelle on Jħus day and All Soullene Day, for bothe dayes 6s. 8d. To powre fowlke onn the said 2 dayes 6s. 8d. To John Worsopp servaunt for thengrossing up of this accompte 3s. 4d. And for a key and a barre of irone for a chest 8d. } £8 15s. 8d.

f. 108v

[**155**] Also in sundry potacyons necessary, that is to say: At the the [sic[119]] eleccyone of the new Wardeyne 12s. 1d. Spent at the awdyte of Master Worsoppe 20s. For the dynner onn Jħūs day £4. For a potacyone to the Assistence whene the went to the busshope of Ely 9d. Also the said accomptauntes axene allowaunce for charges spent upone the proctours and other straungers comyng to Jhus masse as before tyme hathe bene allowede 40s. } £7 12s. 10d.

Also the said accomptauntes axene allowaunce for therrerages of Richarde Peirsone & Robert Shether of the last accompte } £8
Item for therrerages of Henry Storige as aperethe by obligacion } £12
Item for therrerages of William Marke by obligacione as aperethe in the last accompte } £6 13s. 4d.
Item for therrerages of of Walter Sheffelde as aperethe by obligacione in the last accompte 40s., and of this yeres ferme £4 } £6
Item for therrerages of Roger Robyns due in the last accompt 40s., and of this yeres ferme £5 } £7
Item for therrerages of Robert Bristow as aperethe in the last accompte 46s. 8d., and of this yeres ferme £3 } £5 6s. 8d.
Item for therrerages of Hugh Rogers and other as aperethe in the last accompte £3 6s. 8d., and of this yeres ferme £3 6s. 8d. } £6 13s. 4d.
Item for therrerages of John Sestone of the yeres ferme of this accompte } 33s. 4d.
Item for therrerages of Thomas Holme of this yeres ferme of this accompte } 20s.

Summa } £54 6s. 8d.

Summa totalis of alle the chargis and reseitis } £267 16s. 3½d.

Summa totalis of alle the paymentes, disthargis and allowauncis } £118 4s. 7½d.

And so due to the said Fraternitie } £149 11s. 8d.

---

119   Word repeated across line-break.

f. 109r

[**156**] Rest delyverede to William Botery and William Brokett, rescyvours of this accompte } £149 11s. 8d.

The whiche said somme of £149 11s. 8d. the said William Brothers hath delyverede unto the said William Botery and William Brokett before the awdytours according to the ordenaunce. Wherof is put into a chest belonging to the said Fraternitie £80 11s. 8d., remaynyng in the handes of the said William Botery £20, whiche the same William Botery receyvede at the gyving upp of this accompte; and 3 goblettes without covers of sylver parcelle gilte weying 22^{ti} unces, whiche 3 goblettes lyene to pledge for £4, parcell of the said somme £149 11s. 8d., due by Roger Robyns. And £45 parcell of the said somme of £149 11s. 8d. remaynethe in the handes of Master John Browne, late aldermane, as aperethe by obligacione remaynyng in the saide chest }

[157] Obligacions delyverede by thandes of the said William Broders, accomptaunt, unto thandes of the said William Botery and William Brokett, Wardeins for this yere next ensuying, that is to say from Christemas in the 21^{ti} yere of the reigne of kyng Henry the 8th [1529] unto the fest of Christemas then next folowing }

First an indenture of Robert Shether, citezeine and merchaunt taylour of London, and Richard Peirsone of Cambridge, with an obligacione of £40 to perfourme the covenauntes of the said indenture.
Item an indenture of John Tyler of Coventre of the leasse of the dioces of Worcetour, Herfford, Coventre & Lychefelde } [no amount]
f. 109v
Item an obligacione of the same John and of John Tyler his sonne of the towne of Yatt in the countie of Glowcestre, yomane, of £10 6s. 8d. }
Item an indenture of Wa[l]ter Leycetour and John Herfforde of the leasse of the archedeconry of Chestre and the Ile of Man, and an obligacione with condicione of £40 to perfourme the covenauntes of the same indenture.
Item an obligacione with condicione of Henry Storige of £20, to pay £12.
Item an obligacione with condicione of William Marke, John Philip & John Marke of Lyskar[d] of £20, to pay £6 13s. 4d.
Item an obigacione with condicione of Henry ~~Storige~~ Thornetone and James Alysaunder of £10, to pay £7
Item an obligacion of James Huntley of £4, to pay 40s.
Item an obligacione of Robert Bristow of £5.
Item an obligacione with condicione of Hughe Rogers, Richarde Downe

[and] Roger Fermer ~~of 5 marke~~ to pay £3 6s. 8d. for the dioces of Seynt Davyes, Seynt Asse and Bangour.

Item an indenture of Lawrence Awdertone of the leasse of the archedeconry of Chestre & the Ile of Mane, and an obligacione of £10 with condicione to performe the covenauntes of the said indentures.

Item an indenture of John Sestone of Lewes of the leasse of the dioces of Chichestre with an obligacione of £5 to perfourme the covnauntes of the said indentures.

f. 110r

Item an obligacione with condicione wherin the said John Sestone ys bounde in £20 to delyver unto the Wardeins alle maner of bokes, regestres, scrippes, scrowes or munymentes consernyng the names of the bretherne and sustrene of the said Fraternitie.

Item an inventory of the juelles, goodes and ornamentes belonging to the said Fraternitie.

f. 110v

[158] This is thaccompte of William Botery and William Brokett, Wardeins of the Fraternitie or Gilde of the most glorious Name of Jhu' foundede in the crowdes of the cathedralle churche of Seynt Paule of London, frome the fest of Christemas in the yere of our Lorde God 1529^ti and in the 21^ti yere of the reigne of kyng Henry the 8^the unto the fest of Christemas then next ensuyng, that is to saye by the space of one hole yere.

First the said accomptauntes chargene them selves with therrerages in the foote of the last accompte } £149 11s. 8d.

Also with therreragis of Richarde Peirsone and Robert Shether of the last accompte } £8

Also with therreragis of Henry Storige as aperethe by obligacione } £12

Also with therreragis of William Marke by obligacione as aperethe in the last accompte } £6 13s. 4d.

Also with therreragis of Wa[l]ter Sheffelde as aperethe in the last accompte } £6

Also with therreragis of Roger Robyns due in the last accompte } £7

Also with therreragis of Robert Bristow } £5 6s. 8d.

Also with therreragis of the dioses of Seynt Asse, Bangour and Seynt Davyes lettyne to Hughe Rogers and other as aperethe in the last accompte } £6 13s. 4d.

Also with therreragis of John Sestone as aperethe in the foote of the last accompte } 33s. 4d.

Also with therreragis of Thomas Holme as aperethe in the foote of the last accompte } 20s.

Summa } £203 18s. 4d.

f. 111r

[159] Also with the ferme of two tenementes and certeyne londes lying
in the towne and feldes of Uxbridge in the countie of Middlesex and
Bukkingham lettyne to William Bayly and James Standelle for 40s.
by yere payable at the feastes of Seynt Mighelle Tharcheungelle &
Thannunciacione of our Blessede Lady by evyne porcions, that is to say
for the same festes within the tyme of this accompte } 40s.

Also with the ferme of alle the devocions belonging to the saide
Fraternitie of the province of Yorke, the dioses of Lincolne, Ely and
Norwich lettyne to Robert Shether, citezeine and merchaunt taylour of
London, and to Richarde Peirsone of Cambridge by endenture for a yere
within the tyme of this accompte } £24

Also with the ferme of lyke devocyons of the dioses of Worcetour,
Chestre and Herfforde lettyne to John Tyler of Coventre for £10 6s. 8d.
within the tyme of this accompte } £10 6s. 8d.

Also with the ferme of lyke devocions of parte of the countie of Essexe
lettyne to Jamys Huntley for 40s. by yere as aperethe by obligacione
for the tyme of this accompte } 40s.

Also with the ferme of lyke devocyons of the countie of Middlesex and
parte of the countie of Essexe lettyne to Wa[l]ter Sheffelde by yere as
aperethe by endenture for the tyme of this accompte } 40s.

Also with the ferme of lyke devocions of the citie of London lettyne
to the saide Wa[l]ter by endenture for £20 10s. by yere for the tyme of
this accompte } £20 10s.

Also with the ferme of lyke devocions of the dioses of Canterbury
lettyne to John Spynke for £5 by yere as aperethe by endenture } £5

Also with the ferme of lyke devocions of the dioses of Chichestre lettyne
to John Sestone of Lewes by endenture for 33s. 4d. by yere for the tyme
of this accompte } 33s. 4d.

Also with the ferme of lyke devocyons of the dioses of Wyntone and
Sarum lettyne to Thomas Holme for £5 by yere as aperethe by obligacione
for the tyme of this accompte } £5

Summa } £72 10s.

f. 111v

Also with the ferme of lyke devocions of the archedeconry of Chestour
and the Yle of Mane lettyne by endenture to John Hertforde for 33s. 4d.
for the tyme of this accompte } 33s. 4d.

Also with the ferme of lyke devocions of the dioses of Seynt Asse,
Bangour and Seynt Davyes lettyne to [blank] for the tyme of this
accompte } £3 6s. 8d.

Also with the ferme of lyke devocyons of the diose of Exetour, Bathe and Welles lettyne to Henry Thornetone by yere within the tyme of this accompte } £7

Also for waxe offerede before Jhūs } 15s. 5d.
Also of the Wardeins of the Felishippe of Wexchaundlers of London for an annuelle rent of 20s. by yere } 20s.
Also for the hyer of blak sattene hodes } 20s.
Also with the bequest of Hughe Actone, merchaunt taylour } 40s.

Summa } £16 15s. 10d.

Summa totalis **of alle the chargis and reseites** } £293 4s. 2d.

Wherof paide

f. 112r

[160] The said accomptauntes accompte in payment ordenary to be made in the crowdes of the saide cathedralle churche to sundry mynysters of the same church being present and keping dyvyne service there of and in the festes of Transfiguracione and Name of Jhu' and masse of Requiem onn the morow then next and ymmediatly folowing, that ys to saye: First, to the subdeane being present at alle the premissis and singing highemasse in the saide feastes, for either day 2s., in alle 4s. To 8 chauntrey prestes bering copies in the saide festes, in rewarde 13s. 4d. To 12 pety canons 40s. To 6 vykers 16s. 8d. To every highe canone, petycanone, chauntrey prestes, vyker and quorester being present and bering copes in the saide feastes of Transfiguracione and Name of Jhu', 4d., in alle 27s. 2d. To a petycanone synging masse of Requiem and reding the Pistelle and Gospelle at the saide 3 masses and for saying of *Deprofundis* 2s. 10d. For the collacione there made at the highe masse in the festes and Name of Jhū 3s. 4d. To the sextone for garnysshing of the aulters and bering of bokes and other ornamentes 3s. 10d. To 4 veirgers their being attendaunt, to every of them 16d. with 20d. in rewarde this yere, 7s. And to the belle ryngers for their labour in the saide festes besydes 20s. to them paide p quarterly for keping of the dores of the said crowdes, 13s. 8d. *Summa* } £6 11s. 10d.

Also for the masses of Jhu' solempnely by note kepte in the saide crowdes by the subdeane, a cardinalle, a petycanone, 6 vykers and 10 quoresters of the saide cathedralle church in their habettes & surplices, [and] to a chauntrey prest synging masse of Requiem by note every Frydaye ymmediatly aftre Jħus masse with 6 of the quoresters, that is to say: To the subdeane being present 4d. To the petycanone synging the masse of Jhu' 8d. To the chauntrey prest synging the masse of Requiem and every of the vykers 4d. In alle for 47^{ti} Frydayes within the tyme of this accompte } £7 16s. 8d.

Also to the maistre of the saide 10 quoresters kepyng 3 *salves* dayly in the saide crowdes aftre Complayne done in the saide cathedralle church, before the ymages of Jhū, our Blessede Lady and Seynt Sebestyan, takyng for his labour 26s. 8d. at 4 termes of the yere, that is to saye according to the ordenaunce } 26s. 8d.

Also to the belle ryngers of the saide cathedralle churche for their labour and dayly attendaunce in openyng, closyng and shutting of the dores of the saide crowdes, for ryngyng of belles, blowing of orgaynes, lighting and quenching of torches and other lightes, and for sweping and makyng clene of the saide crowdes at 20s. by yere payable quarterly, besydes 13s. 8d. to them allowede in the said festes } 20s.

Summa } £16 15s. 2d.

f. 112v

[161] Also for the rewarde of the Wardeins this yere, lymyttede and taxede by the Rectour, Wardeins and Assistence of the saide Fraternitie according to the ordenaunce } £4

Also for lyveres for clothing for the saide Wardeins with conysaunces of the same [sic] of Jhu, lymyttede in lyke wise by the said Rectour, Wardeins and Assistence } £4

Also to John Worsoppe for makyng and engrossing uppe of this accompte } 20s.

Also to the prechers at Poulys Crosse and Seynt Mary Spyttelle remenbryng and praying for alle the soules of alle the bretherne and sustrene of the saide Fraternitie for 44ti Sondayes and Good Fryday at Poulys Crosse and 3 dayes in Estre Weke at Seynt Mary Spyttelle, at 8d. every of the said dayes } 32s.

Also to the 6 weightes with banners paynetede, conysaunces enbrowerede with Jhūs, going alle the stretes and subburbes of London playing with their instrumentes to gyve warnyng and knowlege to the people of the saide Fraternitie for the saide festes of Transfiguracione and Name of Jhū, according to the said ordenaunce 10s., and in rewarde this yere 3s. 4d. for the tyme of this accompte } 13s. 4d.

Also to the proctour of the saide Fraternitie for the bonefyre before the northe dore of the saide crowdes yerely in the saide evenyng of the fest of the Name of Jhū 2s. 8d. For the cressett lighte for the tyme of this accompte [no amount]} 2s. 10d.

Also for synging brede, brede for holy brede, and for 40^{ti} gallondes of malmesay at 12d. the gallonde, *summa* 40s. Spent in the saide crowdes within the tyme of this accompte } 48s. 6½d.

Also for waxe spent in the said crowdes besyde the waxe foundede by the Wexchaundlers this yere for the tyme of this accompte } 43s. 6d.

Summa } £16 2½d.

f. 113r

Also to the almoynour of Poulis for 10 quoresters of the saide cathedralle churche servying God in their habettes in the said crowdes, aswelle in the said festes of Transfiguracione and Name of Jhū as every Fryday at the masse of Requiem and at the 3 *salves* kepte dayly by the saide Fraternitie } £4 3s. 4d.

Also to Thomas Holme, sextone, attending daily in the saide crowdes, kepyng the vestmentes and other ornamentes belonging to the saide Fraternitie, for a hole yere within the tyme of this accompte } 40s.

Also to Thomas Batone, Richarde Eve, John Loring and William Myssilbroke, pour mene appoyntede to the almes of the saide Fraternitie, keping the crowdes and helping prestes to masse and preying for alle the bretherne and sustrene of the saide Fraternitie, every of them 40s. by yere payable quarterly according to the saide ordenaunce } £8

Summa } £14 3s. 4d.[120]

[162] Also in sundry exspences necessary, that is to say: First, paide to a vestment maker for turnyng of a redde vestment, for rebonde threde and sering candelle for the same 11d. For settyng onn of parelles upone vestmentes and amettes 2d. Paide for a glasse for a paxe which Maistres Grene gave 1d. Paide for grynding of a paryng irone and smalle corde 1½d. Paid for carying of a chest into Jhūs Chappelle 2d. Paid for mending of the loke and for a barre of irone for the same chest 7d. Paide to the bedille of the beggers to kepe pour people out of Jhūs Chappelle 2d. Paide for carying awey of olde hassokkes and other rubbusshe 2d.

---

[120] The amount is in a lighter ink and slightly less formal hand than the preceeding and following text.

Paide for 2 wyping towelles for handes 3d. Paide to the bisshoppe of Londons secreatory and to his chambeleyne for a lettre to the bisshoppe of Ely 20d. Paide for lymmyng of 10 great lettres and 20 small lettres with byce and golde in the boke that Doctour Fayrefaxe[121] gave 10d. Paide for makyng of 5 surplices 20d. Paide for whiting of 12 corporas kerchers and for hallowing of them 5d. Paide for mendyng of a loke and a key of the great chest 2d. Paide for borde and wyre for a wyndow 2d. Paide for lavendre to ley amongest the vestmentes & clothes 1d. Paide for pynnes, hokes, pakthrede [and] russhes 7½d. Paide for 2 barres of irone and a stay 13d. Paide for makyng clene of the glasse wyndowes and for scowering of the candellestyckes, basons, ewers, crewettes and halywaterstok 13d. Paid for 2 Jĥus for 2 hodes 4d. Paide for tewnyng of the orgaynes 20d. Paide for mending of the loke of the Maisters pew 2d. Paide for a hoke to holde opene the wyndow 2d. For pykkyng of the belles and gresse 4d. Paide to the glasyer for glasing of the wyndowes 3s. 4d. Paide for paring and sweping of Jĥūs Chappelle & for mending of a rope 6d. Paide for makyng of a key for the great chest 2d. Paide for an hamper for the chalices and for a loke and a key for the same hamper 10d. Paide for a Jĥus gyvene to a bacheler 2d. Paide to a suffregane for hallowing of 4 chalices[122] and for Thomas Holmes costes to Croydone 2s. 2d. Paide for a tabylle to sett onn Seynt Annes aulter and for mending of a nother 4d. Paide for a pece of white gurdelle rebonde 4d. Paide for a quarter of redde tynselle sattene for Jĥūs aulter 22d. Paide for 4 peces of threde rebonde for vestmentes 8d. Paide for redde, blew and grene threde for vestmentes and sering candelle 8½d. Paide for sowdering and mending of the basone in Jĥūs Chapelle and for a lampe glasse for the same 10d. Paide to a vestment maker for mending of vestmentes, aulterclothes

f. 113v

stoles and other apparelle to them belonging 8s. 3d. Paide for hyring of clothes of arras onn Jĥūs day [and] for cariage and recarriage of them from the Towre and to the Towre 7s. 7d. Paide for bromys 4d. Paid for 2 dozeine of talowgh candelle 2s. Paide for 4 gallondes and a pottelle of lampe oyle 5s. 5d. Paide for wasshing of alle the lynnyng [sic] clothes belonging to the crowdes 10s. Paide for coles, brede and ale at sundry tymes to the pour mene 17d. Paide to the erbe wiff for garlondes, roses, jelofers, erbes and flowers spent in the crowdes onn Jĥūs day 3s. 4d. For 5 barelles of ale 20s. For tappes and treyes 8d. Paide to two womene to draw ale 2s. Paide to Thomas Holme for watching 16d., and to 4 pour mene for watching, 16d. Paide to 4 porters keping the dores 4s. For mete for them and the porters for 2 dayes 2s. 8d. To Walter Sheffelde for his reward 2s. To the quoresters for their rewarde 12d. To

---

[121]   Dr Robert Fayrfax (d.1521). See also [154].
[122]   Symbol in left margin next to this entry.

Ser Richard Gates, prest of Poules, for wexe offered before Jhūs 13s. 4d. For lyveres gyvene to the Wexchaundlers and other bretherne and sustrene of the saide Fraternitie 7s. 4d. To the prestes that saide masse in Jhūs Chappelle onn Jhūs day and Alle Soules day, for bothe dayes 6s. 8d. Gevene in almes to the pour people onn bothe the said dayes 6s. 8d. To John Worsoppis servaunt for engrossing of this accompte 3s. 4d. Paide for 22^ti elles of brisselle clothe for albes and surplices at 5d. the elle 9s. 2d. Paid for 4 yerdes of grene bokeram for vestmentes at 4d. *le* yerde, 16d. Paide for a yerde quarter *dimidium* [half] of white bridges sattene for the frountes of Our Lady aulter 2s. 9d. Paide for 4 yerdes of blew bokeram for vestmentes at 4d. *le* yerde, 16d. Paide for a yerd & *dimidium* quarter of redd bridges sattene for a vestment 2s. 3d. Paide for 3 yerdes of tawny bridges sattene for a vestment at 2s. *le* yerd, 6s. Paide for 4 chalices, wherof one ys silver parcelle gilte weying 14 unces *dimidium* & *dimidium* quarter, one other of silver parcelle gilte weying 14 unces quarter *dimedium*, one other of silver parcelle gilte weying 14 unces *dimidium* quarter, and the 4^the of silver parcelle gilte weying 13 unces, *summa le ounz* 56^ti unces *dimidium* quarter, preice *le ounz* 4s. 4d. *summa,* £12 3s.[123] Paide for 2 payre of endentures of leasse and two obligacions to performe the covenauntes of the same endentures, wherof one payre was for Wa[l]ter Sheffelde and the other payre for John Spynke, at 4s. the payre, 8s. } £20 9s. 5½d.

Also in sundry potacions necessary, that is to say: At the eleccione of the new Wardeyne 9s. 7d. Spent at the awdyte of Maistre Broders 20s. For the dynner onn Jhūs day £4. For a brekefaste gyvene to dyvers of the Assistence onn Jhūs day at Thomas Holmes, 11d. For a potacione at the assymble of Master Croppes 2s. For a potacione at the assymble of Master Speight 20d. Also the saide accomptauntes axene allowaunce for charges spent upone the proctours and other straungers commyng to Jhūs masse as before tyme tyme [sic[124]] hathe byne allowed 40s. *Summa* } £7 14s. 2d.

Summa } £28 3s. 7½d.

f. 114r

[163] Also the said accomptauntes axene allowaunce for tharrerages [of] Richarde Peirsone and Robert Shether in the last accompte } £7 ~~16~~ 13s. 4d.
Item for therrerages of Henry Storige as aperethe by obligacione } £12
Item for therrerages of William Marke by obligacione as aperethe in the last accompte } £6 13s. 4d.

---

[123] Symbol in left margin by this entry for the chalices.
[124] Line-break between repeated word.

Item for therrerages of Walter Sheffelde as aperethe in the fote of the last accompte £6, and in the tyme of this accompte 30s., *summa* } £7 10s.

Item for therrerages of Robert Bristow as apereth in the last accompte } £5 6s. 8d.

Item for therrerages of Hughe Rogers as aperethe in the last accompte } £6 13s. 4d.

Item for therrerages of Thomas Holme of the last accompte 20s., and of this yeres ferme 20s. *Summa* } 40s.

Item for therrerages of Henry Thornetone in the tyme of this accompte } 10s.

Item for therrerages of Caunterbury lettyne to John Spynke } £3[125]

Item for therrrages of of the dioses of Seynt Davide, Seynt Asse and Bangour } £3 6s. 8d.

Item for therrerages of John Sestone } £3 6s. 8d.

Item for therrerages of Roger Robyns due in the last accompte £4, the which said somme of £4 the Assistence releassede and pardonede the saide Roger Robyns } £4

Summa } £62

Summa totalis of alle the charges and reseites } £293 4s. 2d.

Summa totales of alle the paymentes and allowaunces } £137 2s. 4d.

And so due to the said Fraternitie } £156 22d.

Rest delyverede to William Brokett and William Pavyer, reseyvours of this accompte } £156 22d.

f. 114v

The whiche said somme of £156 22d. the saide William Botery hathe delyverede unto thandes of the saide William Brokett and William Pavyer before the awdytous according to the ordenaunce, wherof is put into a chest belonging to the saide Fraternitie £84 22d., remaynyng in thandes of the saide William Brokett £20 which the saide William Brokett reseyvede at the gyvyng up of this accompte. Also remaynyng in thandes of the same William Brokett theise parcelles of plate folowing, that is to saye: 3 goblettes without a cover of silver parcelle gilte weying 22[ti] unces; one other goblett without a cover of silver parcelle gilte weying 9 unces 3 quarter; a salt with a cover of silver parcelle gilte weying 19 unces; and a stonding maser, the fote and the bounde of silver over gilte, weying 7 onzes quarter; which saide parcelles of plate leyene to pledge for £7 due by Roger Robyns, parcelle of the saide somme of

---

[125]   Ambiguous. Could be £2 with a truncated end and a dash from the end of the line.

£156 22d. And £45 parcelle of the same somme of £156 22d. remaynethe in thandes of Maistre John Browne, late aldermane, as aperethe by obligacione remaynyng in the saide chest }

[164] Obligacions delyverede by thandes of the saide William Botery, accomptaunt, unto thandes of the saide William Brokett and William Pavyer, Wardeins for this yere next ensuyng, that is to say frome Christemas in the 22^ti yere of the reigne of kyng Henry the 8^the [1530] unto the fest of Christemas thene next folowing }

First an indenture of Robert Shether, citezeine and mer[char]unt taylour of London, and Richarde Peirsone ~~and~~ of Cambridge, with an obligacione of £40 to performe the covenauntes of the saide endenture.

Item an indenture of John Tyler of Coventre of the leasse of the dioses of Worcetour, Herfford, Coventre and Lichefelde } [no amount]

Item an obligacione of the same John ~~and of John Tyler his sonne of the towne of Yate in the countie of Glowcestr yeomane~~ of £10 6s. 8d.

Item an indenture of ~~Water~~ (Thomas) Leycetour and John Herfforde of the leasse of the archedeconry of Chestre and the Yle of Mane, and an obligacione with condicione of £40 to performe the covnenauntes of the same endenture.

f. 115r

Item an obligacione with condicioun of Henry Storige of £20, to pay £12.

Item an obligacioun with condicione of William Marke, John Philipp and John Marke of Lyskar[d] of £20, to pay £6 13s. 4d.

Item an obligacione with condicione of Henry Thornetone and James Alysaundere of £10, to pay £7.

Item an obligacione of Robert Bristow of £5.

Item an obligacione with condicione of Hugh Rogers, Richarde Downe & Roger Fermere to pay £3 6s. 8d. for the dioses of Seynt Davies, Seynt Asse and Bangour.

Item an endenture of Lawrence Andertone of the leasse of the archedeconry of Chestre and the Yle of Mane, and an obligacione of £10 with condicione to performe the covenauntes of the saide endenture.

Item an indenture of John Sestone of Lewes of the leasse of the dioses of Chuchestre, with an obligacione of £5 to performe the covenauntes of the saide endenture.

Item an obligacione with condicione wherin the said John Sestone ys bounde in £20 to delyver unto the Wardeins alle maner of bokes, registres, scriptes, scrowes and munymentes consernyng the names of the bretherne and sustrene of the saide Fraternitie.

Item an inventory of the juelles, goodes and ornamentes belonging to the said Fraternitie.

Item an endenture of Wa[l]ter Sheffelde of the citie of London, parte

of the countie of Middlesex and the fyve hunderdes of Essexe, with an obligacione of £30 to performe the covenauntes of the saide endentures.
Item 2 endentures of the leasse of londes in Uxbridge lettyne to ~~William Bayly~~ (John Howe[.]borne) and James (Pe[.]e ater) Standelle.
Item an endenture of John Spynke of the (diose of the) countie of Kent with an obligacione of £10 to performe the covenauntes of the same } Ca[.]elle¹²⁶ indenture.
Item 3 single obligacions of Roger Robyns, wherof 2 of them ys £5 a pece and the 3ᵈᵉ 5 merke[s].
Item an an [sic] endenture of Thomas Holmes of the dioses of Salysbury, Wynchestre and the Yle of Wyghte.
Item an obligacione of Wa[l]ter Sheffelde of £4, to pay 40s.
f. 115v
Item an obligacioun with condicione of Henry Storige of £6 13s. 4d. The condicione is that if one William Marke of Lyskarde in the countie of Cornewalle, yomane, John Philippe of the same, yomen, & John Marke of the same, yomane, welle and truely pay £6 13s. 4d.
Item an obligacione with condicione of Davide ap Griffithe ap Ll[ywely]n of Wraxhaum in the lordshippe of Bromefeld in North Wales, yomane, & Robert Johnes of Wraxhaum aforsaide, yomane, of 40s., to pay 23s. 4d.

Per me William Bromwelle
Per me Wylliam Turk
X
The sygne of Roger Barker, one of the awdytours.¹²⁷

f. 116¹²⁸
[165] This is thaccompte of William Brokett and William Pavyer, Wardeins of the Fraternitie or Guilde of the most glorious Name of Jhū foundede in the crowdes of the cathedralle church of Seynt Paule of London, frome the feast of Christemas in the yere of our lorde Gode 1530 and the 22ᵗⁱ yere of the reigne of king Henry the 8ᵗʰ unto the feast of Christemas thene next ensuyng, that is to saye by the space of one hole yere.

First the saide accomptauntes chargene them selves with therrerages in the foote of the last accompte } £156 22d.
Also with therrerages of Richarde Peirson and Robert Shether of the last accompte } £7 13s. 4d.

¹²⁶ Or 'ca.ette'?
¹²⁷ Bromwell and Turk are signatures; the note about Barker is probably hand of main scribe, but uncertain.
¹²⁸ Ruling for this account is in a mix of crayon and hard-point.

Also with therrerages of Henry Storige as aperithe by obligacione } £12
Also with therrerages of William Marke by obligacione as aperieth in the last accompte } £6 13s. 4d.
Also with therrerages of Walter Sheffelde as aperith in the last accompte } £7 10s.
Also with therrerages of Robert Bristow } £5 6s. 8d.
Also with therrerages of the dioses of Seynt Asse, Bangour and Seynt Davyes lettyne to Hughe Rogers and other as apereth in the last accompte } £6 13s. 4d.
Also with therrerages of John Sestone as aperithe in the fote of the last accompte } £3 6s. 8d.
Also with therrerages of Thomas Holme as aperithe in the fote of the last accompte } 40s.
Also with therrerages of Henry Thornetone as aperithe in the last accompte } 10s.
Also with therrerages of the diose of Caunterbury lettyne to John Spynke as aperethe in the foote of the last accompte } £3
Also with therrerages of the dioses of Seynt Davide, Seynt Asse and Bangour as apereith in the fote of the last accompte } £3 6s. 8d.

f. 116v

[166] Also with the ferme of two tenementes and certeyne londes lying in the towne and feldes of Uxbridge in the countie [sic] of Middlesex and Bukkingham lettyne to [blank] Ocbourne, myller of Uxbridge aforesaide, for 40s. by yere payable at the festes of Seynt Mighelle Tharchaungelle and Thannunciacione of our Blessyde Lady by evyne porcions, that is to say for the same festes within the tyme of this accompte } 40s.

Also with the ferme of alle the devocions belonging to the saide Fraternitie of the provynce of Yorke, the dioses of Ely, Lyncolne, Norwiche, Worcetour, Chester and Herfforde lettyne to John Tyler of Coventre for the somme of £34 6s. 8d. within the tyme of this accompte } £34 6s. 8d.
Also with the ferme of lyke devocions of parte of the countie of Essexe lettyne to Jamys Huntley for 40s. by yere as aperith by obligacione for the tyme of this accompte } 40s.
Also with the ferme of lyke devocions of the countie of Middlesex and parte of the countie of Essexe lettyne to Walter Sheffylde by yere as aperithe by endenture for the tyme of this accompte } 40s.
Also with the ferme of lyke devocyons of the citie of London lettyne to the saide Walter by endenture for £20 10s. by yere for the tyme of this accompte } £20 10s.
Also with the ferme of lyke devocyons of the diose of Canterbury lettyne to John Spynke for £5 by yere as aperithe by endenture } £5

Also with the ferme of lyke devocions of the diose of Chichester lettyne to John Sestone of Lewes by endenture for 33s. 4d. by yere for the tyme of this accompte } 33s. 4d.

Also with the ferme of lyke devocions of the diose of Wintone and Sarum lettyne to Thomas Holme for £5 by yere as aperithe by obligacione for the tyme of this accompte } £5

f. 117r

Also with the ferme of lyke devocions of the archedeconry of Chestour and the Ile of Man lettyne by endenture to John Harteforde for 33s. 4d. for the tyme of this accompte } 33s. 4d.

Also with the ferme of lyke devocions of the dioses of Seynt Asse, Bangour and Seynt Davyes lettyne to [blank] for the tyme of this accompte } £3 6s. 8d.

Also with the ferme of lyke devocions of the dioses of Exetour, Bathe and Welles lettyne to Henry Thornetone by yere within the tyme of this accompte } £7

Also of the waxe offeryde before Jhūs and a rynge of sylver of the value of 7d., *summa* } 4s. 3d.

Also of the Wardeins of the Felishippe of Wexchaundlers of London for an annuelle rent of 20s. by yere } 20s.

Also with the bequest of Maistre Croppe,[129] haberdassher } 20s.

Also with the bequest of Maistre Campyone,[130] grocer } 10s.

Summa totalis of alle the chargis and receites } £301 19s. 5d.[131]

Wherof Paide

f. 117v

[167] The saide accomptauntes accompte in payment ordenary to be made in the crowdes of the saide cathedralle church to sundry mynysters of the same church being present and keping dyvyne service there, of and in the festes of Transfiguracione and Name of Jhū and masse of Requiem onn the morow then next and immedyatly folowing, that is to say: First, to the subdeane being present at alle the premisses and synging highe masse in the saide feastes, for either day 2s., *summa* 4s. To 8 chauntrey prestes bering copes in the saide festes in rewarde 13s. 4d. To 12 petycanons 40s. To 6 vycars 16s. 8d. To every high canone, pyty [sic] canone, chauntrey prestes, vykar and quorester being present

---

129   Thomas Cropp, assistant of the Jesus Guild.
130   William Campion, warden of the Jesus Guild 1525/26, 1526/27.
131   The sum 19s. 5d. possibly written over erasure.

and bering copes in the saide festes of Transfiguracione and Name of Jesu 4d. a pece, *summa* 27s. 2d. To a pety canone syngyng masse of Requiem and reding the Pystelle and Gospelle at the saide 3 masses and for saying of *Deprofundis* 2s. 10d. For the collacione there made at the highe masse in the fest and Name of Jhū 3s. 4d. To the sextone for garnysshing of the aulters and bering of the bokes and other ornamentes 3s. 10d. To the 4 veirgers there being attendaunte, to every of them 16d. with 20d. in reward this yere, 7s. To the belle ryngers for their labour in the saide festes besydes 20s. paide to them quarterly for keping of the doores of the saide crowdes, 13s. 8d. *Summa* } £6 11s. 10d.

Also for the masses of Jesu solempnely by note kepte in the saide crowdes by the subdeane, a cardynalle, a petycanon, 6 vycars and 10 quoresters of the saide cathedralle churche in their habettes and surplices, [and] to a chauntry prest syngyng masse off Requiem by note every Fryday ymmedyatly aftre Jhūs masse with 6 of the quoresters, that ys to say: To the subdeane being present 4d. To the petycanone syngyng the masse of Jesu 8d. To the chauntrey prestes synging the masse of Requiem and every of the vycars 4d. *Summa* in all 47ᵗⁱ Frydayes within the tyme of this accompte } £7 16s. 8d.

Also to the maister of the saide 10 quoresters for keping of 3 *salves* daily in the saide crowdes, after Complayne done in the saide cathedralle church, before the ymages of Jesu, oure Blessyd Lady and Seynt Sebestyane, takyng for his labour 26s. 8d. at 4 termes of the yere, that ys to say according to the ordenaunce } 26s. 8d.

f. 118r
Also to the belle ryngers of the saide cathedralle church for their labour and dayly attendaunce in openyng of the dores, closing and shetting of the same dores within the saide crowdes, for ryngyng of belles, blowing of orgaynes, lighting & quenching of torches and other lightes, and for sweping and making clene of the saide crowdes at 20s. by yere payable quarterly, besydes 13s. 8d. to them allowede in the said festes } 20s.

[168] Also for the rewarde of the Wardeins this yere, lymyttede and taxede by the Rectour, Wardeins and Assistence of the saide Fraternitie according to the ordenaunce } £4

Also for lyveres for clothing for the saide Wardeins with conysaunces of the name of Jhu', lymyttede in lyke wise by the saide Rectour, Wardeins and Assistence } £4

Also to John Worsoppe for making and engrossing uppe of this accompte } 20s.

Also to the prechers at Poulys Crosse and seint Mary Spyttelle, remenbring and praying for alle the bretherne & sustrene of the saide Fraternitie for 44^{ti} ~~Fry~~ (Son)dayes and Good Fryday at Poulys Crosse and 3 dayes in Ester Weke at Seynt Mary Spyttelle, at 8d. every of the saide dayes } 32s.

Also to the 6 waytes (with) banners payntede, conysaunces enbrowderyde with Jhūs, going alle the stretes and subberbes of London playing with their instrumentes to gyve warnyng and knowlege to the people of the saide Fraternitie for the saide festes of Transfiguracione and name of Jhu', according to the said ordenaunce 10s. and in reward this yere 3s. 4d., for the tyme of this accompte } 13s. 4d.

Also to the proctour of the saide Fraternitie for the bonfyre before the northe doore of the saide crowdes yerely in the saide evenyng of the fest of the name of Jhu' 2s. 8d. And for cressett lighte for the tyme of this accompte [no amount]} 2s. 10d.

f. 118v
Also for syngyng brede (and) brede for holy brede and for 37^{ti} gallondes and a pottelle of malmesay at 12d. the gallone, *summa* 37s. 6d. *Summa totalis*} 46s.

Also for waxe spent in the saide crowdes besydes the waxe foundede by the Wexchaundlers this yere for the tyme of this accompte, *summa* } 49s. 6d.

Also to [the] amoynour of Poulys for 10 quoresters of the saide cathedralle church serving God in their habettes in the saide crowdes, aswelle in the saide festes of Transfiguracione and Name of Jhu' ~~as~~ every Fryday at the masse of Requiem and at the 3 *salves* kept dayly by the saide Fraternitie } £4 3s. 4d.

Also to Thomas Holme, sextone, attending dayly in the saide crowdes, keping the vestmentes and ornamentes belongyng to the saide Fraternitie for a hole yere within the tyme of this accompte } 40s.

Also to Thomas Batone, Richarde Eve, John Loring and William Myssylbroke, pour mene appoyntede to the almes of the saide Fraternitie, keping the crowdes and helping prestes to masse and praying for alle

the bretherne and sustrene of the saide Fraternitie, every of them 40s. by
yere payable quarterly according to the saide ordenaunce } £8

f. 119r

[169] Also in sundry exspences necessary, that is to saye: First for brede
and drynke to pour mene 12d. To a pavyer for his labour for pavyng of
the crowdes before the rode 4d. For *dimidium* [half] ane unce of silk
rebonde for vestmentes and for the workemanshippe of them 14d. For
bromys alle the yere 9d. For setting onn of the pararras of 4 Lenttyne
vestmentes 4d. For paring of the stayers 3 tymes in the yere 3d. For
setting onn of the pararras of Jħus vestmentes and of 3 amyttes 2d. For
a kay and a stapele & 2 hokes for the stayre doore 6d. For 2 holywater
sprynkylles 2d. For a staff brusshe for to brusshe ymages and wyndowes
with alle 1d. For whiting of corporas clothes 4d. For 2 claspys for the
portas before Jħus 2d. For mending of 2 deskes for masse bokes 3d.
For setting onn of the pararrars of 9 vestmentes 9d. For pynnes, hokes
great & smalle, and for lyne, 3½d. For scrowring of glasse wyndowdes
14d. For scowring of lampe[s], bassons, candylstyckes and cruettes 14d.
For tunyng of the orgaynes 12d. For russhes 2d. For mending of 2
surplices 2d. For a stay of yrone for dores and 2 hokes 3d. For setting
onn of pararrars of 4 holy daye vestmentes 4d. For 2 sackes of coolys
10d. For hawsing of the great belle clapper and hanging of yt 4d. For
mending of other two vestmentes 4d. For setting onn of pararrars of
4 workyng day vestmentes 4d. For 4 dozeine of talough candelle 5s.
For 4 gallondes and a pottelle of lampe oyle 5s. 10d. For wasshing of
clothes alle this yere 10s. For the hyer of clothes of arras onn Jħus day
and for cariage of them to and fro the Tower 7s. 9d. To the herbe wyff
for garlondes, roses, jeloffers, herbys and flowers spent in the crowdes
onn Jħus day 3s. 4d. To Oswalde Dockwra for a clapper for the great
belle 10s. To William Horneby, glasyer, for mending of wyndowes at
Jħus tyde 3s. 4d. For 5 barelles of ale 20s. To 2 womene to draw ale
2s. For tappis and trayes 8d. To Thomas Holme for watching 16d. To
4 other mene for watching 16d. To 4 porters for keping of the dores
4s. To Walter Sheffelde for his rewarde 2s. To the queresters for their
brekefaste 12d. To the pour mene for their dynners onn Jħus day 2s.
To the wardeyne of beggers for his labour 12d. To Sir Richarde Gates,
prest, for waxe offeryde before Jħus 13s. 4d. For lyveres gevene to
the Wexchaundlers and to other bretherne and sustrene 7s. 4d. To the
prestes that sange masses onn Jħus day and onn Alle Sowlys day 6s.
8d. Gevine in almes to pour peopele on bothe dayes 6s. 8d. Gyvene to
John Worsoppis servaunt for thengrossing upp of this accompte 3s. 4d.
Summa } £6 10s. 6d.

f. 119v

[170] Also in sundry potacyons necessary, that ys to say: At the eleccione of the new Wardene 9s. 7d. And at the awdyte of Maister Botery 20s. For the dynner onn Jhūs day £4. For a brekefast gevyne to dyvers of the Assistence onn Jhūs day, with dyvers other potacyons at dyvers assembles, 14d. And for a dynner made at Stephyne Masons for certeyne of the Assistence for making of a clere inventory of alle the juelles, goodes and ornamentes belonging to the saide Fraternitie 5s. 4d. Also the saide accomptauntes axene allowaunce for charges spent upone the proctours and other straungers commyng to Jhūs masse as before tyme hath byne used 40s. *Summa* } £7 16s. 1d.

[171] Also the said accomptauntes axene allowaunce for therrerages of Henry Storige as aperithe by obligacione } £12

Item for tharrerages of William Marke by obligacione as aperithe in the last accompte } £6 13s. 4d.

Item for therrerages of Walter Sheffelde in the last accompte £7 10s. and of this yeres ferme for Middlesex & Essexe 20s. } £7 10s.

Item for therrerages of Robert Bristow as aperithe in the last accompte } £5 6s. 8d.

Item for therrerages of Hugh Rogers as aperithe in the last accompte } £6 13s. 4d.

Item for therrerages of Thomas Holme as aperieth in the last accompte 40s., and of this yeres ferme 20s. *Summa* } £3

Item for therrerages of Henry Thornetone as aperithe in the last accompte } 10s.

Item for therrerages of Caunterbury lettyne to John Spynke as aperithe in the last accompte £3, & of this yeres ferme £3, *summa* } £6

Item for therrerages of the dioses of Seynt Asse, Bangour and Seynt Davyes as aperithe in the last accompte £3 6s. 8d., and of this yeres ferme £3 6s. 8d. *Summa* } £6 13s. 4d.

Item for therrerages of John Sestone as aperithe in the last accompte } £3 6s. 8d.

Item the saide accomptauntes axene allowaunce of 20s. of therrerages of Roger Robyns, which was pardonede and for gyvene by the assent of the hole Assistaunce } 20s.

f. 120r

Summa totalis of alle the charges and receitis } £301 19s. 5d.[132]

Summa totalis of alle the paymentes and dischargis } £120 2s. 1½d.

And so due to the saide Fraternitie } £181 17s. 3½d.

---

[132]   The sum 19s. 5d. written over an erasure.

Rest delyvered to William Pavyer and Richarde Callarde, reseyvours of this accompte } £181 17s. 3½d.

The whiche said somme £181 17s. 3½d.[133] the saide William Brokett hath delvyerede unto thandes of the saide William Pavyer and Richarde Callarde byfore the audytours according to the ordenaunce, wherof is put into a chest belonging to the saide Fraternitie £116 17s. 3½d.,[134] remaynyng in thandes of the saide William Pavyer £20, whiche the saide William Pavyer rescyvede at the gyvyng uppe of this accompte. And £45 parcelle of the saide somme of £181 17s. 3½d.[135] remaynethe in thandes of Maistre John Browne, late aldermane, as aperithe by obligacione remaynyng in the said chest.

William Dawnturey[136]
William Botrye, mercer
Be me John Pyke
Be me Benjamyn Dygby

f. 120v

[172] Obligacions delyverede by thandes of the saide William Brokett, accomptaunt, unto the handes of William Pavyer and Richarde Callarde, Wardeyns for this yere next ensuyng, that is to say frome Christemas in the 23ᵗⁱ yere of the reigne of kyng Henry the 8ᵗʰ [1531] unto the fest of Christemas thene next folowing.
First an indenture of John Tyler of Coventre of the leasse of the dioses of Worcetour, Herfforde Coventry and Lichefelde } [no amount]
Item an obligacione of the saide John Tyler of £10 6s. 8d.[137]
Item an endenture of ~~Thomas Leicetour and John Herfforde~~ (Blanche Leicetour) of the leasse of the archedeconry of Chester and the Ile of Mane, and ann obligacione with condycione of £10 to performe the covenauntes of the same endenture.
Item an obligacione with condicione of Henry Storige of £20, to pay £12.
Item an obligacione with condicione of William Marke, John Philippe and John Marke of Lyskarde of £20, to pay £6 13s. 4d.
Item an obligacione with condicione of Henry Thornetone of [blank] and Jamys Alysaunder of £10. to pay £7.
Item an obligacione of Robert Bristow of £5.

---

133   The sum 17s. 3d. written over an erasure.
134   The sum 17s. 3d. written over an erasure.
135   The sum 17s. 3d. written over an erasure.
136   Signatures. William Dauntsey was a prominent mercer, sheriff of London, and founder of Dauntsey's School in West Lavington. Sutton, *Mercery*, 333, 347, 367, 529.
137   Small dot in margin next to this and rest of entries on folio.

Item an obligacione with condicione of Hugh Rogers [and] Richarde Downe of Ludlowe of £3 6s. 8d. for the dioses of Seynt Davyes, Seynt Asse and Bangour.

Item an endenture of Lawrence Andertone of the leasse of the archedeconry of Chester and the Ile of Mane, and ann obligacione with condicione of £10 to performe the covenauntes of the saide endenture.

Item an endenture of John Sestone of Lewes of the leasse of the diose of Chichester with an obligacione of £5 to performe the covenauntes of the saide endenture.

And other obligacone for delyveraunce of almaner of bokes & regestryes.[138]

f. 121[139]

Item an obligacioun with condicione wherin the saide John Sestone ys bounde in £20 to delyver to the Wardeyns almaner of bookes, regesters, scrippes, scrowes and munymentes consernyng the names of the bretherne and sustrene of the saide Fraternitie.

Item an inventory of the juelles, goodes and ornamentes belonging to the said Fraternitie.

Item an endenture of Walter Sheffelde of the citie of London & parte of the countie of Middlesex and the fyve hundredes of Essexe, with ann obligacione of £40 to performe the covenauntes of the same endenture.

Item 2 endentures of the leasse of the londes of Uxbridge lettyne to William Bayle and Jamys Standisdale.

Item an endenture of John Spynke with ann obligacione of £10 with condicione to performe the covenauntes of the same endenture } [.]*ret indentur'* [140]

Item an endenture of Thomas Holme of the dioses of Sailsbury, Wynchester and the Yle of Wighte.

Item an obligacione of Walter Sheffelde of £4, to pay 40s.

Item an obligacione of Henry Storige of £6 13s. 4d. The condicione is that if William Marke of Lyskarde in the countie of Cornewalle, yomane, John Philippe of the same, yomane, and John Marke of the same, yomane, wele and truely pay £6 13s. 4d.

Item ann obligacione with condicione of Davide ap Griffithe ap Ll[ywely]n of Wraxhaum within the lordeshipp of Bromefelde in north Wales, yomane, & Robert Johnes of Wraxhaum aforsaide, yomane, of 40s., to pay 23s. 4d.

Item an obligacione of Jamys Huntley of Chelmysforde in the countie of Essexe, Parsone Sharpe, and Thomas Turnebulle, fysshemonger, with condicione of £4, to pay 40s.

Item an obligacion of John Donne of Rednour in the Marche [of] Wales

---

138 Added in same hand but smaller script.
139 Small dot in left margin next to each entry on this folio except that of Blaunche Leicetour, which has a small cross next to it.
140 Added, possibly in a different hand, in right margin next to this entry.

and Richarde Dune, haberdassher of London, for 23s. 4d. payable at Barthylmew tyde nexte.

Item an obligacione & ann endenture of Blaunche Leicetour, late the wyff of Thomas Leycetour late of Tabley in Cheshere, esquyer, and Hughe Bordesley of Thelwalle in the same countie, yomane, & obligacione of £10 to performe the covenauntes of the same endenture.

f.121v

[173] This is thaccompte of Rychard Callarde [and] in the name William Paver, late Wardeyne with the saide Richarde of the Fraternitie or Guilde of the most glorious Name of Jhu' foundede in the crowdes of the cathedralle church of Seynt Paule of London, frome the feast of Christemas in the yere of our lorde God 1531^{ti} and the 23te yere of the reigne of kyng Henry the 8th unto the fest of Christemas thene next ensyuyng, that is to saye by the space of one hole yere.

First the saide accomptauntes [sic] chargene them selffes with therrerages in the fote of the last accompte } £181 17s. 3½d.

Also with therrerages of Henry Storige as aperith by obligacione } £12

Also with therrerages of William Marke by obligacione } £6 13s. 4d.

Also with therrerages of Walter Sheffelde in the last accompte } £7 10s.

Also with therrerages of Robert Bristow as aperithe in the last accompte } £5 6s. 8d.

Also with therrerages of Hugh Rogers as aperithe in the last accompte } £6 13s. 4d.

Also with therrerages of Thomas Holme as aperithe in the last accompte } £3

Also with therrerages of Henry Thornetone as aperith in the last accompte } 10s.

Also with therrerages of Canterbury lettyne to John Spynke as aperith in the last accompte } £6

Also with therrerages of the dioces of Seynt Asse, Bangour & Seynt Davyes as aperith in the last accompte } £6 13s. 4d.

Also with therrerages of John Sestone as aperithe in the last accompte } £3 6s. 8d.

Summa } £239 10s. 7½d.[141]

f. 122r

[174] Also with the ferme of two tenementes and certeyne londes lying in the towne and feldes of Uxbridge in the countie [sic] of Middlesex and Bukingham lettyne to John Ocbourne of Uxbridge aforsaide for

---

[141] Possibly a different hand or the main scribe writing this in afterwards and less carefully.

40s. by yere payable at the feastes of Seynt Mighelle Tharchaungelle and Thannunciatione of our Blessyde Lady by evyne porcions, that is to saye for the same festes within the tyme of this accompte } 40s.

Also with the ferme of alle the devocions belonging to the saide Fraternitie of the province of Yorke, the dioces of Lincolne, Norwiche, Worcetour, Chester and Herfforde lettyne to John Tyler of Coventre for the somme of £34 6s. 8d. within the tyme of this accompte } £34 6s. 8d.

Also with the ferme of lyke devocions of parte of the countie of Essexe lettyne to James Huntley for 40s. by yere as aperithe by obligacione for the tyme of this accompte } 40s.

Also with the ferme of lyke devocions of the countie of Middlesex & parte of the countie of Essexe lettyne [to] Walter Sheffelde by yere as aperithe by endenture for the tyme of this accompte } 40s.

Also with the ferme of lyke devocions of the citie of London lettyne to the said Walter by endenture for £20 10s. by yere for the tyme of this accompte } £20 10s.

Also with the ferme of lyke devocions of the dioces of Canterbury lettyne to John Spynke for £5 by yere as aperith by endenture } £5

Also with the ferme of lyke devocions of the dioces of Chichester lettyne to John Sestone of Lewes by endenture for 33s. 4d. by yere for the tyme of this accompte } 33s. 4d.

Also with the ferme of lyke devocions of the dioces of Wintone and Sarum lettyne to Thomas Holme for £5 by yere as aperith by obligacione for the tyme of this accompte } £5

Summa } £72 10s.[142]

f. 122v

Also with the ferme of lyke devocions of the archedeconry of Chestour and the Ile of Mane lettyne by endenture to John Harteforde for 33s. 4d. for the tyme of this accompte } 33s. 4d.

Also with the ferme of lyke devocions of the dioces of Seynt Asse, Bangour and Seynt Davyes lettyne to [blank] for the tyme of this accompte } £3 6s. 8d.

Also with the ferme of lyke devocions of the dioces of Exetour, Bathe and Welles lettyne to Henry Thornetone by yere within the tyme of this accompte } £7

Also of the wexe offeryde before Jhūs } 3s. 9d.

Also of the Wardeyns of the Felishippe of Wexchaundlers of London for ann annuelle rent of 20s. by yere } 20s.

---

142 Possibly different scribe or at least different time from main writing.

Also with the bequest of Maistre Billesdone[143] } 6s. 8d.

Summa } £13 10s. 5d.

***Summa totalis* of alle the charges and receites** } £3~~20~~15 11s.[144] ~~8d.~~ ½d.

Wherof paide

f. 123r

[**175**] The saide accomptauntes accompte in paymentes ordenary to be made in the crowdes of the said cathedralle church to sundry mynysters of the same church being present and keping devyne service there of and in the festes of Transfiguracione and name of Jhu' and masse of Requiem onn the morow thene next and immedyatly folowing, that ys to say: First, to the subdeane being present at alle the premisses and synging highe masse in the saide festes, for either day 2s., *summa* – 4s. To 8 chauntry prestes bering copes in the saide festes in rewarde 13s. 4d. To 12 peticanons 40s. To 6 vykers 16s. 8d. To every highe canone, peticanone, chauntrey prestes, vyker and quorester being present and bering copes in the saide festes of Transfiguracione and Name of Jhu' 4d. a pece, *summa* – 27s. 2d. To a petycanone singing masse of Requiem and reding the Pistelle and Gospelle at the saide 3 masses and for saying of *Deprofundis* 2s. 10d. For the collacione there made at the high masse in the fest and Name of Jhu' 3s. 4d. To the sextone for garnysshing of the aulters and beryng of the bokes and other ornamentes 3s. 10d. To the 4 vergiers there being attendaunt, to every of them 16d. with 20d. in rewarde this yere, 7s. To the belle ryngers for their labour in the saide festes besydes 20s. paide to them quarterly for keping of the doores of the saide crowdes 13s. 8d. *Summa* } £6 11s. 10d.

Also for the masses of Jhu' solempnely by note kepte in the saide crowdes by the subdeane, a cardynalle, a petycanone, 6 vykers and 10 quoresters of the saide cathedralle church in their habettes and surplices [and] to a chauntry prest singing masse of Requiem by note every Fryday immediatly aftre Jhūs masse with 6 of the queresters, that ys to say: To the subdeane being present 4d. To the peticanone singing the masse of Requiem 8d. To the chauntrey prestes singing the masse of Requiem and every of the vykers 4d. *Summa* in alle 47[ti] Frydayes within the tyme of this accompte } £7 16s. 8d.

---

143 John Billesdon, grocer.
144 The number '11' written over erasure.

Also to the maister of the saide 10 quoresters for keping of 3 *salves* daily in the saide crowdes, after Complayne done in the saide cathedralle church, before the ymages of Jhu, our Blessyd (Lady) & Seynt Sebestyane, taking for his labour 26s. 8d. at 4 termes of the yere, that is to say according to the ordenaunce } 26s. 8d.

Summa } £15 15s. 2d.[145]

f. 123v

Also to the belle ryngers of the saide cathedralle church for their labour and daily attendaunce in openyng of the dores, closing and shetting of the same dores within the saide crowdes, for ryngyng of belles, blowing of orgaynes, lighting and quenching of torches and other lighetes, and for sweping and making clene of the saide crowdes at 20s. by yere payable quarterly, besydes 13s. 8d. to them allowede in the saide festes } 20s.

[176] Also for the rewarde of the Wardeyne this yere, lymyttede and taxede by the Rectour, Wardeins and Assistence of the saide Fraternitie according to the ordenaunce } £4

Also for lyveres for clothing for the saide Wardeins [sic] with conisaunces of the Name of Jhu', lymyttede in lyke wise by the saide Rectour, Wardeins and Assistence } £4

Also to the prechers at Poulys Crosse and Seynt Mary Spyttelle remenbring and praying for alle the bretherne and sustrene of the said fraternitie for [blank] Sondayes and Goode Fryday at Poulys Crosse and 3 dayes in Ester Weke at Seynt Mary Spettelle at 8d. every of the saide dayes } 31s. 4d.

Also to the 6 waightes with banners payntede, conysaunces enbrowderyde with Jhūs, going alle the stretes and subberbes of London playing with their instrumentes to gyve warnyng and knowlege to the people of the saide Fraternitie for the saide festes of Transfiguracione and Name of Jhu', according to the said ordenaunce 10s., and in rewarde this yere 3s. 4d. for the tyme of this accompt } 13s. 4d.

Also to the proctour of the saide Fraternitie for the bonfyre before the northe dore of the saide crowdes yerely in the saide evenyng of the fest of the Name of Jhu' 2s. 8d., and for cressett light 2d., for the tyme of

---

[145]   Again, possibly a different scribe or added subsequent to main text.

this accompte } 2s. 10d.

Also for singing brede, brede for holy brede, and for 38 gallondes and a halff of malmesey at 10d. the gallonde, *summa* 32s. 2d. *Summa totalis*} 39s. 4½d.[146]

Summa } £13 6s. 10½d.[147]

f. 124r
Also for waxe spent in the saide crowdes besydes the waxe foundede by the Wexchaundlers this yere for the tyme of this accompte, *summa* } 40s.

Also to the almoynour of Poulys for 10 quoresters of the saide cathedralle church serving God in their habettes in the saide crowdes, aswelle in the saide festes of Transfiguracione and Name of Jhu' as every Fryday at the masse of Requiem and at the 3 *salves* kept daily by the saide Fraternitie } £4 3s. 4d.

Also to Thomas Holme, sexton, attending dailey[148] in the said crowdes, keping the vestments and ornamentes belonging to the saide Fraternitie, for a hole yere within the tyme of this accompt } 40s.

Also to Thomas Batone, Richarde Eve, John Loring and William Misselbroke, pour mene appoyntede to the almes of the saide Fraternitie, keping the crowdes and helping prestes to masse and praying for alle the bretherne and sustrene of the saide Fraternitie, every of them 40s. by yere payable quarterly according to the saide ordenaunce } £8

Summa } £16 3s. 4d.

[177] Also in sundry exspences necessary, that ys to say: First for bandes and colors for surplices & setting onn 5d. To a pavyer and his laborer for the paving of the chapelle a day a pece 13d. For lyme and sande for the same 8d. For *dimidium* [half] a 100 of paving tyle 18d. Item a glasse for the lampe 1d. For paryng and sweping 4d. For the prikyng of a masse of Master Rowces[149] into the great boke of Jhūs 20d. For wasshing of clothes 10s. For 5 gallondes and a quarter of lampe oyle 7s. 11d. For

---

146 This entry is in the same hand but smaller and more cramped as though added as an afterthought.
147 This and the following sub-totals at the foot of folios are in a smaller and less formal hand than main text.
148 Curious hybrid 'ey' letterform at end of word.
149 See Mateer and New, 'In nomine Jesu', 516 and n. 52.

setting onn pararrars, macalles, aulbes and mending of vestmentes 2s. 8½d. For brede, ale and chese for the pour mene 7d. For mending of the orgaynes 14s. 6d. For 2 peces of hungre lether for the belowes of the saide orgaynes and for their labour 5d. For the sothering of a candelstyk onn Jhūs aulter 3d. For bromes 4d. For mending of 2 masse bokes of Jhūs and our Lady 10d. For whiting of corporas kerchers, white stope, & for halowing of them 8d. For scowring of the glasse wyndowes 14d. For scowring }

f. 124v

of lampes, bassons, candelstykes, cruettes and the halywaterstoke 13d. For russhes 4d. For rosses & lavender for the clothes 1d. For the hemmyng of wyping towelles for the aulters 4d. For a key for the medylle dore in Jhūs Chappelle 3d. For the glewing of a creste of Jhūs aulter and for the glewing of a toppe of a pewe 10d. For a funnelle for the botelle 1d. For mending of the lanthorne before the Rode 5d. For hemmyng of dyves aulter clothes & halowing 7d. For gryndyng of a paring shovelle and pakthrede 2d. For 2 halywaterstykes 2d. For garnettes of wyer for the tabulle onn Jhūs aulter 2d. For carying of a lode of duste 2d. For burnysshing of silver bassons 16d. For setting onn of 24 Jhūs onn their [sic] hodes 4d. To the bedelles whene they toke downe the clothes 6d. To 4 prestes at Barthylmewtyde to say masse 10d. For 3 sakkes of coles 13½d. For 4 dozeine of talough candelle 5s. For the makyng of 2 barres for the deske for Jhūs masse 5d. For a chene for a prymmar 2d. For a pece of tape for gurdelles 3d. For hemmyng of 4 coverynges of canvas for the aulters 3d. For glewing of 2 paxes 1d. For the hemmyng and werkyng of 8 chales clothes 7d. Spent for hanging of the clothes for 12 quarter 2s. 8d.[150] To a carpenter for 7 dayes & *dimidium* 5s. For pynnes, nayles, hokes, lyme, pakthrede and russhes 2s. 5d. For drynke for them the same tyme & in rewarde 4d. For *dimidium* 100lb & 3 quarter of 1lb. of yrone 8s. 4d. To a masone for 4 dayes 2s. 4d. For the hyer of clothes of arres and for cariage to and fro the Tower 7s. 7d. For 18 yerdes & a quarter of dyaper for aulter clothes 18s. 3d. For 12 elles canvas for the saide aulters 4s. 8d. To the herbe wiff for garlondes, rosses, jeloffers, herbes & flowers spent in the g crowdes onn Jhūs day 3s. 4d. For 5 barelles of ale 20s. To 2 womene to draw ale 2s. For tappes & trayes 8d. To Thomas Holme for watching 16d. To 4 porters for keping of the dores 4s. 8d. To 4 other mene for watching 16d. To Walter Sheffelde for his rewarde 2s. To the quoresters for their brekefaste 12d. To the poer mene for their dynner onn Jhūs day 2s. 8d. To the wardeyne of beggers for his labour 12d. To Sir Richarde Gates, prest, for wexe offeryd before Jhūs 13s. 4d. For lyveres gyvene to the Wexchaundelers & to other bretherne and sustrene 7s. 4d. To the prestes

---

[150] Two small letter 'a's in left margin at entries for hanging of the cloths and drink in reward.

that sange masses on Jh̄s day & onn All Sowlys day 6s. 8d. Gevene in almoyes to poer people onn bothe dayes 6s. 8d. To the 4 poer mene for their dynner the morow aftre Jh̄s day 12d. *Summa totalis*}

Summa – £9 7s. 3d.

f. 125r

Also in sundry potacions necessary, that ys to say: At the eleccione of the new Wardeyne 9s. 7d. And at the audyte of Master Brokett 20s. For the dynner on Jh̄s day £4, and for dyverse potacions made to the Assistence 13s. 7d. } £6 3s. 2d.

Summa } £6 3s. 2d.

[178] Also, the said accomptauntes axene allowaunce for therrerages of Henry Storige as aperith by obligacione } £12

Item for therrerages of Walter Mark ~~by obligacione~~ as aperith by obligacione } £6 13s. 4d.

Item for therrerages of Walter Sheffelde in the last accompte £7 10s., of this yeres ferme for London 31s. 4d., and for the ferme of Middlesex & parte of Essexe 40s. } £11 16d.

Item for therrerages of Robert Bristow as aperith in the last accompte } £5 6s. 8d.

Item for therrerages of Hugh Rogers as aperith in the last accompt } £6 13s. 4d.

Item for therrerages of Thomas Holme as aperith in the last accompt £3, and for this yere ferme 20s. } £4

Item for therrerages of John Spynke as aperith in the last accompt £6, and of this yeres ferme £5 } £11

Item for therrerages of Seynt Asse, Bongour and Seynt Davyes as aperith in the last accompt £6 13s. 4d., and of this yere ferme £3 6s. 8d. *Summa* } £10

Item for therrerages of John Sestone as aperith in the last accompte £3 6s. 8d., & for the tyme of this accompte 33s. 4d. *Summa* } £5

Item for therrerages of James Huntley for parte of Essexe } 50s.[151]

Item for therrerages of Henry Thornetone in the tyme of this accompte } £3 10s.

Item for therrerages of of John Tyler } £4 6s. 8d.

Item for therrerages of Wylliam Paver } £21 6s. 7½d.

Summa } £102 17s. 11½d.

f. 125v

---

151 There is an ambiguous mark at the end of this line so it could be 40 (xl)s.

***Summa totalis* of alle the charges & receites } £325 11s. ½d.**

***Summa totalis* of (alle) the paymentes & distharges } £163 13s. 9d.**

And so rest due to the saide Fraternitie over and a bove the saide arrerages } £161 17s. 3½d.

Off the which sayde somme £161 17s. 3½d., ys put into a chest belonging to the saide Fraternitie in the presens of the audytours according to the ordenaunce before made £116 17s. 3½d., and £45 parcelle of the saide somme of £161 17s. 3½d. remaynyng in the handes of Master John Browne, late alderman, desseassede, as aperith by ann obligacione remayning in the handes of Richard Calarde, this accomptaunte.

Be me Wyllyame Brothurs[152]
Be me William Broket
[sign rather like I U]

[A leaf, presumably containing the debts still owing for the year, has been removed between folios 125 and 126.]

f. 126r

[**179**] This is thaccompte of Richard Calard and Rauff Aleyne, Wardeyns of the Fraternytie or Guylde of the most glorious Name of Jhu' founded in the crowdes of the cathedralle churche of Seint Poule in London, form the feast of Christemas in the yere of our lorde God 1532[ti] and in the 24[the] yere of the reigne of kynge Henry the 8[the] unto the feast of Christemas thene next ensyyng, that is to say by the space of one hole yere.

Fyrst the said accomptaunces chargene them selffes with tharrerages in the fote of the last accompte } £161 17s. 3½d.
Wherof £45 remayned in the handes of Master John Browne, late alerman.[153]
Also with tharrerages of Henry Storige } £12
Also of Walter Marke } £6 13s. 4d.
Also of Walter Sheffelde } £11 16d.
Also of Robert Bryscowe } £5 6s. 8d.
Also of Hughe Rogiers } £6 13s. 4d.
Also of Thomas Holme } £4
Also of John Spynke } £11

[152] Signatures.
[153] This entry has been added by the same scribe but in a smaller script.

Also with tharrerages of Seint Asse, Bangor and Seint Davyes as aperith in the last accompte } £10

Also of John Sestone } £5

Also of Jamys Huntley for parte of Essexe } 40s.

Also of Henry Thornetone } £3 10s.

Also of John Tyler } £4 6s. 8d.

Also of William Pavyer } £21 6s. 7½d.

Also with the somme of £4 which he receyved of the same William Pavyer the day of the eleccion of this accomptaunt } £4

Also with the bequest of Master Browne } 40s.[154]

Also with a rynge of baas golde which was offred to Jhu' and solde by this accomptant for 10s. 6d. } 10s. 6d.

Summa } £271 5s. 9d.

f. 126v

[180] Also with the ferme of two tenementes and certeyne londes lying in the townes and feldes of Uxbrige in the countie [sic] of Middlesex and Bukingham letten to John Ocborne of Uxbrige aforsaid for 40s. by yere payable at the feastes of Seint Mighell Tharchaungell and the Annunciacion of our Lady by evyne porcions, that is to say for the same feastes within the tyme of this accompte } 40s.

Also with the ferme of all the devocions belonging to the said Fraternitie within the province of Yorke, the dioces of Lyncolne, Norwyche, Worcetor, Chester and Herforde, lettene to John Tyler of Coventre for the somme of £34 6s. 8d. within the tyme of this accompte } £34 6s. 8d.

Also with the ferme of like devocions for parte of the countie of Essexe lettene to Jamys Huntley for 40s. by yere as aperithe by obligacion for the tyme of this accompte } 40s.

Also with the ferme of like devocions for the countie of Middlesex and parte of the countie of Essexe lettene to ~~Bryscow~~ (Walter Sheffelde) by yere as apperith by endenture for the tyme of this accompte } 40s.

Also with the ferme of like devocions of the citie of London letten to the said Walter by endenture for the somme of £20 10s. by yere for the tyme off this accompte } £20 10s.

Also with the ferme of like devocions of the dioces of Canterbury lettene to Crakynthorpe for £5 by yere as aperith by the last yere } £5

Also with the ferme of like devocions of the dioces of Chichestre lettene to John Sestone of Lewys by endenture for 33s. 4d. by yere for the tyme of this accompte } 33s. 4d.

Also with the ferme of like devocions of the dioces of Wintone and

---

[154]   John Brown, haberdasher.

Sarum lettene to Thomas Holme for £5 by yere as aperith by obligacion for the tyme of this accompte } £5

f. 127r

Also with the ferme of like devocions of the archdeconry of Chester and the Ile of Mane letten by endenture to John Hartforde for 33s. 4d. for the tyme of this accompte } 33s. 4d.

Also with the ferme of like devocions of the dioces off Seint Asse, Bangor and Seint Davys letten to John Phillipps for the tyme of this accompte } £3 6s. 8d.

Also with the ferme of like devocions for the dioces of Exetour, Bathe and Welles lettene to John Amadas, sergiant at armes, by yere within the tyme of this accompte } £7

Also with the waxe offered before Jhūs – 4s. 3d.

Also of the Wardeyns of the Felyship of Waxe Chaundelers of London for an annuell rent of 20s. by yere } 20s.

Summa } £85 14s. 3d.

Summa totalis of all the charges & receytes } £357

Wherof paiede

f. 127v

[181] The said accomptauntes accompte in paymentes ordinary to be made in the crowdes of the saide cathedrall church to sundry mynysters of the same churche beyng present and keping divine service there of and in the feastes of ~~tha~~ the Transfiguracion & Name of Jhu' and mas off Requiem onn the morowe then next and immediatly folowing, that is to say: Fyrst, to the subdeane beyng present at all the premysses & singing highe masse in the said feastes, for either day 2s., *summa* – 4s. To 8 chauntery prestes beryng copes in the said festes in rewarde 13s. 4d. To 12 petycanons 40s. To 6 vycars 16s. 8d. To every high canon, petycanone, chauntery prest, vyker and querester beyng present and bering copes in the said feastes of the Transfiguracion and Name of Jhu' 4d. a pece, *summa* 27s. 2d. To a petycanone synging masse of Requiem and reding the Gospell & Pistell at the said 3 masses and for saying *Deprofundis* 2s. 10d. For the collacion there made at the highe masse in the feast and Name of Jhūs 3s. 4d. To the sexteyne for garnysshing of the aulters & bering of the bokes and other ornamentes 3s. 10d. To the 4 vergiers there beyng attendaunt, to every of them 16d. with 20d. in rewarde this yere, 7s. To the bell ryngers for their labor in the said feastes, besides 20s. paied to them quarterly for keping of the dores of the saide crowdes 13s. 4d. *Summa* } £6 11s. 6d.

Also for the masses of Jhu solempnely by note kepte in the said crowdes by the subdeane, a cardynall, a petycanone, 6 vykers and 10 queresters of the said cathedrall churche in their habettes and surplices [and] to a chauntery prest singing masse of Requiem by note every Fryday immediatly after Jhus masse with 6 of the queresters, that is to say: To the subdeane beyng present 4d. To the petycanone singing the masse of Requiem 8d. To the chauntery prestes singing the masse of Requiem and every of the vykers, 4d. *Summa* in all 45 Frydayes within the tyme of this accompte } £7 16s. 8d.

Summa } £14 8s. 2d.

f. 128r

Also to the maister of the said 10 queresters for keping of 3 *salves* dayly in the said crowdes, after cumplyne [sic] done in the said cathedrall churche, before the images of Jhu', our Blessid Lady and Seint Sebastiane, taking for his labour 26s. 8d. at 4 termes of the yere, that is to say according to the ordynaunce } 26s. 8d.

Also to the bell ryngers of the said chathedrall [sic] church for their labour and dayly attendaunce in openyng of the dores, closyng and shetteing off the same dores within the said crowdes, for ringing of belles, blowing of organs, lyghting and quenching of torches and other lyghetes, and for sweping & making clene of the said crowdes at 20s. by yere payable quarterly, besides 13s. 8d. to them alowed in the said feastes } 20s.

[182] Also for the rewarde of the Wardeyne[s] this yere, lymyted and taxed by the Rector, Wardeyns and Assistence of the said Fraternitie according to the ordenaunce } £4

Also for lyveres for clothing for the said Wardeyns with conysaunces of the Name of Jhu, lymitted in likewise by the said Rector, Wardeyns & Assistens } £4

Also to the preachers at Poulys Crosse and Seint Mary Spittell remembryng and praying for all the brethene and sustrene of the said Fraternitie for 47 Sondayes and Good Fryday at Poulys Crosse and 3 dayes in Esterweke and [sic] seint Mary Spittell at 8d. every of the saide dayes } 34s.

Also to the 6 weyghetes with banners paynted, conysaunces enbrodered with Jhus, goyng all the stretes and suburbes of London playing with their instrumentes to gyve warnyng and knowledge to the people of the said Fraternytie for the said feastes of Transfiguracion and Name of Jħu, according to the said ordenaunce 10s. and in rewarde this yere 3s. 4d. for the tyme of this accompte } 13s. 4d.

Summa } £12 14s.

f. 128v

Also to the proctor of the said Fraternitie for the bonfire before the northe dore of the said crowdes yerely in the said Evenyng of the feast of the Name of Jħu, 2s. 8d., and for cresset lyghte 2d. } 2s. 10d.

Also for wax spent in the said crowdes in the tyme of Maister Pavyer 12s., and for waxe spent in the tyme of this accomptaunt 50s. 10½d. } £3 2s. 10½d.

Also for singing brede and for brede for holy brede 8s. 6d., and for 46 gallons of malnesey at 10d. the gallone, 38s. 4d. *Summa* } 46s. 10d.

Also to the almener of Poulys for 10 queresters of the said cathedrall church servyng God in their habites in the said crowdes, aswell in the said feastes of Transfiguracion and Name off Jħu as every Fryday at masse of Requiem, and at 3 *salves* kept dayly by the said Fraternitie } £4 3s. 4d.

Also to John Worsoppe for makyng and engrosing of Maister Pavyers accompte 20s., and to his clerke 3s. 4d., and for makyng and engrosyng off this accompte to hym & to his clerke as off olde tyme hath beene accustomed, 23s. 4d. *Summa* } 46s. 8d.

Also to Thomas Holme, sexteyne, attending dayly in the said crowdes, keping the vestmentes and ornamentes belonging to the said Fraternitie for a hole yere within the tyme of this accompte } 40s.

Also to Thomas Batone, Richard Eve, William Myssylbroke and [blank] Penyfader, poueremen appoyntid to the almes of the said Fraternitie, keping the crowdes, helping prestes at masse & praying for all the bretherne & susterne off the said Fraternitie and all Christen soules, every of them havyng yeerely 40s. payable quarterly according to the ordenaunces } £8

Summa } £22 2s. 6½d.

f. 129r

[183] Also in sondry expenses necessary, that is to say: First, for the hire of arras occupied in Jhus Chapell 6s. 2d. Paied for carying of the treasor chest to Master Calardes 3d. Paied for a bottell with a gurdell to fetche malmesey yne [sic] 5d. Paied for mending of the haspe of the greate chest and nayles for the same 6d. Paied for mending of a forme, nayles ande workemanship 5d. Paied for arresting of Spynke, proctor of Kente, and for ~~arresting~~ a drynking at his arest 9d. Paied for a key for the organes and mending of the lok 4d. Paied for the redemyng of certeyne regestry bookes which remayned in the handes of Robert Briscow 10s. Paied for wasshing of 16 corporas kyrchers 4d. Paied for mending of the lok for the greate chest of irone 4d. Paied for mending of a surples color 1d. Paied for the dyner of 4 pouere mene watching onn Jhus daye 2s. 8d., and for there dyner the next daye folowing 16d. Paied for lyveres gyvene to the Waxchaundelers and to other, the bretherne and susterne of the said Fraternitie 7s. 4d. Paied to prestes singing masse onn Jhus day and onn Alhallone Day 6s. 8d. Paied and delte to pouere people the said 2 dayes 6s. 8d. Paied to 4 porters keping the dores onn Jhus day 4s. Paied to a clerke which sat 3 dayes in Poulys with Walter Sheffelde to knowe the parffit rescyte of the same Walter 4s. Paied for 2 burdeyns of russhes 4d. Paied for a 100 of pynnes 1½d. Paied for scoryng and clensyng of the glasse wyndowes 14d. Paied for scowering of bosens, candelstykkes, crewettes and hollywater stok 13d. Paied for a brekefast to the queresters 16d. Paied to Thomas Holmes for his watching 4 nyghetes 16d. For lavender spyke for the clothes 1d. Paied for 2 keyes for a pewe and a tylle 6d. Paied for halywater stykkes 4d. Paied for a glasse for the lampe 1d. Paied for the lok for the Maisters pewe 2d. Paied for a lanterne to hange before the rode & for wyer for the same 11d. Paied for a bawderyk for the greate bell 10d. ~~Paied~~ Paied for hokes and pakthrede 1½d. Paied for pykkyng and gresyng of the greate bell [no amount]. Paied for a kylderkyne of single bere 12d. Paied to a glasier for mending of the wyndowes in Jhus Chapell 3s. 4d. Paied for takyng downe of the clothes that garnysshed Jhus Chappell 2d. Paied for garlondes and erbes spent in Jhus

f. 129v

Chapell 3s. 4d. Paied for serching of Spynkes obligacion 2d. Paied to Walter Sheffelde in rewarde 2s. Paied for 5 barrelles of ale 20s. Paied to 2 womene for drawing of the same ale 2s. Paied for tappes, trayes and white cuppes 8d. Paied for paring of the stayers and makyng clene of the crowdes and for bromys at sondry tymes 13d. Paied (for drinke) to the pouere mene 5d. Paied for setting of parrars onn awbes at sondry tymes 3s. 2d. Paied for 7 gallons of lampe oyle 7s. 4d. Paied for mending of the pavement in Jhus Chapell 12d. Paied for rybonde to amende Jhus cote ½d. Paied for 3 quarters of colys for the pouere men 12d. Paied for the lampe & for the basone 1d. Paied for 2 dosene of talough candell 2s. 6d. Paied for a basket to cary dust yn 1½d. ~~paide~~ Paied for a rope for the bell at Jħūs dore ande the hanging up of the same 7d. Paied for mending of the stayre at Jħus dore into Poulys 6d. Paied for wasshing of clothes all this yere 10s. Payed for mending of a fourme and for a ledge 3d. Paied for writing new of a tabyll before Jħus fote 8d. Paied for graving of 4 letters upone 4 chalyces 4d. Paied for mending of a fote before Seint Sebastyane and for mending of the halywater stok 20d.

Summa } £6 4s. 5d.

Also in potacions necessary, that is to say: At the eleccione of a new Wardeyne 13s. 8d. And atte awdyte of Master Pavyer 20s. For the dynar on Jħus day £4. For a potacion made the 17 day of Janyure atte eleccione of fyve of the Assistence and for reformacone of certeyne causes 4s. 2d. For a potacione made the 23^{ti} day of May for the eleccione of 2 of the Assistence and for causes consernyng Master Pavyer[155] 19d. And for the brekefast made at Thomas Holmes howce on Jħus Day 3s. 4d. And for charges spente upone the proctors and other strangers commyng to Jħus masse as before tyme hath beene used 40s. For mending of a boke at Jħus awter 3d. Also for chaunging of yll money 12d.

Summa } £8 4s.

f. 130r

[184] Also, the said accomptauntes askene alowance for tharrerages of Henry Storage as aperithe in the last accompte } £12
Item for tharrerages of Walter Marke by obligacion as aperith in the said last accompte } £6 13s. 4d.
Item for tharrerages of Walter Sheffelde in the last accompte £11 16d., and of this yeres ferme 40s. 8d. } £13 2s.
Item for tharrerages of Robert Brystow as aperith in the last acompte £5 6s. 8d., and in this yere for the ferme of Middlesex and parte of Essexe 30s. } £6 16s. 8d.
Item for tharrerages of Hugh Rogiers as aperith in the last accompte } £6 13s. 4d.
Item for tharrerages of Thomas Holme in the last accompte £4, and of this yeres ferme 20s. *Summa* } £5
Item for tharrerages of John Spynke as aperithe in the last accompte } £11
Item for tharrerages of (John Phillips, proctour, for the dioes of) Saynt Asse, Bangor and Seint Daves as aperithe in the last accompte £10, and of this yeres ferme (£3) 6s. 8d. } £13 6s. 8d.
Item for tharrerages of John Sestone as aperithe in the last accompte } £5
Item for tharrerages of William Pavyour 26s. 7½d., wherof his wyff

---

155   William Pavor, late warden.

was pardoned and forgevene by the assent of all the hole Assistence } 26s. 7½d.

Item for tharrerages of Jamys Huntley this yere } 40s.

Item for tharrerages of Henry Thornetone as doth apere by obligacione } £4

Item for tharrerages of John Tyler this yeres ferme } £5

Item the said accomptaunt axethe allowance of £4 which he delyvered unto Rauffe Aleyne the day of the eleccion of the same Rauff } £4

Summa } £95 18s. 7½d.

f. 130v

Summa totalis of all the charges and receytes } £357

Summa totalis of all the paymentes and dyscharges } £159 11s. 9d.

And restithe due to the said Fraternytie over & above the said arrerages } £201 8s. 3d.

The whiche said somme of £201 8s. 3d., and also ann image of Jħus of silver with a foote of tree over gilte, item 2 basons of silver and parcell gilte, ande a grete maser with a brode bonde withe a bosse in the middes of silver and gilte, the said accomptant hathe delyvered into the handes of the said Rauff Aleyn and William Turke before the awditors according to the ordynaunce. Wherof is put into a chest belonging to the said Fraternitie £181 8s. 3d., and remaynyng in the handes of the saide Rauffe £20 and all the parcelles of plate above namede.

Per me William Botrye mercer[156]
Per me John Scampyne

f. 131[157]

[185] Obligacions delyvered by thandes of the said Richard Callard, accomptant, unto thandes of Rauf Aleyne and William Turke, Wardeyns for this yere next ensuyng, that is to say from Cristmas in the 25 yere of the reigne of kynge Henry the 8the [1533] unto the feast of Cristmas then next ensuyng.

Fyrst ann obligacion of John Tyler of Coventry of £10 6s. 8d.

---

[156] Signatures. It is possible that one or more additional names has been lost through historical trimming of the folio.

[157] Smaller than previous folios with large hole on gutter side starting halfway down, tears at head and foot, some staining.

Item ann endenture of Blaunche Leicetor of the lease of the archedeaconry of Chester and the Ile of Mane, and ann obligacion with condicion of £10 to performe the covenauntes of the same endenture.

Item ann obligacion with condicone of Henry Storege of £20 to pay £12.

Item ann obligacion with condicion of William Marke, John Phillip and John Marke of Lyskard of £20, to paye [£]5 13s. 4d.

[Item a]nn obligacion with condicion of Henry Thorneton [lost] [and] [Ja]mys Alizaunder of £10, to pay £7.

[Item a]nn obligacion with condicion of Robert Bristow of £5.

[Item an] obligacion with condicion of Hugh Rogers [Richar]d Downe of Ludlowe of £3 6s. 8d., for the [dioces] of Seint Davys, Seint Asse & Bangor.

[Item] ann endenture of Laurence Anderton of the [text lost] of the archediaconry of Chester and the Ile [of] Mane, and ann obligacion with condicion of £10 to [per]fourme the covenauntes of the same endenture.

Item ann endenture of John Sestone of Lewys of the lease of the dioces of Chichestre with ann obligacion of £5 to perfourme the covenauntes of the same endenture, and an other obligacion for the delyverance of almaner of bokes & regestryes.

Item ann obligacion with condicion wherin the saide John Sestone is bounde in £20 to delyver to the Wardeyns almaner of bokes, regestres, escriptes, scrowes and mynymentes consernyng the names of the brethren and susterne of the said Fraternitie.

Item ann obligacion with condicion of Roger Wayte, John Crosse & Hen[ry] Lacy.

f. 131v

Item ann inventory of the juelles, goodes & onamentes belonging to the said Fraternitie.

Item ann indenture of Walter Sheffelde of the citie of London and parte of the countie of Middlesex & the fyve hundredes of Essexe, with ann obligacone of £40 to perfourme the covenauntes of the same endenture.

Item two endentures of the lease of the londes in Uxbridge lettene to William Bayle & Jamys Standisdayle.

Item ann endenture of John Spynke with ann obligacion of £10 with condicion to perfourme covenauntes.

Item ann endenture of Thomas Holmes of the dioces of Salysbury, Wynchester & the Ile of Wyghte.

Item ann obligacion of Walter Sheffelde of £4 to pay 40s.

Item ann obligacion of Henry Storege of £6 13s. 4d. The condicion is that if William Marke off Lyskard in the countie of Cornewall, yomane, [John] Phillipp of the same, yomane, and John Mar[ke] [text lost] the same, yomane, wele & truly pay £6 11[text lost[158]]

---

158   Probably 12 or 13 because last numeral visible is 'i' not 'j'.

Item ann obligacion with condicion of David ap G[ruffyd] ap Ll[ewely]n of Wraxhaum within the lordeship of Bromf[eld] in Northwales, yomane, & Robert Johns' of Wrax[ham] aforsaid, yomane, of 40s. to pay 23s. 4d. Item ann obligacion of Jamys Huntley of Chelmesford [lost] in the countie of Essexe, Parsone Sharpe and Thomas Turnebull, fysshemonger, of £4 with condicion to pay 40s.

Item ann obligacion of John Donne of Rednour in the merches of Walys and Richard Dunne, haberdassher of London for 23s. 4d.

Item ann endenture made betwene Master John Colet, late Rector of the said Fraternitie, William Bromwell, mercer, and John Monke, waxchaundeler, then Wardens of the said Fraternitie, onn the one parte, and William Hawkyns of London, salter, on the other parte consernyng londes & a quyterent in Uxbridge.

Item ann obligacion wherin John Phillipps ande other stondene bounde to pay 33s. 4d., payable at Cristmas & Ester last past.

f. 17r[159]

[186] This is thaccompte of Rauffe Aleyne and William Turke, Wardeyns of the Fraternitie or Guilde of the most glorious Name of Jhu' founded in the crowdes of the cathedrall churche of Seint Paule of London, from the feast of Cristemas in the yere of our lorde God 1533 and in the 25[the] yere of the reigne of kynge Henry the 8th unto the feast of Cristemas then next ensuyng, that is to say by the space of one hole yere.

Fyrst the said accomptauntes chargen them selffes withe tharrerages in the fote of the last accompte } £201 8s. 3d.

Also with tharrerages of Henry Storidge as apperith by obligacion } £12
Also with tharrerages of Walter Marke by obligacion } £6 13s. 4d.
Also with tharrerages of Walter Sheffelde as apperith in the last accompte } £13 2s.

Also with tharrerages of Robert Bryscowe as apperith in the last accompte } £6 16s. 8d.

Also with tharrerages of Hugh Rogiers as apperith in the last accompte } £6 13s. 4d.

Also with tharrerages of Thomas Holmes as aperith in the last accompte } £5

Also with tharrerages of John Spynke } £11
Also with tharrerages of Seynt Asse, Bangour and Seynt Davys as aperith in the last accompte } £13 6s. 8d.

Also with tharrera[ges of] John Seston } £5
Also with th[arrerages of] Jamys Huntley } 40s.

---

159 There is a large hole in the folio three-quarters of the way down on the gutter side. This and the following account are bound out of order in the current format of the manuscript (see Introduction, p. 33).

Also with [tharrerages] of Henry Thornetone as apperith by obliga[cion] } £4

Also with tha[rre]rages of John Tylere } £5

Also with £4 which he receyved of Richard Calarde at the eleccion of his accompte } £4

Summa } £296 3d.

f. 17v

[187] Also with the ferme of two tenementes and certeyne londes lying in the townes [sic] and feldes of Uxbridge in the counties of Middlesex and Bukingham letten to John Ocbourne of Uxbridge aforsaide for 40s. by yere payable at the feastes of Seint Mighell Tharchaungell & Thannunciacion of our Lady by evene porcions, that is to say for the same feastes within the tyme of this accompte } 40s.

Also with the ferme of all the devocions belonging to the said Fraternitie within the province of Yorke, the dioces of Lyncolne, Norwyche, Worcetour, Chestour & Herforde letten to John Tyler of Coventry for the somme offe £34 6s. 8d. within the tyme of this accompte } £34 6s. 8d.

Also with the ferme of like devocions for parte of the countie of Essexe letten to Jamys Huntley for 40s. by yere as apperith by obligacion } 40s.

Also with the ferme of like devocions for the countie of Middlesex and parte of the countie of Essexe letten to Walter Sheffelde by yere as aperithe by ~~obligacion~~ endenture for the tyme of this accompte } 40s.

Also with the ferme of like devocions for the citie of London letten to the said Walter by endenture for the somme of £20 10s. by yere for the tyme of this accompte } £20 10s.

Also with the ferme of like deuoc[ions of the] dioces of Canterbury letten to Crakynthorp [...]e } £5

Also with the ferme of like devocions of [the dio]ces of Chichestre letton to John Sestone of Lewes by endenture for 33s. 4d. by yere for the tyme of this accompte } 33s. 4d.

Also with the ferme of like devocions of the dioces of Wintone and Sarum letten to Thomas Holme for £5 by yere as aperith by obligacion for the tyme of this accompte } £5

Also with the ferme of like devocions of the archedeaconry of Chester and the Isle of Man letten by endenture to John Hartforde for 33s. 4d. for the tyme of this accompte } 33s. 4d.

Also with the ferme of like devocions of the dioces of seint Asse, Bangor and Seint Davys letten to John Phillippes for the tyme of this accompte } £3 6s. 8d.

f. 18r

Also with the ferme of like devocions of the dioces of Exetour, Bathe and Welles lettene to John Amydas, sergiaunt at armys, for the tyme of this accompte } £7

Also with wax offered before Jħus } 8s.

Also of the wardeyns of the Felysship of Waxchaundelers of London for an annuell rent of 20s. by yere } 20s.

Also of the bequest of Master Doctour Edmondes[160] } 5s.

Also receyved of the executours of Henry Thorneton for tharrerages by hym due the day of his decease, over and above tharrerages of £4 abovewryttene } £3

Summa } £89 3s.

Summa totalis of all the charges & receytes } £385 3s. 3d.

Wherof paide

f. 18v

[188] The said accomptauntes accompte in paymentes ordynary to be made in the crowdes of the (said) cathedrall church to sondry minestres of the same churche beyng present and keping divine service there in the feastes of the Transfiguracion and Name of Jhu' ande masse of Requiem on the morowe then next & ymmediatly folowing, that is to say: First, to the subdeane beyng present at all the premysses and singing high masse in the said feastes, for either day 2s., *summa* 4s. To 8[the] chauntry prestes bering copes in the said feastes in rewarde 13s. 4d. To 12 petycanons 40s. To 6 vycars 16s. 8d. To every high canon, petycanon, chauntry preste, vycar and querester beyng present and bering coopes in the said feastes of the Transfiguracion and Name of Jhu' 4d. apeace, *summa* - 27s. 2d. To a petycannon singing masse of Requiem and reding the Gospell & Pistell at the said 3 masses and for saying *Deprofundis* 2s. 10d. For the collacion there made at the highe mas in the feast and Name of Jhu' 3s. 4d. To the sexteyne for garnysshing of the aulters and bering of the bokes and other ornamentes 3s. 10d. To the 4 vergiers there beyng attendant, to every of them 16d. with 20d. in rewarde 7s. To the bell ryngers for their labour in the said feastes beside 20s. paied to them quarterly for keping of the dores of the said crowdes 13s. 4d. } £6 11s. 6d.

Also for masses of Jhu' solempnely by note kepte within the said crowdes by the subdeane, a cardynall, a petycanon, 6 vicars and 10 queresters of the saide cathedrall churche in their habittes and surplices [and] to a chauntry prest singing masse of Requiem by note every Fryday ymmediatly after

---

[160] John Edmonds (d. 1533), canon of St Paul's Cathedral.

Jhus masse with 6 of the queresters, that is to say: To the subdeane beyng present 4d. To the petycanon singing the masse of requiem 8d. To the chauntry prestes singing the masse of Requiem and every of the vicars 4d. *Summa* of all 46 Frydayes within the tyme of this accompte } £7 13s. 4d.

Also to the maister of the said tenne queresters for kepyng of thre *salves* dayly in the said crowdes, after complyne doone in the said cathedrall churche, before the images of Jhu', our Blessed Lady and Seint Sebastyane, taking for his labour 26s. 8d. at 4 termes of the yere, that is to say according to the ordynaunces } 26s. 8d.

f. 19r

Also to the bell ryngers of the said cathedrall churche for their labour and dayly attendaunce in openyng, closing and shetting of the dores within the said crowdes, for rynging of belles, blowing of organs, lygheting and quenching of torches and other lyghtes, and for sweping and makyng clene of the said crowdes, at 20s. by yere payable quarterly besides 13s. 8d. to them alowed in the said feastes } 20s.

[189] Also for the rewarde of the Wardeyne[s] this yere, lymitted and taxed by the Rectour, Wardeyns and Assistence of the said Fraternitie according to the ordynaunce } £4

Also for lyveres for clothing for the said Wardeyns with conysaunces of the name of Jhu', lymytted in lykewyse by the said Rectour, Wardeyns and Assistence } £4

Also to the preachers at Poulys Crosse and Seynt Mary Spyttell, remembryng and praying for all the brethern and susterne of the said Fraternitie for 44^ti Sondayes and Good Fryday at Poulys Crosse and thre dayes in Esterweke and [sic] Seint Mary Spyttell at 8d. for every of the said dayes } 32s.

Also to the 6 weighetes with banners paynted, conysaunces enbrowdered with Jhus, goyng all the stretes & suburbes of London playing with their instrumentes to gyve warnyng and knowledge to the people of the said Fraternitie for the said feastes of Transfiguracion and Name of Jhu', according to the said ordynaunce 10s. and in rewarde this yere 3s. 4d. for the tyme of this accompte } 13s. 4d.

Also to the proctour of the said Fraternitie for the bonfire before the northe dore of the said crowdes yerely in the evenyng and of the feast and Name of Jhu' 2s. 8d., and for cresset lyghte 2d. } 2s. 10d.

Also for waxe spente in the said crowdes in the tyme of this accomptaunt } £3 3s. 6d.

Also for singing breide and for breide to make hoolye breide 8s., and for 36 gallons and a quarte of malnesey at 10d. the gallone, *summa* } 38s. 2½d.

Also to the almener of Poulys for 10 queresters of the said cathedrall churche servyng God in their habittes in the said crowdes, aswell in the feastes of the Transfiguracion and Name of Jhu' as every Friday at masse of Requiem and at 3 *salves* kepte dayly by the said Fraternitie } £4 3s. 4d.

f. 19v

Also to John Worsoppe for makyng and engrosing of this accompte 20s., and to his clerke 3s. 4d. } 23s. 4d.

Also to Thomas Holmes, late sextene, attendyng dayly in the said crowdes, keping the vestmentes ande ornamentes belonging to the said Fraternitie for one half yere 20s., and to Richard Skotheroppe his successor for one other half yere 20s. *Summa* } 40s.

Also to Thomas Butler, Richard Ewe, Wylliam Mystelbroke and Thomas Penyfather, pouere men appoynted to the almes of the said Fraternitie, keping the crowdes, helping prestes at masse and praying for all the bretherne and susterne of the said Fraternitie and all Cristen soules, every of them havyng yerely 40s. payable quarterly according to the ordenaunce. *Summa* } £8

Also for lyveres gyven to 5 pouere mene, that is to say to Walter Sheffelde, proctour, and to the 4 almes mene, 3 yardes & *dimedium* [half] apece, *summa* 17 yerdes at 3s. 4d. the yarde } 58s. 4d.

Summa } £50 6s. 4½d.

[190] Also in sondry expences necessary, that is to say: Fyrst, for the hier of arras occupied in Jhus Chapell 4s., ande other costes therto apperteynyng 23d. Paied for bromes and paryng of the stayers at sondry tymes 13d. Paied for brede and ale to poore men at sondry tymes 4½d. Paied to a mason for a staple and leade for the forme before Jhu' 3d. Paied for setting on (of thapparell) of 4 Lenton vestmentes 4d. Paied for sowing 2 blak clothes for the roode 1½d. Paied for mending and sowing of 2 Lentone vestmentes 2d. Paied for mending 3 vestmentes

ande for 4 stoles ande for satten of bridges, for setting onn of thapparell of a blak vestment, ande for *dimedium* yarde of bokram, 18½d. Paied for mending of a vestment with white hartes 8d. Paied for collering of thre surplices 6d. Paied for a longe brusshe for the wyndowes 1½d. Paied for 4 quarters of cooles 16d. Paied for 4 plates for the pillers 4d. Paied for a lampe 1d. Paied for a lether bag for a chales 4d. Paied for 5 dosene taloughcandelles 6s. 3d. Paiede for 4 gallons and one pottell of lampe oyle at 16d. the gallone, 6s. Paied to the wyff of Thomas Holme, sextene, for a gowne cloth for her said husbonde now

f. 20r

deceessed 9s. 7d. Paied for wasshing the clothes all this yere 11s. 8d. Paied to prestes singing masse onn Jhus Day and Allhallowene Day 5s. 4d. Paied & delte in almes on the said 2 dayes 6s. 8d. Paied to 4 porters keping the dores in the said feastes 4s. Paied for the dyner of 4 pouere mene 2 dayes 4s. Paied to 2 wemene for drawing of ale 2s. Paied for tappes and trayes 8d. Paied for 5 barrelles of ale at 3s. 8d. the barrell 18s. 4d. Paied for erbes and garlondes in the said feastes 3s. 4d. Paied for lyveres gyvene to the Waxchaundelers and other the bretherne & susters of the said Fraternitie 7s. 4d. Paied for the hire of the Sadlers Hall in the feast of Jhu' aforsaide 4s. 4d. Paied to Walter Sheffelde for his rewarde in the said feastes 2s. Paied to a clerke which sat with the said Walter 3 dayes in the crowdes to knowe the perfecte recepte of the same Walter and to helpe to overse the bokes 4s. Paied to 4 pouere mene for watching 3s. Paied for 39lb. of irone to mende the clapper of the greate bell at 4d. the lb., with the werkemanship 13s. Paied and gyven in rewarde to Master Rauffe Sadler,[161] chamberleyne unto Master Secretory,[162] to put his maistership in rembrance to obteyne of the kynges grace a supplicacion for Jhus Bretherhed, one aungell noble,[163] 7s. 6d., & 2 suger loves waying 13lb. at 6d. the lb., 6s. 6d. Item gyven to Master Richard Cromwell for like entent, two suger loves waying 14lb. at 6d. the lb., 7s. Also gyvene to Master Popler[164] for like entent, two crownes of the sonne,[165] 9s. 4d. Paied to John Worsoppe for makyng 2 supplicacions in parchement to the kynge for opteynyng of a lycence that the proctors myghte collecte and gather the devocions of the bretherne and susterne of the said Fraternitie, 3s. 4d. Item for writing of 4 copies of the suffrages of the said Fraternitie of Jhu' 3s. 4d. Item for writing in parchement 2 tymes the corporacion of the said

---

[161]   Sir Ralph Sadler (d. 1587). see *ODNB* 'Sadler, Ralph'.

[162]   Thomas Cromwell (d. 1540), 1st earl of Essex. See *ONDB* 'Cromwell, Thomas'.

[163]   An angel noble was usually worth 6s. 8d.

[164]   William Popley, royal servant; for example see in *Letters and Papers, Foreign and Domestic, Henry VIII, Volume 13 Part 1, January–July 1538*, ed. J. Gairdner (London, 1892), nos 226, 247, 248.

[165]   The French *ecu d'or au soleil*. I am grateful to Dr Martin Allen for this information.

Fraternitie graunted by Kynge Henry the VIth and the confirmacone of kynge Henry the 7th 13s. 4d.

Summa } £8 15s.

f. 20v

Also in potacions necessary, that is to say: At the eleccion of a new wardeyne 13s. 8d., and at the awdyt of Master Callarde 20s. For the dyner on Jhus Day £4, and for a brekefast on Jhus Day at Holmes house to the Assistence 3s. 4d. *Summa* } £5 17s.

Summa ut praedicatur

Summa totalis of all the paymentes & discharges } £64 18s. 4½d.

[191] Also the said accomptauntes askene allowaunce for the arrerages of Henry Storydge as aperethe in the last accompte } £12

Iteme, for tharrerages of Walter Marke by obligacone as aperith in the last accompte £6 13s. 4d. } £6 13s. 4d.

Iteme, for tharrerages of Walter Sheffelde in the last accompte £13 2s., and of this yeres freme £5 9s. 4d. } £19 20d.

Item for tharrerages of Robert Bryscowe as it apperithe in the last accompte £6 16s. 8d., and of this yeres ferme 40s. for the ferme of Middlesex, *summa* } £8 16s. 8d.

Item for tharrerages of Hugh Rogiers as apperith in the last accompte £6 13s. 4d. } £6 13s. 4d.

Iteme, for tharrerages of Thomas Holme, *defuncti*, in the last accompte £5, and this yere £5. *Summa* } £10

Item for tharrerages of John Spynke as aperithe in the last accompte £11 } £11

Item for tharrerages of John Phillippes, proctour, for the dioces of Seint Asse, Bangor and Seint Davys as aperith in the last accompte £13 6s. 8s., [sic] ande of this yeres ferme £3 6s. 8d. *Summa* } £16 13s. 4d.

Item for tharrerages of John Sestone as aperith in the last accompte £5, and of this yeres ferme 33s. 4d. *Summa* } £6 13s. 4d.

Item for tharrerages of Jamys Huntley as aperithe in the last accompte 40s., and for this yeres ferme 40s. } £4

Item for tharrerages of John Amadas for this yeres ferme } £7

Item for tharrerages of John Tyler as aperith in the last accompte £5, and of this yeres ferme £34 6s. 8d. *Summa* } £39 6s. 8d.

f. 21r

Iteme, for tharrerages of John Harte for the archedeaconry of Chester and the Isle of Mane for the tyme of this accompte } 22s. 6d.

Also for tharrerages of Crakynthorpe for the dioces of Canterbury for this yeres ferme } £5

243

Summa } £154 10d.

Summa totalis of alle the charges & receptes } £385 3s. 3d.

Summa totalis of all the paymentes, allowaunces & discharges } £64 18s. 4½d.

Summa of the arrerages - £154 10d.

So restithe due to the said Fraternitie over and above the said arreges } £166 4s. 1½d.

The which said somme of £166 4s. 1½d. and also an immage of Jħus of silver & gilte with a fote of tree over gilte, 2 basons of silver parcell gilte, and a greate maiser with a brode bonde with a bosse in the middes of silver & gilte, the said accomptauntes have delyvered into thandes of the said William Turke & Rogier Barker before the auditours according to the ordinance. Wherof is put into a chest belonging to the said Fraternitie £ 146 4s. 1½d., and therof remayneth in thandes of the said William Turke £20 and alle the parcelles aforesaid.

Memorandum[166] that the auditors of this accompte have founde the Richard Calard charged hym self in his accompte with £4 which he receyved of William Pavior, where he shulde not have charged hym self for yt was to hymself due according to the ordynaunce in the tyme of his accompte. And in likewise the said Richard Calard charged Rauff Aleyne with the said somme of £4 which he shulde not have doone. Wherfore the said auditours, considering the premysses, in consciens have alowed the said Rauff Aleyne the saide somme of £4 over and above the alowaunces abovewrittene, and so remaynethe clere to the said Fraternitie £142 4s. 1½d.

Per me William Broket[167]
Per me Rycharde Calarde
Per me Walter [... .]ett
Per me Edwarde Dormer

f. 21v

[192] Obligacions delyvered by thandes of the saide Rauffe Aleyne,

---

[166] Small 'a' added in left margin at start of this entry. Same hand but much longer lines than the main text.
[167] Signatures. The third and fourth were cut in half when pages trimmed, presumably for current binding, and the lower portion pasted next to Broket's and Calard's signatures.

accomptaunt, into thandes of William Turke & Rogier Barker, ~~for~~
Wardeyns for this yere next ensuyng, that is to say from Cristemas in
the 26 yere of the reigne of kynge Henry the 8th [1534] unto the feast
of Cristmas then next ensuyng.

Fyrst an obligacion of John Tyler of Coventry of £10 6s. 8d.

Iteme an endenture of Blaunche Leycetor of the lease of the archedeaconry
of Chester and the Isle of Mane, and an obligacion with condicion of
£10 for the perfourmance of the covenauntes of the same endentures.

Iteme, an obligacion with condicion of Henry Storidge of £20, to pay
£12.

Item an obligacion with condicion of William Marke, John Philippe
and John Marke of Lyskard of £20, to pay £6 13s. 4d.

Item an obligacion with condicion of Henry Thornetone and Jamys
Alexaunder of £10, to pay £7.

Item ann obligacion with condicion of Robert Briscow of £5.

Item an obligacone with condicion of Hughe Rogiers and Richarde
Downe of Ludlowe of £3 6s. 8d. for the dioces of Seint Davis, Seint
Asse & Bangour.

Item an endenture of Laurence Anderton of the lease of the archediaconry
of Chester & the Isle of Mane, with ann obligacone for the perfourmaunce
therof.

Item ann endenture of John Sestone of Lewes of the lease of the dioces
of Chichestre & ann obligacion of £5 for the trewe perfourmaunce of
the covenauntes of the same endentures, & ann other obligacion for the
delyvere of almaner of bookes & regestres.

Item an obligacion with condicion wherin the saide John Cestone is
bounde in £20 to delyver to the said Wardeyns almaner of bookes,
regestres, escriptes, scrowes and mynymentes consernyng the names
of the bretherne & susterne of the said Fraternitie.

Item an obligacion with condicion of Roger Wayte, John Crosse and
Henry Lacy.

Item an inuentory of all the juelles, goodes and ornamentes belonging
to the said Fraternitie.

f. 22r

Item an indenture of Walter Sheffelde of the citie of London and parte
of the countie of Middlesex and the 5 hundredes of Essexe, with an
obligacone of £40 for the perfourmaunce of the covenauntes of the
same endentures.

Item two endentures of the lease of the londes in Uxbridge lettene to
William Bayly & Jamys Standisdoyle.

Item an endenture of John Spynke & ann obligacone with condicone
of £10 to perfourme the couenntes therof.

Item an endenture of Thomas Holmes of the dioces of Salysbury,
Wynchestre & the Isle of Wyghte.

Item an obligacion of Walter Sheffelde of £4, to pay 40s.
Item ann obligacone of Henry Storedge of £6 13s. 4d. with condicone
that if William Marke of Lyskard in the countie of Cornewall, yomane,
John Philip & John Mark of the same, yomene, do pay £6 13s. 4d.
Item an obligacion with condicion of David ap Gryffithe ap Ll[ewel]in of
Wrexhaum withyn the lordeship of Bromefelde in Northwalys, yomane,
& Robert Johnes of the same, yomane, of the somme of 40s., to pay
23s. 4d.
Item ann obligacion of Jamys Huntley of Chelmesforde in the countie
of Essexe, Parsone Sharpe & Thomas Turnebull, fysshemonger, of £4,
to pay 40s.
Item an obligacion of John Donne of Rednour in the Merches of Walys
& Richard Donne, haberdassher of London, of 23s. 4d.
Item an indenture made betwene Master John Colett, late Rectour
of the said Fraternitie, William Bromwell, mercer, and John Monke,
waxchaundeler, then Wardeyns of the said Fraternitie on the one parte,
and William Hawkyns of London, mercer salter, on the other partie,
consernyng londes & a quytrent in Uxbridge.
Item ann obligacone wherin John Philippes & other stonde bounde to
pay 33s. 4d. payable at Cristmas and Easter.
Item an obligacion with condicion wherin John Tyler & other stondene
bounde to in £40, to pay £38 payable at Cristmas & Mydsomer next.
Item an obligacion of John Sestone of £6 13s. 4d., to pay £4 3s. 4d.
Item ann obligacion with condicion of John Philippes & other of £6,
to pay £4, payable at Cristmas & Ester.
Item an obligacion with condicion of John Aleyne & other of £6, to
pay £3 at Cristemas & Mydsomer nexte.

f. 22v [Blank]
f. 23r
[193] This ys thaccompt of Wylliam Turke and Rogier Barker, Wardeyns
of the Fraternitie or Guylde of the moost glorious Name of Jhu founded
in the crowdes undre the cathedrall church of Seint Paule of London,
from the feast of Cristemas in the yere of our Lorde God 1534[ti] and in
the 26[the] yere of the reigne of kynge Henry the 8[the] unto the feast of
Cristemas then next ensuyng, that is to say by the space of one hole yere.

Fyrst[168] the same accomptaunces chargen theym selffes with tharrerages
in the fote of the last accompte } £166 4s. 1½d.
Also with tharrerages of Henry Storige } £12
Also with tharrerages of Walter Marke } £6 13s. 4d.
Also with tharrerages of Walter Sheffelde } £19 20d.

[168] 'Fyrst' smudged as though either written over erasure or with pen overloaded with ink.

Also with tharrerages of Robert Bryscowe } £8 16s. 8d.

Also with tharrerages of Hugh Rogiers } £6 13s. 4d.

Also with tharrerages of Thomas Holmes as apereth in the last accompt } £10

Also with tharrerages of John Spynke } £11

Also with tharrerages of John Philippes [as] apereth in the last accompte } £16 13s. 4d.

Also with tharrerages of John Sestone } £6 13s. 4d.

Also with tharrerages of Jamys Huntley } £4

Also with tharrerages of John Amadas } £7

Also with tharrerages of John Tyler thelder } £39 6s. 8d.

Also with tharrerages of John Harte } 22s. 6d.

Also with tharrerages of Crakynthorepe as apereth in the said last accompte } £5

Summa } (£)320 £26 4s. 11½d.

f. 23v

[194] Also with the ferme of two tenementes and certeyne londes lying in the towne and feildes of Uxbrige in the counties of Middlesex and Bukingham lettene to John Ocborne of Uxbrige for 40s. by yere payable at Myghelmas and Ester, that is to say within the tyme of this accompte } 40s.

Also with the ferme of all the devocions belonging to the said Fraternitie within the dioces of Lyncolne, Norwich, Worcetour, Chester, Hereforde, Wintone and Sarum lettene to John Tyler the yonger for } £29 6s. 8d.

Also with the ferme of all the devocions belonging to the said Fraternitie within the province of Yorke lettene to Henry Hasilwood of Yorke for } £10

Also with the ferme of like devocions for parte of the countie of Essexe lettene to George Blakborne for } 26s. 8d.

Also with the ferme of like devocions for the countie of Middlesex and parte of Essexe lettene to John Newyll for } 20s.

Also with the ferme of like devocions of the citie of London lettene to Walter Sheffelde for } £20 10s.

Also with the ferme of like devocions of the dioces of Caunterbury lettene to John Aleyne for } 46s. 8d.

Also with the ferme of like devocions of the dioces of Chichester letten to John Sestone for } 26s. 8d.

Also with the ferme of like devocions of the archedeconry of Chester and the Ile of Mane lettene to Blaunche Leicetor and Hugh Bardesley her sone for } 53s. 4d.

Also with the ferme of like devocions of the dioces of Seint Asse, Bangor and Seint Davys lettene to John Philippes and Gyttowe for } £6

247

Also with the ferme of the devocions of the dioces of Exetour, Bathe and Welles letten to John Amadas for } £7

Also with the ferme of the devocions of the dioces of Sarum lettene to William Graver for } £3 6s. 8d.

Also with an annuell rent of 20s. payable yerely by the Wardeyns of the Felyship of Waxchaundelers of London to the said Fraternitie } 20s.

Summa } £85 16s.

Summa totalis of all the charges and receytes } £406 11½d.

Wherof paiede

f. 24r

[195] The said accomptauntes accompte in paymentes ordynary to be made in the crowdes of the saide cathedrall church to sondry ministres of the same church beyng present and keping divine service there in the feastes of the Transfiguracion and Name of Jhu' and masse of Requiem onn the morow folowing, that is to say: First, to the subdeane beyng present at all the premysses and singing highe masse in the said feastes, for either day 2s., *Summa* - 4s. To 8 chauntry prestes bering copes in the said feastes 13s. 4d. To 12 petycanons 40s. To 6 vycars 16s. 8d. To every highe canone, pety canone, chauntry preste, vycar and querester beyng present and bering copes in processione in the said feastes 4d., *summa* 27s. 2d. To a pety canone singing masse of Requiem and reding the Gospell and Pistell at the said thre masses and for saying *Deprofundis* 2s. 10d. For the collacone there made at the highe masse in the saide feastes 3s. 4d. To the sexteyne for garnysshing of the alters & bering of bokes & other ornamentes 3s. 10d. To every of the 4 vergiers there beyng attendant 16d. apece & 20d. in rewarde, 7s. To the bell ryngers for their labour in the said feastes besides 20s. to them paied quarterly for keping the dores of the said crowdes 13s. 4d. *Summa* } £6 11s. 6d.

Also[169] for masses of Jhu' solempnely by note kepte in the said crowdes by the subdeane, a cardynall, a petycanone, 6 vycars and 10 queresters of the said cathedrall church in their habettes and surplices, that is to say: To achauntry [sic] prest singing masse of Requiem by note every Fryday ymmediatly after Jhus masse with 6 of the queresters [blank]. To the subdene beyng present 4d. To a petycanone singing masse of Requiem 8d. To the chauntry prestes singing masse of Requiem & every of the vicars 4d. *Summa* of all 47[ti] Frydayes within the tyme of this

---

[169]   'Also' at the start of this and the subsequent paragraph are written in lighter ink and larger script, seemingly added subsequent to the main text.

accompt } £7 16s. 8d.

Also to the master of the said 10 queresters for keping thre *salves* dayly in the said crowdes, after complyne done in the said cathedrall churche, before the images of Jhu', our Blessed Lady and Seint Sebastyane, takyng for his labour yerely 26s. 8d. payable at foure termes according to the ordynaunce } 26s. 8d.

f. 24v

Also to the belle ryngers of the same cathedralle church for their labour & daily attendance in openyng, closing and shitting of the dores within the said crowdes, for rynging of belles, blowing of organs, lyghting & quenching of torches and other lyghtes and for sweping & making clene of the said crowdes, 20s. by yere payable quarterly besides 13s. 4d. to them allowed in the said feastes } 20s.

[196] Also for the rewarde of the Wardeyne this yere, lymyted and taxed by the Rectour, Wardeyns ande Assistence of the said Fraternitie according to thordinaunce } £4

Also for lyveres to be gyvene for clothing of the saide Wardeyns with cognisaunces of the name of Jħu, lymytede also by the said Rectour, Wardeyns and assistence } £4

Also to the prechers at Poulys Crosse and Seint Mary Spyttell remembryng and praying for all the bretherne and susterne of the said Fraternitie for 44ti Sondayes and Good Fryday at Poulys Crosse and 3 dayes in Esterweke at Seint Mary Spyttell at 8d. for every of the said dayes } 32s.

Also to the 6 weyghetes with banners payntede, conysaunces enbrowdered with Jħus, goyng all the stretes and suburbers of London playing with their instrumentes to gyve warnyng and knowlege to the people of the said Fraternitie of the said feastes of Transfiguracion & Name of Jħus, according to the ordynaunce 10s. ande in rewarde this yere 3s. 4d. *Summa* } 13s. 4d.

Also to the proctour of the said Fraternitie for the bonfyre before the northe dore of the said crowdes yerely in the evenyng of the said feast 2s. 8d., and for cressit lyghte 2d. *Summa* } 2s. 10d.

Also for wax spent in the said crowdes within the tyme of this accompt } 54s. 10d.

Also for singing brede and for brede to make holly brede, 8s. 1½d., and for 35 gallons & *dimidium* of malnesey at 10d. the gallone, *summa* } 37s. 8½d.

Also to the almener of Poulys for 10 queresters of the (same) cathedrall church servyng God in their habittes in the said crowdes, aswell in the feastes of the Transfiguracion and Name of Jhu' as every Friday at masse of Requiem and at the 3 *salves* kepte dayly by the said Fraternitie } £4 3s. 4d.

f. 25r
Also to Richard Scotherope, sexteyne, attending dayly in the saide crowdes, keping the vestmentes & ornamentes of the said Fraternitie for one hole yere } 40s.

Also to Thomas Butler, Richarde Ewe, William Mystelbroke and Thomas Penyfather, power mene apoynted to the almes of the said Fraternitie, keping the crowdes, helping prestes at masse and praying for all the bretherne ande susterne of the said Fraternitie and all Cristen soules, every of them havyng yerely 40s. payable quarterly } £8

Summa } £45 18s. 10½d.

[197] Also in sondry expenses necessary, that is to say: First, for the hire of arras 5s., ande for other costes therto belonging 2s. 1d. Paied for bromes & paring the stayres at sondry tymes 13d. Paied for brede & ale to pouere mene at sondry tymes 6d. Paied for mending of awbes and surplices 2s. 4d. Paiede for nayles to mende the dore where the wyndow was brokene, ande for nayles to mende the cheste & for a plate 4d. Paied for coles 16d. Paied for pynnes and taype 6d. Paied for mending the pavementes both within and without the crowdes and for morter and stone 6d. For russhes 4½d. Paied for a key for one of the pew dores 4d. For a fourme and a ladder 10d. For mending 3 holys over the dore 3d. For scowring the grete lampe at Jḣus aulter and mending the botom therof 8d. Also for scowring the hollywaterstok, 12 candelstykkes, 4 basons & 8 creuettes 3 tymes 2s. 10d. For a bag to put in the satten hoodes 2d. For sponging and making clene of the best alter clothes 8d. Paied for wasshing the clothes all this yere 13s. 4d. Paied for 8lb. of leade to make fast a barre of irone 6d. Paied to a glasier to amende the wyndow and for nayles 14½d. Paied to a smyth for mending the grete irone cheste by the aulter 3d. Paied to a glasier for sytting of 8 fote of glasse in ann other wyndow 16d. Paied to a glasyer for mending of a wyndowe on the south side 3s. Paied to the glasier for new sytting and scowerryng awyndowe onn the north side

2s. 7d. Paied to prestes singing masse onn Jħus Day and Alhollowen Day 5s. 4d. Paide and delte in almes onn the said 2 dayes 7s. Paied to 4 porters for keping the

f. 25v

dores in the said feastes 4s. Paied for the dyner of the same 4 porters 2 dayes 2s. Paied for the queresters brekefast 8d. Paied to 2 womene to drawe ale 2s. For tappes and trayes 8d. For 5 barrelles of ale 18s. 4d. For erbes and garlondes 3s. 4d. For lyveres gyvene to the Waxchaundelers and other the bretherne and susterne of the said Fraternitie 7s. 4d.[170] Paied for the hire of the Sadlers Halle 4s. 8d. Paied to Walter Sheffelde for his rewarde in the said feastes 2s., and to Richarde Scotherope for hys watching and attendaunce in the said feastes. 16d. Paied to a clerke which satt with the said Walter 3 dayes in the said crowdes to knowe the perfecte recepte of the same Walter and to helpe to overloke the bokes 4s. Paied to the foure bedemen for their attendance and labour in the saide feastes 3s., and to Richard Scotherope for his attendance and dyner 9d. Paied for 4 doseyne candelles 5s. Paied for 3 gallons of lampe oyle 3s. 6d. Paied to the porters for watching the crowdes the next nyghte after the wyndowe was brokene 4d. Paied for a barre of irone for the wyndowe waying 10lb. *dimidium* 15½d. Paied to a mason to sett up the barre in the wyndowe 8d. Paied for 40lb. weight of bell ropes 5s. Paied to Thomas Piersone, servant to John Worsoppe, for writing this accompte 3s. 4d. Paiede to a carpenter for 12 quarters and for setting up of them aboute 4 pillers, ande for 32^{ti} hokes of irone to bere up the same quarters ande for making of 32^{ti} hooles to sett in the same hokys, and for 200 of grete hokes to hange the clothe of arras onn, 14s. 8d. Paied for drynke to the werkemen 3d. Item gyven to Maister Popley to get the kynges seale out *dimidium* a conger and a turbut price 3s. 4d. Item gyvene hym more at certeyne other tymes a conger, 2 places, 2 soules, a turbut , a gurnarde, a chyne of calver salmone and a quarter of calver salmon, price 11s. 2d. Also, gyvene to Ser John Aleyne[171] for like entent *dimidium* a conger price 2s. 4d. Item paied to John Worsoppe for entryng into the boke 2 patentes and for diverse other wrytinges 6s. 8d.

Summa } £8 5s. 11½d.

f. 26r

Also in potacions necessary, that is to say at the eleccion of the newe Wardeyne 13s. 4d., and at the awdet of Master Aleyne 20s. For the dyner on Jħus Day £4 } £5 13s. 4d.

Summa ut praedicatur

---

[170] Possible strikethrough first 'i' of 'iiij', so possibly 3d.
[171] Sir John Aleyn, (d. 1545) mercer, mayor of London. Barron, *London*, 352.

Also paied to Master William Botery, mercer, for a pece of blak Lukes weluet which was gyvene by thassent of thassistence for a lycence to be had for the proctors to gether the devocions of weldisposed people } £12

Also paied to Master Rauffe Aleyne by thassent of the said Assistence for that he was overcharged in his accompte, as aperethe in the same his accompte } £4

Summa } £16

Summa totalis of all paymentes & discharges } £75 18s. 2d.

[198] Also the said accomptauntes askene allowaunce for tharrerages of Henry Storege } £12

Also for tharrerages of Walter Marke } £6 13s. 4d.

Also for tharrerages of Walter Shelffelde as apereth in the last accompte £19 20d., ande of this yeres accompte £7 6s. 8d. *Summa* } £26 8s. 4d.

Also for tharrerages of Robert Bryscowe as apereth in the last accompt } £8 16s. 8d.

Also for tharrerages of Hughe Rogiers } £6 13s. 4d.

Also for tharrerages of Thomas Holme as doth apere in the last accompt } £10

Also for tharrerages of John Spynke } £11

Also for tharrerages of John Philippes as apereth in the last accompt } £16 13s. 4d.

Also for tharrerages of John Sestone as apereth in the last accompt £6 13s. 4d., and of this yeres ferme 10s. *Summa* } £7 3s. 4d.

Also for tharrerages of Jamys Huntley as apereth in the last accompt } £4

Also for tharrerages of John Amydas as aperethe in the last accompt £7, and of this yeres ferme £5. *Summa* } £12

f. 26v

Also for [tharr]erages of John Tyler thelder as apereth in the last accompt } £39 6s. 8d.

Also for tharrerages of John Harte as aperethe [in] the last accompt } 22s. 6d.

Also for tharrerages of Crakynthorpe as apereth in the last accompt } £5

Also for tharrerages of John Aleyne for this yeres ferme } 16s.

Also for tharrerages of John Tyler the yonger for this yeres ferme } £29 6s. 8d.

Also for tharrerages of Henry Hasylwood for this yere } £3

Also for tharrerages of John Newyll for Myddlesex this yere } 5s.

Also for tharrerages of Blanche Leicetour for this yeres ferme } 8s.

Also for tharrerages of William Grover which shalbe due and payable at Marche next commyng, as apereth by obligacion } 33s. 4d.

Summa } £202 6s. 6d.

Summa totalis of all the charges & receytes } £406 11½d.

Summa totalis of all the paymentes & discharges } £75 18s. 2d.

Summa totalis of all the arrerages } £202 6s. 6d.

So restith due to the said Fraternitye over & above the arrerages } £131 8s. 5d.

[199] The which said somme of £131 8s. 5d., and also an image of Jħus of silver and gilte with a fote of trey overgilte, 2 basens of silver parcell gilte, and a greate mayser with a brode bonde with a bosse in the myddes of silver and gilte, the said accomptauntes have delyvered into thandes of the said Rogier Barker and John Skampyone before the auditors according to the ordynaunce. And therof is put into a chest belonging to the sayd Fraternitie £111 8s. 5d., and remaynnyng in the handes of the said Rogier £20 and all the parcelles of plate aforsaid.

By me Rauff Aleyn[172]
Per me Johannus Pery
Per me William Wilkynson[173]

---

172 Signatures.
173 It is likely that a final folio has been lost from this account, but it is impossible to verify this with the manuscript bound in its current form.

APPENDIX I:
THE 1552 INVENTORY OF GOODS
IN ST FAITH'S, LONDON
(TNA, E117/4/5)[1]

f.1 [blank recto and verso]
f.2r
[200]
Fa[ith] W(t)M.[2]

The certificate and declaracion of John Lewys,[3] one of the churche wardeynes of Saynte Faithes in the Citey of London, and Robert Toye, deputie to Symon [Co]stone the other church wardene there, made to the articles minerstred & delyvered to the same churche wardens the eleventh daye of Julie [in] the syxte yere of the reigne of oure sovereigne Lorde Edwarde the Syxt, [1552] by the grace of God kinge of Englonde, Fraunce, and Irelande, Defender of the Faithe, and in earthe of the Churche of Englonde and also of Irelande imediate under God the Supreame Hedd, by the Lorde Maior of the Citey of London and other oure soveraigne lordes Commissioners by his Majestie appoynted to take the survey of the churche goods and ornamentes within the sayde Citey.

To the fyrste of the sayed articles wee do certife [and] declare that Roger Hunte, clerke of the Admiraltie, & Henry Tabb, stacyoner, nowe deceased, were churche wardeyns there the fyrste yere of the raigne of our sayed soveraigne lo[rd] the Kinge that nowe ys.

To the seconde wee declare that wee the sayed John Lew[ys] & Robert Toye have yet remayninge and appurteyninge to the sayde parishe churche of Saynte Faithes aforesayd twoo chaleyses with patentes [sic] of sylver

---

[1] For a discussion of the manuscript, especially in relation to its mis-binding and idiosyncratic foliation, and for editorial conventions, please see Introduction: Editorial Conventions. I am grateful to Claire Martin for photographs of this document.

[2] Heading in left margin, almost certainly in a different hand to the main text. The letters presumably stand for the Virgin Martyr.

[3] Lewys was a Proctor of the Court of Arches and one of the senior Wardens of the Jesus Guild when it was restored in 1556; see Introduciton.

and gylte, wherof the one waies fower and fortie ownces, and thother one and twentie ownces scante.[4] Also one whole sute of crymosone or redd velvett vestim[entes] embrodred, with twoo aultare clothes of the same; one cope of white damaske; a cope of bodkyne worke; a vestiment of redd damaske; a herse clothe; and twoo table clothes of olde sylkes with a cope and a vestiment of olde velvett, ripped and brokene; wone bell; and certene other olde table clothes, towelles, albes, and surpleses, with other lumber of lytle value.

To the thirde we saye that other inventary or transcriptes of the goodes, plate, juelles or ornamentes of the sayede churche thene wee have in the nexte article precedent mentyoned & rehersed, wee are not hable to delyver unto your [sic], for that neithe[r] in the bysshoppes register of London nor in any book of the sayed churche orelles where, wee cane fynde any mentyone of any perticulers of thee same, nor there hath bene any inventaries or particulers made or kept of the same thiese twentie yeres past by the churche wardeynes there, or any other as farre as wee can learne or knowe.

f.2v

[201]

To the fourth and laste article wee declare that this laste yere paste wee the sayed John Lewys and Robert Toye, beinge thene churche wardeynes of the sayed parishe, by the expresse consent, advise, and appoyntment of the parishenours aforesayed, in consideracion that our late parishe churche was lytle ande not hable to conteyne the whole people of that parishe, beinge of late yeres muche increasede, and also so darke that in the brightest sommer daye of necessitie for lighte there were candelles burnte in the same, and by reasone thereof so fustie and unsavery that in sycknes tyme yt mighte be occasione of muche infectione of the people there, and for diverse other laufull & honest consideracions movinge, the same parishioners have solde & bestowed for thopteyninge of the late chappell called the crowdes to be our parishe churche, and to furnishe ande adorne the same to that purpose, aswell in glasse, yrone, pavementes, lyme, waynescott, workemanshipp and other necesaries, as more particulerly hereafter ensuethe of the sayed churche goodes. Fyrste, unto one [blank] Tompsone, a broker dwellinge in Saynte Katheryns by the Tower of London, the twentye of September in the fyfte yere of the raigne of our sayde soverayne lorde the kinges majestie that nowe ys, certene olde vestimentes ande churche stuffe, in grosse all togthers the particulers wherofe (bycause the greatest parte therof

---

4   'A. viz 3 coopes, a vestyment and 2 tunykles' written in left margin in a different hand next to this entry.

was olde, rottene & brokene),[5] wee dyde not note in wrytinge nor are not hable at this tyme to expresse the same, for the summe of two and twentie poundes.

Item, solde the same daye to William Bull one olde and torne vestiment of grene and white velvett reysed for fyve shillinges.

Item, solde unto one [blank] Grace[6] a goldesmythe dwellinge in Chepesyde, the eighte of Februarye thene next followinge, a crosse parcell gylte, poinz fower score and tenne ownces; one lesser crosse all white, poinz nyntene ownces three quarters; a pyxe gylte, poinz three and thirtie ownces three quarters; a payer of candelstickes white, poinz fower and twentie ownces & half; a censure white, poinz thirtie ownces & a half; a paxe gylte, poinz tenne ownces three quarters; a shipp for encence white, poinz tenne ownces & a quarter; a cople of cruettes white, poinz syxe ownces & a half; and certene brokene peces of sylver, poinz three ownces and a halff[7] at fyve shillinges the ownce one with another. *Summa* - £57 7s. 6d.

Item, the same daye solde to Master Gregory Rayltone,[8] onne of the clerkes of the kinges majesties signet, one chalice parcell gylte with a patent, poinz twentie ownces at fyve shillinges the ownce, *summa* - £5.

Item, solde to John Lewys a pece of sylver wherin was a cristall, poinz fower ownces & a quarter at fyve shillinges the ownce, *summa* – 21s. 3d.

Item, solde the tenthe daye of February aforesayede to M[ist]res Crooke a wydowe, a marbell stone for a tomble [sic] for tenne shillinges.

Item, the

f.3Br

twentythe of Februarye sold to Roger Sylvester and Aleyne Ganelyne,[9] marblers, seven score pounde of olde & brokene lattyne for syxe and fortie shillinges & eighte pence.

Item, lykewise solde a lytle awter stone off marbell for three shillinges and fower pence. Item, three & fortie poundes of olde yrone at three hal[f]pens the pounde, *summa* fyve shillings and fower pence.

Item, twoo frames of wood for aulters ande twoo stones belonginge unto the same, an olde pulpytt, a frame of a sepulchr[e] & an olde dore, and certene olde somers [sic], joystes & lathes, to dyveres and sondry persons whose names for that the parcelles were of sm[all] value wee dyde not take remembraunce of, nor do not nowe remember, for twoo & thirtie shillinges & fower pence.

5   Brackets are in-text and contemporary .
6   Possibly Richard Grace, d. 1560, TNA, PROB 11/43/172.
7   'halff' written over erasure.
8   Gregory Railton, d. 1561. See C. H. Garrett, *The Marian Exiles: A Study in the Origins of Elizabethan Puritanism* (Cambridge, 1938), no. 338, pp. 265–6.
9   For Sylvester and Ganelyne (Gammon), see J. Bayliss, 'New Thoughts on A Sixteenth-Century Workshop', in *The Monuments Man: Essays in Honour of Jerome Bertram*, ed. C. Steer (Donington, 2020), 234–54, 237, 239, 252–4.

Summa totallis of all which goodes as aforesayede solde dothe amounte to fower score tenne poundes, elevene shillinges ande fyve pence.

A[ll] other goodes, plate, juelles or ornamentes of the sayede parishe chur[ch] wee do not fynde or knowe to be solde sythens the fyrst yere of the raigene of our sayede soveraigne lorde the kinges majestie that nowe ys. The value of which goodes solde as ys a[s] saide was imployed to thuse aboutsaide as hereafter perticulerly ensueth.

[202]

In primis, by the agrement of the parishe paide to the Deane and Chaptre of Paules the thirtie daye of June the yere of our lorde God a thousande, fyve hundreth, fyftie ande one, for thobteyninge of their good will & consent for a lease of the sayede crowdes to be had & made for the terme of fower score and nyntene yeres to the sayed parshe of Saynte Faithes to be used and enjoyed for a parishe churche } £14

Item the laste of June to one Master Grymstone,[10] pretendinge righte in the sayed crowdes, for his good will & delyverye of the kayes of the same whiche were in his possessione to us the churche wardenes aforesayed, to bye hym a sattene dublett } 40s.

Item payede to Roger Sylvester, marbler, the syxte of Julie for his labour ande toles in takinge downe thalters & a stondinge tombe in the sayede crowdes } 4s.

Item the 11[the] of Juliie to three laborers for seven dayes worke aboute the sayede awlters & diggene & caringe awaye [th]e rubbishe } 5s. 6d.

Item for bredd ande dryncke to the sayed laborers for forberyinge their ydell howers } 3s. 3d.

Summa - £16 12s. 9d.

f.3Bv

[203]

Item payed to twoo carpynters for fower dayes worke in takynge downe the chappell in the bodye of the crowdes and settinge up of the qwere } 4s.

Item to a free masone for a dayes worke ande an halfe } 15d.

Item geven to a laborer that hurte hym selfe in his worke } 4d.

Item for a newe kaye for the dore towardes the churche yarde } 6d.

Item for a pounde of candelles } 2d.

Item for fyve baskettes to cary rubbishe } 10d.

---

10   Possibly Edward Grimston, listed as liable for taxation in the royal household in 1552 (TNA, E115/177/46) who may be synonymous with Edward Grimston MP (d. 1600). See History of Parliament 'Grimston, Edward'.

Item for bromes } 2d.

Item the 18th of Julie to Goodmane Capper, joyner, and his boye for sevene dayes worke, twelve pence a daye hyme selfe and syxe pence to his boye } 10s. 6d.

Item to Mathewe Jonsone, joyner, the same daye for syxe dayes worke at lyke rate } 6s.

Item the same daye to Richarde Hardy, joyner, for three dayes worke after the same rate } 3s.

Item for 4^{II} duble ponchyons } 3s. 4d.

Item for sawinge of twoo of the same punchyons } 3d.

Item for makinge of fower dogges ande fower spykens of yrone } 7d.

Item to the joyners for drynkinges the weke aforesaide } 5d.

Item to Hughe the under sextene for laboringe the same weke and tendinge upone the workemene and shotinge and openynge the churche dores } 12d.

Item the 20th daye of Julie for three duble punchions } 3s.

Item the same daye for thirtene duble quarters } 6s.

Item the 23th of Julie to a cuple of laboerers that holpe the marbler, for one dayes labour } 16d.

Item the same daye to Sylvester the marbler for a dayes worke } 12d.

Item the 24th of Julie to the three joyners for fower dayes worke } 12s.

Item to [th]e joyners boye for 4 dayes worke the same daye } 2s.

Item the same daye to Hugh thunder sextene for 2 dayes worke } 12d.

Summa – 58s. 8d.

f.3Ar

[204]

Item for makinge of 2 chesylles & one crowe [bar] of yrone } 6d.

Item for drynke to the joyners this weke } 4d.

Item the 30^{ty} daye of Julie for halfe a pounde of gloue } 3d.

Item the same daye for bromes } 2d.

Item for candelles the same daye } 2d.

Item the fyrste of Auguste to Harry Watsone, playsterer, for fower dayes worke } 4s.

Item to James Estone his laborere for fower dayes worke } 2s. 8d.

Item to John Fremane, playsterer, for 2 dayes worke } 2s.

Item to Richerde Abrigg and Christopher Bryane, playsterers, for three dayes worke } 6s.

Item to Richerde Becquett and Robert Smythe, laborers, for twoo dayes worke } 2s. 8d.

Item to Arnolde the laborer for a dayes worke } 8d.

Item to John Robyns ales Capper the joyner for 6 dayes worke } 6s.

---

^{II}   The number 4 written over erasure.

Item to Mathewe Jonsone, joyner, for syxe dayes worke } 6s.
Item to Richerde Hardy, joyner, for syxe dayes worke } 6s.
Item to Phillipp [th]e joyners boye for syxe dayes worke } 3s.
Item to Hughe thunder sextone for syxe dayes worke } 3s.
Item to the joyners in drynckinges this weke } 7d.
Item the 7th of Auguste to Harry Watsone, playsterer, for fyve dayes worke } 5s.
Item to Harry Watsones laborer for fyve dayes worke } 2s. 8d.
Item to John Fremane, playsterer, for fyve dayes worke } 5s.
Item to John Fremanes laborer for fyve dayes worke } 2s. 8d.
Item gevyne to the playstereres for a rewarde } 4d.
Item payed to John Robyns ales Capper, joyner, for syxe dayes worke } 6s.
Item to Richerde Ardye, joyner, for syxe dayes worke } 6s.
Item to Mathewe Jonsone, joyner, for syxe dayes worke } 6s.
Item to John Twydie, joyner, for fyve dayes worke } 5s.
Item to Phillipp the joiners boye for fyve dayes worke } 3s.
Item to Hughe the under sextene for his wekes labour } 3s.
Item to his wiff for twoo dayes laboure for wasshinge and wypynge the pewes } 12d.
Item to [th]e Goodmane Smythmane for cuttinge the fote of a marble pyller } 2s. 8d.
Item for fower and twentie paimes [sic] of syse for to white the walles } 2s.

Summa } £4 14s. 4d.

f.3Av

[205]
Item for half a busshell of heyre [sic] } 4d.
Item for a pounde of candelles } 2d.
Item for dryncke for the joyners this weke } 6d.
Item for the mendinge of the crowe [bar] of yrone [th]e same daye } 2d.
Item the 12th of Auguste for nayles of sondry sortes as shall apeare in the irne mongers byll } £3 4d.
Item the same daye for a hundrethe & twoo lode of lyme } 6s.
Item the same daye for 12 single quarters at 3d. a pece } 3s.
Item the 14th of Auguste to the glasyer for twoo and thirtie foote of newe glasse for the wyndowe in the quere at sevene pence the fote } 18s. 8d.
Item for settinge of syxtene fote of olde glasse in the same wyndowe at three pence a fote } 4s.
Item for mendynge of a hedd of one of the panys in the same wyndowe } 4d.
Item for 24 fote of olde glasse newe sett in the wyndowe in the myddle isle } 6s.

Item in the same wyndowe for sevene & twentye fote of newe glasse } 15s. 9d.

Item the 15th of Auguste to John Robyns, joyner, for his wayges, his twoo menns [sic] ande a boyes [sic] for syxe dayes } 21s.

Item [th]e same daye to Richarde Ardye, joyner, for 6 dayes werke } 6s.

Item to John Pyforde, tyler, for three dayes worke } 3s. 6d.

Item to William Swanesone, tyler, for fower dayes work } 4s. 8d.

Item to Richarde Wrighte, laboroer, for 4 dayes worke } 2s. 8d.

Item to Robert Messinger, laborer, for 3 dayes worke } 2s.

Item to Hughe thunder sextene for 6 dayes } 3s.

Item for drynke this weke } 16d.

Item the same daye for syxe loade of lyme } 4s.

Item Thursdaye the 20th of Auguste for twoo laborers worke for that daye } 16d.

Item Saterdaye the 22th for trymmynge and mendynge of the organes } 5s. 2d.

Item to a tylar for the same daye for settinge of the same ande doinge other jobbes } 16d.

Item to his laborer for that dayes worke } 8d.

Summa } £8 11s. 11d.

f.4r

[206]

Item the same daye to John Robyns, joyner, for hym self, his mane and his boye, for fyve dayes } 12s. 6d.

Item to John Twydie, joyner, for fyve dayes worke } 5s.

Item to Richerde Ardye, joyner, for fower dayes worke } 4s.

Item to Hughe thunder sextene for syxe dayes worke } 3s.

Item the same daye to twoo wemene for wasshinge and swepynge } 12d.

Item to Ambrose Crowler the smythe for twoo duble casementes } 20s.

Item for drynkinges this weke to joyners, playsterers ande other workemene } 18d.

Item for twelve single quarters occupied this weke } 3s.

Item the 26th of Auguste to the smyth for locke ande kaye to the vestry dore & certen other jobes } 4s. 4d.

Item for a pounde of candelles } 2d.

Item Saterdaye the 29th of Auguste to John Robyns the joyner for hyme self, his mane ande his boye for fyve dayes } 12s. 6d.

Item the same daye to Richerde Ardye, joyner, for 5 daies } 5s.

Item to Hughe theunder sextene for fyve dayes worke } 2s. 6d.

Item for drynke this weke } 4d.

Item the fyrste of September for fyftene wainscotes at twentie pence a pece } 28s.

Item the same daye for 18 single quarters and twoo duble } 6s.
Item for the cariage of the wainscottes and quarters } 8d.
Item for a payer of joyntes for a pewe dore } 4d.
Item the fyft [sic] of September for half a pounde of glewe } 3d.
Item the same daye to John Robyns, joyner, for his worke, his mane and his boye for syxe dayes } 15s.
Item to Hughe the under sextene for syxe dayes work } 3s.
Item to Richerde Ardye for syxe dayes worke } 6s.
Item in bredde ande dryncke this weke } 10d.
Item the 8th daye of September for syxe duble quarters } 3s.
Item the same daye for 200 fote of selinge borde } 12s.
Item twoo single qwarters } 6d.
Item the 12th of September for a locke and kaye for the dore next the churche yerde } 6s. 10d.

Summa - £7 17s. 3d.

f.4v

[207]

Item for a duble case of yrone for the wyndowe nexte the pulpytt } 13s.
Item the same daye to John Robyns for his mane, hyme self and his boye for syxe dayes worke } 15s.
Item to Richerde Ardye for syxe dayes worke } 6s.
Item to Hughe thunder sextene for syxe dayes werke } 3s.
Item to the glasyer } 30s.
Item for sawinge of 13 carses of waynscotte } 2s. 2d.
Item for bredd and dryncke this weke } 8d.
Item the 15th of September for three hundrethe of selinge borde } 18s.
Item for fyftie single quarters } 12s. 6d.
Item for syxtene duble quarters } 8s.
Item for the cariage } 4d.
Item the 16the of September for three rafters } 3s.
Item for twoo poundes of candelles } 3½d.
Item the 19the of September for the sawinge of twelve carse of waynscote } 2s.
Item to John Robyns for his mane, his boye ande his owne wayges this weke } 15s.
Item to Richerde Ardye, joyner, for his wekes waiges } 6s.
Item to Hughe thunder sextene for his wekes waiges } 3s.
Item for drynkinges to the joyners this weke } 10d.
Item to the glasier this same daye } 9s. 6d.
Item the 26th of September to John Robyns for hyme self, his mane & his boye for 5 dayes worke } 12s. 6d.
Item to Richerde Hardye, joyner, for fyve dayes } 5s.
Item to Hughe thundersextene for fyve dayes } 2s. 6d.
Item for bredde and dryncke } 9d.

Item the thirde of October to John Robyns for his wages, his mane and his boye for fower dayes worke } 10s.
Item the same daye to Richerde Ardye, joyner, for fower dayes worke } 4s.
Item for dryncke this weke } 6d.
Item to Hughe thonder sextene this weke } 16d.
Item for twoo loikes & kayes & hynges for the scedilles[12] in the qwere & for a vyce for the church dore } 4s.
Item the 10th of October for 25ty single qwarters } 6s. 3d.

Summa } £9 15s. 5½d.

f.5r

[208]

Item three hundrethe and eighte fote of selinge borde at syxe shillinges the hundreth } 18s. 3d.
Item for the carriage of the same } 4d.
Item for twoo pounde of glewe } 10d.
Item for eighte pounde of candelles } 16d.
Item for John Robynson, his mane & his boye for syxe daies } 15s.
Item for Richerde Hardie for syxe dayes worke } 6s.
Item to Harry Ponder, joyner, for fower dayes worke } 3s. 4d.
Item to Hughe thunder sextene for his attendance [th]is weke } 18d.
Item the 12th of October for three hundreth of planche borde at syxe shillinge the hundrethe } 18s.
Item the same daye for half a hundreth clapborde } 5s. 6d.
Item half a quarterne of waynscote } 27s. 6d.
Item for the cariage of the waynscote } 6d.
Item for the cariage of the planche borde } 3d.
Item the same daye to Goodmane Capper for his breckfaste } 3d.
Item to John Langeforde, joyner, for three dayes worke the last weke } 3s.
Item Saterdaye the 17th of October for the sawinge of eighte waynscottes } 20d.
Item for drynke this weke } 18d.
Item for candelles } 6d.
Item for half a pounde of glewe } 3d.
Item to Goodmane Capper for hyme self, his mane and his boye for syxe dayes worke } 15s.
Item to Harry Ponder, joyner, for syxe dayes worke } 6s. 6d.
Item to Richerde Hardy, joyner, for syxe dayes work } 6s.
Item to John Burges, joyner, for three dayes worke } 3s.
Item to John Longeforde, joyner, for fyve dayes worke this weke } 5s.
Item to the sextene this weke } 2s.

---

12   Probably sedilia, the seats for officiating clergy.

Item Saterdaye [th]e 24th of October for 2 duble quarters } 12d.
Item for eighte pounde of candelles [th]is weke paste } 16d.
Item for the joyners drynckinges this weke } 18d.
Item for 12 pair pewe henches after 20d. the payer } 20s.
Item for half a pounde of glewe } 3d.
Item [th]e same daye to Harry Ponder, joyner, for 6 dayes worke } 6s. 6d.
Item to Richerde Hardye, joyner, for syxe dayes worke } 6s.
Item to John Burges, joyner, for syxe dayes worke } 6s.
Item to John Langforde, joyner, for syxe dayes worke } 6s.

Summa } £9 11s. 7d.

f.5v

[209]
Item to Goodmane Capper for hym self, his mane and his boye for syxe dayes } 15[s.]
Item to Hughe thunder sextene for this weke } 2s.
Item the laste of October for candelles [th]is weke past } 13d.
Item a pounde of glewe } 5d.
Item syxe and thirtie single quarters } 9s.
Item syxe duble quarters } 3s.
Item a hundrethe planche borde } 6s.
Item for the cariage of bordes and quarters } 3d.
Item to Goodmane Capper for his worke, his mane and his boye for fyve dayes worke } 12s. 6d.
Item to Richerde Hardye for fyve dayes worke } 5s.
Item to Ponder the joyner for fyve dayes worke } 5s.5d.
Item to Langeforde & Burges, joyners, for fyve dayes worke } 10s.
Item to Hughe the under sextene } 3s.
Item for half a dosene henges for womene[s] pewes } 10s.
Item for drynke ande fyar } 20d.
Item the 7th of November to the smythe for three payer of hynges, three sprynges & twoo boltes } 10s.
Item to Goodmane Capper for his worke this weke and his mane and his boye } 15s.
Item to Langforde, Burges & Hardy for [th]is weke labour } 18s.
Item to Ponder the joyner } 6s. 6d.
Item to Hughe the sextene } 3s.
Item for sawinge of waynscotte } 6d.
Item for fower spyck nayles } 2d.
Item for fyre and dryncke this weke } 2s.
Item for candelles this weke } 13d.
Item for a pounde of glowe } 5d.
Item for three quarters of borde } 4s.
Item for fower lode of lyme } 2s. 8d.

Item the 14th of November for fower waynscottes } 8s.
Item for a quarter of clapborde } 2s. 9d.
Item for candelles and coles } 18d.
Item for drynckinge this weke } 2s. 1d.
Item to Goodmane Capper for hym self, his mane & his boye } 15s.
Item to John Longeforde, joyner, for this weke } 6s.
Item to Richerde Ardye for fyve dayes weke } 5s.

Summa } £9 8s.

f.6r

[210]

Item to Master Ponder for syxe dayes worke } 6s. 6d.
Item to Burges the joyner for syxe dayes worke } 6s.
Item to Hughe thunder sextene for this weke worke } 3s.
Item the 21th of November to Capper the joyner for hyme self, his mane
and his boye for syxe dayes } 15s.
Item to Ponder the joyner } 6s. 6d.
Item to Ardy, Burges & Langforde for syxe dayes } 18s.
Item to Hughe the under sextene } 3s.
Item for candelles and drynecke this weke } 3s. 2d.
Item for twoo hundrethe of planche borde } 12s.
Item for twoo waynescottes } 5s.
Item for twoo duble quarters and 26 single quarters } 7s. 8d.
Item for a pounde of glewe } 6d.
Item for a payer of hynches for the pulpytt } 2s. 4d.
Item for twoo stayes with twoo [th]eser for the grates } 3s.
Item for tynnynge and mendinge of 12 payer of hinges } 14d.
Item the 27th of November to Ponder the joyner for syxe dayes
werke } 6s. 6d.
Item to Ardy, Longforde & Burges for 6 daies worke } 18s.
Item to Goodemane Capper for hyme self, his mane and his boye for
syxe dayes } 15s.
Item to the sextene } 3s.
Item for candelles this weke } 18d.
Item for dryncke and coles } 21d.
Item for half a quarter clapborde } 17d.
Item syxtene quarters } 4s.
Item to the smythe for a staye for the roufe of the pulpytt, twoo stayes
for twoo of the lytle p[e]wes, eightene nayles for the pulpytt ande the
bolte of the pulpytt ande mendyng of the hynches } 3s. 6d.
Item to Richerde Ardye, one of the joyners, at his departinge, for a
rewarde } 12d.
Item for dubbers and pendates for the pulpytt } 2s. 8d.
Item for halfe a hundrethe of planche borde } 3s.

Item Saterdaye the fyrst of December to Ponder the joyner for three dayes worke } 3s. 3d.

Item to Burges the joyner for fyve dayes worke } 5s.

Item to Capper for hyme self, his mane ande his boye for fyve dayes worke } 12s. 6d.

Summa } £8 14s. 11d.

f.6v

[211]

Item for a hundrethe of selinge borde } 6s.

Item for twoo and twentie single qwarters } 5s. 6d.

Item for candelles } 10d.

Item for a pounde of glewe } 6d.

Item for turninge of twoo dubbers for the pulpitt } 2d.

Item for Hughe thunder sextene for fyve dayes } 2s. 6d.

Item to the marbler for removinge of the greate stone } 9d.

Item for drynke this weke } 20d.

Item Saterdaye the 12th of December to the smythe for a deske for the pulpytt, 4s. 8d. For a payer of hynges, 20d. For a ringe for the pulpytt, 4d. For a payer of handelles for the cover of the fonte, twoo shillinges & eighte pence } 9s. 4d.

Item for syxe dayes worke to Goodmane Ponder, joyner } 6s. 6d.

Item to Burges for syxe dayes } 6s.

Item to Capper, his mane & his boye for 6 daies } 15s.

Item to the sextene } 3s.

Item for a hundrethe of clapborde } 11s.

Item for a waynscott } 2s. 3d.

Item for syxe single quarters } 18d.

Item for drynke this weke } 2s.

Item for candelles } 16d.

Item for a pounde of glewe } 6d.

Item in rewarde to Capper and Tyse towardes the reperacions of their towelles } 3s. 4d.

Item Saterdaye the nyntenthe daye of December to Ponder the joyner for 6 dayes worke } 6s. 6d.

Item to Burges for syxe dayes } 6s.

Item for candelles this weke } 10d.

Item for drynkinge this weke } 12d.

Item for planche borde } 2s. 8d.

Item for fower single quarters } 12d.

Item for half a pounde of glewe } 3d.

Item to Hughe the sextene for this weke } 3s.

Item to the joyners boye } 2d.

Item for brome } 1d.

Item paide for the mendinge of twoo olde surpleses } 8d.

Summa } £5 22d.

f.7r

[212]

Item for a lether thonge for the bellowes of the organes } 4d.

Item for makinge of fower surpleses of olde albes } 16d.

Item for ivey and holly to sett aboute the churche at Cristmas laste paste } 8d.

Item for a rope for the bell of Saynt Faythes } 3s. 4d.

Item payed for three newe lockes for the doctoers pues and tenne kayes to the same } 8s. 6d.

Item payed for mendinge of the locke and for makinge of twoo newe kayes to Master Argalles pewe } 16d.

Item for mendinge of twoo lockes, one upone the dore of Master Dockwreys[13] pewe & thother upone Master Costons } 12d.

Item payed to [th]e smythe for mendinge of the locke of the dore of [th]e particion next my Lorde Mayores seate } 2d.

Item paide the 12ᵗʰ of February to Capper [th]e joyner for his worke, & for Tyce his servautes worke, & for his boye for three dayes & a half in mendinge of certene pewes } 8s. 9d.

Item the same daye for fower single qwarters } 12d.

Item for 12 fote of quarter borde } 9d.

Item for dryncke unto theme those dayes } 6d.

Item for a pounde of glewe } 6d.

Item for glasinge of the windowe that commethe owte of Blandes house the skynner[14] } 11s. 4½d.

Item payed to the irnemonger for nayles occupiede aboute churche worke as apeareth by his bylle of perticulers } 41s. 4d.

Item for twoo spalters[15] [sic] in Englishe in quarto for the quere } 3s. 8d.

Item for fower paper bookes to pryck songes in for the quere } 16d.

Item for drawinge, wrytinge & ingrossinge of the accompte exhibited before the parishoners upone the parisshe, seconde daye of Apriell last past, and for the sayed churchewardeynes paynes & travelles overseenges the workes, ande towardes recompence of the losse of their tyme aboute the same, gevyne and allowyd by the parishoners } 53s. 4d.

Item the syxte daye of Apriell in the yere of oure Lorde a thousande,

---

13 Possibly the same man or a relative of the Oswald Dockwra paid for a bell-clapper in the 1530/31 Jesus Guild accounts **[169]**.

14 Almost certainly Adam Bland, later Skinner to the Queen (Elizabeth I). TNA, C3/19/65, N. Carlisle, *Collections for the history of the ancient family of Bland* (London, 1826), 123–4.

15 That is, Psalters.

fyvehundrethe, fyftie and twoo, to John a servaunte of one Fraunces, a carpynter, for twoo dayes worke aboute the particioune in the longe entrye towardes Paules } 2s.

Summa } £7 14½d.

f. 7v

[213]

Item to Robert Wethers & James Quynye, carpinters, for three dayes worke there lykewise } 6s.

Item for syxe single qwarters } 18d.

Item for a pounde of candelles } 3d.

Item to a smythe for makinge (of) yrone worke for the same particone } 4s. 2d.

Item to Goodmane Capper, joyner, for fower dayes worke for hyme selfe and his boye occupied aboute the doctores pewe ande mendinge of other pewes there } 6s. 8d.

Item to Olyver Kelam and Benjamye Hall, laborers, for fower dayes worke in removinge of stones and other lumber } 5s.4d.

Item for half a pounde of glowe } 3d.

Item for drynke to the workemene this weke for forbearinge their odd howres } 8d.

Item for fower paper bookes for the churche in folio for pryck songes } 4s.

Item to the irne monger the 16th of Apriell as maye apeare by his byll of perticulers } 4s. 6d.

Item for fower lode of lyme } 2s. 8d.

Item for candelles } 3d.

Item for a plancheborde } 16d.

Item for three single qwarters } 9d.

Item for a kaye and mendinge of a locke at the farther dore of the store house } 8d.

Item for a rynge for the vestry dore & a spyk nayle } 4d.

Item for a brycke layer & his laborers for 2 daies worke } 3s. 4d.

Item for three laborers for twoo dayes } 4s.

Item to the joyner and his boye for 4 dayes worke } 6s. 8d.

Item for drynke for the workemene this weke } 12d.

Item payed to Roger Hunte for redemptione of the greater of the aforesayed twoo chalices, with his patent beinge in pawne with hyme for 52s. 1½d. } 52s. 1½d.

Item for the conceyvinge and drawinge of a dede of the sayede crowdes to be usede & enjoyed for the parishe churche of St Faithes for ever, beinge perused & penned by learnede mene at sondry tymes } 20s.

Summa } £6 6s. 5½d.

f.8r

[214]

Item afterwardes for drawinge, wrytinge, ingrossing ande registringe of a payer of indentures for the sayede crowdes to be used to the perpose aforesayed for terme of yeres for that the Deane ande Chapter ande the sayed parishoners coulde not conclude uppone, the fyrste dede devised as abovesayede ande for a pounde of pepper and other duties for the sealinge therof } 26s. 8d.

Item for drawinge and engrossinge of this present Certificate exhibited to the kinges majesties Commissioners } 10s.

Summa } 36s. 8d.

Summa totallis [sic] } £98 11s. ½d.

So yet apperethe the parishe yett to be indetted above the totall summe of all that was solde in sevene poundes, nyntene shillinges, sevene pence halpenye.

And yett the churche restyth not fully fynyshede, specially in glasse for all the wyndowes benethe the particoune of the sayed churche, and dyverse other thinges necessarye hereafter more particulerly to be shewyd at tyme convenient.

Per me Johannem Lewyes[16]

Per me Simonem Costone

Thomas Petyt

Wylliam Bulle

[16] The names all appear to be individual signatures; that of Lewyes is followed by an elaborate flourish. Lewyes was a proctor of the Court of Arches and senior Warden of the Jesus Guild when it was restored in 1556; see Introduction, pp. 15–16.

APPENDIX II:
WARDENS OF THE JESUS GUILD
MENTIONED IN BODLEIAN MS
TANNER 221[1]

[215] RALPH ALEYN, warden 1532/33, 1533/34
Aleyn, nephew of Sir John Aleyn (mayor 1525–6, 1535–6), was a grocer, and served as master of the Grocers' Company on three occasions, in 1539–41, 1542–43, and 1544–45.[2] He was also a member of the Merchant Adventurers' Company, and acted as appointer of ships for certain ventures in 1527.[3] Aleyn held civic office, representing Aldersgate, Billingsgate and Queenhithe wards as alderman between 1534 and 1546,[4] and serving as sheriff in 1545–6.[5] He was a wealthy man: in the 1541 Subsidy, he was assessed on £1333 6s. 8d. in goods and chattels and, in his will also of 1541, bequeathed the sum of £2,000 to his wife, Anne.[6] Although Aleyn was generous to his wife and appointed her co-executor with his brother Thomas, rector of Stevenage (Herts.), he stipulated that at all times when managing his post-mortem estate Anne should consult with Thomas 'to whom I have fully declared my secrete mynde'. He did not specify in his will where he was to be buried but, when he died in 1546, was interred in his parish church of St Matthew Friday Street and commemorated there by a monument.[7]

[216] ROGER BARKER, warden 1534/5
Barker, an innholder, also served the Jesus Guild as an assistant and

---

1   For wardens identified from other sources, see E. A. New, 'The Cult of the Holy Name of Jesus in Late Medieval England, with Special Reference to the Fraternity in St Paul's Cathedral, London, c.1450–1558' (unpub. Ph.D. thesis, University of London, 1999), Appendix 4.
2   A. B. Beaven, *The Aldermen of the City of London*, 2 vols (London, 1908–13), i, 20–47.
3   *Acts of Court of the Mercers' Company 1453–1527*, ed. L. Lyell and D. Watney (Cambridge, 1936), 333, 566.
4   Beaven, *Aldermen of the City of London,* i, 20–47.
5   C. M. Barron, *London in the Later Middle Ages* (Oxford, 2004), 354.
6   *Two Tudor Subsidy Assessment Rolls for the City of London: 1541 and 1582,* ed. R. G. Lang, LRS 29 (1993), **36**; TNA, PROB 11/31/406.
7   J. Stow, *A Survey of London*, ed. C. L. Kingsford, 2 vols (Oxford, 1908), i, 322.

as an auditor of the annual accounts in 1529/30 **[164]**. On that occasion
he made his mark rather than signing his name, but this could have
been the result of infirmity rather than illiteracy. Barker was actively
engaged in land transactions and legal matters and was remarkably well-
connected, purchasing land in Shoreditch with his wife Johanna and in
conjunction with Sir Richard Gresham and Robert Hogan, a master cook
in the king's household.[8] Barker was co-executor for Hogan alongside
Gresham, a role taken on by his wife after his own death.[9] Barker also
acted as overseer of the will of William Botry **[218]**, another warden of
the Jesus Guild.[10] He had a close attachment to the Jesus Guild for, in
addition to serving as an officer on a number of occasions, he made a
bequest of 40s. to it in his will of 1539, stating 'wherof nowe I am one
of the same assistaunce'.[11] Barker was also a brother of the guilds of
the Rood and of St Ursula in his parish church of St Lawrence Jewry,
although his bequests to these fraternities were considerably smaller
than his gift to the Jesus Guild. Barker requested burial 'againste the
myddell of the aulter' in the Holy Rood chapel in St Laurence Jewry,
and asked his executors to establish a year-long chantry there. He also
bequeathed a gilded standing cup and 20s. to the Innholders' Company
on condition that they attended his burial and prayed for him.

[217] HENRY BENET, warden 1459–post 1471

Henry Benet was one of the earliest known wardens of the Jesus Guild
and was named in the letters patent granted in 1459 **[2]**. He was a
clerk of the Privy Seal by 1453, a post that he held until after 1471, and
clearly an active royal servant.[12] It is possible that he was a member of
the prominent Benet family of Newbury in Berkshire, not least because
he was a constable of the town, and was sent there in 1470 to arrest
John Bedford, a local yeoman.[13] The Benets of Newbury were involved
in the cloth trade, particularly fulling; and, adding further weight to
the suggestion that Henry was part of this clan, in 1453 he was also
appointed constable of a number of commotes in Cardiganshire (now

---

8   Roger's wife is named as Jane in his will, in which he bequeathed her 10 acres of
     pasture in Shoreditch, TNA, PROB 11/31/406; this land had been purchased in 1532
     from Edward Elryngton (named as Edward Holder in Barker's will), LMA, Q/HAL/237.
     Barker acted alongside Gresham and Hogan in the late 1520s; see, for example, LMA,
     E/MW/C/332.
9   Several documents survive from the execution of Hogan's will; see, for example, LMA,
     E/MW/C/339. Johanna/Jane Barker continued her husband's role as executor for at least
     one exchange, LMA, E/MW/C/333/1–2.
10   TNA, PROB 11/25/428.
11   TNA, PROB 11/28/589.
12   *CPR* 1452–61, 143, 480.
13   *CPR* 1467–77, 251. For Newbury's role in the cloth trade, see M. Yates, *Town and
     Countryside in Western Berkshire, c.1327–c.1600: Social and Economic Change*
     (Woodbridge, 2007); J. Lee, *The Medieval Clothier* (Woodbridge, 2018), 61, 255, 301.

Ceredigion), which was an important area for wool production.[14] Benet was sent to arrest the disruptive Bedford for a second time in 1471, the same year in which he accepted the gift of land and property in Uxbridge on behalf of the Jesus Guild [10].[15] Benet does not appear in the records of central government after this date, and his will, if he made one, has not been located.[16]

[218] WILLIAM BOTRY, warden 1528/29, 1529/30

A mercer and merchant adventurer, Botry was both wealthy and well connected. He was almost certainly from Norfolk, holding the manor of Thorpe Market and other lands in the county.[17] He was also related to the prominent mercers of Norfolk origin, Sir Richard and Sir John Gresham, to whom he left the residue of his estate; he also appointed them executors of his will and named them, along with Thomas Gresham, as his 'cosyns'.[18] Botry was apprenticed to Richard Golofer and admitted into the Mercers Company in 1486 and, by the late 1490s, was already a major importer of buckram.[19] In 1502, Botry received a part payment for a consignment of silks delivered to the household of Elizabeth of York, and he was a major supplier to the Great Wardrobe under Henry VII and Henry VIII.[20] Botry was an active member of the Mercers' Company, serving as a warden on several occasions.[21] He was a parishioner of St Laurence Jewry and, like fellow Jesus Guild officer Roger Barker [216] (who was appointed overseer of his will), was a member of the Rood and St Ursula guilds in that parish.[22] Botry left 40s. to the Jesus Guild and appointed Barker as overseer of his will, while fellow Jesus Guild warden John Worsopp [239] was one of the witnesses.[23] Botry does not appear to have had any surviving children

---

[14] *CPR* 1452–61, 143, 163.

[15] *CPR* 1467–77, 287.

[16] He is not the same Henry Benet of Newbury who made his will in 1485 and died in that or early in the following year, PROB 11/7/287. I am grateful to Dr Christian Steer for this reference, and for helpful suggestions about how to trace the Benets of Newbury.

[17] TNA, PROB 11/25/428.

[18] Sir John Gresham was seised of Thorpe Market on his death in 1547, see F. Blomefield, 'North Erpingham Hundred: Thorp-Market', in *An Essay Towards a Topographical History of the County of Norfolk*, 11 vols (London, 1808), viii, 171–5.

[19] A. F. Sutton, *The Mercery of London. Trade, Goods and People 1130–1578* (Aldershot, 2005), 222, 466, 533; 'List of Members of the Mercers' Company from 1347', (Unpublished typescript list held at Mercers' Hall, compiled 1915), 34.

[20] *Privy Purse Expenses of Elizabeth of York: Wardrobe Accounts of Edward the Fourth*, ed. N. H. Nicolas (London, 1830), 67; *The Great Wardrobe Accounts of Henry VII and Henry VIII*, ed. M. Hayward, LRS 47 (2012), xxx n. 134, xxxii, 18–19, 37, 45–6, 79, 83–5, 102, 104, 118, 122–3, 137, 154 – among many other examples; *Acts of Court of the Mercers' Company*, ed. Lyell and Watney, 246, 269, 274, 424–8, 671–3.

[21] Sutton, *Mercery*, 558.

[22] TNA, PROB 11/25/428.

[23] TNA, PROB 11/25/428. The final witness was Thomas Piersone, almost certainly the

of his own, but he bequeathed £10 to Alice Norris (Norryce) 'whom I have broughte upp of charitie'.[24] His wife, Alice, predeceased him, and he requested burial as close to her as possible in the Lady chapel of his parish church.

[219] WILLIAM BROKET, warden 1529/30, 1530/31

Broket was born in Alnham in Northumberland and his sister, Jennet, still lived in the county at the time of his death in 1536.[25] Broket may already have had London connections when he moved south to become a goldsmith since a kinsman, Robert Broket, was named as an alderman of the Goldsmiths' Company in William's will. Broket appears to have been a diligent master to apprentices and served his Company as renter warden in 1504/5 and as warden in 1508/9.[26] He also remembered the Goldsmiths' in his will, bequeathing them 10 marks for a memorial drink and 40s. to be distributed among the poor of the Company.[27] Broket does not appear to have held civic office but certainly mixed with the highest levels of London society.[28] Broket was predeceased by his wife, Johanne, and they do not appear to have had any surviving children.[29] He does, however, appear to have had strong connections both with an extended family and with friendship networks, making bequests to various siblings, nephews and nieces and cousins, and appointing his nephew, Henry Holland, and friend, Thomas Atkinson, a cutler, as his executors.[30] Broket also left 10 marks to support Richard Shyrte, 'scoler of Oxenford', who may have been yet another kinsman. Broket did not mention the Jesus Guild in his will, but he did leave bequests to the guild of the Pappey and the parish clerks' Fraternity of St Nicholas, to

---

same man as the scribe for the 1534/5 Jesus Guild accounts [197] who was named as servant of John Worsopp.

[24] TNA, PROB 11/25/428. The money was to be given to Alice by John Gresham on the occasion of her marriage, or if she were in need.

[25] TNA, PROB 11/25/603.

[26] TNA PROB 11/25/603. Broket bequeathed £20 and half the tools in his workshop to his apprentice Laurence Hoosye and 10 marks and the other half of his tools to goldsmith Matthew Messenger 'nowe being my serv[a]nt', so perhaps recently past his apprenticeship; T. F. Reddaway and L. M. Walker, *The Early History of the Goldsmiths' Company, 1327–1509*, (London, 1975), 341.

[27] TNA, PROB 11/25/603.

[28] For example, in 1519 he acted alongside fellow goldsmith and former sheriff of London, Henry Worley, in a feoffment, LMA, Q/CMW/18. Broket's overseers were mercer George Medley and haberdasher Edward Dormer (to whose wife Katherine he bequeathed some of his widow's wearing gear), probably a member of the prominent mercer family of that name, see Sutton, *Mercery*, 426, 529–30, 558.

[29] Broket's wife is not named in his will, but is called 'Johane, his wife, formerly Sterne' in a Chancery case of 1515x18, TNA, C 1/415/74.

[30] TNA, C, 1/415/74 also discloses that Holland received the residue of Broket's estate, from which he was to establish a twenty-year obit.

which he had been admitted in 1506.[31] Broket requested burial in his parish church of St Peter Westcheap, close to the pew where a Master Palmer 'knelyde in'.

[220] WILLIAM BROMWELL, warden 1506/7, 1518/19, 1519/20

William Bromwell was apprenticed to Richard Gowle, and admitted into the Mercers' Company in 1490.[32] He was appointed as one of the supervisors of the work on the new Mercers' hall in 1517 (along with Benjamin Digby, an assistant of the Jesus Guild [147]), and served as their warden in 1513 and 1522.[33] Bromwell was an active and well-connected man, the son-in-law of Sir Michael Dormer, mayor of London, 1541–2 (who was also one of his executors), and had as an apprentice David Appowell, a future benefactor of the Mercers'.[34] He was very wealthy, with substantial property holdings and being able to act as cash creditor, although was himself once arrested on an action of debt.[35] Bromwell was also a merchant adventurer, and was elected as warden of that Company in 1527.[36] Bromwell, who acted as an assistant and auditor of the Jesus Guild as well as warden, bequeathed it 40s. in his will of 1536, and made a separate bequest of 6s. 8d. to each of the Guild's four almsmen, giving some of his 'wering gere' to Thomas Penyfather, one of these men [182, 189, 196].[37] Bromwell also made several bequests to individual members of the Jesus Guild, including either a gown or 40s. to scrivener John Worsopp [239], a fellow warden, and four yards of black cloth to the widow of Sir Thomas Baldry (d. 1534), a mercer and also assistant of the Jesus Guild.[38] Bromwell's long and detailed will of 1536 requested burial in his parish church of St Thomas the Apostle (in the Vintry) as near his pew as possible, a trental of masses followed by a month of daily masses, the continued support of Stephen Malyn

31 *The Bede Roll of the Fraternity of St Nicholas*, ed. N. W. James and V. A. James, LRS 39, 2 vols (2004), **444**.
32 'List of Members of the Mercers' Company from 1347', 34, 585; *Acts of Court of the Mercers' Company,* ed. Lyell and Watney, 271, 543–70.
33 Sutton, *Mercery*, 364, 558.
34 Bromwell names Dormer's wife as his mother-in-law in his will, TNA, PROB 11/27/23; and see Sutton, *Mercery*, 522, 529–30. Bromwell was older than Dormer, so presumably his wife was the daughter of Dormer's wife by one of her previous marriages.
35 Bromwell was acting as creditor as early as 1499, TNA, C241/273/27. In addition to bequeathing a considerable amount of property, mainly for charitable purposes (*Calendar of Wills Proved and Enrolled in the Court of Husting, London, 1258–1688*, ed. R. R. Sharpe, 2 vols (London, 1889–90), ii, 650, 692–3), in 1519 he acted as creditor to scrivener Robert Cressy, who defaulted on a loan of 100 marks (although Bromwell forgave him £6 13s. 4d. of this in his will), TNA, C 131/105/2. George Monoux, a draper and mayor of London (Barron, *London*, 350), took the action of debt along with his wife Anne, executrix and late the wife of draper Robert Watts, TNA, C 1/317/51.
36 *Acts of Court of the Mercers' Company,* ed. Lyell and Watney, 567.
37 TNA, PROB 11/27/23.
38 Baldry had also been apprenticed to Richard Gowle, Sutton, *Mercery*, 222.

'which I kepe of almes to scole till he can wryte and rede', and the bequest of books including his 'Inglisshe boke called *Vitas Patru*' to his mother-in-law, and 'the hole volume of Frossard' to Oliver Leder, gentleman.[39] Land and tenements given by Bromwell to support his obit and poor relief at St Thomas' were valued in 1548 at £4 16s.[40]

[221] WILLIAM BROTHERS, warden 1527/28, 1528/29

William Brothers, who may well have originated from Huntingdonshire, was admitted to the livery of the Drapers' Company by apprenticeship in 1501–2, and served as their warden in 1519–20 and 1525–26.[41] Brothers was also a merchant of the Calais Staple, and named as principal plaintiff in a case to recover debts in Calais.[42] He was wealthy enough to have contributed to Cabot's voyage to Newfoundland in 1521, and was assessed on £800 in the Lay Subsidy of 1541, being the third-highest taxpayer in his parish of St Mildred Poultry.[43] Brothers certainly had substantial property holdings, devising seven tenements in London to the Drapers' Company to support a perpetual chantry in Whittington's College for fellow draper and London mayor William Bailey (d. 1533) and others in his first will, made in 1542.[44] Brothers made a second will, in October 1545, in which he detailed a substantial number of pious provisions, including a sermon to be delivered by a 'well learned' man and the establishment of a chantry in St Katherine's chapel in St Mildred Poultry, the church in which he and his wife Anne were buried.[45] He also

---

[39]   TNA, PROB 11/27/23. For an important recent study of literary culture in late medieval London, see C. M. Barron, 'What Did Medieval London Merchants Read?' in *Medieval Merchants and Money: Essays in Honour of James L. Bolton*, ed. M. Allen and M. Davies (London, 2016), 43–70 (at 52 n.37).

[40]   *London and Middlesex Chantry Certificate, 1548*, ed. C. J. Kitching, LRS, 16 (1980), **95**.

[41]   Brothers made bequests to maintain the sepulchre light and the bells at 'Wydon', TNA PROB 11/31/614; this may have been Wyton (Hunts.), which had three bells in 1552, 'Parishes: Wyton', in *The Victoria County History of Huntingdon: Volume 2*, ed. W. Page, G. Proby and S. Inskip Ladds (London, 1932), 253–4. A. H. Johnson, *The History of the Worshipful Company of the Drapers of London*, 5 vols (Oxford, 1914–22), ii, 265, 271, 468.

[42]   TNA, C 1/946/56–58.

[43]   Johnson, *Worshipful Company of the Drapers*, ii, 265, 468. *Two Tudor Subsidy Assessment Rolls*, ed. Lang, **70**.

[44]   Johnson, *Worshipful Company of the Drapers*, ii, 356–8. This may have been a refoundation or to provide additional support, for Bailey himself is credited with founding the chantry, Johnson, *Worshipful Company of the Drapers*, ii, 61 n.; Bailey, along with his wife Katherine, was buried in the church of St Michael Paternoster Royal (rebuilt by Whittington and adjacent to his college and almshouse), Stow, *Survey*, i, 243.

[45]   PROB 11/31/614; Stow, *Survey*, i, 262, ii, 330 records a 'marble' tomb on the north side of the church which was said to be Brothers'. A bequest of £40 to support a priest for six years was recorded in the 1548 Chantry Certificate for St Mildred Poultry; the Certificate for the Drapers' included two perpetual chantries endowed by Brothers, see *Chantry Certificate*, ed. Kitching, **100, 224**.

bequeathed £10 and a gown to 'my chapleyn', suggesting that he may have maintained a household chapel. William Brothers was predeceased by Anne and does not appear to have had surviving children, but he remembered various relatives and a godson in his second will, which was proved in August 1547. He was also a cousin of William Campion [224], another warden of the Jesus Guild.

[222] JOHN BROWN, warden 1516/17, 1517/18
The career of John Brown falls into two parts. He began as a painter-stainer, working for the royal household from *c*.1502, appointed king's painter in 1511/12, and created the first known sergeant painter in the following decade.[46] In 1524 he was excused from this office on the grounds that he was 'impotent and feeble', although Brown seems to have maintained some activity as a painter because, in 1532, he bequeathed a number of craft-specific tools, granting some to a servant who was to continue to work for his wife.[47] Whatever the situation, Browne did not settle for a quiet retirement but continued to lead a life full of professional and civic responsibilities. He transferred to the Haberdashers' in May 1523 and, by his death, was among the wealthiest men in his new Company.[48] Brown was assessed on £1000 in the forced loan imposed on London in 1523 and, by the time of his death in 1532, had acquired a substantial portfolio of properties in the city and suburbs of London.[49] Just before he switched Companies, Brown was elected an alderman, representing the wards of Farringdon Without (1523–24) and Farringdon Within (1524–27).[50] Brown married twice, and appears to have had good relationships with both wives; he had children with his first wife, Alice, several of whom predeceased him, while his second wife, Anne, was the principal beneficiary and sole executor of his will.[51] Brown, a parishioner of St Vedast Foster Lane, made numerous pious bequests in his will of 1532, including a gift of 40s. to the Jesus Guild. He also bequeathed his best primer 'that John Worsopp gave me' to

46 E. Waterhouse, *Painting in Britain 1530 to 1790* (London, 1978), 15; E. Auerbach, *Tudor Artists* (London, 1954), 144; *Great Wardrobe Accounts*, ed. Hayward, 109. The date at which he became 'sergeant painter' is disputed: the first article on the subject suggested that the title was created when Brown was appointed as king's painter, 'The Serjeant-Painters', *The Burlington Magazine for Connoisseurs*, 84 no. 493 (1944), 81–2; Auerbach, *Tudor Artists*, suggested a subsequent appointment, and Waterhouse, *Painting in Britain*, states 1527.
47 W. A. D. Englefield, *The History of the Painter-Stainers' Company of London*, (London, 1923), 51–2; TNA, PROB 11/24/279.
48 I. W. Archer, *The History of the Haberdashers' Company* (Chichester, 1991), 36–7.
49 TNA, E179/251/15B, f. 59; E. Auerbach, 'Vincent Volpe, the King's Painter', *Burlington Magazine*, 92 no. 569 (1950), 222–9 (at 227 and n., which cites the entry for Brown as on f. 60); TNA, PROB 11/24/279.
50 Beaven, *Aldermen of the City of London*, ii, 20–47.
51 TNA, PROB 11/24/279.

Richard Callard, both fellow wardens of the Jesus Guild [223, 239]. Despite his transfer to the more prestigious Haberdashers' Company, Browne remembered the Painter-Stainers' Company, bequeathing 20s. to the poor of the craft, and providing them with a new company hall, the transfer of which property he entrusted to Richard Callard.[52]

[223] RICHARD CALLARD, warden 1531/32, 1532/33

Richard Callard, a native of Tavistock in Devon, styled himself 'esquire' in his will (1544), but was a prominent member of the Painter-Stainers' Company and involved in the acquisition of their new hall in 1532.[53] Callard successfully requested to be discharged from the list of potential aldermen in 1535 on the grounds that the expense would be too great.[54] Either Callard was being 'economical with the truth' or he suddenly acquired considerable wealth for, in 1541, he was assessed in the Subsidy on £2000 in London and a further £50 in Middlesex (he had a house in Islington).[55] Richard Callard married twice. From his will, he appears to have been particularly close to his first wife, Alice, with whom he had four daughters, three of whom predeceased him.[56] His second wife, Lady Anne, was widow of Sir John Clerke and, although he bequeathed her 200 marks and plate, these details were separately recorded in an indenture, and she was excluded from any involvement in the affairs of his estate.[57] Instead of his wife, Callard appointed his surviving daughter, Elizabeth, and her husband, Thomas Hayes, as his executors, and his brother and widowed son-in-law as overseers. Callard, a parishioner of St Vedast Foster Lane, made a notably orthodox will in which he sought intercession for his soul; he bequeathed 'all my synnes to the dyvill from him they came' and requested that a sermon should be preached soon after his death by a 'Catholycke Doctor or Bacheler of dyvynytie'. He also requested a twenty-year chantry in his parish church and named the chaplain who was his choice as chantry priest, who had previously been celebrating in a neighbouring parish.

---

52 Englefield, *Painter-Stainers'*, 51–2
53 Callard bequeathed £5 to the poor householders in the parish of Tavistock, where he was born. TNA, PROB 11/30/209; Englefield, *Painter-Stainers'*, 52.
54 Beaven, *Aldermen of the City of London*, ii, xxxvii.
55 *Two Tudor Subsidy Assessment Rolls,* ed. Lang, **100**. Callard was assessed at £1500 in 1544, *Two Tudor Subsidy Rolls*, ed. Lang, liii and lxxv (Table V).
56 TNA, PROB 11/30/209. Callard gave very precise instructions about his burial with his wife and three daughters.
57 The Hayes and Clerke families of Islington appear to have been related, while Callard's daughter Elizabeth married a John Clerke at some point between 1544 and 1556, with one of Callard's properties passing to the Clerke family through that route, A. P. Baggs, Diane K. Bolton and Patricia E. C. Croot, *A History of the County of Middlesex: Volume 8, Islington and Stoke Newington Parishes*, ed. T. F. T. Baker and C. R. Elrington.

[224] WILLIAM CAMPION, warden 1525/26, 1526/27

Campion was a member of both the Grocers' and the Merchant Adventurers' Companies, although he does not appear to have held office in either; he did, however, serve as a warden of London Bridge in 1513.[58] William Campion was related to his namesake, another grocer who died in 1520; he had two daughters with his wife Amy (all three survived him), and was the cousin of William Brothers [221], another warden of the Jesus Guild, making him overseer of his will in 1530.[59] Campion made a bequest of 10s. to the Jesus Guild and wished to be buried by his pew in the Lady Chapel of his parish church of St Mary Magdalen Milk Street. He was also a member of the parish clerks' fraternity of St Nicholas, and his name was entered onto the bede roll of this guild in 1519.[60]

[225] HENRY DACRES, warden 1522/23, 1523/24

Henry Dacres (or Dakers) served the Jesus Guild as an assistant, and as an auditor of the accounts in 1515/16, 1520/21 and 1524/5, in addition to his term as warden. Dacres may have been related to Barnard Dacres, a fellow merchant tailor, whose obit that company supported in Austin Friars; Henry himself served as master of the Merchant Taylors' Company in 1514.[61] Henry Dacres held civic office, serving as alderman of Farringdon Without from 1526–28, and was clearly wealthy, able to act as creditor for large sums and bequeathing substantial property to his wife and son.[62] Dacres married twice and had strong attachments to both his wives, requesting burial with his first wife, Elizabeth, and bequeathing six tenements and the residue of his estate to his second, 'moost lovyng' wife, Alice, for her 'manyfolde kyndenes' to him. This hints at her possible role as a carer for an elderly husband, for Dacres refers to his 'great feblenes impotence and age' in his will of 1537. Dacres was a parishioner of St Dunstan in the West and requested a perpetual obit and a ten-year chantry there. He was buried with his first wife under a memorial brass already in position, although the date of

---

58 *Acts of Court of the Mercers' Company,* ed. Lyell and Watney, 333; Sutton, *Mercery,* 337, where he is named as a member of the Adventurers' deputation sent to the royal court in June 1515; property was transferred from a stationer to William Campion, grocer, and Simon Ryce, mercer, wardens of London Bridge in 1513, C. P. Christianson, *A Directory of London Stationers and Book Artisans 1300–1500,* (New York, 1990), 78.

59 *Bede Roll of the Fraternity of St Nicholas,* ed. James and James, **280, 610**; TNA, PROB 11/24/152.

60 *Bede Roll of the Fraternity of St Nicholas,* ed. James and James, **595**.

61 *The Merchant Taylors' Company of London: Court Minutes, 1486–1493,* ed. M. Davies (Stamford, 2000), 68; M. P. Davies and A. Saunders, *A History of the Merchant Taylors' Company* (Leeds, 2004), 270.

62 Beaven, *Aldermen of the City of London,* i, 156, ii, 26–7; in 1510/11 Dacers acted as creditor for a debt of £100, C 131/258/4; TNA, PROB 11/27/489.

his death was never added.[63] Dakers was survived by his son, Robert, and by three daughters, one of whom became an important patron of the Clothworkers' Company.[64]

[226] ELLYS DRAPER, warden 1523/24, 1524/25

Ellys Draper, who may have been from Derby and certainly had connections there, was a haberdasher and, by 1509, a member of the Merchant Adventurers' Company.[65] In common with a number of the wardens, he had served the Jesus Guild both as an assistant and as an auditor, signing the accounts in 1517/18 and 1519/20; he bequeathed 40s. to the fraternity, although this is not recorded in the Guild accounts.[66] Draper also remembered the Haberdashers' in his will and bequeathed them a silver-gilt cup with the wheel of St Katherine engraved on the foot. He was a parishioner of St Peter Westcheap when he made his will in 1527, but also left bequests to St Mary Magdalen Milk Street and so may previously have lived in that parish. Draper's wife Elyn predeceased him and, while his will made no mention of children, he remembered a number of relatives, including two sisters, a nephew, and nieces; he also remembered a Robert Neweparte, 'whiche I have brought uppe of a childe'.

[227] RICHARD FORD, warden 1459–post 1471

Richard Ford, a royal servant, was the second warden named in the 1459 letters patent granted to the Jesus Guild, and was well established in his professional career by this date. In 1439/40 he had been one of several men entrusted to hold the manor of Kingsbury, Middlesex, on behalf of Christina Coke and, in 1448, was appointed a clerk of the exchequer.[67] He was promoted as remembrancer of the exchequer a few years later, although problems arose which obliged him to petition parliament to regain his position.[68] Ford was married by 1450, at which date he and

63 C. Steer, '"Under the tombe that I have there prepared": Monuments for the Tailors and Merchant Tailors of Medieval London', in *Memorializing the Middle Classes in Medieval and Renaissance Europe*, ed. A. Leader (Kalamazoo, 2018), 107–27 (at 113 and fig. 4.2).
64 https://www.clothworkersproperty.org/benefactors/packington-dame-anne.
65 Draper demised land in Derby that he had inherited from his father and, in 1527 when he made his will, had a sister living in the town, TNA, PROB 11/24/306; Archer, *Haberdashers' Company*, 36–7; *Acts of Court of the Mercers' Company*, ed. Lyell and Watney, 333.
66 TNA, PROB 11/24/306. Draper dated his will 16 July 1527 but named no executor. His nephew William Billingesley, his principal beneficiary, was granted administration of Draper's estate in February 1532.
67 *Calendar of Feet of Fines for London and Middlesex, vol. 1 Richard I–Richard III*, ed. W. J. Hardy and W. Page (London, 1892), 209 (no. 68); *CPR 1446–52*, 127. I am grateful to Dr Jessica Freeman for discussion on Richard Ford.
68 TNA, SC 8/28/1393.

his wife, Mercy, were granted land in Surrey and, from 1458 onwards, he was usually described as 'gentleman' in official documents.[69] Richard Ford was living in the parish of St Clement Danes by 1470, although he held land on the Hoo peninsula in Kent and his duties as a royal servant frequently took him away from London.[70] In August 1470, for example, he was one of several men commissioned to supervise the swan-upping on the Thames and, in March 1478, was appointed as keeper of the king's park at Chipmanholt, Devon, which post would probably have required occasional visits to the west country.[71] Ford had two sons, Richard (who predeceased him) and Anthony, but little else is known about his family.[72] He died at some point between November 1484 and December 1486, possibly intestate.[73]

[228] HENRY HILL, warden 1513/14, 1514/15

Haberdasher Henry Hill remains a shadowy figure, despite wealth and connections. He was identified as the son of a Johanna Hylston in a 1490s case concerning land in Essex, so may have originated from that county and had possibly adapted his name.[74] It is also possible that he was related to John Hill, a fellow haberdasher, or to the mercer family of the same name, and he had connections with members of the Pinners' and Wiresellers' Company.[75] Henry Hill was involved in trade with Antwerp and had either a shop or house in Milk Street, whence a servant of his was allegedly 'taken away' by a fellow haberdasher.[76] Hill was a brother of the parish clerks' fraternity, and an assistant and auditor as well as warden of the Jesus Guild [20, 22.h, 47, 74, 89]. He died sometime after June 1523.[77] The main purpose of his Husting wills

69 *CPR 1446–52*, 312; *Calendar of Plea and Memoranda Rolls*, ed. A. H. Thomas, vols 1–4; ed. Philip E. Jones, vols 5–6 (Cambridge, 1924–1961), v, 152.

70 For Ford's Kent lands, see, for example, TNA, C 146/9880, C 1/83/57.

71 P. M. Barnes, 'Chancery *corpus cum causa* file 10–11 Edward IV', in *Medieval Legal Records edited in memory of C. A. F. Meekings*, ed. R. F. Hunnisett and J. B. Post (London, 1978), 450; *CPR 1467–77*, 222; *CPR 1476–85*, 68.

72 Richard and Mercy Ford were defendants in a case of 1483x85 taken by their daughter-in-law that names her late husband as Richard, while Anthony was named as Ford's son in a 1484 receipt, TNA, C 1/65/66, C 47/37/9/34.

73 A feoffment to use of the last will of Richard Ford is dated 20 December 1486, in Nottingham University Library, Department of Manuscripts and Special Collections, Mi 6/177/75.

74 Henry Hill was named as son of 'Johane Hylston' as plaintiff in a case of detention of deeds relating to land in Maldon and Chelmsford, TNA, C 1/206/28

75 John Hill, haberdasher, d. 1516, TNA, PROB 11/18/367; Henry Hill acted as executor to wireseller William Parker (d. 1500), *The Pinners' and Wiresellers' Book, 1462–1511*, ed. B. Megson, *LRS* 44 (2009), **95**.

76 TNA, C 1/272/58, C 1/180/2.

77 *Bede Roll of the Fraternity of St Nicholas*, ed. James and James, **424**; Hill appointed Edward Miryll and Peter Tumor, grocers, and William Crowe, a pewterer, as his executors and made two wills dated 16 June 1521 and 15 June 1523, LMA, Husting

was to establish a chantry for Bishop Richard Fitzjames (1506–22), dedicated to Jesus, the Blessed Virgin Mary and St Jerome, in St Paul's Cathedral, although it is unclear why Hill shouldered this duty.[78] There may, however, have been a continuing family connection with the chantry, for the chaplain at the time of its dissolution was a John Hill.[79]

[229] THOMAS HYNDE, warden, 1520/21, 1521/22

Thomas Hynde was another mercer and merchant adventurer who held office both in his company and in the Jesus Guild. Thomas may have been a relative of the mercer William Hynde and, although his parents were buried in St Stephen Colman Street, he had family connections with Hunsdon in Hertfordshire.[80] He had been apprenticed to Richard Lakyn, was admitted into the Mercers' Company in 1490 and, by 1502, was clearly well established for, in that year, he and another mercer received £129 16s. 6d. in part payment for goods supplied to Elizabeth of York.[81] Hynde prospered, perhaps in part because he was the son-in-law of the mercer mayor William Brown the elder, and himself served as warden of the Mercers' Company in 1513 and 1523, on both occasions serving alongside fellow Jesus Guild officer Thomas Baldry.[82] Hynde was also active in the Merchant Adventurers' Company, being one of their representatives in a Star Chamber case of 1512.[83] Hynde was elected sheriff of London in 1526 but asked to be excused from this office, perhaps because of age or infirmity (he died in 1528).[84] Thomas Hynde made no mention the Jesus Guild in his will (1528) but he made several bequests to other wardens and brothers of the Fraternity.[85] Benjamin Digby, a fellow mercer who was an assistant and auditor of the Jesus Guild [147, 171], received a gold memorial ring, while he named Thomas Baldry and William Botry [218] as executors; scrivener and notary John Worsopp, another warden [239], was one of the witnesses of Hynde's will. Hynde made numerous pious bequests, including a tun of wine to Syon Abbey and £5 to the Observant Friars at Greenwich, and he wished to be buried before the image of St Anne in his parish church, St Antholin.

Rolls of Wills and Deeds, 240 (28, 29); *Calendar of Wills Proved and Enrolled in the Court of Husting*, ed. Sharpe, ii, 634–5.

[78] Hill was one of several London merchants who founded chantries in St Paul's for members of the clergy, M.-H. Rousseau, *Saving the Souls of Medieval London: Perpetual Chantries at St Paul's Cathedral, c.1200–1548* (Farnham, 2011), 35.

[79] *London and Middlesex Chantry Certificate*, ed. Kitching, 108.

[80] Sutton, *Mercery*, 225; TNA, PROB 11/23/75.

[81] 'List of Members of the Mercers' Company from 1347', 221; *Privy Purse Expenses of Elizabeth of York,* ed. Nicolas, 60.

[82] Sutton, *Mercery*, 524–5, 558.

[83] Sutton, *Mercery*, 340.

[84] Beaven, *Aldermen of the City of London,* ii, xxxvii.

[85] TNA, PROB 11/23/75.

[230] STEPHEN LYNNE, warden 1522/23, 1523/24

Lynne (d. 1528) was a haberdasher who, as a successful businessman, had acquired several properties in London by the time of his death. He is not known to have held any company or civic office but did, however, make a substantial bequest to the Haberdashers.[86] Nothing is known about Lynne's origins (although his toponym is suggestive of Norfolk ancestry), and he does not appear to have had any surviving children, although he was survived by his wife Johanne. He was a parishioner of St Sepulchre without Newgate, and a brother of three guilds in that parish (Our Lady, St Stephen and Corpus Christi); but he requested burial within the Lady Chapel of Greyfriars in London, to which house he bequeathed £20 for a daily Mass and *De profundis* and established an eight-year obit.[87] Lynne did not make a bequest to the Jesus Guild, but he named Ellys Draper [226], a fellow warden of the Jesus Guild and a haberdasher, as his sole executor.

[231] JOHN MATTHEW, warden 1515/16, 1516/17

Matthew was of Welsh ancestry, possibly from Llangollen since he left 40s. to the church there.[88] He was a leading baker, twice serving as master of his company and a prominent figure in the bakers' opposition to the construction of new bread ovens on the Bridge in 1521.[89] Matthew was also a yeoman of the chamber to Henry VII and attended the king's funeral; he maintained personal connections with members of the household, bequeathing a gold ring to fellow Welshman Evan ap Rice, yeoman proctor to the king.[90] Matthew, who was a member of the parish clerks' fraternity, requested burial near his pew in the parish church of St Michael, although he did not specify which of the seven London

---

86   In 1503/4, Lynne and fellow haberdasher, Robert Holderness, were named as creditors for the sum of £21 in a Westminster Staple debt case, TNA, C, 241/275/117; he bequeathed a substantial number of properties in his Husting will made in 1528, LMA, Husting Rolls of Wills and Deeds, 241 (10), *Calendar of Wills Proved and Enrolled in the Court of Husting*, ed. Sharpe, ii, 637.

87   Lynne's testament is dated 7 July 1528, and proved 6 October 1529, TNA, PROB 11/23/199; his testament was witnessed by James Payne, a Franciscan, suggesting that Lynne had a strong connection with the mendicant house. Lynne died on 10 September 1528, *The Grey Friars of London: Their History, with the Register of their Convent and an Appendix of Documents*, ed. C. L. Kingsford (Aberdeen, 1915), 81–2.

88   LMA, Commissary Register, MS 9171/10, fols. 36–37v. Matthew's will, dated 10 February 1524, names his mother as Gladys, who was still alive at the time.

89   G. Phillips, *1666 and All That: A History of the Bakers' Company* (Cambridge, 1993), 117, 222.

90   'Henry VIII: May 1509, 1–14', in *Letters and Papers, Foreign and Domestic, Henry VIII, Volume 1, 1509–1514*, ed. J. S. Brewer (London, 1920), 8–24, where Matthew was named as a 'harbegour' and Evan ap Rice as 'porter'. He was identified as yeoman of the chamber in the will of Thomas Exemew (d. 1528), who made a bequest to support the obit in his memory, LMA, Husting Rolls of Wills and Deeds, 241 (9); *Calendar of Wills Proved and Enrolled in the Court of Husting*, ed. Sharpe, ii, 636.

churches dedicated to the saint this was.[91] Strong personal devotions can be identified from his will, where his numerous pious bequests included those to the London Charterhouse and the Trinitarian Friars at Hounslow (Middx.), Matthew declaring that he was a 'brother' of both houses. Matthew also bequeathed 40s. to the Jesus Guild, to be spent upon new altar cloths, and made William Bromwell [220], a fellow warden, the overseer of his will. He was survived by his wife Katherine, to whom he devised property in the parish of St Michael.

[232] JOHN MONKE, warden 1506/7, 1513/14

Monke acted alongside fellow waxchandlers as a creditor in a case of debt in 1497/8 and was, by 1500, master of his company, an office he held again in 1516.[92] He is also known to have supplied the paschal and sepulchre lights for the Bridge chapel in 1501/2.[93] Monke was one of the wardens at the time of the re-organisation of the Jesus Guild, and acted as auditor of the Fraternity accounts in 1518/19, 1520/21 and 1523/24. He appears in the annual accounts until 1526/27, in which year he was granted 10s. in alms with the assent of the Guild assistants [138]. This was a very unusual move and might suggest age-related infirmity; his will (if indeed he made one) has not been located.

[233] WILLIAM PAVER, warden 1530/31, 1531/32

William Paver (sometimes Pavior or Paviour) was the only warden identified between 1507 and 1535 who was not a member of a London trade or craft guild, and the only one known to have committed suicide. Paver was elected as the common clerk of London in June 1514 and served in this capacity until his death in May 1533.[94] As well as being active in the Jesus Guild, William Paver and his wife, Dorothy, were also members of the Luton guild of the Holy Trinity and of the London parish clerks' fraternity.[95] On May Day 1533, Paver oversaw the execution of James Bainham, a relapsed heretic; Bainham made a speech confirming his beliefs and declared that he was a true Christian, to which Paver is said to have replied, 'Thou liest, thou heretic! Thou deniest the blessed sacrament of the altar'.[96] According to the chronicler Edmund Hall,

91 *Bede Roll of the Fraternity of St Nicholas*, ed. James and James, **329**.
92 TNA, C 241/272/13; J. Dummelow, *The Wax Chandlers of London*, (London, 1973), 169.
93 *London Bridge: Selected Accounts and Rentals, 1381–1538*, ed. V. Harding and L. Wright, *LRS* 31 (1995), **385**.
94 B. R. Masters, 'The Town Clerk', *Guildhall Miscellany* 3 (1969), 55–74 (at 72); Barron, *London in the Later Middle Ages*, 364.
95 *The Accounts of the Guild of the Holy Trinity, Luton: 1526/7–1546/7*, ed. B. Tearle, Publications of the Bedfordshire Historical Record Society 91 (2012), Pl.3 (rough notes on their admission in 1515), and 76 (a dirge held for William); *Bede Roll of the Fraternity of St Nicholas*, ed. James and James, **595, 596** (admission for both William and Dorothy in 1519).
96 J. Foxe, *The Acts and Monuments of John Foxe*, ed. G. Townsend and S. R. Cattley, 8

Paver vehemently opposed any dilution of traditional Catholicism, and declared that if the Gospel were allowed in English he would cut his throat.[97] A few weeks later Paver did indeed kill himself, an act which John Foxe recorded as the 'Marvelous judgement of God against ... an open enemy of his word'.[98] Although Hall was apparently disappointed by the fact that Paver did not actually cut his throat ('but he brake promes, for as you have hard he hanged hymself'), he was rather more sympathetic than Foxe, and clearly wondered about Paver's state of mind at the time of his death.[99] There is no mention of Paver's suicide in the records of the Jesus Guild, an understandable omission since suicide, even if prompted by religious anxiety, was a mortal sin, but the Guild did relieve Paver's widow of her husband's debts [184].

[234] JOHN PYKE, warden 1524/24, 1525/26

Pyke was a member of the Goldsmiths' Company, serving as one of their wardens in1495–6 and in 1501–2, on the latter occasion alongside Bartholomew Reed, a wealthy benefactor of the Jesus Guild.[100] Pyke was comparatively young when he held high office in his company, for he acted as auditor for the Jesus Guild in 1530/31 and died in 1533. John Pyke was well-connected and wealthy. His wife Isabella was the daughter of mercer John Hosyer, who served the Jesus Guild as an assistant [22.h], and the couple were given £200 at the time of their marriage, as well as lifetime gifts and bequests.[101] Isabella Pyke was also named as a 'cousin' by Sir William Brown, the mercer who died in 1514 during his term as Mayor of London.[102] John and Isabella Pyke had two daughters, both under-age in 1518, when their grandfather died; only one was mentioned in John's will of 1533, so the other possibly predeceased him.[103] At the time of his death, John Pyke was a parishioner of St Vedast but had previously lived in St Peter Westcheap; he left 'tithes forgotten' to both parishes.

[235] JOHN SANDELL, warden 1514/15, 1515/16

Vintner John Sandell's origins are unknown but, by 1514, he was sufficiently established to take out a sixty-year lease on the Mitre at the corner of Cheapside and Old Jewry, where the officers of the Jesus

---

97   E. Hall, *Hall's Chronicle: Containing the History of England &c.* (London, 1809), 806.
98   Foxe, *The Acts and Monuments*, v, 65. The incident is discussed in S. Brigden, *London and the Reformation* (Oxford, 1991), 217–18.
99   Hall, *Hall's Chronicle*, 806.
100 Reddaway and Walker, *Early History of the Goldsmiths*, 340.
101 PROB 11/20/128.
102 PROB 11/17/567; Sutton, *Mercery*, 525–6 – he was confused with his namesake even by the mid sixteenth century.
103 PROB 11/25/29.

Guild met on occasion [36].¹⁰⁴ Sandell served as master of his company
in 1522–23 and made bequests to their priest, to their hall, and to poor
people lodged within.¹⁰⁵ He was prominent in the Jesus Guild, serving
as warden and assistant, and as an auditor of the accounts in 1519/20 and
1522/23. Sandell died in 1532 and requested burial in the Lady Chapel
of St Thomas of Acre, close to the Mitre, rather than his parish church,
St Mary Colechurch. He made no specific bequest to the Jesus Guild
in his markedly orthodox and pious testament, but evidently admired
anchorites, leaving bequests to those at Westminster, Northampton, St
Alban's and Walsingham, as well as those nearby at London Wall and
without Bishopsgate. Sandell was survived by his wife Agnes and son
Richard, the latter also being involved in the wine trade.¹⁰⁶

[236] RICHARD SMYTH, warden 1517/18, 1518/19

Richard Smyth was a merchant tailor and yeoman of the queen's robes.¹⁰⁷
He was enrolling apprentices as early as 1476/7 and served two terms as
warden of his company before being elected master in 1502–3.¹⁰⁸ Smyth
was a brother of the parish clerks' fraternity (admitted in 1504) and the
fraternity of the Pappey as well as member of the Jesus Guild in St
Paul's, and he made bequests to all three in his will.¹⁰⁹ Smyth wished
to be buried in a tomb he had commissioned in his parish church of
St John the Evangelist, but bequeathed torches to four other London
parishes, and to churches in Staffordshire and Essex. Smyth named his
son, John, and John Billesdon, a grocer and fellow member of the Jesus
Guild [174], as executors.

[237] WILLIAM TURKE, warden 1533/34, 1534/35

William Turke also served as an assistant and auditor of the Jesus Guild.
In the Guild records he is identified as a fishmonger and, therefore,
almost certainly a member of the Turke family active in that company
in the fifteenth and sixteenth centuries.¹¹⁰ The William Turke assessed at

104 D. J. Keene and V. Harding, 'St. Mary Colechurch 105/19', in *Historical Gazetteer
of London Before the Great Fire Cheapside; Parishes of All Hallows Honey Lane,
St Martin Pomary, St Mary Le Bow, St Mary Colechurch and St Pancras Soper Lane*
(London, 1987), 518–26. Sandell's widow continued to lease the property until her death
in 1545.
105 A. Crawford, *A History of the Vintners' Company* (London, 1977), 285; PROB 11/24/235.
106 Richard Sandell was engaged in frequent correspondence concerning the purchase
and sale of wine in the late 1540s and early 1550s. See, for example, TNA, SP 46/7/
fo102–102d.
107 For Smith's activities in supplying the royal court, see *Great Wardrobe Accounts*, ed.
Hayward, 19 and n. 51.
108 *Merchant Taylors' Company*, ed. Davies, 253–5, 283, 301.
109 *Bede Roll of the Fraternity of St Nicholas*, ed. James and James, **426**; Smyth made his
will in March 1524/5, but probate was not until June 1527, TNA, PROB 11/22/345.
110 The William Turke, fishmonger and citizen of London, named in documents relating to

£200 in the 1541 Subsidy may well have been the Jesus Guild warden, since his parish, St Magnus, was dominated by fishmongers.[111] The most prominent member of the family in this period was Richard Turke (d. 1558), alderman and sheriff of London, although he and his kinsman William would hardly have seen eye-to-eye over religious matters, since Richard was a noted supporter of the Edwardian Reformation.[112]

[238] STEPHEN WARD, warden 1519/20, 1520/21

Stephen Ward was elected as master of the Waxchandlers Company in 1522, a year after he had served as warden of the Jesus Guild.[113] Nothing is known about his professional career prior to this date, but he served as an assistant of the Jesus Guild [20] and as an auditor of their accounts [98]. He was possibly a parishioner of St Christopher le Stocks for, as well as mentioning a fraternity dedicated to that saint, he requested burial in a tomb 'made as is apon Thomas Carter'; in 1513 Thomas Carter, priest, had requested that a 'marbilstone' with his name and date of death should be laid over his grave in the church of St Christopher.[114] Ward also left torches to the guilds of Our Lady and St Anne in his parish church, and to a fraternity in Stepney, suggesting a connection with that location, too. Ward was survived by his wife, Margaret, and son, Robert, the former being made his executrix. His overseer was John Colyns, a mercer said to be an 'unsuccessful businessman', but who is remembered today for his involvement in the book trade.[115]

[239] JOHN WORSOPP, warden 1526/27, 1527/28

John Worsopp was apprenticed to scrivener John Mane in 1490, admitted to the Scriveners Company in 1493, and served as a warden of the same company.[116] In 1497/8 he was paid for his professional services by the

---

land in Essex and Kent in the 1470s and 1480s was probably the Jesus Guild William Turke's father, Essex Record Office, D/DL T1/478, TNA, C 1/58/47. Fishmonger Walter Turke, sheriff in 1334–5 and mayor in 1349–50, may have been founder of the dynasty, Barron, *London in the Later Middle Ages*, 329 and 331. Unless he changed companies just before death, the Jesus Guild William Turke cannot be the man whose will was recorded in the London Consistory Court in 1541, *London Consistory Court Wills, 1492–1547*, ed. I. Darlington, *LRS* 3 (1967), **148**.

[111]   *Two Tudor Subsidy Rolls*, ed. Lang, **43**.

[112]   Richard Turke's will, made in 1552, was distinctly Protestant, PROB 11/35/344; see D. J. Hickman, 'The Religious Allegiance of London's Ruling Elite, 1520–1603' (unpub. Ph. D. thesis University of London, 1995), 91–2, 114, 121.

[113]   Dummelow, *Wax Chandlers*, 169.

[114]   Warde's will was made on 19 March 1527 and proved in October 1529, GL MS 9171/10, Commissary Wills, f.132v. Thomas Carter's will was made and proved in 1513, *Consistory Court Wills*, ed. Darlington, **62**.

[115]   Sutton, *Mercery*, 444.

[116]   *Scriveners' Company Common Paper 1357–1628,* ed. F. W. Steer, LRS 4 (1968), 13, 24, 26 n 4.

Pinners' and Wiresellers' Company and, by 1512, had become sufficiently well established for the prior of Canterbury Cathedral to request that payments owed to the Priory were made at his house.[117] He was a notary and court-hand writer, and drew up and witnessed a number of wills, including those of several wardens and brothers of the Jesus Guild.[118] Worsopp had a number of apprentices and 'servants' who worked for him in a professional capacity, some of whom were responsible for writing the accounts and other records of the Jesus Guild.[119] He appears to have been successful and well-connected for, as well as networking within the Jesus Guild, he was godfather to Mary, daughter of Sir John Gresham, and also had property in London and Surrey.[120] Worsopp was active in the Jesus Guild between 1516 and 1534/5, and acted as receiver and auditor of the accounts on several occasions, for example **[140]**. He made a bequest of 40s. to the Guild in his last testament, with the interesting proviso 'if the same Fraternitie doo contynue'.[121] He was also a member of the parish clerks' fraternity, being entered onto the Bede Roll in 1510; this may have been a family tradition, for another John Worsopp was listed among the dead of this fraternity in 1474.[122] Worsopp was a parishioner of St Vedast and his wife Lettice, two sons and four daughters survived him.[123]

---

117   *Pinners' and Wiresellers' Book*, ed. Megson **49, 50**; Canterbury Cathedral Archives and Library, CCA-DCc-ChAnt/B/362. Despite his success, in the year that he died Worsopp was accused of providing false information that led to the imprisonment of a merchant tailor, TNA, C 1/853/44.

118   See also J. Luxford, 'The Testament of Joan FitzLewes: A Source for the History of the Abbey of Franciscan Nuns without Aldgate', in *Medieval Londoners. Essays to Mark the Eightieth Birthday of Caroline M. Barron*, ed. E A. New and C. Steer (London, 2019), 275–95.

119   See Introduction, p. 23.

120   TNA, PROB 11/27/356. Worsopp's testament was dated 28 August and will 12 September 1538; both were proved on 7 November 1538.

121   TNA, PROB 11/27/356.

122   *Bede Roll of the Fraternity of St Nicholas*, ed. James and James, **169, 501**. The John Worsopp who died in 1474 was a draper, however, and more likely a direct ancestor of the Worsopps involved in the luxury fabrics trade, PROB 11/6/248; and *Great Wardrobe Accounts*, ed. Hayward, *Great Wardrobe Accounts*, ed. Hayward, 83 n. 34.

123   The wording in his will suggests that three of his daughters, two married and one widowed, may have been from a previous marriage.

SELECT GLOSSARY

Sources: *OED*; *MED*; *Anglo-Norman Dictionary* https://anglo-norman.
net ; Osbourne's *Concise Legal Dictionary*; L. F. Salzman, *Building in
England Down to 1540. A Documentary History* (Oxford, 1952); F. L.
Harrison, *Music in Medieval Britain* (London, 1958); J. Mayo, *A History
of Ecclesiastical Dress* (1985); R. W. Pfaff, *The Liturgy in Medieval
England A History* (Cambridge, 2010); *English Medieval Industries*,
ed. J. Blair and N. Ramsay (London and New York, 1991); *St. Paul's:
The Cathedral Church of London, 604–2004*, eds D. Keene, A. Burns
and A. Saint (New Haven, 2004); *Mass and Parish in late Medieval
England: The Use of York*, ed. P.S. Barnwell, C. Cross and A. Rycraft
(Reading, 2005).

almonyner (almoner). Official who distributed alms. At St Paul's, also
the master of the choristers.

amytte (amit, amice). Rectangle of cloth worn around the neck as part
of a priest's mass vestments.

anthems. Antiphons, texts sung before and after a Psalm or canticle,
occasionally sung alone.

apparels (also parawbes). Decorated squares of cloth, mainly added
to albs.

arrages. Debts (also something due, outstanding balance).

asshen. Made of ash wood.

aube, awbe (alb). Full-length white vestment worn over a cassock,
usually tied at the waist.

baas gold. Meaning uncertain, possibly equivalent to modern low caret gold.

baners (banners). Flags, usually square.

besines. Business.

bokram (buckram). Fine linen.

billes of parcelles. Statements of payments.

book of parcelles. Itemized account of commercial transactions.

Bressle / Brussles (Brussels) cloth. Cloth from Flanders, usually the Brussels area.

burden. Load.

by note. Sung and/or accompanied by music.

by even porcions (portions). In equal parts.

calver. Fresh.

capace. Of legal capacity.

Cardinals (of St Paul's). The two senior minor canons at St Paul's Cathedral.

cassed and adnulled. Quashed and annulled (from *cassetur billa / breve*, let the bill / writ be quashed).

collacion (*collatio*, collation). Exposition on Scripture or a theological treatise, in the Jesus Guild context presumably forming the basis of a sermon.

Comen Place. Court of Common Pleas.

conger. Conger eel.

conisaunce, conusauns, conysaunce. Device, badge, pennon.

convenient. Suitable.

coropras (corporal). Cloth on which the chalice and paten were placed for consecration during Mass, and with which the vessels subsequently were covered.

Crowdes. Popular name for the large crypt chapel beneath the east end of Old St Paul's Cathedral (from *cruta*, Latin for crypt).

De profundis (**'Form the depths'**). Opening words of Ps. 129, part of the Office of the Dead but also widely used as part of general devotions and commemorations.

droppes (drops). Either pendant 'jewels', probably made of metal, or teardrop-shaped decoration on cloth.

either. Both.

ell. Measurement, usually for cloth. An English ell was 45 inches.

emoluments. Profits from offices/dues/rewards/salary.

empcions, empacions. Purchases.

emproment. Commission.

engrossing, ingrossing. Drafting and, usually, writing up fair copy in a legal form.

eve. Vigil, evening before a liturgical feast.

every of them, everich of them. Each of them.

for the time being. Now, current, present.

garnets. Hinges.

garnisshing (garnishing). Decorating, equipping.

gogeons (gudgeons). Axles attached to the headstock of a bell, often covered in metal.

green geese. Young geese, goslings.

grey amys (grey amice). At St Paul's Cathedral, the grey fur tippet worn by canons to distinguish themselves from other clergy.

gurnard. A salt-water fish.

hogshead. Barrel containing 63 gallons.

Hollond cloth. A type of linen produced in the Low Countries.

holy bread. Bread distributed after Mass to those who had not received the Eucharist.

incontinently. Immediately.

in ernest. Part payment given in advance.

jollifers (gillyflowers, *Dianthus caryophyllus*). Clove-scented flower, ancestor of the modern pink and carnation.

kerchers. Cloths.

kilder, kilderkyn (kilderkin). Cask containing half a barrel (16 gallons of ale or 18 gallons of beer).

latten. Yellow-coloured copper alloy similar to brass.

lawpe (laupe). A loop of cloth, rope, leather, etc.

Lukes welvet. Velvet from Lucca (Italy).

lymmyng (limning). Illuminating/decorating a manuscript or document, usually with gold leaf.

lymnyng of the corporacion. Meaning uncertain. Possibly decorating an original copy relating to the foundation of the Guild.

lynkes (links). Torches made of tow and pitch.

lyverees, lyveries (liveries). Usually small metal or cloth badges with a specific device, but occasionally a garment in identifiable colours or with a device or badge.

male ingigne (*malengine*). A wicked plan or bad intent.

malnesey (malmsey). Sweet wine.

mazer. Drinking-bowl or cup without a foot or only a shallow base; traditionally made of wood, usually with a metal rim or external band, but sometimes made completely of metal.

Maisters of Paules. Meaning uncertain; possibly the canons.

macalles. Probably maniples (maniple: strip of cloth, usually ornamented, hung over the left wrist of a priest at mass).

meting and bowding (c.f. metes and bounds). Measuring or checking the legal boundaries of land and property.

mortmain. Alienation of land to institutions.

Nomine Jesu. Name of Jesus. In the ordinances and accounts, usually the celebrations of the annual Feast or weekly Jesus Mass.

Normandie cloth (Normandy cloth). A type of linen from northern France.

noted. With music (liturgical manuscripts).

pair of organs. Pipe organ (a single instrument, possibly so named because of the set of bellows).

palys (palis). An enclosure.

parcel gilt. Partially gilded.

parclose. Screen within a church for sub-divisions within the main building.

perser. A pointed tool used for piercing or boring.

peticanons (petty canons). Minor canons of St Paul's.

Placebo and *Dirige*. Office of the Dead (from the first words of the main part of the Office).

planche, plaunche. Large boards, planking.

plenar (plenary). Full.

polen wax. High-grade beeswax used for church candles, often imported from Eastern Europe.

portus (portiforium). Breviary, a manuscript containing the liturgical Offices for the public celebration of the Canonical Hours.

potacion. An occasion of drinking.

pottell. Half a gallon.

premisses. Above-stated, previous (usually above-stated matters).

pricked, pricking. To write down music by way of notation.

prickett. Spiked candlestick.

prymmar (primer). Book of Hours.

punchoun (ponchyon). A wooden strut or a load-bearing post.

quarry. Small, diamond-shaped piece of window-glass.

quarter (weight). 8 bushels.

quarter (length). 9 inches.

quarters (carpentry). Pieces of wood, usually 4" wide and 2–4" thick, used as upright studs in partitions or frames.

queresters. Choristers.

remain. Balance of account.

reperacions. Expenses for upkeep, maintenance/costs of repairs.

rishes. Rushes.

sacring bell. Bell hung outside a church, rung before and at specific points during a service.

Salves. Antiphons (also see anthems).

sanctus bell. Small bell within a church rung by altar servers.

sarcenet. Silk cloth.

satten of Bridge. Satin from Bruges.

sconse. Candlestick fastened to a wall.

scrippes and scrowes. Small pieces of parchment or paper.

several. Separate, different.

signes manuelles. Sign manual or signature.

singing bread. Large communion wafers used by the clergy at mass.

sothering. Possibly soldering.

specialties. Sealed contract or agreement.

spyck nayles (spike nails). Large nails, usually of iron.

spirituall (spiritual). When used in relation to people, a man or men in Holy Orders.

staple. Shaped metal bracket from which a bell clapper is suspended.

spriggs. Small square-bodied nails.

stay. Fixed, upright part of the apparatus for hanging a bell.

steropp, stirrup (stirrup). Part of the apparatus for hanging a bell.

suffrages. Standard sets of memorials appended to Offices.

superalteryes (super-altars). Portable altars, most often used on an unconsecrated surface.

table. Small board with image or text (or both).

tewke. Cloth, possibly from Tewkesbury.

thaccompt. The account.

verder (verdegris). Green (the colour, not necessarily the specific dye).

vicars. In St Paul's Cathedral, the vicars choral.

waites. Paid musicians.

yerely. Annually

INDEX

This Index is to the section numbers of the edited text and the appendices. The names of persons and places are listed under their usual modern spelling, with variants found in the manuscripts listed in parentheses. When an individual's occupation is known this is noted, even if this information has been obtained from sources other than the edited text.

Abrigg, Richard, plasterer 204
Acton (Actone), Hugh, merchant
     tailor 126, 159
Acts of Parliament
  Ordinances of Corporations Act
     1503 3n.
Albrowe, John, mercer 10a.
Aleyn (Aleyne)
  Sir John, mercer, sheriff and mayor
     of London 197, 198, 215
  Ralph (Rauff), grocer 179, 184,
     185, 186, 191, 192, 194, 197,
     199, 215
  Anne, wife of 215
Alexander (Alysaunder, Alizaunder),
     James 149, 157, 164, 172, 185
Alnham (Northumb.) 219
Alwyn (Alwyne, Ailwyn), Nicholas,
     mercer/waxchandler, mayor of
     London 11
Amadas (Amydas), John, sergeant at
     arms 180, 187, 191, 193, 194, 198
anchorites 235
Anderton (Andertone), Lawrence
     (Laurence) 149, 164, 172, 185,
     192
Andrew, Walter 82
Antwerp 228
Appowell, David, mercer 220
Argalle, Master 212
Armagh, (arch)diocese of 128, 135,
     143
Arnold the labourer 204
Atkinson, Thomas, cutler 219
Audley, Thomas, 1st Lord Audley,
     Chancellor of England 19

Badbe, John 84
Bafforde, Roger, mercer 13

Baily (Baille, Bayle, Bayly, Baylly),
     William, draper, mayor of
     London 25, 50, 40, 60, 69, 77,
     84, 92, 101, 110, 120, 128, 135, 143,
     151, 159, 164, 172, 185, 192
Bainham, John 233
Baker, John, of Southwark,
     innkeeper 67, 75, 82
Baldry, Thomas, mercer, mayor and
     sheriff of London 13, 20, 22.h
Bamen (Bamene, Banene, Bavene),
     William, almsman 32, 45, 55, 64,
     72, 80
Bardsley (Bardesley, Bordesley),
     Hugh (*see also* Leicestor,
     Blaunche) 172, 194
Barker, Roger, innkeeper 19, 21.a, 21.b,
     164, 191, 192, 193, 199, 216
  Jane (Johanna), his wife 216
Baron (Barone), John, chaplain 10.a,
     10.b, 10c. 10.d
Bath and Wells, farm of the diocese
     of 25, 40, 48, 50, 60, 69, 77, 84,
     92, 101, 110, 117, 128, 135, 143, 151,
     159, 168, 174, 180, 187, 194
Bayntone (Batone), John, almsman 79,
     86, 95, 104, 114, 122, 123, 130, 137,
     145, 153, 161, 168, 176, 182
Becquett, Richard, labourer 204
Bedford, John 217
Belamy, Master 63
Belle, Master 63
Benet (Benett), Henry, clerk of the office
     of the Privy Seal 2.a, 2.c, 10.d, 217
Berde, William 20
Berelle, Robert, grocer 77
Billesdone (Billesdon), [John],
     grocer 174
Bishop, Master 51

Thorpe Market (Norf.) 218
Toye, Robert, deputy churchwarden of
 St Faith's 200, 201
Turke (Turk)
 Richard, sheriff of London 237
 Walter, fishmonger, mayor of
  London 237
 William, fishmonger 237
 William (Wylliam), fishmonger,
  warden of the Jesus Guild 19,
  21.a, 21.b, 164, 184, 185, 186,
  191, 192, 193, 237
Turnbull (Turnebulle, Turnebull),
 Thomas, fishmonger 172, 185, 192
Turnour
 Edmond, of London, gentleman 67,
  69, 74, 77
 Thomas, shearman 58
Twydie, John, joiner 204, 206
Tyler (Tylere)
 John 25, 38, 40, 50, 60, 65, 69, 71,
  77, 81, 84, 90, 92, 97, 99, 100,
  101, 106, 108, 118, 126, 127, 132,
  133, 134, 138, 140, 141, 142, 148,
  178, 179, 184, 186, 191, 192
 John, clerk of Jesus 60
 John, of Coventry, 'the elder' 58,
  67, 69, 75, 77, 84, 90, 92, 99,
  101, 108, 110, 118, 119, 125, 126,
  127, 128, 133, 135, 141, 143, 146,
  149, 151, 157, 159, 164, 166, 172,
  174, 180, 185, 192, 193, 198
 John, his son, of Yate (Yatte)
  (Glouces.), 'the
  younger' 149, 157, 164,
  194, 198
Tyse, servant of John Robyns alias
 Capper 211, 212

Uxbridge (Middx.), rent of land and
 property in (*see also* Jesus Guild,
 Uxbridge) 25, 40, 50, 60, 69, 77,
 84, 92, 101, 110, 120, 128, 135, 143,
 151, 159, 164, 166, 172, 174, 180,
 186, 187, 192, 194

Vaughan (Vaughauin), Richard 24, 37,
 39, 47, 49, 57, 59, 66
Vowelle, William, gentleman 4.k

waits of London 8.b, 8.f, 30, 42, 51, 62,
 70, 79, 86, 94, 103, 113, 122, 130,
 137, 145, 153, 161, 168, 176, 182,
 189, 196

Walker, John 10.a, 10.d
Wallis (Walles, Wales), John,
 almsman 32, 45, 55, 64, 72
Ward (Warde), Stephen (Steven),
 waxchandler 20, 66, 74, 76, 81,
  82, 83, 89, 92, 97, 98, 238
 Margaret, wife of 238
 Robert, son of 238
Warenne, Robert, skinner 38
Warham, William, archbishop of
 Canterbury and chancellor of
 England 3
Watson (Watsone), Harry,
 plasterer 204
 his labourer 204
Watts, Robert, draper 220n.
 Anne, wife of (*see also* Monoux,
  Anne) 220n.
Waynfford, William, esquire 10.a
Wayte, Roger 185, 192
Wellis, Thomas 38
Wethers, Robert, carpenter 213
Wilkynson, William
Williams (Wylliams), Nicholas, of
 Chepstow 67, 69, 74, 75, 77, 81
Winchester, farm of the diocese of 25,
 40, 48, 69, 77, 84, 92, 101, 110, 120,
 128, 135, 143, 151, 159, 164, 166, 172,
 174, 180, 185, 187, 192, 194
Wolsey, Thomas, (d. 1529) cardinal
 archbishop of York and papal
 legate 71, 123, 154
Worley, Henry, goldsmith, sheriff of
 London 219n.
Worsopp (Worsoppe), John, scrivener
 (*see also* Pierson, Thomas) 20,
  47, 51, 58, 62, 68, 70, 71, 72, 79,
  80, 86, 94, 103, 112, 122, 130, 131,
  132, 133, 134, 137, 140, 141, 142,
  145, 148, 149, 153, 155, 161, 168,
  182, 189, 190, 197, 218, 220, 222,
  229, 239
 Lettice, wife of 239
 servant of 72, 95, 115, 123, 131, 138,
  146, 154, 162, 169
Wright (Wrighte), Richard,
 labourer 205
Wyminghaum (Wynnygham), John,
 almsman 32, 45, 55, 64, 72
Wyndout (Wyndeoute), Thomas,
 mercer 13
Wyton (Hunts.) 221n.